MY OMAHA OBSESSION

Searching for the City

Miss Cassette

Foreword by Chris Ware

University of Nebraska Press

Lincoln

Library of Congress Cataloging-in-Publication Data
Names: Cassette, Miss, author. | Ware, Chris, writer of
foreword.
Title: My Omaha obsession: searching for the city / Miss
Cassette; foreword by Chris Ware.
Description: Lincoln: University of Nebraska, [2020]
Identifiers: LCCN 2020010788
ISBN 9781496207616 (paperback)
ISBN 9781496224699 (epub)
ISBN 9781496224705 (mobi)
ISBN 9781496224712 (pdf)
Subjects: LCSH: Omaha (Neb.)—Buildings, structures,
etc. | Omaha (Neb.)—History—Anecdotes. |
Architecture, Domestic—Nebraska—Omaha. | Omaha
(Neb.)—Biography—Anecdotes. | My Omaha Obsession
(Website)
Classification: LCC F674.O543 C37 2020 |
DDC 978.2/254—dc23
LC record available at https://lccn.loc.gov/2020010788

Set in Whitman by Laura Buis.

For my beloved grandmother, who exposed me to the finer things in life. Not one for public displays of emotion or exposition, she did reveal, when I was very young, that in discreet moments of deep despair, the beautiful music of Billie Holiday and a record table could ease a good cry. And that has made all the difference.

One way to open your eyes to unnoticed beauty is to ask yourself, "What if I had never seen this before? What if I knew I would never see it again?"

RACHEL CARSON

Contents

Foreword

CHRIS WARE

A s a graphic novelist who's been working for the past couple of decades on a historical book set in Omaha, I am on a perpetual quest for photo references. I so envy those lazy words-only novelists who, in only a few short phrases, can conjure up a shopping mall or a screen door or a whole town without actually having to draw anything. But we cartoonists can't fake out the reader; we're always on the lookout, quite literally, for anything and everything that can contribute to the veracity of our graphic claims.

Such was the aim of my Google image search one day, a couple of years ago, when I stumbled upon the *My Omaha Obsession* website. Rummaging for photos of the area around where I grew up—I was born in Omaha, splitting my time between a home near Benson and my grandparents' house a bit farther west—I suddenly found, cascading down my browser window, a veritable deluge of maps and photographs of the neighborhoods of my childhood, all anchored in a long, text-heavy web page that began, "I remember fake falling asleep in the backseat of my family's car, driving home after special nights in downtown Omaha."

Nonplussed, I paused. "Fake falling asleep?" Who starts an architectural history blog like that? I read on: "I would close my eyes on 480 because I loathed it and still do," Describing the sensation of passing through, and over, the hilly topography of a town—my hometown—with eyes closed, this writer, a "Miss Cassette," went on to discuss a particular screen door for which she felt a special sense of anticipation as well as her "steal(ing) squinted sightings" (eyes open now) of passing landmarks from the back seat of her family car, in which, "like a springer spaniel" she "would rush from backseat window to backseat window, to get a peek."

I hadn't bothered to breathe for a few seconds, I think. I was maybe even a little bit miffed. "Goddammit, I thought I was the only person in the world who cared about this stuff," I said to myself. I, who lay in the back seats of our car as a kid, also fake falling asleep as I passed favorite, familiar Omaha landmarks. Questions began to cascade down my own mental web page: What was this site? Who *was* this person?

Thus began my own obsession with *My Omaha Obsession*. The author, the mysteriously named Miss Cassette, offers no name or government-issued personal information—a finger in the eye of the internet, and of blogs in particular, where the celebration of oneself has been virtually de rigueur for two decades—though chinks regularly show through her Proustian rabbit hole of a website. As a kid, she liked Nancy Drew and spying on her neighbors. She made up her own houses, drawing pictures of them and even building them from cardboard "on the floor of her beloved grandmother's kitchen." She loved old movies. Old handwritten letters in the backs of drawers, secret stairs off kitchen, buckled brick paths. The same stuff, really, that we all like, whether we remember it or not. Mostly, however, she really likes looking. Looking through land deeds, Sanborn fire insurance maps, and the records of the Douglas County tax assessor. Looking through newspapers, old advertisements, and census records. And especially looking at houses. A self-described "mansion-hungry" flaneur, she looks at buildings, businesses, and places that others might pass by without a thought, asking: Why do I like that house so much? Who lived there? And most important, what *happened*, anyway?

And as this book voluminously attests, she gets answers. Through vertiginous research, careful combing of archives and the distillation of essential, almost microscopic detail, Miss Cassette brings to life the broken pediments, busted sidewalks, and beautiful homes of Omaha and its neighborhoods with a fine-grained redolence one normally only expects to find in literature. Capturing the curiosity born of idle neighborhood wanderings and harnessing it to the power of the internet, she has, it seems, crafted a new approach, if not a new genre, for writing about history, or, more properly, the places and spaces in which we all, however sensately or inchoately, live out our lives.

It's patently irresponsible to try to suss out and sum up any sort of standard approach to scholarship that Miss Cassette generally takes, but I'll do it anyway. Nearly all of her stories start with a house. Sometimes it's grand, sometimes it's just something one might drive by and forget about, but for some reason it's taken her fancy. So begins her "stakeout," a sort of circuitous flirtation around a property, taking in the details from the polite distance of the curb. Photos are perhaps snapped—north, south, east, west. Then, like all good stalkers, she rushes back home to Google it. Maps, satellite photos, county records, newspaper articles, and obituaries well up and then flesh out the original distinguished owners and family members, its inheritors and later inhabitants and eras, nearly always up to our present, insensitive day. Through excited and often lovely (and funny) writing, she connects historical photos, interior images, and newspaper articles that hint at the quotidian details of a home's forgotten life; interviews with neighbors, family members, and even an old owner or two might add to the mix. Before you know it, snippets of invisible, imagined conversations with people who died long before you were born start to coalesce and float through your mind, and you begin to feel a dizziness at the tendrils of dates untangled—and entangling. And that's when you realize it: she's gotten you to fall in love with a house.

Or at least sort of. I've never experienced anything quite like it, but nearly every story (she calls them "stories") about the houses and buildings she chooses instills in me a sense of affection for a particular locale that I'd previously reserved for the places in which I lived as a child. This is no small feat. And it's not just homes; she also does restaurants, businesses, notable people, Easter egg hunts. No detail is too small, no pebble too tiny to gently roll over and see what's underneath. The desire to find spaces to accommodate and dignify private nostalgias, the indefinable longing for just the briefest returning taste of one's childhood, the all-too-common dream plot of discovering the "door to that giant room that you never knew about"—all of these ineffabilities seem to inform her quests. Not surprisingly, euphoria, infatuation, adoration, besottedness, and yearning characterize her prose. Yet sadly, many of the stories end up with an ineptly renovated and unrecognizable home and/or some oldster living forgotten in a sad apartment on Pacific or 108th Street. I recall a recent entry in which really all that survived of one wiped-clean home was the original, genuinely unremarkable banister of a staircase, yet after Miss Cassette's lengthy weaving of a vast intertwined magic web of story, finally seeing a picture of that banister made my eyes well up. Why? I dunno.

I've long suspected that there was something enchanting, magical, and indescribably mysterious about the hills and homes of Omaha because they've formed not only my memories but the shapes of my memories too; I can close my eyes and sense the geography of the town itself, a landscape dotted by the homes and landmarks of my childhood but also improbably overlaid by family and friends and places from my life since moving away. Really, however, my Omaha obsession could just as easily be your Poughkeepsie obsession. While what Miss Cassette offers the reader is inarguably centered in our shared hometown, it also acts as an indirect, general instructional manual of how to be aware of one's surroundings wherever you are. How to *pay attention*. That brick foundation buried in the weeds didn't just get there on its own; someone put it there. And not only did someone put it there; someone made the bricks. And those someones had mothers and fathers and maybe even spouses and families who lived there or helped build the place. And what were they like? What did they care about, think about, and live for? Nowadays, it's not so hard to find out, using, miraculously, the same thing that tells you what Kim Kardashian wore last night. For Miss Cassette the "sense of connection with buildings" she feels so deeply is really a sense of connection with the world that so many of us have been internetted and mass-entertained right out of. Alive to her surroundings, she's alive to life itself. Personally, I think she's rediscovered a little piece of the secret to happiness, and this book might help you find it too. It's not that difficult: as my grandmother used to tell me whenever I was bored, go outside and take a walk around the block. Have a look around. You might be surprised at what you see.

Introduction

Having written about Omaha photographs on my personal Facebook page for many years, I launched the *My Omaha Obsession* website in early March 2016. In those early days my interests were finding obscure local photos and writing brief histories, along with family memories of the particular image. It expanded from there . . . but the obsession had really begun in my childhood. I began writing and illustrating books at the age four, although at that time I was apparently fixated with living on a flying carpet, not a Shingle style house. I have always loved houses, big and small, and the strange awareness of how one's environment can shape feeling and memory.

Later I began designing houses on paper—of course, usually mansions— and graduated to creating cities of cardboard on the linoleum floor of my grandmother's kitchen and in my family's basement. At one point my father's friend, a real architect, taught me how to draw up "blueprints," or the floor plans of my designs, which kicked my interests into high gear.

I immediately gravitated to Nancy Drew, my life heroine, whom my mother introduced me to at a young age. This started me on an early path to finding other like-minded girls for a club and planning our Benson neighborhood stakeouts, spying on almost everyone within a five-block area, making a habit of keen observation, note-taking, cassette tape recording, and learning how to collect fingerprints from spy books we would check out of the old Benson library: baby powder and Scotch tape!

All the while, I simply couldn't get enough of my growing fascination with the movies of the silent era through the 1950s, the original *Upstairs, Downstairs* series, scary backless wardrobes, hand-painted and neon signs, pocket doors, imagined private ballrooms on the top floors of homes, hidden mansions, ghosts, alleys with spray paint, ornate dollhouses, spiral staircases, flowered tea sets, cigarette holders, elaborate private gardens, Sears homes, reading, third-floor hallways that whistle, oil paintings, long red fingernails, fireplaces, buckled brick paths, parquet wood floors, beveled and leaded glass, old handwritten letters in the backs of drawers, antiques, towers, servants' quarters, back elevators, high privacy fences of brick, uniforms of any kind, secret stairs off of kitchens, music from all eras, vintage clothes especially involving intricate beadwork, ghost signs, and forgotten attic windows.

My Omaha Obsession is not just a book; it is a long walk 'round our Omaha streets through the years. If it bores you to walk 'round Omaha's streets, peer in the windows of glorious homes and mysterious buildings, and try to infer all of the whos and whats in the whodunit, you might long ago have chucked this whole bit aside. And yet, here you are . . . curious. If this is your first visit to the places I've covered in the *My Omaha Obsession* website and you would like to go on a stakeout with us, then this is the perfect moment to welcome you. Do you have a trench coat perchance? Are you prone to wearing the collar up day or night? Do you like to lurk around puzzling brick buildings, searching for hidden ghost signs, or do you have an obsession with delightful manhole covers, secret overgrown gardens, and their ivy-covered mansions? Oh, you say you've even got a dark fedora? Good . . . this is looking good. Magnifying glasses or Wayfarers are usually a must, but today, today of all days, we'll all need a good flashlight. Now let's look over our shoulder before we continue because I've got a hunch many are going to want to follow us on this underground case.

I hope that *My Omaha Obsession*'s pages fill you with the wonder and enchantment I sense as I research each clue. I hope to inspire a slowing down, to engage a part of you that used to wander, and that my adventures encourage you to look for the little architectural details all around. It was all right in front of us not too very long ago.

With love especially to my Omaha friends,
Miss Cassette

Note to the Reader

These are really ghost stories through and through—even if you do not believe in ghosts. Many of you wandered in for the Omaha history, the images and the architecture. I welcome you, regardless. But these are ghost stories, and you should know what you're getting into. Eighty years ago a person turned that brass doorknob to the hallway linen closet. A ghost sign is well preserved between the adjoining buildings, waiting to be discovered. One hundred years ago that well-worn cobblestone was set in place by a human hand. It remains beneath the concrete that is below the asphalt, its patina perfectly embalmed. All evidence of life. The sandstone treads have been filed away by generations of hard leather-soled shoes, and the wooden steps display a smooth favored footing of someone's auntie and five more after her to the attic above. Like Lewis Carroll's *beausage*, these aged clues all around us are the worn history, the beauty of past peoples. Even if you do not believe in them, they were just here. And maybe still are.

MY OMAHA OBSESSION

1. 4025 Izard Street. Photo by author.

CHAPTER 1

The Mysteries of 4025 Izard Street

B efore I tell you one of the best stories you will ever hear, I have a confession to make. It is a confession that does not paint me in the best light, and I risk having you think less of me. I guess that is a part of confessing. I will just get to it and air this admission so that I can spend more time explaining myself. So here it is: I trespassed and spent time on the property of today's mystery story.

Now allow me to recount the backstory. When I was in my teens and twenties, I was very curious. As you have certainly picked up by now, I have long been obsessed with architecture and large, gorgeous homes. Like many of my curious friends, I was prone to high adventure—honestly, more a carefree kid than a building sleuthhound at that point. Sometime in the late 1980s or early 1990s, a friend of mine moved into an attic apartment on Cuming Street, near the Cuming Street Food Mart. It was named something else back then but still was a little hinky, even for those days. This attic apartment was in one of those old, titanic Walnut Hill neighborhood homes that had long ago been broken up into apartments. I remember there was a perilous set of stairs winding up the side of the home, which scaling with a group was an adventure in and of itself. As the night wore on, one friend in the group wanted to show the rest of us something he had found recently: a castle. Stupendous, we thought.

We all packed up and headed back down those treacherous stairs to find that night's enterprise. After a very short walk and a cut through an alley, he did, indeed, show us a castle. I was absolutely affected by its glory. A silence fell over the group. We all cleared the fence with ease and, in memory, walked the large property, being as quiet and respectful as could be, considering we were intruding. The small castle looked like

2. Alley on southwest side of the home at 4025 Izard Street. Photo by author.

it was built of stone, and it was in the back corner of a large property. I estimated it to have been built in the 1960s for someone's children. I have never forgotten that magical, late-night encounter from twenty-six some odd years ago. I would continue to take newcomers by the castle for the next few years—although always viewed from the alley, reverently from a car.

When I began to think about starting the website *My Omaha Obsession*, I knew that the castle was a Forever Mystery in my mind, needing to be solved. The twists and turns in the research of this story alone have provided months of intrigue for me. I found the castle itself to be just one part of the puzzle. It has truly taken on a life, and I allowed it to. So let me begin to tell you one of the best little Omaha secrets you will ever hear and assure you that Joslyn Castle has nothing on this Walnut Hill treasure.

LAY OF THE LAND

The house at 4025 Izard Street is tucked away, geographically speaking. You might never have met its acquaintance unless traveling on foot. An east-west street, Izard was named in honor of Mark W. Izard, third territorial governor of Nebraska, by Governor Thomas B. Cuming in the mid-nineteenth century. Conveniently, Cuming Street is a mere block south. Although Izard runs throughout Omaha, mind you, a few jogs here and there, this particular stretch of Izard Street—Fortieth Street through Forty-Second Street—is bound on the east side by the Mercer Mansion. Farther to the east, Mercer Boulevard and Mercer Park Road continue to add buffer with additional blockage contributed by curving Lincoln Boulevard. West of Forty-Second Street down to Saddle Creek–Radial Highway is largely defined by industrial buildings, although houses continue past Forty-Fifth Street. Like most of the Walnut Hill neighborhood, there are lots of kinks and quirks—making it all the more fascinating.

Just three doors down from the Mercer Mansion, 4025 Izard, is one of the remaining single-family dwellings from this majestic part of town. Its beauty is breathtaking, even to this day. The house at 4025 has always held its head high, thanks to a series of restoration-minded, community-focused owners. I was pleased to find that the Reconnaissance Survey of 2003 for the Omaha City Planning Department identified 4025 Izard Street for it architectural significance and recommended that it should be eligible for the National Register of Historic Places. The house was prominently featured in the report as a superb example of the popular Queen Anne style, displayed in its irregular form, decorative shingle work,

3

3. Front, north-facing elevation of 4025 Izard Street. Photo by author.

porch, spindles, turrets, and tall chimney. I found a number of homes in the Walnut Hill neighborhood listed in this 2003 report.

THE BEGINNINGS OF 4025 IZARD

Through my research I found that J. B. Mason built 4025 Izard in 1890. J.B., also known as James Bayne Mason, was a local architect, perhaps, a less mentioned contemporary of John Kiewitt and F. A. Henninger. Mason was born in Scotland in 1846. He was originally an agricultural implement maker in Morrison, Illinois, according to the 1880 federal census. By 1886 he had made his way to Omaha. The 1891 city directory found him living at 4025 Izard, occupation listed as "draughtsman" for the first time. An English word, *draughtsman* (or *draftsman* in American English today) describes a person who prepares technical drawings and plans under the direction of an architect or engineer. By 1896 he was listed as an "architect" in private practice. I discovered Mason's office was at 309 South Seventeenth Street. This address no longer exists, but it looked to be just east of the Douglas County Courthouse. In the 1920s that office would house the Omaha Stationery Company. He also had an office at the Paxton Building through the years.

Mason lived in this house of his design for a number of years with his wife, Maria, and their three children, Mable, Claude, and Nancy. It is significant that he built 4025 Izard just five years after Dr. Samuel Mercer had built the infamous Mercer Mansion at 3902 Cuming Street. The rising Walnut Hill neighborhood was one of the most prestigious areas in Omaha, and Mason, no doubt, wanted to have his home situated in this up-and-coming part of town. The two must certainly have brushed shoulders at this time. Using over twenty types of wood and the finest materials available to an architect at that time, Mason's home was as large as it was beautiful. From different sources I found some conflicting information. A number of websites reveal there are 6 bedrooms, 3.5 baths, for a total of 4,583 square feet, and other sites, such as the Douglas County Assessor, reported the home as having been built in 1900, with 5 bedrooms, 2.5 baths, and 3,584 square feet. This discrepancy may be due to the additional square footage of the carriage house, which was added in 1910, now an apartment. I wondered if this incredible architect, credited with designing numerous buildings and private homes around Omaha, had also created the castle for his children. I couldn't find anything about that in the records.

A NEW OWNER

Clues led me to J. A. Swanson, or Johnathan A. Swanson. Swanson bought the house at 4025 Izard, living there from 1907 through 1921. In those years Swanson was president of King-Swanson Company. An immigrant boy from Sweden, Swanson came to America by himself at age fifteen. He secured a job in Stanton, Iowa, working at a general store and post office. He later moved to Omaha and worked at Hellman Clothing and Hayden's Clothing department, where he became a buyer and manager. He then established King-Swanson Company, a men's clothing shop.

4. King-Swanson advertisement from *Omaha World-Herald*, March 10, 1911.
"To fellows who appreciate tasty furnishings."
Reprinted with permission from the *Omaha World-Herald*.

Oddly, in the years 1916 and 1918, the name W. O. Liljenstople was listed at 4025 Izard in addition to Swanson. I soon uncovered that Liljenstople was a prominent local banker employed with the United States National Bank. I wondered if the two families shared the large Izard Street home at that time. After 1918 the home is listed singularly in Swanson's name again.

After four years Swanson sold his interest in the King-Swanson Company and, along with a partner, bought the renowned Omaha business the Nebraska Clothing Company. By 1921 Swanson and his family had moved from 4025 Izard and were splitting their time between a 160-acre farm near Florence, a lake cottage in Paynesville, Minnesota, and the Incredible, To-Die-For House at 418 North Thirty-Eighth Street in Omaha. Obviously, Swanson was a success. He died in 1929 at age sixty-four. His son, Otto, would go on to run Nebraska Clothing Company and later form Inclusive Communities along with other prominent local business leaders.

I could find no indicator that the castle was built during Swanson's ownership of the property. At this point in the mystery research, I figured that any one of these wealthy owners could have hired someone to build their children a castle and it would never make the news.

ANOTHER PROMINENT OWNER

Puzzling, the next few years were difficult for me to piece together due to the 1922 city directory being missing from the library. The 1923 city directory had 4025 Izard listed as "vacant." The 1924 city directory was also missing from the library. I found in a 1923 *Chemical & Engineering News*, the American Chemical Society newsletter, that a Mr. F. J. "Fred" Mleynek had been a newly elected council member of said society between October 15 and November 15 of that year. His address was listed as "4025 Izard Street, Omaha, Neb." Those breadcrumbs led me to the *Chemical Bulletin* 10, no. 11, which stated "F. J. Mleynek, Class of '23, Chemical Engineer, is now located with the testing laboratory of the Union Pacific Railroad of Omaha." So, although I was not exactly sure what years Mr. Mleynek lived at 4025, there were pieces of evidence that he occupied it at some point during those three years and worked at Union Pacific.

AN OBSCURED OWNERSHIP

In 1925 "A. E. Fletcher, physician" had bought the home at 4025 Izard Street. By 1928 the Omaha City Directory listed the property as "A. E. Fletcher phys @ Park Hospital." I thought maybe it had listed this address referring to his place of business. In some years the directories would list a homeowner's profession—including a business office address. (Honestly, there is a whole lot of variation from year to year in the city directories.) It wasn't until I found the 1934 listing of 4025 Izard under "Park Hospital" with no owner's name that I became completely confused. This is where the story began to take flight for me. I thought there must have been some kind of mistake. I needed to know more.

5. Park Hospital angle. Northwest angle of 4025 taken from Izard Street in
October 1928. The sign above the door reads "Park Hospital." From the Nathaniel
Dewell Collection, Nebraska State Historical Society, RG 3882.PH0021-0040-3.

Even more confounding still was the 1939 listing for 4025:

Asa Fletcher
Park Hosp
D-Flo Chemical Co.
Urego Chemical Co.

I was intrigued. I asked the librarian if she had ever seen that many company names listed after a home address. She had not. I guessed that maybe
Dr. Fletcher had sat on the board of all of those companies. The librarian
thought that might be the case also. It was so odd that there were different phone numbers listed for each business but all had the same address.

I began to cross-reference information in the city directories in an
attempt to find Park Hospital, D-Flo Chemical Company, or Urego Chemical Company. There were no listings or acknowledgments of these com-

6. East view of the house and grounds at 4025 Izard Street, October 1928.
From the Nathaniel Dewell Collection, Nebraska State Historical Society,
RG 3882.PH0021-0045-2.

panies in the Omaha business pages, which I thought was mighty strange.
I knew then that I would have to dig a little deeper into this Dr. Asa
Fletcher character.

What I found was the best waiting-to-be novel ever. Asa Fletcher was
born in 1884 in Ohio. Through volume 11 of the *National Eclectic Medical Association Quarterly*, from 1920 (years before Fletcher moved into
4025 Izard), I learned "Dr. Asa Fletcher has changed his address from
1041 North 33rd Street to 3328 North 27th Street, Omaha." The quarterly
also featured medical treatments such as "Plant Protein Therapy" and
"Metaphysic Passionmania." Page after page displayed photos of plants
as medicine. I was fascinated and immediately knew I would need to
report these findings to Mr. Cassette, whose own obsession is plants.

Under his "new" address (thanks to the Eclectic Medical Association)
from this time, I traced him to the 1920 U.S. Census: 3328 North Twenty-
Seventh Street: Asa Fletcher, thirty-eight; Flossie Fletcher, twenty-seven;

Wallace Krieg, twenty-five; Ethel Hardin, twenty-five; Katherin Krieg, fifteen; Donna B. Fletcher, two. Who in the heck were all of these people? I wondered if the Fletchers had a large servant staff. (I later learned that Asa's wife's, Flossie's, maiden name was Krieg. These must have been her siblings.)

I began to look into eclectic medical practices, wondering if it was like homeopathy or the alternative medicine of today. Apparently much like today, the practice used a varied prescription of natural cures alongside different substances and exercise-based recuperation. It was popular in the last part of the nineteenth and first half of the twentieth centuries. An eclectic doctor would utilize botanical remedies, Native American use of therapeutic plants, organic science, and natural medication and would counsel patients and offer cures via mail. The word *eclectic* alluded to those doctors who utilized whatever was found to be gainful to their patients. According to Wikipedia: "Standard medical practices at the time made extensive use of purges with calomel and other mercury-based remedies, as well as extensive bloodletting. Eclectic medicine was a direct reaction to those barbaric practices as well as a desire to restrict Thomsonian medicine innovations to medical professionals."

I learned the last eclectic medical school closed in Cincinnati in 1939. Fletcher was from Ohio. It was all clicking. I was fascinated to imagine that Fletcher was an eclectic doctor and was running an alternative, private hospital out of his home. That all made me think he might just be the kind of daring fellow to build a castle in his backyard.

Later I found in the "Alphabetical List of Registrants of Trade-Marks" from the *Official Gazette of the United States Patent Office* that Dr. Fletcher had applied for a number of patents through the years. In 1920, under the name "Urego Chemicals Laboratories," Fletcher had filed a patent for "Skin Preparations for Certain Purposes, No. 131.653." There were numerous "Skin Preparation" patents over time. I was beginning to understand that Urego Chemicals Company (from the city directory) was one of Fletcher's companies offering naturalistic cures through the mail. I was so thrilled to find that he was an inventor. There were additional pat-

Dr. Asa E. Fletcher.

Dr. Fletcher had this lasting quality
mind when he constructed it for although
is just 46, he says he is going to live long
than any of his family.
Therefore to enjoy his castle through
his lifetime it had to be built with substan
for he recalls four great grandparents re
well, his maternal grandmother's father e
mother, and his maternal grandfather's p
ents as well. His grandmother's mother li
to help prepare the dinner for her one h
dredth birthday.
"However, if through any chance
shouldn't live as long as I expect to"

7. Donnabelle, age 11, and her father, Dr. Asa Fletcher, from 1928
Omaha World-Herald article. Is anyone else excited that her name was
Donnabelle? Reprinted with permission from the *Omaha World-Herald*.

ents under the D-Flo Chemicals Company name as well. I found a great
advertisement for D-Flo from June 2, 1935, boasting, "It lasts Forever!"

"HE HAS A CASTLE IN HIS BACK YARD"

Soon after, I found what I had been craving—an article from the *Omaha
World-Herald* from 1928 named, "He Has a Castle in His Back Yard," complete with photos and illustrations. I about died. I exclaimed much too
loudly for the library, "He built the castle!!!" I went up to the research

desk and excitedly told the young librarian what I had unearthed. Of course he didn't know what I was squealing about.

This article was a true delight to read—whimsical and well written but too long to scan in a viewable size to reproduce here. I will include just a few of its details. Dr. Fletcher's castle was built of many different stones that he collected from everywhere. He modeled it after a Normandy castle. He also built a pergola. There was a Venetian pool filled with lily pads, blooming flowers, and goldfish. There was a rock border outlining the pool and stepping-stones of all colors. He built the castle "because he saw the chance of creating something beautiful and artistic to grace his grounds; second, for a retreat from duties close at hand; and third, to typify in stone and mortar things that in life, have impressed him." It is twenty-two feet high, sixteen feet in diameter. The actual family home–hospital contained "20 or more rooms," with twenty-one different kinds of wood, and "many fireplaces faced with pottery from Holland." Donnabelle, his daughter, then eleven, along with her two parents, would often "gather in the castle in the cold weather for an evening of story telling, wienie and marshmallow roast." Now this was very good stuff. I was beside myself—and I had been wrong. He didn't build the castle for children. He built it for himself. The article contradicted what I had previously read about Fletcher having been born in Ohio, and also my assumption that his medical degree was from a Cincinnati eclectic medical school was incorrect.

Probably my second favorite printed clue in all of this treasure trove of material was an ad from March 9, 1930. This simple ad in the *Omaha World-Herald* gave me an idea of what Dr. Fletcher was trying to accomplish at Park Hospital. It was for "those who do not care to be operated upon." Miss Cassette endorses this statement.

On March 12, 1932, I came across the *World-Herald* article, under the heading of New Incorporations, "Urego Chemical Company; capital, 25 thousand dollars; A.E. and Flossie K. Fletcher and R. Rhoades, incorporators." That was quite the chunk of change for 1932.

August 1933 brought two different *World-Herald* articles about a grand party that was to be held at 4025 Izard. A "Castle Carnival"–themed party

8. Park Hospital advertisement, 1938. Reprinted with permission from the *Omaha World-Herald*.

described Donnabelle and friends hosting it as part of the Job's Daughters group. Over the years there would be mentions of Donnabelle's involvement with Bethel 13, Order of Job's Daughters.

MORE ANSWERS AND EVEN MORE QUESTIONS

By 1938 Dr. Fletcher was running ads in the newspaper that described Park Hospital as an "invalid and convalescent hospital." The ad further describes the facility: "Quiet, Restful, Homelike. Specially trained nurses and physicians. Very low rates, especially for those wishing to make this their home. Park Hospital. 4025 Izard. Omaha." I was beginning to wonder who, exactly, worked at Park Hospital. All of the want ads that I saw throughout the years were worded similarly: "Young Lady to learn to be nurse aid. No tuition to pay. We furnish board, room, laundry, books and laboratory equipment. Nor breakage fee to pay. Liberal salary while learning. Apply in person. Park Hospital." Now that sounded like a good deal. Who knows how many young gals worked there over the years? It would appear from the various ads that the staff was made up of women, young women, who were trained in the various eclectic medical modalities.

According to the 1940 U.S. Census, Donnabelle Fletcher was now twenty-two years old and still living at home. Asa was fifty-eight, Flossie was forty-seven, and Della (one of their mothers?) was seventy-seven years old. Servants or hospital staff at the time included Lucille Store, twenty-three, Doris Vetter, twenty-one, and Margaret McPhodden, nineteen years.

I discovered Donnabelle Fletcher's wedding announcement in the September 1940 *World-Herald*. She married Jack Witte Croft, and the wedding was held at the Fletcher home . . . of course. I can just see that glorious event and the backyard all decorated. I wondered if the patients and staff were involved in family functions.

FLETCHER VACATION

The *World-Herald* ran a curious little story from April 10, 1949, about a vacation Asa and Flossie Fletcher took to the Florida Keys. From the writing and photo captions, I began to deduce that (possibly) people thought the Fletchers to be odd. I could be wrong about that. There was a mocking tone to the report, and truth be told, a sea monster sighting, a hospital in their home, a castle, an inventor, and an eclectic medical practice might have been too much for conservative Omaha society to handle. I wish I could know what the university told Fletcher when he brought in those animal carcass photos.

Another photo from the April 10, 1949, article showed the couple with their basket of sponges from their vacation. The caption reads, "Dr. and Mrs. Asa Fletcher . . . collect sponges, too." I could be wrong, but to me the implication was "We are very weird."

I was sad to find that in July 1955, Dr. Asa Fletcher had died.

In the castle article he had stated that he would outlive his whole family, which did not come to pass. There are indicators that Fletcher might be buried at Westlawn or Hillcrest Cemeteries, and I do plan to investigate this further. This obit mentions his castle and the sea monster—which I love.

9. Dr. Fletcher and "tusk," 1949. Reprinted with permission from the *Omaha World-Herald*.

TRANSITION PERIOD

The property at 4025 Izard then went vacant. I can't help but wonder how the shuttering of Park Hospital went. Apparently, Flossie Fletcher moved to Palm Springs, California, at some point. She died there in 1986. Mr. Owen Moore bought the property next. I found his name listed in a 1957 directory. From 1961 till 1972 Bryan Wilson owned the house.

I had to laugh when I came across a April 5, 1979, *World-Herald* write-in. A reader penned a letter asking if anyone knew where she could get a bottle of Urego. I like to think that by the late 1970s some older woman still had her jar or bottle of 1940s Urego Cream. I know this to be a distinct possibility from looking in my grandmother's medicine cabinet as a child—ancient blue and brown bottles with hand-typed prescriptions taped on. Even the *World-Herald* couldn't solve this poor woman's query . . . but now we know the answer and from where that great, natural medicine came.

NEW ERA AND SOME QUESTIONS ANSWERED

Not too long ago Mr. Cassette and I were walking along Izard Street to get some photos of the outside of 4025. I was pleased to see how well maintained the property was. I had done quite a bit of research about the current owners and knew they are very active in the Walnut Hill Neighborhood Association. In 2011 they were involved in gathering community support to educate and advocate for changes at the Cuming Street gas station due to problematic drinking, drugs and troubled youths. True stewards of 4025 Izard and fierce supporters of Walnut Hill, this couple has worked very hard to create community. I didn't want to impose myself, but when one of the owners approached us out front on that day, I was so pleased. I found them to be lovely and gracious but appropriately cautious. I explained myself and that I was writing a story about 4025. The owners have a good understanding that people are drawn to the castle and their gorgeous property. They only request that people ask permission before taking photos and entering their gardens. During this discussion I confessed to them that I had broken their rule as a kid. It felt good to come clean. Mr. Cassette and I were allowed to walk the property with them and take photos. If my editor would allow, I would have shared all the photos taken at that lucky encounter. (You will just have to visit my website to get a proper peek!) There was a colorful stone path that Dr. Fletcher had created. To the sides would have been the original stream. We discovered very happy moss growing on Fletcher's collected stones. The winding stairs of the castle were still intact. Where the pond had been, once filled with lily pads and goldfish, was an empty basin. There was a lovely stone path bridge going over the once full stream. Photographs taken at the time of Dr. Fletcher's Park Hospital reveal the earlier splendor.

10. Castle view. Note the amazing head sculptures placed just so.
Photo courtesy of the Fletcher and Taylor families.

The current owners reported they had bought the property from Mrs. Bryan Wilson. They shared a fantastic panoramic black-and-white photo taken at the time that Fletcher was running the Park Hospital. There were gnomes and yard sculptures with faces visible in the plantings. I could imagine by the beautiful photograph that it must have been a very healing, spiritual place in its day. At the very least, it was engaging. It still is. One of the owners said they were not sure when the grotto was taken down. There had been a pond with a stream encircling the castle and a stone path that had very large crystals lining the walk. We could see the pergola was still intact, made with broken concrete, which Mr. Cassette called urbanite. There is a fence around the property constructed of the same material.

Being curious, I needed to walk up that wraparound staircase up the side of the castle again. It was still a thrill. I couldn't believe how high

11. The mysterious grotto, now gone, with the carriage house
in the distance. Just dying . . . I love grottoes. So breathtaking.
Photo courtesy of the Fletcher and Taylor families

up it felt. I feel a little teary now as I think about it. I could look through
the windows into the structure but did not go in this time. As we walked
around the grounds, one of the owners gave us some other information.
She shared that she had heard Dr. Fletcher had used electroshock therapy (which doesn't really seem in line with the homeopathic field) and
had invented a therapeutic drink made of urine. She called it the Park
Hospital Sanatorium. She alluded to the people of Omaha viewing Dr.
Fletcher as something of a quack in his day—that he was an outsider. I
cannot be sure if any of this is true, only that she had heard these things.
What I can say for sure is that no matter his skill in the medical realm,
what he created in his backyard was and still is a beautiful thing—serene,
filled with variety and fantasy. It is simply compelling to imagine the
Park Hospital and its park like setting of the 1920s. It must have been so
quiet back then. I dream that is why he named it the Park Hospital. As
his obituary states, Dr. Fletcher left Omaha a landmark. In that fitting
way I believe he did outlive his relatives. I find comfort in that.

12. (*top*) The enshrouded pergola. Dark and majestic. Photo
courtesy of the Fletcher and Taylor families.

13. (*bottom*) Current pergola. Photo by author.

CHAPTER 2

The Adventure of Twenty-Fifth Street

I saw the house on Twenty-Fifth Street properly, for the very first time, early one afternoon in the middle to late 1990s when I was out driving in South Omaha. Or on a hunt, as I now say. House Hunting. Mansion Chasing. Building Stalking. I am sure you understand what this means. I would have liked to omit the fact that I was probably munching on Corn Nuts, smoking cigarettes, and gulping away at an original-flavor Slurpee as I headed down that brick paved road, but I can't ignore those details. That was my idea of a fine summer snack back then, and I now see these details as part of my anecdotal, early-detective shtick.

Let me start by giving some background information. I had never really known much about South Omaha up to that point. Growing up in Benson, we rarely had much occasion to drive south. I was that kid, like so many, who made a big dramatic to-do about the stockyards' smell as we inched ever closer on the freeway. As a child, I remember we would travel south infrequently, to eat at Johnny's Café on South Twenty-Seventh and also to visit Joe Tess Place on South Twenty-Fourth. My parents had met there on a blind date for catfish—a favorite family story. I do remember playing various South Omaha grade schools in volleyball and basketball, where we were customarily met with a fierce pride and bois-terous mystique that seemed so foreign to us young Bensonites. Truth be told, those drives south seemed like a whole city away from what I perceived as Omaha. I now know that it truly was its own city prior to 1915. Throughout high school I would begin to frequent the numerous and well-stocked thrift stores in the Twenty-Fourth Street area, and there was a short time when Drastic Plastic Record Store called South O home. By then I had a few friends in the music scene who lived south. I knew

14. House at 3825 South Twenty-Fifth Street, from a southwest
angle, with porte cochere. Photo by author.

the well-worn path and quite enjoyed it, even though I knew so little of
South Omaha's history.

In recollection I had probably turned off of Twenty-Fourth on one such
thrift store venture that day. The building at 3825 South Twenty-Fifth
Street. What a find! It was the proper porte cochere that beguiled me. I
hadn't seen many of those around in South O. Not only did 3825 impress;
it seemed downright intimidating. Self-possessed. It seemed to hold an
unusual position on the street—right on the corner of Twenty-Fifth and
D. It was both off the beaten path and right out in front, where anyone
could find it. The mature trees seemed much older than I was accus-
tomed to and better somehow. There were some shrubs, which I loved,
with rough patches of grass. But where were all of the other mansions?
It seemed unusual for a house of this magnitude to be next to a row of
common flats. There were some lovely homes in the area but none displaying the haughtiness of 3825, nor any that inspired that hair-raising
quality. It didn't quite make sense to me.

The yard and house were built up, on a bank—imposing, like all elements of the brick home. The windows were tall and gave the impression

of staring down at its admirers. Highland Park was directly across the street, having ensured an excellent view for decades. All of this chilling glory, which I admit I couldn't resist, stayed with me. A brick estate such as this, especially when it is on a brick paved street, across from a large park, leads to daydreaming and extended, tangled bits of playing pretend house in my mind. I couldn't imagine the who and the what and the how a person could acquire such a place. The house at 3825, even in those days, seemed worn in some respects, although still beautiful. I hoped it hadn't been broken up into apartments. As the years went by, I would stop visiting the mysterious 3825.

Then, a *My Omaha Obsession* reader wrote to inquire about 3825 South Twenty-Fifth Street. I was absolutely compelled to research this property the moment I wrote her back. I had no idea of the colorful stories within the house's walls.

EARLY FACT-FINDING MISSION

I began my mission by spending what might seem to many people I know an outlandish amount of time gathering information on 3825. The Douglas County Assessor showed the property as having been built in 1900. I could find no immediate proof of this. Because of the way different years of the city directory are represented—some years do not offer a street guide, and some years show blurry, indecipherable photocopies of the original—I could not find 3825 listed properly until the year 1918. I found the owner's name listed as "Geo Parks." George Parks. In years 1923 through 1930 I found "Geo Parks contr" had owned 3825 as well as having been listed irregularly in different years at nearby addresses 3718–3821. I had a hunch that maybe there had been more large houses originally north of 3825, where the flats now stand. I imagined he was a contractor and might have built or owned other buildings on the block. By 1931, 3825 South Twenty-Fifth Street was listed as "vacant." The home was listed as vacant in 1932 also. I had to find out who this contractor George Parks was.

I could not find any information about the original architect or the builder. The Omaha Planning Department did not have 3825 in its data-

15. George Parks. Photo from *Omaha: The Gate City and Douglas County,
Nebraska; A Record of Settlement, Organization, Progress and Achievement*, vol. 2,
by Arthur C. Wakeley (Chicago: S. J. Clarke Publishing Co., 1917).

base either. The Nebraska State Historical Society could find no record
of the house or George Parks. I would have to go exploring elsewhere.

HISTORY OF GEORGE PARKS

In my research I discovered George Parks built the home at 3825
South Twenty-Fifth Street in 1901. In fact, the home was so well known

16. Cudahy Packing Plant holding pens, 1923. From the KM3TV/
Bostwick-Frohardt Photograph Collection at the Durham Museum.

and often visited in its day that it was called the George Parks House.
This fact has apparently fallen off the books, until now. Unbeknownst to
me, George Parks was regarded as one of Omaha's, and South Omaha's,
most important leaders in the late 1800s. From *Omaha: The Gate City and
Douglas County, Nebraska; A Record of Settlement, Organization, Progress
and Achievement*, written in 1917 by Arthur C. Wakeley, I learned that
George Parks occupied a lofty "position among the most prominent and
substantial residents of Douglas County." An emigrant of County Armagh
(where he apprenticed in bricklaying and masonry), by way of Chicago,
Parks and his wife, Margaret, were brought to Omaha in 1888 to build
the Armour-Cudahy packing plant in South Omaha. In 1890 it became
simply Cudahy Packing Company.

He spent a full year erecting all the brick and ironwork in connection
with the plant. Parks had previously made a name for himself in the
construction and bricklaying business in Chicago and was courted by

South O's growing Union Stockyards Company. The stockyards began its long history in 1883, when Wyoming cattle baron, Alexander Hamilton Swan, together with six Omaha businessmen, accumulated the necessary capital and land and formed the Union Stockyards Company of Omaha.

Aside from being an Irishman, which is tops in my book, my inquiry led me to believe that George Parks was big-time in Omaha. As president of the National Construction Company, Parks would go on to build, become contractor or subcontractor for, every major South Omaha packing plant. According to *100 Years of Omaha Stockyards*, by 1910 there were ten slaughtering houses and packing plants located in South Omaha. Parks's name and expertise won him contracts throughout the United States, where he erected packing plants, hotels, warehouses, and train stations, constructed sewers, and undertook paving projects. Known for efficient, quality work, he paved most of South Omaha and quite a bit of downtown Omaha, employing many men. Of note, he built the Cudahy Ice House at Seymour Lake and the Omaha Wool & Storage Company warehouse—one of its incorporators was Charles H. King, President Gerald Ford's grandfather.

George Parks was also president of the George Parks Company of Omaha. It only made sense that in May 1916 Parks became a city commissioner. As a city official, he would further oversee the department of street cleaning and maintenance. He was in numerous men's fraternal organizations, including Woodmen of the World. I found so many articles about his service work as well as men writing into the local papers touting his fine work and character. It was really pretty awe-inspiring.

THE GEORGE PARKS HOUSE

Is it any wonder that a man so well known for his South Omaha brickwork would create a redbrick home in the very place that made him famous? Boasting twenty-five rooms, 3825 South Twenty-Fifth Street was known for its beautiful, steep pitched roof, stained glass windows, and eleven fireplaces. The Parks House cost a whopping $10,000, making it one of the two most expensive houses built that year. Just so there is no confusion, you must first know that 3825 South Twenty-Fifth Street is a Very Large House. One source listed it at nine bedrooms and five baths, at 7,868 square feet. Another listed it with nine bedrooms, four and half baths, at 6,644 square feet. Another still listed it with 8,284 square feet of living space with five and a half baths. If any of these portray a sliver of the truth, 3825 is an immense property.

THE PARKS APARTMENTS

One of the most interesting facts that I stumbled across was learning George Parks also built the row of flats directly to the north of house. (These were the apartments I thought had arrived after some incredible old homes were destroyed.) Constructed in 1901, the same year as his family home, they were known as the Parks Apartments. I was floored. From what I could find, there were seven separate addresses. In time these were listed as fourteen separate apartments. It is possible that these larger apartments were broken up over the years to make room for more renters. It was so fun to see all of the names of renters over the years. As George was known for employing "most of young South Omaha," I couldn't help but wonder if he rented to them too. Around this time I came across the brilliant "National Register of Historic Places Multiple Property" report by Jennifer Honebrink, which clearly described the history of row houses and attached dwellings in Omaha. Fascinating. She reported that from 1890 to 1930 the rise of the streetcar, providing a connection to all parts of the city (Dundee, Benson, South Omaha), coincided with the rise of attached dwellings. "A growing number of row houses with more than three units per row" was illustrated by numerous Sanborn maps. By 1918 the rise of attached dwellings had doubled. Throughout the study it was noted that the row houses were quite adaptable in that they could easily change from single-family dwellings into single-sex boardinghouses or a shop; one even moonlighted as a hospital. I began to understand how the "apartment numbers" of the George Parks flats could have changed and/or doubled over time.

Additionally, there was a large carriage house built behind the 3825 Parks House in the same year. I would find out more about the carriage

17. The Parks Row Houses as they look today, directly to the north of 3825 South Twenty-Fifth Street. Photo by author.

house later. G. Wm. Baist's *Real Estate Atlas of 1910* revealed the house, apartments, and carriage house for the first time—thanks to the Omaha Public Library archives. I was fascinated to find that Highland Park had always been across the street, to the west.

THE PARKS FAMILY

Just as intriguing as their large house and successful lives, George and Margaret Parks also had fourteen children together. Fourteen. From what I found, one of their children, Marie, died in infancy in 1893. All fifteen of the Parks family lived at 3825 South Twenty-Fifth Street. After inspecting Ancestry.com, I learned that while still living in Chicago, George Parks had sent for his then widowed mother, Catherine Hughes Parks. She later died in Omaha, in 1911. This tells me that she possibly lived in 3825 as well. And surely they had some servants living in the home. Maybe on that third floor? That must have been quite the lively house. I am not sure if you lived in this manner, but having that many

28

people around sounds like a kind of heaven to me. The more the merrier. Local newspapers credited Margaret with accomplishing social and charitable work while raising thirteen children. Her "maternal opinions" were sought after, and she was interviewed as a local expert. I should say.

A SOCIAL CENTER OF SOUTH OMAHA

The Parks House had become a true social and political center in both Omaha and South Omaha. I found many newspaper articles citing meetings held at the home over the years. I was delighted to find breadcrumbs leading to Buffalo Bill Cody. He had been an animated guest at the Parks House. Over the years George, Margaret, and their thirteen children also entertained Irish president Eamon De Valera, U.S. president Woodrow Wilson, and William Jennings Bryan. It can be assumed that every big name in Omaha and the region must have been a guest at some point, as the couple loved to socialize and valued community.

Also discovered were thirtieth and fortieth wedding anniversary articles in the local papers describing incredible parties held in the home. "Such a gathering of intellect and combination of decorative effect has never been witnessed as existed at this wedding anniversary last night." Described were the dancing, hundreds of guests, "the north half of the home devoted to pleasure," and the large basement arranged with tables "with heaps of good things calculated to satisfy the most epicurean tastes of the guests." Oh, how divine is that? The full, finished basement was described again in one of their daughters' wedding reception write-ups. It is interesting to imagine a finished basement of this time period, appropriate for parties of this magnitude.

I am not sure why, but it felt too sudden to hear when I came across the news that George Parks died on May 2, 1930. He was buried at St. Mary's Cemetery at Thirty-Third and Q. I am not absolutely certain, but I have reason to believe that Margaret died the very same year. In fact, this notice in the *Omaha World-Herald* gives me reason to believe that she might have died previous to George. Oddly, George Parks died without leaving a will.

Parks Estate Estimated $65,000; Left No Will

The estate of the late George Parks, contractor, who died May 2, will amount to at least 65 thousand dollars, according to a valuation filed in county court today. There is no will and the estate will be divided between seven daughters and four sons. Joseph Murphy, South Omaha real estate man, is administrator.

18. News of Parks's death from the *Omaha World-Herald* archives, May 31, 1930. Reprinted with permission from the *Omaha World-Herald*.

A SECOND LIFE FOR 3825

The exploration into the history of 3825 South Twenty-Fifth became even more vibrant with the next discovery. I found Heafey & Heafey, Inc., took ownership in the 1933 city directory. I had heard a rumor that 3825 had been a funeral home at some point, but reading the news made the pieces fall into place. Heafey & Heafey Mortuary was another longtime, respected pioneer business in Omaha.

According to *Omaha Memories: Recollections of Events, Men and Affairs* by Edward Morearty, Patrick C. Heafey was another Irishman, originally from Country Kerry. He arrived in Omaha in 1878. Initially employed at Union Pacific Railroad, Heafey would transition into the undertaking business with P. J. Barrett. Together they formed Barrett & Heafey Funeral Home, located at 216 South Fourteenth Street. After Barrett retired, Morgan Heafey, brother of Patrick, entered the business. A new partnership of

Old Parks Residence to Be Funeral Home

The old George Parks home at, Twenty-fifth and D streets has been purchased by Heafey & Heafey, funeral directors, and is being remodeled into a mortuary.

19. Brief article announcing Heafey & Heafey's purchase of 3825 South Twenty-Fifth Street, August 3, 1932. Reprinted with permission from the *Omaha World-Herald*.

Heafey & Heafey later moved to Twenty-Sixth and Farnam. Patrick would go on to become a member of the fire and police board, county coroner, governor's staff, and Omaha water board. Patrick was in a number of fraternal organizations and no doubt had rubbed shoulders with George Parks. Patrick Heafey passed away in 1921. The gorgeous tombstone of Patrick Heafey can be found at Holy Sepulchre Cemetery on Leavenworth Street.

By 1933 John C. Heafey had become funeral director of Heafey & Heafey. I learned that after the Depression many families could not afford to maintain their large homes and mansions. Funeral homes began to move into these once privately owned homes. There were many mansions on Farnam Street, now gone, in the Gold Coast district of Omaha, that later became funeral homes. The Parks House had sat empty for almost two full years after the death of George and Margaret. It is understandable that not many people in the early 1930s would have been able to afford and maintain a house such as that.

It is strange to me, but by May 23, 1934, I found, the Highland Park Improvement Club was holding a "special meeting" at 3825. No men-

31

tion of the meeting being held at a funeral home. I found that odd, but maybe a funeral home was not an unusual meeting place in those days.

Upon deeper probing in the 1938 city directory, I discovered the John C. Heafey family was living in the mortuary. I was completely tingly. Was this possibly as cool and weird as the HBO show *Six Feet Under*? Of course I knew this used to be a fairly common practice, but by today's standards—shudder to think or absolutely enthralled? You decide! By 1945 John C. Heafey had a small 9 after his name in the city directory, denoting nine people resided at 3825. By 1950 there was a 7 after his name. At this point I knew I had to reach out to Heafey-Heafey-Hoffman-Dworak-Cutler Funeral Chapels, as it is now called, to see if I could speak with a relative of John C. Heafey.

THE TOM HEAFEY INTERVIEW

I found Tom Heafey, son of John C. Heafey, to be absolutely gracious. What a sport he was to lend his time and share his family memories. According to Tom, the Heafey & Heafey Funeral Home started in 1882, where the W. Dale Clark Library is now downtown at Fourteenth and Farnam Streets. Later the business moved to South Twenty-Fourth Street, a site that eventually became the Brown Derby restaurant. "We all went to St. Bridget's nearby and knew the Parkses from church." (I later confirmed time and time again that the Parkses were longtime members of St. Bridget's.) "My father bought the Parkses' house. They had raised thirteen kids in the house!" He also added, "They say Parks used the leftover bricks from his jobs and that built that big, old house." Another interesting anecdote that Tom shared was that "one of the Parkses' daughters was born, raised, had her wedding reception in the basement, rosary, wake, and funeral at that very house." I worked to confirm this information but could not find specific records about it . . . yet.

"The house was huge! My folks lived in the house on the second floor. There were six bedrooms there. So did my uncle and other employees over the years." Tom shared that he had lived there as well. When he was older, he lived there with his wife. When I asked him if he raised a family there, he expressed: "That was no place for children. We had

The Finer Funerals For Less

Use Our Insured Time Payment Plan – Up To 36 Months

AMPLE OFF STREET PARKING

3522 FARNAM

PHONE 345-1251

3825 SOUTH 25th

PHONE 733-0246

20. Heafey & Heafey advertisement scanned from the Omaha City Directory. The image depicts the company's two locations.

moved out by then." This statement has stayed with me since talking to him because . . . wasn't he raised there as a child?

He explained that many Creighton students had lived in the house and carriage house off and on. The main floor was used as a chapel and funeral home visitation rooms. The lower back of the first floor was for embalming and funeral prep. The upper rooms were used as family bedrooms. There was a large recreation room in the basement that was used for family gatherings or funeral luncheons. These were the glorious rooms previously described in the press that the Parkses used for their large parties. Funeral home storage was also in the basement. I don't know why, but this felt like a shivery commingling.

Tom remembered 3825 being "filled with beautiful woodwork. The carriage house was solid oak with tile around the sides. There were two full apartments in the carriage house where mortuary staff or students lived." Apparently, there were numerous stalls for the horses of bygone years with a full turntable for cars. I didn't know this, but the early cars had no "reverse." This meant a car would have to be pushed

21. Southwest view of the home at 3825 South Twenty-Fifth
Street, now sans porte cochere. Photo by author.

back out of a carriage house or garage when a person wanted to leave. A turntable allowed the car to be turned in the correct direction to drive out of a carriage house with ease. Heafey said that the turntable could not accommodate the larger hearses as the years went by, and they no longer used it.

Tom shared another scrumptious detail. There is a full basement in the carriage house, and there is or was a tunnel connecting that carriage house basement to the mansion. I found that this was a common trend in mansions with carriage houses at this time period. Very forward thinking when a person considers our weather here in Nebraska. Also, my beautiful porte cochere, previously mentioned, lent itself nicely to the funeral home—a proper detail when letting a mourning family in and out of a hearse. I began imagining what life would be like growing up in a mortuary. Living where you work would be odd enough, in that your private life was never properly shadowed from view. Adding children to the picture of a domesticated funeral home seemed complicated; it was probably considered bad form to leave one's bike on the lawn.

On that note, I found in the January 8, 1973, *Omaha World-Herald* that a daughter was born to Ben and Debbie Funk of 3825 South Twenty-Fifth Street. Perhaps they were Heafey & Heafey employees or some of the students Tom had mentioned.

FUNERAL HOME INQUIRY

By 1975 I had unearthed an interesting change in the directory. The buildings at 3809 through 3821 South Twenty-Fifth Street, previously the Parks Apartments (Row Houses), were listed under the San Francisco Apartments. Additionally, James B. Heafey was registered as living at 3825, no longer John C. I found that John C. Heafey passed away in 1972. He is buried at Holy Sepulchre Cemetery also. I am not entirely sure that James B. was the "uncle" Tom spoke of.

Tiptoeing through the Omaha Obits site, I learned further history about the timeline of Heafey & Heafey. Heafey & Heafey Funeral Homes operated both 3552 Farnam Street and 3825 South Twenty-Fifth Street from 1930 through the 1960s. By the 1980s the company had only one location, at 3825 South Twenty-Fifth.

The funeral industry would go through another shift in the 1980s, when funeral home corporations began buying up the small, family-owned mortuaries. Heafey & Heafey survived the trend, and continues to flourish to this day, by joining with other private, locally owned mortuary businesses. In 1982 Heafey & Heafey and Hoffman Mortuaries joined forces. They maintained three locations during this period, at 7805 West Center Road, Twenty-Fourth and Dodge Streets, and 3825 South Twenty-Fifth. According to the *Omaha World-Herald*, funeral director Leo A. Hoffman died in 1984.

The year 1987 brought another name change or ownership change of hands. The San Francisco Apartments became the Towne Center Apartments. There continued to be seven different apartment listings all under that name.

In 1990 there was yet another funeral home merger, the existing company becoming Heafey-Heafey-Hoffman-Dworak-Cutler Funeral Chapels. This new, larger mortuary had three locations at 7805 West Center Road, Twenty-Fourth and Dodge Street, 3825 South Twenty-Fifth, and 2466 South Sixteenth Street. That year is also the last date I found the funeral home listed at 3825.

PERPLEXING CHAPTER IN THE HISTORY OF 3825

There are a number of points going forward that I am doubtful of and am going to attempt to lay out for your inspection. Either I need to do more digging in these areas to get the chronological order correct or the history of the house was truly this confusing. Confusing point number 1: Tom Heafey stated that at some juncture the "Landmark Preservation group" approached them about wanting to own 3825 South Twenty-Fifth Street. "They were just getting started, and they wanted the house. They wanted it in a form of a donation, and I just couldn't do that." Tom said Heafey-Heafey-Hoffman-Dworak-Cutler wanted out of 3825 simply because of the times. "The trend is always to move west. From our beginnings on Fourteenth and Farnam. Always west." The funeral company was not able to donate the house to the new Landmark group, but I think we can assume from perplexing pieces of the puzzle that the funeral home was looking for a buyer long before 1990.

Confusing point number 2: An *Omaha World-Herald* article I found from August 2, 1979, summarized that United Catholic Social Services had intentions to buy 3825 South Twenty-Fifth Street. Its idea was to "house up to 20 youths who have undergone treatment for alcoholism or chemical dependency." Apparently, the idea was that fourteen- to nineteen-year-olds would remain in the home for four to six months, I assumed, like a halfway house. The neighbors balked, taking issue with safety. Oddly, the article referred to 3825 as a "former mortuary." But by all other accounts Heafey & Heafey, in all of its stages, was consistently operating out of 3825 until 1990. I began to wonder if they owned the building but had moved their business long before. Perhaps like the Parks estate, finding a buyer for 3825 proved difficult. I could understand the barrier, in that it was a very large estate and subsequently carried the stigma of having been a mortuary for decades.

Confusing point number 3: According to the *World-Herald* article from September 12, 1979, the permit was granted for the United Catholic Social Services group care home. "Four residents of the area opposed the plan, saying it was inappropriate for the area." I maintain that this point has continued to confound me. James B. Heafey was living at 3825 in 1979, according to all accounts, as well as running the mortuary from this site. I began to wonder if the Highland neighbors fought this to such an extent that the group home never came to pass—in which case the Heafey & Heafey family was still carrying the ownership. I could find no proof that the group home ever took ownership or formally got off the ground at Twenty-Fifth.

MORE CLUES AND EVEN MORE QUESTIONS

Things began to get back on track for me when I found a real estate transfer from January 31, 1993: "Thomas P. Heafey to Gregory T. Nelson for $50,000." This piece fit tidily with a comment Tom Heafey had made near the end of our talk. He said: "A couple bought it and wanted to start a bed-and-breakfast. They never did. I never heard what happened with that." Additionally, I found in the Omaha City Directory of 1995 that Greg Nelson and Holly Winters owned the home. I figured they were the couple who had wanted to start the B&B. Can you imagine the marketing of a funeral home–turned–guest inn? Now that would have been fabulous.

According to my findings, in October 15, 1995, there was another real estate transfer listed from Gregory T. Nelson to Richard L. Larson for $135,000. Within two years the couple had likely made some nice improvements, adding value to the home, but for whatever reason had decided to move on. I did not know why, but I am fairly certain the bed-and-breakfast never came to fruition. The 1998 city directory showed that R. M. Suiter and Richard Larson were living at 3825. Again in May 1999, another real estate transfer was filed from Richard Larson to Richard J. Larson for $124,000. The city directory of 2003 showed Image Ad Specialties, an advertising and promotional company, had taken over ownership. Additional names of Roxanne Suiter and Dorothy Suiter were listed under this title. I was pretty sure that these people had a connection with or were one and the same as the previously mentioned R. M. Suiter from 1998.

I found 3825 South Twenty-Fifth Street was listed as part of the 2005 *Reconnaissance Survey of Portions of South Omaha*. In this survey the home was one of seventeen individual properties identified as good candidates for designation as an Omaha landmark and an appropriate future listing in the National Register. I was overjoyed.

Later, after corresponding with Trina Westman of Urban Design and Historic Preservation at Omaha Planning, I learned that 3825 South Twenty-Fifth Street had been surveyed as part of the 1980 Landmarks, Inc., survey. Trina also included information gathered from page 68 of the survey, a document that showed building additions and alterations to 3825 in 1937 and 1972 under the Heafey organization. It would appear that in 1937 architects N. Carter & Son designed an addition. The builder was listed as L. Kocher at a cost of $650. J. Heafy, listed as builder, would make another addition in April 1972 for $1,000.

MYSTERIOUS TURN OF EVENTS

Mysteriously, 2009 found Richard Larson Jr. listed as owner of the house again. Perhaps he was partner in Image Ad Specialties? I have reason to believe that Richard J. Larson then sold, lost, or was losing the house to foreclosure in 2010. There was also a Richard Larson who passed away in December 2010. I am not sure what the cause of his death was, only that he was a young man, at fifty-five years of age. A neighbor tipped me off that our Mr. Larson is still alive and well. What is known for sure is that at some point in 2011, the house at 3825 South Twenty-Fifth Street, unfortunately, fell into foreclosure. This is where things got a little more peculiar.

Miss Cassette happens to know a wide variety of people and, being brave in nature, is not afraid to call upon contacts if it means rooting out an investigation. I knew I would have to get dirty and call up a contact in the foreclosure business. A secondary cleaning company or a "foreclosure clean-out company" is another business involved in the foreclosure process. Often the bank or another entity will hire a sweep-out crew to come in and clean, organize, and empty a home after the last owners have moved out or been locked out by the bank. Part of cleaning out a foreclosed property entails photographing the condition that the house was in prior to entrance, documenting all work done, and taking photos afterward to show its condition. I only wish I could include all of the images at the *My Omaha Obsession* website, but that would fill a whole book. The website shows photos from when the house was on the market again, not the cleaning crew's post-cleanup photos.

THE CLEANING TEAM INTERVIEWS

In talking to the foreclosure clean-out crew of 3825 South Twenty-Fifth, I learned many, many things. Some memories are still bothersome to those who helped clean it out that summer. One member of the crew, when asked why the house might have been in foreclosure, thought "a man had bought it for his wife and she died suddenly. He was left with all that house and no money." She remembered the house was filled with antiques, and "it was like he moved what he could with the limited time he had. He left the rest of the furniture." The house was in a worn-down condition, but the team was awestruck by the sheer size and obvious past glory of the estate.

Apparently, there were a couple of big rooms in the basement, which looked "updated." One appeared to be an office-type space, and the other side they perceived to be storage space for the funeral home items. "As you walked toward the other end of the basement, it got creepy where the outside door came down into the basement. I assume this was the entrance for bringing bodies down for embalming. There was a large concrete room. There was a large furnace, or maybe it was a cremation stove. There was another room you could access by walking through this room. This where there was still a long narrow table in it, but we only had our camera flashlights so we didn't spend a lot of time exploring this. It was moldy, smelly, and cold. Off the initial concrete room were about four to five small narrow stairs that went down even further than the basement into a cellar-like room." There were shelves there but nothing in the room other than rusted cans of what they believed were embalming powders or fluids. The cans in storage were shaped similarly to Bickmore Mortician's Embalming Powder, a popular brand. With great zest I share Bickmore's marketing slogan: "Allays all disagreeable odors." One should hope.

Miss Cassette began to wonder, were these cans left over from the funeral home days, similar to when a homeowner of the past leaves clues for homeowners of the future? Mr. Cassette and I found a curious storage area in our early 1940s home filled with leftover linoleum tiles, extra paint, fantastic 1940s metal blinds, wood trim, bags of original hardware, curtains, and a square of old carpet—but nothing like Bickmore Mortician's Embalming Powder. Apparently, that was not the only thing left behind. The mold was so bad the cleaning women had to wear masks because they could hardly breathe on their own.

One member of the cleaning company was working at the site alone one day—the only person with access to the property. She had just finished cleaning one of the renovated bathrooms on an upper floor and had moved into another area of the home. As she was coming back through the house, she observed a small, lit candle found flickering on the edge of the Jacuzzi tub she had just cleaned. This was terrifying to the worker, as she did not remember there being a candle in the bathroom at all, nor did she light the candle. After that experience she had other workers accompany her to the large property.

Another of the cleaning staff reported on a different day, "I placed a camera on the kitchen counter, and we all went up to the third floor to work. When we came back down, the camera was on the floor on the other side of the kitchen with the batteries out—like it was thrown across the room." All three cleaning crew members agreed: "Just creepy feelings in general the moment you walk in there. Not a good feeling."

NEWEST CHAPTER FOR 3825

At this point out of respect of those personally involved, I am going to omit the owners' names. This has come up in the past as an issue of privacy, and I certainly want to be sensitive to all involved. My research again

22. Front elevation, western-facing 3825 South Twenty-Fifth Street. Much improvement has been made to the structure and landscaping. Photo by author.

led me to another real estate transfer in the summer of 2012 from Mr. M to Ms. A for ninety-five thousand dollars. I am not sure if Ms. A is part of a local investments company, but at some point 3825 South Twenty-Fifth Street went on the books under the name of I. Investments LLC. I. Investments continue to operate its business and the management of its many properties out of 3825. Most likely, Mr. C, principal employer, lives there, and possibly others live there as well.

I knew I had to call the police just to be sure I beat the bushes. From the Omaha Police Department records department, I learned that the OPD had received a "destruction of property" call in 2015. Upon the officers' arrival, the owner claimed someone (unknown to this day) had apparently thrown a brick through the large, glass-plated front door. Ironic. The vandal reportedly "ran toward the Highland Towers." The Highland Tower is a few blocks north of 3825. I could find no other crimes associated with this property.

Incidentally, the Parks Apartments are currently owned by 3809 South Twenty-Fifth Street LLC under the auspices of the Omaha Group LLC, an investment group out of Denver, Colorado. They purchased the historic Parks Row Houses in 2015. The flats are again listed as fourteen separate units.

I honestly don't know how I managed to walk so jauntily down Twenty-Fifth Street after hearing what I had been told by the cleaning crew. I knew I had to get photos, though. My only thought when my mind ventured to chilling places or fear on that walk around the property was that I hoped a spirit or spirits would understand my curiosity. An odd hope that there could be a mutual understanding. My eye was drawn upward to the truly spectacular property. Where was my porte cochere? I couldn't believe it was missing. It was still intact in the photos taken during the foreclosure sale. I was saddened. After many years of neglect due to changing owners (and who has that much money, after all?), the years post–Heafey & Heafey had altered the old girl's character. I could see the new owners were working to bring her back to glory. She retained an individual pride and beauty. Great interest had been shown in the garden surrounding the property, and there were telltale signs that someone moves around the estate frequently. It may seem childish, but as I walked down the brick road to my car, I hoped that the house and all inside, whatever shape or form, knew it was a treasured part of Omaha history.

CHAPTER 3

For the Love of Rose Lodge

I had written Rose Lodge on a manila file folder, an early target investigation that I had hoped to explore in my first months at this sleuthing business. Eventually, the folder was buried like so many of my dead-of-night epiphanies piled up around this study. We don't really have a wood-paneled study that I can haunt about in, but if we did, I know exactly how it would look and feel and smell. It would most surely involve hiring a distinguished man of taste, a spirited centenarian specter, to come in and set things up to his liking, arranging leather-bound volumes, adjusting brass picture lights on equestrian paintings, and turning a weathered, leather globe just so and resting in a crackly chair in old gray suede Hush Puppies, most likely prompting the smoking of a pipe. A guild of golden retrievers would also be employed to lay about the gloriously large Persian rug as to subsume all of their good-scented-ness and profuse shedding. Actually, the group of retrievers could stay on as family members, no longer employed, but most likely the older gentleman presence might have to go after a time because his good-natured shadow of a wife would surely miss him, and I abhor shuffling about in the middle of the night and gargling early in the morning. Well . . . you clearly can see how I would fancy my dark wood–paneled study and how that might have been the perfect place to pleasurably toil away on my latest mystery. Back to the matter at hand: Rose Lodge.

My Dear Watsons, Rose Lodge has been permanently moored in my memory since childhood. I know I am not the only one with those keen thoughts. Yes, this was one of the very first moments when I realized that fried chicken was a true delicacy, quite different from any home-cooked serving before. And yes, I nattered on and on about Bishop's Buffet fried chicken in my article "For the Love of Bishop's Buffet: Why, Oh Why, Did They Close?" but Rose's was different. In the words of Father of Miss Cassette: "The secret was in the flaky crust. They were known for their 'secret recipe.'" If by chance you don't recall, there was always an air of intrigue within the community regarding Rose Lodge's secret recipe. This Omaha institution was a True Cassette Family Favorite, even from my grandmother's time. As each savory piece of evidence presented itself along this investigation, I soon could not deny that my family favorite had a Very Colorful Past, unbeknownst to me. As it turns out, the beloved family fried chicken enterprise wasn't always so family friendly. And this only brought up more questions. I knew we had a mystery to solve.

A word of warning, however, must be issued to all New Wise Readers. Any regular will tell you. I like to play around on side streets and get lost on each trail. I am not a very tidy narrator. As you by now have picked up, there will be an almost insurmountable pile of irrelevant personal details. Even Mother of Miss Cassette only reads my every twentieth word. (It is true. She was taught to speed-read, and she really cannot kick this dreadful habit.) If you cannot bear my wanderings, you can always skip ahead to part 2, "The Official Rose Lodge," but honestly, you will probably find more meanderings there as well. Is this new adventure best read over three afternoons or a full week in bed suffering with a spring cold? For myself I think you should take your time, reading it like chapters in a book, rather than small sections, but I will let you make those decisions. Fellow sleuthhounds will know to get out their pads and pencils now, for this story could be a small tome unto itself. The clues will mount up to something Treacherously Wonderful.

PART 1

The Beginning

My early discovery was the first official advertisement for Rose Lodge from July 2, 1937, announcing its new location on Seventy-Ninth and Dodge Streets. This seemed way out west as a child. The drive from Benson seemed to last an eternity, making it all the more special. Many of

IT'S NEW . . .
. . . IT'S DIFFERENT

ROSE LODGE

79th and Dodge Sts.
(formerly Rose's, 230 S. 68th Ave.)

Opening Saturday
July 3rd

CONTINUING SERVING OUR
DELICIOUS CHICKEN AND
STEAK DINNERS

SPECIAL!
FRIED CHICKEN
SANDWICH **40c**

Your Favorite Beer
In Bottles
Served Ice Cold **10c**

23. Advertisement for the Rose Lodge from July 2, 1937. "It's New . . . It's Different
ROSE LODGE." Reprinted with permission from the *Omaha World-Herald*.

you will recognize it as the home of O'Daniel Honda of Omaha, across
the street from Wild Oats Market, now Natural Grocers.

My opening mystery clue in the ad read, "Formerly Rose's, 230 S.
68th Ave." What was this? As a sleuth, one must always jot these hints
down . . . and I knew I would want to see if there was still a building at
an old address. I was not exactly able to pinpoint the location right off.
During this time, by fluky fortune, a *My Omaha Obsession* reader (aka
operative), named Bill Glaser wrote me an email. He astutely picked

24. The house at 230 South Sixty-Eighth Avenue on
that bitterly cold day. Photo by author.

up an indication from one of my articles, "I Wish I Could Have Gone
To: The Cave under the Hill," that I soon would be writing about Rose
Lodge. He sent along a photo of 230 South Sixty-Eighth Avenue, along
with a little story of how he became acquainted with one of the Rouse
boys who lived in this home in the 1960s. I was floored to see this glorious photo and instantly thought it looked like a Dundee-Fairacres affair.
At that point I was very turned around and was not completely sold that
Rose Lodge had potentially started in this beautiful home. Could Bill be
mistaken? I thought to myself.

I was easily able to look up 230 South Sixty-Eighth Avenue through
the Douglas County Assessor's site, and by George, there it was. Still
standing in all its glory. I had thought maybe a prior incarnation of Rose
Lodge had stood there, predating the home—more of a proper restaurant? But the Assessor's site said the pretty home was built in 1926. If
that year was correct, that meant that Rose's Restaurant, as it apparently
was called then, had been operating out of this house. But how? I would

need to have a good look, and a quick drive over to Sixty-Eighth Avenue became of utmost importance. As I wheeled down the avenue, I shortly realized this was a block that I had spent quite a bit of time at in my early high school years, with a classmate living right up the way. I found 230 to be all the more breathtaking in person . . . right on the corner of Sixty-Eighth and Farnam. It was a nice wide lot with room to stretch. I noted the larger tract was uncommon in this part of town, but it suited the broad, formal symmetry of the residence. Impressive.

So I was engulfed in glory once again. I walked the quiet avenue on that cold day, sizing up each beautiful house with very different eyes than I had in high school. The building at 230 South Sixty-Eighth Avenue was a beautifully strange fit for this neighborhood. I spun around on my sleuthing heels—yet another mystery involving the entangled lives and the comfortable halls of the Omaha well-to-do. And here I thought this story would be a simple fried chicken piece. From that moment on, I was on the case.

Early Hints

I had the Rose Lodge advertisement from the summer of 1937, giving me the perfect clue to the origins of the early Rose's. It was a shameless scurry to the W. Dale Clark Library in downtown Omaha, where I cracked open that 1937 city directory—long exhale. There was no restaurant named Rose's

or Rose

or Rose Lodge

but under the surname of Rose, I found "Wm. Rose h 230 S. 68th Ave." Things were looking good. I penciled William Rose into my field notebook. By the 1938 Omaha City Directory I found "William Rose Restaurant" listed in the restaurants section, not in the cross street address section. It read "79th SE corner Dodge." So I knew it had officially arrived; meanwhile, William Rose was listed as "r 230 S. 68th Ave." A lower case r stood for "residence." I was beginning to put together that Mr. Rose had indeed been operating a restaurant out of his beautiful home and then moved it out west. When I jumped back to the 1928 city directory, I was surprised to see "Rose, Wm." had listed his business as "real estate" and the address was still "h. 230 S 68th Ave."

There was no city directory in the year 1927. So I pedaled back to 1926. There was no address for 230 South Sixty-Eighth Avenue at that time. Rose's place of employment was listed as 505 World Herald Building, although what he did there I cannot be sure. I thought I had read the word *toilet* as a descriptor but had decided not to dwell on that. The year 1926 had brought the newly built Omaha World-Herald Building to the northwest corner of Fifteenth and Farnam.

Rose's residence in 1926 was listed vaguely at "74th and Douglas." I do hope you feel compelled to write this down with your tiny golf pencil. When I flipped to the street guide in the same directory, the closest address to Seventy-Fourth and Douglas was at 7315 Douglas, owned by H. C. Linahan. Not a mention of Rose in cross-reference. I assumed Seventy-Fourth and Douglas was very likely farmland, and the directory didn't always specify a house address back then. I would learn much more about this area when I fell into my Twenties Club investigation.

Early Rose Clues

It was all a swirling conundrum in the beginning, and why was that? I now wonder. Why was I so surprised that a fellow with the surname of Rose had named and owned Rose Lodge? I mean, it only made perfect sense. Oddly, I persisted in wanting Rose Lodge to have been named after a woman or like the flower on the tall sign I faintly remembered. Soon after, I learned that William Rose had married a woman name Rose, and that is when I decided this was the Most Perfect Story Ever. I told Mr. Cassette, Mother, and Stepfather Cassette about the discovery one night while waiting for a table in front of the fireplace at the Drover. "Rose Rose!" I exclaimed. "Her name was Rose Rose? Can you beat that?" No one seemed to think this was as spectacular as I. That was when I knew I had gone mad.

I dug back to the 1920 U.S Census. In 1920 William Rose was twenty-nine years of age, his profession listed as "Moving Picture Thr." The location for this profession or theater, if I understood this correctly, was "Own Place." His position was listed as "Employer." Rose Rose was

then twenty-three and listed as "Saleswoman," "Show.," "Wageworker."
The young couple lived at 1017 Homer Street. According to the Douglas
County Assessor's website, this home is still alive and well and upright.
I always like to see that. The 1017 Homer Street cutie was built in 1918.
The couple would own or live at this address until 1926. As the bread-
crumb path would lie out before me, I would later come to believe that
1017 Homer was a movie theater front for a very different kind of busi-
ness. This will make more sense later.

Multiple Addresses

Things would get more complicated when I found a notice of property
sale in the "West Leavenworth" area, as it was coined, in July 1925. It
showed the transfer of the "Northwest corner of Forty-fifth and Mayberry streets" from Emily M. Safarik to Rose Rose for $7,700. I tracked
this plot of land to the Morton Meadows area. This corner appears to
be now properly named 916 South Forty-Fifth Street. According to the
Douglas County Assessor, this quaint home and fine corner lot, conveniently right down the street from La Casa, was built in 1924.

Let us have a pause and a quick brushup. This will certainly bore those
among you who question my dalliances, but I think it is important to
clarify the vast, enduring subtleties that have begun to pile up around this
wood-paneled study. I remembered that by 1928 William Rose had listed
his business as that of "real estate." If you are tracking with me so far,
we had learned that Rose had something to do with toilets at the *Omaha
World-Herald* business, owned some sort of theater, was in real estate, and
would later own a restaurant. The Rose couple owned a number of properties in 1925, which were most likely investments, and it would appear
that at least a few of the properties were listed in Rose Rose's name. The
Roses were tied to Forty-Fifth and Mayberry, 1017 Homer Street, and
Seventy-Fourth and Douglas. I would find even more properties later.

Omaha Prohibition

There were a number of questionable events that happened in 1925,
leading me to believe that the Roses were involved in the Omaha under-

world. Of course what caused a goosey-ness with the police and the press in those dry days was quite different by today's standards. In 1917 conservative Nebraska was quick to become a dry state, with nation-wide Prohibition not officially beginning until around 1920. According to the incredible book *Cigars and Wires: The Omaha Underworld's Early Years* by Jon L. Blecha, statewide Prohibition did not mean that Omaha adhered to the rules. The alcohol did not stop flowing, nor did the gamblers stop betting, and the sex trade . . . well, it flourished. In fact these three trades, surely enhanced by Prohibition, were laced up in the corrupt Omaha political structure.

The Rose Mystique

I nosed around and found evidence that in 1925 William Rose owned yet another property in the Fort Calhoun area. Rose had claimed this house as his residence as well, but it was later found to be an illegal drinking establishment and "club." This house or club was subsequently destroyed in a mysterious fire, leading the Globe and Rutgers Fire Insurance Company to resist payment. The company insisted that William Rose had misrepresented the property for residential purposes, whereas it later discovered it was used for "social purposes." This was not the only fire the Roses would encounter.

Things Get Hinky

August 1925 exposed Omaha to a troubling local case, one that has a modern ring to it. The Roses came to the rescue when Omahan Dr. Charles E. Barnes was charged with violating the Harrison Drug Act after his eighteen-year-old secretary, Miss Josephine Nepodal, claimed the doctor had used her name and names of her family members to write prescriptions for morphine tablets. Dr. Barnes was caught selling morphine, specifically, to one Fred M. Mapes, a patient whom he had treated for three years due to a nervous breakdown, "the drink habit," and anxiety brought on post-army service. Miss Nepodal claimed innocence when the doctor sent her to "many different drug stores, secured the prescriptions and turned them over to the doctor" over and over again.

GIRL CHIEF WITNESS AGAINST DR. BARNES

Secretary Says Names of Kin Used in Fake Pre-scriptions.

FREE DOCTOR ON BOND

Dr. Charles E. Barnes, held for trial yesterday by Commissioner Mame Mullen after a hearing on charges of violating the Harrison Drug act, was released from the county jail at 6 o'clock last night. His bond for 10 thousand dollars was signed by William Rose.

The bond offered by Rose was turned down earlier in the evening, department of justice officials demanding 20 thousand dollars worth of property as security for 10 thousand dollars bond. Investigation of Rose's holdings satisfied the officers later.

Dr. Barnes went directly to his room at the Fontenelle hotel after his release and there refused to answer all phone calls.

According to federal officials, Miss Josephine Nepodal, 18-year-old secretary to Dr. Barnes, will be the principal witness against him when he is tried on the charge of selling

ACCUSED DOCTOR

FEDERAL WITNESS.

Dr. Charles E. Barnes.

Miss Josephine Nepodal.

army," Mapes told the World-Herald "I have been nervous. For the last three years I have been going to

scription made out to her July 14, 1925, calling for six tablets, one-fourth grain morphine, with the di-

25. The claim against Dr. Barnes spelled out in black and white from August 1925. Reprinted with permission from the *Omaha World-Herald*.

The young secretary would get thirty morphine prescriptions filled on days that Mapes came to the office. wow. The federal agents eventually found over two hundred prescriptions that had been filled at various drugstores all over town.

They say Dr. Barnes had been threatened by a number of "outside parties" who had grudges against the doctor. It was specified these grudge holders were not the police or federal agents. Apparently, the well-known Dr. Barnes had been a witness in the trial of Roscoe "Fatty" Arbuckle following the death of Virginia Rappe in San Francisco. Coincidentally, Dr. Barnes had formally treated Miss Rappe as a patient while in Chicago. This was a terrible story, an early Hollywood disgrace, that my grandmother had told me about when I became enraptured with "old movies" as a teenager.

It is intriguing to note that when Dr. Charles Barnes was searched, they found a "powder puff and rouge in his pocket." Later, when he

appeared in court, his eyebrows had been shaved off. Andrew Durant, a close friend of Barnes, was in his office when the arrest happened. An "actor specializing in female impersonations," Durant was also taken into custody for questioning.

So this is all very engrossing, you will surely admit, but why on earth is Miss Cassette dragging on and on about it and what does it have to do with the Roses? Well, William "Billy" Rose of 1017 Homer Street and his wife, Rose Rose, came forward that very day to offer bond for Dr. Charles Barnes—apparently a good friend, or were they business partners of some sort? The department of justice officials had turned down Rose, demanding twenty thousand dollars worth of property as security on a ten thousand–dollar bond. The Roses could produce, and Barnes was allowed to walk.

The Second Mysterious Rose Fire

As if a fire at their Fort Calhoun Speakeasy and involvement with a morphine scandal wasn't enough, in August 1926 the Roses had another home they owned set ablaze after an explosion following a peculiar set of events. You will recall that William and Rose Rose owned a home on Seventy-Fourth and Douglas. This palatial spread allegedly sat unfurnished and, come to find out, was only used as a distillery, even though it was "just off Dodge Road in a neighborhood of expensive homes." It was a "large two and a half story structure, handsomely finished inside."

A moonshine still, estimated to have cost $10,000 (about $135,000 by 2017 calculations), was found installed in the Roses' basement at Seventy-Fourth and Douglas. Evidently, the still exploded, setting fire to the interior of the home. The still towered nearly twenty feet, and the first floor of the home had been chopped away to make room for it. Gulp. "Occupying half the basement was a huge concrete and brick vat, 10 feet long, 10 feet wide and about five feet deep. It would contain five thousand gallons." On the morning after the fire, it was full of grain mash. Additionally, the cellar steps had been chopped away and replaced by a ladder, leading up into a double garage (I don't have to tell you that this

SEIZE 750 BOTTLES ALLEGED TO BE OF BEER

William Rose Denies Illegal Possession; Mash Is Confiscated.

William Rose, Sixty-ninth and Farnam streets, arrested shortly afternoon Wednesday when Federal Prohibition Agent A. C. Anderson and deputy sheriffs found 750 bottles of alleged beer in the basement of his home, was released later under $250 bond on a charge of illegal possession of intoxicating liquor.

Fifteen gallons of mash, a few quarts of alleged whisky, and several crocks were also confiscated

26. Later in the day, this additional article was released after the arrest of William Rose, August 1925. Reprinted with permission from the *Omaha World-Herald*.

was a rarity in those days!) built onto the house. Cars could be loaded in the garage without detection from the outside. I was getting the idea that this was a serious operation. Deputy Sheriff Phillips held that the Rose moonshine outfit was one of the largest ever uncovered in Omaha. Oddly, neighbors said they had never seen anyone coming or going about the substantial home. Meanwhile, William Rose contended that he had sold the house just recently to a man named Ready out of Wyoming. Inexplicably, the Roses were found at a neighbor's house across the street.

Curiouser and Curiouser

Following the explosion at the Seventy-Fourth and Douglas Street property, officers then searched the Rose residence, finding and confiscating 750 bottles of beer, fifteen gallons of mash, a few quarts of whiskey, and several crocks in their basement. The Rose residence was listed as "69th and Farnam." I knew I had found the official link to 230 South Sixty-Eighth Avenue, even thought the article was one block off. Bill Rose denied connection to the still explosion and insisted that the alcohol seized from his basement on Sixty-Ninth (Sixty-Eighth) Avenue was "for his own use."

If you are anything like Miss Cassette, these traces only brought up more questions, more connections, and more excitement. Before we go much further into the fascinating Roses, let us back up a bit and examine the history of the Sixty-Eighth and Farnam area, as we now know the time frame that the Roses supposedly occupied 230 South Sixty-Eighth Avenue. Grab your magnifying glass.

The Charles L. Vance Clues

My self-induced chills and thrills only further fueled the hunt as I drove straightaway to the Douglas County Register of Deeds Office. I knew that 230 South Sixty-Eighth Avenue was in Sunset Terrace, formally identified as Lot 25, Block 0. I soon uncovered that this property also included Lot 24, which explained the wide corner expanse I had become giddy over.

According to the deed, on June 2, 1925, "Charles L. Vance et al." sold 230 South Sixty-Eighth Avenue to Rose Rose. By paging through the large book, I could see that Charles L. Vance had sold all of the nearby lots on this and other blocks south. I later found he had owned all of the land that would later be developed into the Sunset Terrace addition. But more on Sunset Terrace later. I am not exactly sure of how the Vances came to acquire the land on Sixty-Eighth Avenue. I have reason to believe that it was an early investment, but it could have been an inheritance from Mrs. Vance's side of the family. They possessed a large swath from Dodge to Howard Streets on what would become Sixty-Eighth Avenue. From what

27. Hayden Brothers Department Store was at Sixteenth and Dodge Streets. Interior of Hayden Brothers men's hat department, 1922. From the KM3TV/ Bostwick-Frohardt Photograph Collection at the Durham Museum.

I could ferret out, Charles Lyall Vance was born in or around Clarinda, Iowa, in 1873. He married his wife, Lena, and together they had sons Charles L. Vance Jr. and Verne W. Vance. Both boys would graduate from Creighton Law School and become local attorneys. The senior Charles Vance was a well-known advertising executive for the Hayden Brother Department Store and was often interviewed in the local newspapers as the spokesman for the store.

I had previously mentioned this fine department store when writing "The Mysteries of 4025 Izard Street." I found that John A. Swanson had been a buyer and manager at Hayden Brother's before going on to establish King-Swanson Company and later the renowned Nebraska Clothing Company. For your records Swanson was former congressman Brad Ashford's great-grandfather.

By 1930 Charles and Lena Vance had bought the mansion at 3110 Chicago Street, situated in the Gifford Park area. It probably shocks no one to hear I simply worship this home. To find that I missed the chance at a desirable tour when it was for sale recently really breaks my heart. Cracker magnate Joseph Garneau Jr. built the palatial home in 1890. Allegedly, Garneau left town for New York with hopes of starting a wine importing business, whereby Thomas Kilpatrick took ownership until his death in 1916. The Thomas Kilpatrick Company was one of Omaha's most well-loved department stores, down at 1509 Douglas Street. Mr. Vance retired from Hayden Brothers in 1931, after working there for more than twenty years.

Son Charles Jr. died suddenly at home after a bout of pneumonia. At age thirty-three he left a wife and four small children. Charles Sr. and Lena would later move to a house at 205 South Twenty-Fifth Avenue, where Charles Sr. would die in 1946. He had been a lifelong Mason and active in local musical organizations. Lena Vance died in 1949 following complications from a surgery. The address 205 South Twenty-Fifth Avenue is now home or very near to the Salvation Army thrift store. This short avenue runs perpendicular to Douglas. The Vance house would have been closer to Douglas Street. There were at one time a number of large homes in this area, which were later converted into rooming houses. Its history is covered thoroughly in my article "Mysteries of Omaha: 2561 Douglas Street" (at my website). Attorney Verne Vance, their youngest son, would go on to live at 2510 Country Club Avenue, in the fantastic Country Club area. I only wish I could share all of the photos from the website with you in this book.

The Sunset Terrace Puzzle

Have we fallen in the nettles yet? I do hope you are still with us and finding this an endless cycle of delight. Let us circle back to Sunset Terrace, as I seem to remember promising I would tie this into a precious little bow. The development along Sixty-Eighth Avenue from Dodge to Howard Streets is called the Sunset Terrace addition. This development was created in September 1924 and was touted as "Adjoining Fairacres."

"You'll Want a Lot in Sunset Terrace," boasted an advertisement from September 25, 1924. In an article from that October, I learned the sightly new addition of Sunset Terrace was "recently platted and has been placed on sale this week by a syndicate of Omaha men." The addition was only forty-six lots and not exactly selling like hotcakes. "Improvements are being pushed to completion as rapidly as possible," one article read. I was not sure what that meant but was more hung up on the syndicate of Omaha men idea. Did that mean that Charles L. Vance et al. was the head of this syndicate? I would later come to believe that this was an investment and that Charles and partners had purchased and developed this west neighborhood. Another great ad from July 16, 1926, encouraged, "Own a Piece of the Earth!" A bit later, after the Roses had purchased 230 South Sixty-Eighth Avenue, this advertisement ran. I enjoy the twelve-point address intended to attract just the right, moneyed crowd. Each statement included a bellwether wink to the young, up-and-coming, new money, West Omaha crowd.

West Dodge in 1925

According to Bradley H. Baltensperger's *Nebraska: A Geography*, Omaha began expanding westward along Dodge, then known as Lincoln Highway, with the growing popularity of the automobile. The 1910s through the 1920s brought a need for quick, urban sprawl, passing through and annexing existing villages and towns such as Benson and Dundee. Remarkably, Fairacres Village (now Fairacres neighborhood), one of the most desirable Omaha areas, held out until 1941.

230 South Sixty-Eighth Avenue Mention

I reached a number of roadblocks in my search for deeper Sunset Terrace clues. The *Reconnaissance Survey of Selected Neighborhoods in West-Central Omaha including Fairacres, Dillon's Fairacres, Mel-Air and Others: Nebraska Historic Buildings Survey* prepared by Mead & Hunt, Inc., in 2009, included 230 South Sixty-Eighth Avenue in its survey. It is a great little book, available at the W. Dale Clark Library, but rather light in comparison to other Omaha surveys. Other than a formal nod to the building design and inclusion in the historic neighborhood survey, I could uncover no further details on 230 in the study.

Origins of 230 South Sixty-Eighth Avenue

Let us again find our bearing and revisit the original deed. We know that Vance had sold the plat to Rose Rose in June 1925. It is believed that by 1926 William and Rose had constructed their large residence, originally costing more than $30,000. Thirty thousand dollars in 1926 had the same buying power, roughly, as $405,000 in 2017. Oddly, this property is currently valued just a bit higher ($25,000 more), according to the Douglas County Assessor site. This whole area around Sixty-Eighth Avenue is so very lovely, and I encourage you to go visit when you can sneak away. The Fair Ridge, Fair Park, and Drury Manor developments include some of the finest hidden gems in Omaha. I love how Sunset Terrace is nestled in there in such a cozy manner.

Sadly, all of this busybodying about could not produce information on the architect of 230 South Sixty-Eighth Avenue. Perhaps the current homeowner will come forward with the juicy details. What I was able to uncover through newspaper articles was that 230 South Sixty-Eighth Avenue started life very much as it appears today. The brick and stucco home had ten rooms, including four bedrooms, full maid's quarters, multiple baths, and a double garage. The grounds were landscaped with a fishpond and flowerbeds. More clues would appear later.

The survey of 2009 labeled the design as a Spanish Colonial Revival style. Ignorant as I am of all the technicalities, I knew, at the very least, from the formal layout of 230, taking into account the year that it was built, the property would be of the American Revival period—the emphasis on "correct" interpretation of the past, the formality and "good taste," spread to these smaller suburban home models during these years. The stucco and low-pitched clay tile roof was a nod to the Spanish style, as were the hood moldings, arched transoms, fluted columns, and adorable fanlights. But 230 is missing some key elaborations such as the wrought iron balconies, strap hinges, and the casual asymmetrical layout. I observed Georgian formality with serious Italian Renaissance revival

28. Southwestern angle of house at 230 South Sixty-
Eighth Avenue. Photo by author.

hints in 230's commitment to symmetry, balanced proportions, and classical details. The fanlights displayed above the double-hung sash windows
also adhered to this style.

In a vice grip between *The Visual Dictionary of American Domestic Architecture* by Rachel Carley and *A Field Guide to American Houses* by Virginia
Savage McAlester, I am leaning toward calling this fine Midtown home
a mix of the Eclectic movement, purely an American hybrid with serious hints at the Georgian, Italian Renaissance, and Spanish styles. The
simple hipped roof without a prominent porch, with the small classical
columns, rounded arches above the door, first-story windows, and one-
story matching enclosed side wings—all signs of the Italian Revival. The
stuccoed walls were perfected after World War I.

The Spanish Revival is seen in the little eave overhang and the fact
that there are no bracket details. If I could only peak inside and see what
the interior revealed! These side wings, by the way, could have been an

early addition to the home. I have found proof of a number of homes in this exact mixed style from this time period. And I might be wrong, wrong, wrong, chums, but I trust you will correct me.

The Newest Report from 230 South Sixty-Eighth Avenue

According to the last sale of the residence, 230 South Sixty-Eighth Avenue was described on Zillow as a two and a half–story "mansion." Again, you know my thoughts on Omaha and its overexaggeration of mansion status, which I adhere to wholeheartedly! It gives us a much-needed thrill. "You will appreciate the original woodwork, wood floors and French Doors. There's also original beveled glass and 9 foot ceilings. The main level has 2 fireplaces, a Living Room, a Formal Dining Room & a Sunroom perfect for curling up with a cup of coffee or a good book. The kitchen has been nicely updated and has a large Pantry, a built in desk area and a neat Breakfast Nook. All bedrooms are generously sized. The 3rd level has a 5th bedroom and a Full Bath. Outside in the expansive yard you'll discover a gazebo, hot tub, many beautiful flowers and plantings, plus quaint pathways that lead to a tranquil pond. See this one of a kind mansion today!" Let it be known that if you have been in this home, either as a guest or on a real estate tour, we want to hear from you.

The Bootleggers of Sixty-Eighth Avenue

Before you assume that the Roses had cleaned up their act, moving into the fried chicken field, let me assure that there are still plenty more underworld pointers to sift through. You may want to review your operative notes at this point—but the big reminder is that the Roses' home at Seventy-Fourth and Douglas had blown up in August 1926. A few months later, in December, William Rose sold the Sixty-Eighth Avenue residence and the Forty-First and Leavenworth property to his brother, Henry Q. Rose, for $45,000. A real estate transfer from *Omaha World-Herald* of December 21, 1926, showed that Adelaide Fogg sold property on Forty-Second and Farnam to Nathan Somberg (see "The Quest for Miss Adelaide Fogg" at my website). The fact that William, Rose, and Henry continued to live together in the palatial south Fairacres abode tipped me off to a

29. A 1929 interior view of a bar in the home of George Brandeis. There are two tables with small chairs sitting around them. There is a bar with four stools in front of it, with three casks behind it. This was not the Roses' home but is used to illustrate how a private home might feature a "bar" at that time. From the KM3TV/ Bostwick-Frohardt Photograph Collection at the Durham Museum.

very strong likelihood of the ongoing Rose hooch business. They most likely needed to move the property out of William and Rose's names for some reason. With the frank, daring smile of an Irishman, I dug further.

It was rather hard to ignore the West Omaha speakeasy scandal from November 1927, both for neighbors and the rest of the town. As the story goes, "30 well-dressed persons fled hurriedly" from the Rose home on Sixty-Eighth Avenue after a nighttime Prohibition raid. The Rose family had been running both a club and a bootlegging outfit in their home. William Rose was named as the "operator of the bootlegging place." Interesting to note the distinction of "30 well-dressed persons" by the reporter. This was surely an indication to the general public that the Roses weren't just operating some backwoods riffraff roadhouse, even

61

though their speakeasy was considered on the edge of town. This was a moneyed establishment.

"Dry Officers Raid," shown in the newspaper on November 12, 1927, disclosed the Rose raid produced more than one hundred gallons of whisky and a charcoal aging plant. A new $1,500 automobile owned by one Allen Oliver was also seized on a charge of "transportation." So, while this area was recognized as a beautiful neighborhood, the Roses were using this covert environ as an unlawful hush-hush nightclub. I was beside myself.

Apparently, a neighbor had called in the Rose enterprise and reported of a shooting in the neighborhood. Can you imagine all that racket on sleepy little Sixty-Eighth Avenue? Through further digging, I located proof that James Kazakas, neighbor at 117 South Sixty-Eighth Avenue, alleged that he had been threatened by William Rose. This threat apparently prompted Kazakas to call in the federal raid. Wow. The Kazakas home at 117 South Sixty-Eighth Avenue is across the street and up two doors from the Rose residence. This home, according to the Douglas County Assessor, was erected in 1926, the same year as the Roses' home. All of the other houses on the block were built in the 1940s, except for 114 South Sixty-Eighth. Because of the Great Depression from 1929 through 1939, most residential construction halted across the country. But according to the Douglas County Assessor, 114 South Sixty-Eighth Avenue was thought to have been built in 1930, making it only the third home on the block after the initial Sunset Terrace launch five years earlier. It is a lovely home.

What I would hypothesize is that the Roses were used to having the block to themselves, except for that pesky Kazakas. I cannot be sure what happened between James Kazakas and William Rose, only that Rose ended up paying a five hundred–dollar peace bond (an order from the court requiring a person to keep the peace and be on good behavior for a period of time).

A sidenote worth mentioning: The other great little houses on Sixty-Eighth Avenue are all of the minimal traditional house trend of the 1940s. I recommend *Small Houses of the Forties* by Harold E. Group, an incredible collection of homes with illustrations and floor plans, if you want to know more about this movement. It is interesting to note the style and

30. Looking southwest on Dodge Street from about Sixty-Eighth Avenue. There is a vet's office on the street with a car parked in front. Farther down the hill you can see some other buildings. The photo is from about the 1940s, but it illustrates how desolate and undeveloped the western part of Dodge was at the time. From the KM3TV/Bostwick-Frohardt Photograph Collection at the Durham Museum.

larger size of two original homes at 117 and 230, followed by 114 in 1930, which speak to the times. Potentially, Sunset Terrace might have been a very different neighborhood had those lots sold quickly in the 1920s. Also obsession worthy: the curious Farnam Street footpath, found just south east of the Rose home. The Farnam Street thoroughfare, running just south of the Rose house, was blocked off and turned into a footpath years ago. University of Nebraska Omaha is just east of Sunset Terrace (and other developments), with Elmwood Park and Elmwood Golf Course directly to the south of UNO. It is doubtful that Farnam Street was ever a direct route to the Roses from downtown Omaha.

Another Speakeasy Bust and the Fate of the Rose Ducks

In early December two large vice squads headed out into liquor raiding action from midnight until early one morning. The list of arrests and the incredible club names from back in the day were simply fascinating. I wish I could include it all here. "Samardick Hits Bootleggers" from December 3, 1927, the *Omaha World-Herald* proclaimed: "The first place raided was that of William Rose, 230 South Sixty-Eighth Avenue, where 59 gallons of whisky were found and 30 gallons of beer mash. Others arrested there were Mrs. Rose, a brother, Henry Rose, and Walter Mulfinger." Days later the strange headline "Raid Fatal to Ducks" appeared. I am not the only one to decipher which of these elements is more odd than the next. The Roses evidently kept seven live ducks in their basement in a swimming pool. When William Rose gave bond in federal court for the December raid, he reported that two of his seven ducks had been killed due to the fumes and dumping of whiskey and beer mash in their basement pool. The conclusion that I would prefer to assume is that the Roses moved their ducks into the basement for the winter from their well-known pond in the garden. But it only conjures visions of a wading pool in the basement. I need to get in that house and look for clues.

The Missing Link and the Auction

By spring of 1928 a missing witness marked William Rose's federal liquor trial. Witness Harvey Draeger testified that he and a "man named Porter" had bought liquor on three separate occasions from Rose. Rose's attorney called Draeger into question, as earlier "Porter" had testified in the preliminary that he had actually made the buys. It was later surmised that Porter was a felon with a colorful past of his own. Conveniently, this Porter character had gone missing. Now friends and fellow detectives, I am only presenting evidence. You can draw any conclusion that you feel comfortable with. Regardless, Rose was found guilty on six counts of liquor indictment after nearly three hours of jury deliberation. Apparently, our man Rose started a fight with Draeger out in the courthouse hall.

Two days before the jury returned a verdict in William Rose's court case, the beautiful Rose estate was to be put up for auction. The gorgeous corner lot was "the largest," "highest-priced" home in Omaha ever to be offered at auction (as of 1928), and 230 was "placed on block" in what was thought to establish a precedent for real estate to come. The article cited that expensive California homes were often purchased at auction in this manner. I couldn't help but feel sad for the Roses and for the house.

Puzzling Sale

A mysterious Lone Pine, Nebraska, rancher named P. Jensen was rumored to have placed the highest bid, at $18,100, in the May 28, 1928, auction. Interestingly, P. Jensen's main competitor in a bidding war was the Omaha chief of police, who was no doubt quite familiar with the Rose establishment. Detectives, what do we make of that? William Rose offered all home furnishings as well, valued at $4,000 for $1,000 cash but had no takers. Things got even more hinky when I discovered that the mysterious P. Jensen never took ownership of the house. In fact brother, Henry Q. Rose continued to own the home-speakeasy for a number of years following the raid and auction. Was Jensen brought in as a guise? He reportedly had been in South Omaha at market that day, with a shipment of cattle. Was this a smokescreen to get the police department off their backs? I cannot be sure. It all seemed a little flimsy when I found an article about the "home of William Rose in Fairacres" being padlocked in November 1928 due to Prohibition violations but was not ordered "permanently closed." I began to suspect the Roses of having some serious social connections in Omaha.

A Sleight of Hand

For the next couple of years the Roses kept themselves well under the radar. A prowl around found them conspicuously missing from local papers and in court records. I have significant reason to believe this was all by design. In the spring of 1930 Henry Q. Rose sold 230 South Sixty-

Eighth Avenue back to Rose Rose. It was announced in the paper as the largest city property transfer, at forty thousand dollars.

Who Were the Roses?

As much as I snooped around, I would have difficulty recovering much personal information about the Rose family. This dilemma would continue throughout the investigation, leaving me to theorize all sorts of fantastic storylines. Their photos were not in the newspaper. Their exploits were not documented in the Society Pages. They were not known for hobnobbing in any fashion other than owning a fabulous house on the outskirts of Fairacres, where liquor was made and served up. It wasn't until I located the 1930 U.S. Census that I found a tad more detail of the clan. Rose Rose was estimated to have been born in 1896. In 1930 she was thirty-four. Her parents were from "Czecho-slovakia." She had no occupation listed. From my sleuthing it would appear that Rose Rose never gave birth to any children. Much later I would learn that her maiden name had been Celak. Her mother was Marie Celak. Rose had three brothers (Charles, Henry, and Edward) and two sisters (Besse and Mary). Upon brother Charles Celak's death in 1956, he was listed as having lived at 1019 Homer Street. I noted that this was one house away from the Roses' property at 1017. Did they own more homes on that block? I warned you I went mad.

In the same 1930 Census, William Rose was listed as age forty. His parents were from Berlin, Germany. Much later I would learn that William was born and raised in Omaha. His brothers were listed as Henry, Jack, and Otto Rose. I wondered if the Rose surname had been Germanized or Americanized from a proper Jewish name. I was not able to find William Rose listed within the Nebraska Jewish Historical Society burial registry. In 1930 Rose was listed as a "manager in Real Estate." Henry Rose, William's brother, was then thirty-four and was listed as the "gardener in the home." I liked that very much. I fancied Henry was the one behind the planning of fishponds and flowerbeds. I imagined him gardening in brown tweed wool pants on that fine, large corner.

Gunfire on Sixty-Eighth Avenue

Unfortunately, Bill Rose was in and out of court through the early 1930s. He continued to serve jail sentences much as he had before. In yet another raid on the 230 South Sixty-Eighth Avenue home, this time called the "residence of Mrs. Rose Rose," a prohibition agent fired his gun after Rose Rose "grabbed at his wrist." Mrs. Rose was charged with attempting to destroy liquor seized as evidence. Later it was revealed that the agent, Frank Haas, had been pointing the weapon at William when Rose purposefully struck the agent's arm. The bullet went into the wall. I wonder if we could still find this clue? U.S. commissioner Mary Mullen was assigned the case, and for those with long memories, you may remember her as daughter of the Arthur Francis Mullen clan in the adventure entitled "The Curious Case of the French Fairytale Cottage: Part 1" (at my website).

The Fried Chicken Connection

With all of the bootlegging shenanigans, I was beginning to wonder where or when that delicious fried chicken would enter the picture. I am sure you are wondering the same. I was beside myself when, near the end of the investigation, I found an ad from the late 1970s honoring many of the early Omaha businesses. It was there that I found Rose Lodge had been serving Rose's Famous Fried Chicken since 1934. An early advertisement educated me that Rose's Famous Fried Chicken was open 362 days a year. So, although we know that the Roses had not yet moved to the Seventy-Eighth and Dodge location, we had our definitive answer about chicken and steak dinners having been served out of 230 South Sixty-Eighth Avenue. Now in those days it was known as Rose Restaurant, sometimes called Rose's and also the William Rose Restaurant. For a period it was known as Rose's Roadhouse. I was beside myself with the imagery of Mildred's Fine Foods from one of my favorite disturbing Joan Crawford movies, *Mildred Pierce*. The idea of a glorious restaurant in a glorious home. . . . I weakened.

Just because homemade food was being served up did not mean the Roses had intentions to go gentle into that good night—just yet. By 1934

31. Why here he is now—police captain Frank Rose sitting at his desk and laughing. Photo by John Savage, May 1949. But the Roses were in trouble with the law so much. Maybe they might have been in trouble more, had it not been for the captain brother? From the *Omaha World-Herald* / John Savage Collection at the Durham Museum.

the couple had brought slot machines into their restaurant-bar enterprise. "Raid of the roadhouse operated by William Rose at 230 South 68th Avenue," read the article. This raid was part of a new slot machine–focused drive-by vice, with two machines being confiscated at the Roses'. One was said to be a nickel machine, the other a quarter machine.

Yet Another Fire

It was many nights that I carried my lonely flashlight to bed, obsessively exploring, in a fine sweep, miles of newspaper articles. Mr. Cassette and a number of furry friends snored pleasantly in unison as I paused and studied each enchanting Rose document. At that point it did not surprise me to learn that Rose Rose also owned a great little home at 4751 Capitol. In a suspicious fire being credited to "pyromaniacs," the Roses were once again in the news. Was this fire, set in the basement, a personal vendetta against the Roses or an inside job? Two men were seen running from the fire into the street in the wee hours of the morning. This tidy but peculiar article revealed that Rose Rose was the sister-in-law of police captain Frank Rose, only adding to the family mystery. Bill Rose's brother was the police captain? Hmm.

Long-Awaited Arrival

By May 1935, two years after Prohibition ended, Rose Rose was finally granted a beer license. The press made a point to mention that the commissioner had previously objected to the license until it could be determined that the application was not made for William Rose. Another signal that the Roses had respectably arrived in Omaha was a short mention in the 1937 Society Page. "Mrs. Fred DeVore will entertain 28 guests at dinner this evening at Rose Rose's Country Club in celebration of Mr. DeVore's birthday." Country Club, indeed. It was in that very same year that the Roses would move way out west, as everyone thought in those days, and solidify their beloved restaurant in the Omaha annals, leaving behind their colorful past.

PART 2

The Official Rose Lodge

I still cherish the enduring, if not fuzzy, memory of Rose Lodge. When pressed, I was upset by how very dim the fine points of this vision had become after all these decades. The restaurant really wasn't much of a looker, by today's standards. In fact, I fondly remember it looking like something of an old farmhouse with an addition built around it, which only served to remind me how very far we had driven from Benson to get there. I might have made up that farmhouse-with-the-addition bit, but through my mind there drifted a strong visual. It was like that early delight when one realizes that Gorat's Steakhouse, Marks Bistro, Gold-

32. I searched and I searched for the Rose Lodge property. This aerial view
of the Beverly Hills Shopping Center, renamed Plaza, at Seventy-Eighth
and Dodge Streets, shows the area, looking southwest. New Tower Motor
Inn is seen just north of Rose Lodge, across Dodge, October 1955. From the
Omaha World-Herald / John Savage Collection at the Durham Museum.

berg's in Dundee, and La Casa Pizzeria were actually built around small
Midtown homes. Comforting and comfortable. Customers would park
out front on the Beverly Drive side and enter through a west-facing door.
There seemed to be a hidden quality to that southern end of Beverly Drive
that isn't there now. Perhaps there was a hedge or wall of trees to the very
south of Rose Lodge? I can't be sure. I do remember the very tall Rose
Lodge sign, which could be seen as we inched west along Dodge toward
our destination. The entryway seemed small. I recall a red interior, maybe
with red vinyl chairs or booths? The walls seemed dark and inviting, like a
back room at the old Trovato's Italian in Dundee but much larger. In fact,
the restaurant seemed to keep going and going as the hostess would bring
us to our table. Rose Lodge was a very special place to me in those days,
and I remember going there for special birthdays or after an Ak-Sar-Ben
family show. I didn't know how lucky I was. Unfortunately, as much as I
explored, I could find no historic photos of the real Rose Lodge.

Beverly Hills

IS SELLING. We are locating a lot of good people in this beautiful acreage tract, on Dodge Street, west of Fairacres. Several nice homes will be built at once.

Think of It!

One acre (equal to six city lots) for $1,100 to $1,600, and straight WEST on Farnam Street and only 5 MILES from 16th Street.

Buy Now!

A producing home site, and in a few years—Omaha crowding westward—will make each LOT worth all you are paying for an ACRE.

TOMORROW is not the time to buy Real Estate; you must act TODAY while prices are low.

Call our salesmen today, while you can get choice location.

Beverly Hills Company

| The Byron Reed Company 1612 Farnam Street. Tel. Douglas 297. | Charles W. Martin & Company 742 Omaha Nat'l Bk. Bldg. Tel. Tyler 187. |

33. August 11, 1918, Beverly Hills Company advertisement.
Reprinted with permission from the *Omaha World-Herald*.

Early Tracks

I need hardly mention to you, fellow detectives, that when I embarked on this fresh treasure hunt into the second incarnation of Rose Lodge in West Omaha, I was very soon to discover a whole new heap of clues. I promise you we will soon draw a plan on Rose Lodge, but first let us take a wide-lens view.

I knew we had a year to start from: 1937—a base from the first advertisement of the new Rose Lodge location on July 2—a decisive stroke of luck that set this whole mystery in motion. "It's new, it's different, Rose

Lodge." The Rose couple could now proudly offer "your favorite beer" without fear of repercussions.

I pulled myself together and again headed for the Douglas County Register of Deeds Office. According to the early deed, Josephine H. Weidenfeller had sold the farmland, which would later house Rose Lodge, to the Beverly Hills Company on February 14, 1918. I found the name Josephine Weidenfeller in the newspaper dating back to 1906; evidently, she was selling gobs of Omaha property. Under J. H. Weidenfeller there were even more sales. This woman owned everything! Of particular interest was the 1912 sale of a large residence on Thirty-First Avenue between Davenport and Chicago, "opposite the Yates Residence."

The year 1918 was a significant one for the new Beverly Hills Company. The realtors began buying up huge swaths of land in this area. In an article from 1925 the Byron Read Company was listed as the realtors in charge of Beverly Hills. An announcement of Dr. John Mack having bought fifteen acres of "Beverly Hills property in the West Dodge district, lying south of the peony farm in the vicinity of 84th Street," piqued my interest. This mention of the peony farm is an old reference to what would become Peony Park. This whole area from Seventy-Second west along Dodge was basically farmland.

Somehow, in August 1931, the plat changed hands from Bart E. Frank and wife to Gladys C. Johnson. It was noted in the deed that Bart Frank had died. I cannot be sure if he was an early investor in the Beverly Hills Company and/or if he was farming the area of Seventy-Eighth and Beverly Drive. Was the Rose Lodge his original farmhouse? Gladys C. Johnson and husband later sold the property to Mrs. Rose Rose on July 22, 1938. By July 1939 Rose Rose had Metropolitan Utilities District complete work on the restaurant. I was unreasonably elated. This must have meant that the Roses had rented the farmhouse for a year before buying it.

Not Out of the Woods

By all accounts, while the Roses were becoming established as successful, well-respected entrepreneurs, they still had their brushes with the police. "Mrs. Rose Rose, operator of an inn near Omaha," was hit with a temporary liquor license suspension for serving beer and liquor after closing hours shortly after the place opened. These busts would happen frequently in the early years on West Dodge. Of note, the Seventy-Eighth (curiously sometimes called Seventy-Ninth) Street and Dodge location was not considered within the Omaha city limit. For that matter Seventy-Eighth was not yet called Beverly Drive, and Dodge Street was still a highway bringing western travelers into Omaha. Not even the *Streets of Omaha: Their Origins and Changes* book of which I am so fond could peg the year that South Seventy-Eighth became Beverly Drive. The first mention of newfound Beverly Drive was from a July 22, 1922, announcement in the *Omaha World-Herald*. I will assume, as should you, that it was named after the burgeoning Beverly Hills development.

The Green Gables Connection

Sometime in the mid-1930s William Rose bought the Green Gables Tea Room, formerly at 2552 Leavenworth. I surmised Rose attained the business in October 1936—a real estate deal that offered up a "large home in Florence" in conjunction with a "former Green Gables Tea Room." Friends, this was no ladies' tearoom. Police stormed the Green Gables as often as the Rose home in Sunset Terrace. By the 1940s, under the new name the Green Gables Inn, Rose had established a proper drinking establishment at Seventy-Second and Dodge. In other documents I found that it was also known as a steak house in the 1940s. Advertisements calling for Green Gables's waitresses, from the late 1940s, offered "transportation and a furnished home," leading me to wonder if the Green Gables Inn was also built around an original house or if the Roses had so many real estate properties that they were able to rent to their employees. Regardless, it was an unusual offer. I would find a fantastic photo from the John Savage collection showing a group of men and police standing in a doorway, looking at confiscated pinball machines. It was described as "Pinball Machine Raid," the image captured in 1939. I cannot say with surety that this photo was from the Green Gables pinball machine seizure, but I do have articles from 1937–39 showing the Green Gables Inn at Seventy-Second and Dodge was often subject to weekend raids. The slot machines—"one armed bandits," as they were called—and pinball cash payoff machines were the focus of the busts. The pinball "actuated the slot machine device for the payoff." In one Green Gable raid the police were happy to yield $3.40 for the county treasurer.

By the time I had discovered all of this Green Gables business, I began to feel a little dizzy. I suspected the business as being on the southwest corner of Seventy-Second and Dodge, where Kenny's Steakhouse had been when I was a girl. Later that corner became Borders Bookstore, and now is home to the digital library Do Space. With hands trembling I went to the Douglas County-Omaha GIS (DOGIS) site and investigated. Indeed, there was a smaller business just to the east of Kenny's Steakhouse until the mid-1950s. Was the Green Gable Inn east of Kenny's Steakhouse, or did Kenny's take over after the Green Gable closed in 1950? My brief exploration led me to believe that Kenny's Steakhouse officially opened in 1950. The two buildings are depicted on the southwest corner of Seventy-Second and Dodge on this aerial map of approximately 1950. It is interesting to see that Douglas Street cut across this corner in a diagonal fashion and would remain until Borders Bookstore came to the corner in the 1990s.

Charlie Hutter

You will meet Charles Hutter Sr. in "The Curse of the Clover Leaf Club." Charlie Hutter made news as a bootlegger during Prohibition, and he did so again in 1943, this time for killing a young farmer in front of the Green Gable Inn. Hutter, surprisingly a former Sarpy County sheriff known for his deep ties in the Omaha underworld, was featured prominently in the news during the Prohibition era. As the story goes, Charlie Hutter, then fifty-five, and a twenty-three-year-old Grant Fallon of Elkhorn were said to have gotten into a fight at the Green Gable Inn. There were varying accounts of three men arguing with a man in a car, later identified as Hutter. Fallon was said to have punched Hutter four times before the fatal shot. Fallon's friends claimed that Hutter drove into one of their cars in the lot and that they did nothing to provoke the shooting. Charlie Hutter's doctor attested to his swollen jaw and evidence of a good punching from

34. Charles Hutter sitting in a jail cell for murder, December 6, 1943. From the *Omaha World-Herald* / John Savage Collection at the Durham Museum.

that night. The friends reported to a night of drinking at the Ten Mile Inn on West Dodge Road, followed by a stop at Rose Lodge, and then on to Green Gable Inn for nightcaps. Hutter was charged with second-degree murder. I told you this Rose goose chase would circle back to the *Cigars and Wires: The Omaha Underworld's Early Years* book. For all of the dark Rose exploits, their only mention in this book was the murder in their Green Gable Inn parking lot.

The Demise of the Green Gable Inn

As the Rose fate would have it, the Green Gable Inn oil furnace exploded one Thursday morning in 1948, burning and blowing a large hole in the restaurant floor. Not surprisingly, by April 1950 William Rose was ready to move on, running an ad that read: "Lost our lease. Miscellaneous restaurant equipment and fixtures for sale. 7205 Dodge. Green Gables. Complete fixtures and stock of Green Gables Steakhouse. Conducted by Walnut Hill Auction Co." By the way, 7205 Dodge Street is the exact address of the Do Space digital library.

The Real Rose Lodge

No more willy-nillying about, I scolded myself. If I do say, this has been a fantastically fun dawdle. But let us pull ourselves together at least for the mere appearance of this detective's endeavor. I pulled the collar of my pea coat up and strode into the stacks. From the official record I presumed part of the popularity and appeal of the fried chicken and steak dinners at Rose Lodge was that they were served up anytime, day or night. The prices were reasonable at any budget. They were open every day of the week, and their ingenious location welcomed folks from the country as well as the city. Rose Lodge was close to the new Peony Park amusement park at Seventy-Eighth and Cass, making it a great place to stop for a meal after a day of play or an evening event. The DOGIS 1941 aerial of the Rose Lodge area made plain that this was still largely the countryside. In one article from 1946, I found Omar Bakery entertaining its returning veterans at a special Rose Lodge dinner, to be followed by a hockey game at the Ak-Sar-Ben Coliseum. Eighty guests were expected, leading me to believe that Rose Lodge had expanded quite a bit from that original farmhouse. It would smartly adapt into a patio area, boasting its May 1946 "outside beer license granted." In 1947 the Roses moved into selling package beer for their customers on the move. They also had a full bar in-house called Rose's Tavern.

New Digs

Rose Rose sold 230 South Sixty-Eighth Avenue to Estrella L. Rickerd in January 1940. It is believed that the Roses sold this Sunset Terrace home to move into a dwelling adjacent to the Rose Lodge restaurant. The 1955 aerial photo by John Savage displayed other structures surrounding the restaurant, much larger than I had remembered. I found verification that other tenants would live there as well. Were they employees, family, or renters? I was intrigued. In July 1944 the Roses were selling "three choice acres at 79th and Dodge: city water, gas, electricity. Rose Lodge," leading me to believe the couple had bought up surrounding lots either early on or after their initial purchase.

Death of William "Bill" Rose

William Rose died in June 1953 at a hospital after a sudden illness. From an earlier advertisement of 1944, I found traces that William had at one time run for county commissioner of the third district. In this ad I discovered Rose was a Republican, born and raised in Douglas County, and had been a member of the American Legion. But his main claim to fame was that he was "famous for his Fried Chicken and Steak Dinners at the ROSE LODGE." I do regret not finding out more about Bill Rose because by headlines alone, he was a very colorful person. His early death must have been quite the shock for our Rose Rose. His obit from June 28, 1953, revealed he was only fifty-six years of age. One day later another obit ran, listing his age as sixty-three, also giving the clue that he was buried at Hillcrest Cemetery.

That Secret Recipe

Throughout the 1940s and 1950s I found many, many ads stating: "Sell Us Your Spring Chickens. Rose Lodge." There are also rumors that Rose Rose raised her own chickens out back, but I could not find solid proof of this. During this time period Harlan Sanders, the original Colonel Sanders, was developing his signature Kentucky Fried Chicken recipe, but the Omaha community believed Rose Lodge had already perfected the art. Father of Miss Cassette had this to say: "The name of the best 1950s fried chicken place ever was Rose Lodge. Chicken was different then—it wasn't gooey like now. The chicken was more toned from walking around—not just sitting on a perch eating feed with growth hormones. Rose's drew people from all over the place. It was famous, kind of like King's Drive-In in Lincoln. Really tasty, flaky crust—they were known for that crust, and it was even much better than my mom's or grandmother's." I soon discovered a boatload of write-ins to the *Omaha World-Herald* over the years from hungry Rose Lodge fans looking to score that secret recipe. Also frequently requested was the Roses' secret coleslaw recipe.

New Neighbors in 1955

Aside from amassing a monumental family business in the 1950s, Rose Lodge found some new neighbors mid-decade. The year 1955 brought the brand-new Beverly Hills Plaza to the north side of Dodge. The H. A. Wolfe Realty Company was behind the venture. The 76th and West Dodge Drive-In, or "The Drive-In," as it was called, opened in 1948 and could accommodate 550 cars in its day.

Meanwhile, as stated in the 1955 Omaha City Directory, the Lawrence Ortman family was living at our old fixation, 230 South Sixty-Eighth Avenue. I backtracked and found the family had taken ownership in 1945, after buying the home from Ms. Rickerd.

A Fifties Collaboration

As only the humorous universe could arrange, Rose Rose, the once Prohibition-balking proprietor, began loaning out her "high way café" to St. Timothy's Lutheran Church congregation on Sundays. Mrs. Rose allegedly installed a rented organ in the dining room for her Sunday guests. My favorite quote of this whole investigation was the sly *Omaha World-Herald* nod-wink: "Many a hungry wayfarer, misled by all those parked cars, stopped in for a snack. These is no record that any of them remained after being advised it was church time."

Mysterious Clues of the 1960s

Valuable as is this information, or exhausting, depending on your personality type and true mettle, even Miss Cassette wondered where the chest of gold would rest. I found that Rose Lodge began bringing even more money in by selling its famous fried chicken to other restaurants, a real feather in the cap for these other businesses. It was a win-win. Alberto's down on Fifth and Pierce was one of many restaurants that served up Rose's fried chicken. Oddly, April 11, 1961, was the absolute last time I found mention of Rose Rose in conjunction with Rose Lodge. It was an advertisement for new waitresses. And then . . . poof. Nothing.

By March 1962 articles of incorporation had been filed for Rose Lodge, "Omaha restaurant and cabaret," with $100,000 authorized capital stock. The incorporators were listed as Joy Drucker and Marie Marik. Was the idea of a Rose Lodge corporate charter more confusing or the fact that the restaurant was known as a cabaret? You be the judge.

Concurrently, the 1962 Omaha City Directory revealed that Mr. William A. Rouse, an employee of the Lutheran Medical Center, now owned 230 South Sixty-Eighth Avenue. Through examination I found the Rouse family had actually bought the property back in October 1958 from Margaret Ortman. This touched back full circle with my friend Bill Glaser, who had written that he knew the Rouses in the 1960s. What a tidy puzzle piece that turned out to be.

Sidenote Confessional

By the by I am wondering if you are as famished as I? To quote Nancy Drew, my life inspiration, "All this mystery solving makes me hungry!" A few deeply private words about fried chicken: Now some will say fried chicken is unhealthy and greasy and all sorts of hideous whispers. I have proudly and outwardly been a vegan and a vegetarian and a pescovarian and all sorts of other *isms* too, but my thoughts on (and true love of) fried chicken always remained the same. I savored it. I craved it. It is the consummate sneak food, in my shameful opinion. Kind of like a hot dog. Fried chicken is like the cousin of the hot dog. Delicious. Perfect. I've never had fried chicken, even from the lowliest of the fast food restaurants, that wasn't absolutely heavenly. There. I said it. My secret is out.

Point of Obscurity

A little-known secret was revealed to me along the path. In 1964 Rose Rose sold Rose Lodge and moved to Florida to retire, according to her family. I found proof that Harvey Craig, Rose's brother-in-law, was later the restaurant manager in the 1970s.

35. Ad from 1964 from the *Omaha World-Herald*. "For the best,
go to Rose's on Sunday. How can fried chicken taste so good?"
Reprinted with permission from the *Omaha World-Herald*.

Following the breadcrumbs, I am not sure if he and his wife, Mary
Celak Craig, later divorced or not. I do know that Rose would retire to
Port Charlotte, Florida, where sister Mary resided. I was not able to track
who this specific owner was until just recently, as Rose Lodge had already
changed into an Inc. As it turns out, two Omaha attorneys bought Rose
Lodge in the 1964. August Ross, who had worked in foreclosures with
Douglas County for sixteen years, began a private practice with Robert E.
O'Connor Jr. Later the two became co-owners of the famous Rose Lodge.

This concealed lead was one that ultimately evaded the Cassette family
entirely as the newspaper never officially announced Rose's retirement.
There was another rumor that said Rose stayed on as a manager of Rose
Lodge, even after she sold it—only later moving to Florida. I couldn't be
sure. But I was saddened to learn that I had probably never seen the real

Rose Rose in all of my times going to the Rose Lodge. The Deeds Office would prove that Rose Rose continued to own the land past 1964, so maybe she had only sold the business portion initially? Surely the new owners wanted to portray the successful Rose Lodge as business as usual. No doubt this could only mean that Rose Rose's secret fried chicken recipe was sold with the restaurant.

Big and Little Papio Fight

Through the mid-1960s Omaha city ordinances arose that prohibited the construction of buildings along the Big and Little Papio Creeks within 150 feet of the Little Papio centerline and 200 feet on either side of the Big Papio, arguing that it was a floodplain. The Little Papio Creek, as you may recall, runs directly east along the Rose Lodge property. Rose Lodge, Inc., among other companies, filed action against the City of Omaha, claiming that the ordinances were taking private property for public use without compensation and that flood control measures were already in place. The businesses were able to block the city from enforcing the zoning laws in their suit, stating that the laws constituted "a forerunner to condemnation." When government seizes property from a private party, it is also called eminent domain. By 1967 the City of Omaha paid Rose Lodge $56,615 for a parcel of land for the Papio Creek flood control work. I was able to verify the city bought a large parcel from Rose Lodge, Inc., and Rose Rose, dated 1977. Previous to that, Rose Rose formally sold off a part the original Rose Lodge parcel as well as the strip adjacent to Rose Lodge, Inc., in May 1967. In 1979 Rose Rose sold the "whole property" to Rose Lodge, Inc. The Roses must have amassed numerous lots along this block when they lived there.

PART 3

Hints of the 1970s and 1980s

My father wasn't the only one who thought Rose Rose was still frying up that delectable chicken in the back kitchen, deep into the 1970s. Bill Gonzalez, of the Durham Museum Photo Archives, remembered that between 1977 and 1978 he had a delivery route with Carpenter Paper

Company. He delivered the "to-go materials" to Rose Lodge during that time period. "There was a good-size gal with big forearms who would always come out of the back. I remember bloody chicken on her apron and a hairnet." This woman would make Bill sit down and wait as she fried him up a pound of gizzards for his route. She seemed delighted that he loved those fried gizzards. He fondly recollected this familiar pattern. Later he'd drive around with those hot gizzards on the passenger seat, merrily eating as he went on with his deliveries. Not a bad deal. Who was this generous mystery woman if not our Rose Rose?

I contacted Amy Mather, one of *My Omaha Obsession*'s operatives at the Omaha Public Library, about looking into the library's fabulous menu collection. Unfortunately, the library does not have a Rose Lodge menu in its archives. I hope a reader will come forward with this request! I found evidence of Don Gatch managing Rose Lodge in the early 1970s. Gatch would go on to open his own old-fashioned chicken eatery at R. D. Cluckers in Miracle Hills Square.

The End Is Near

Tip-offs pointed to Robert's wife, Agnes O'Connor, who helped to manage Rose Lodge as well Tom Ross, August's son, in the late 1970s. Although the partners openly admitted, decades later, to having bought Rose Lodge for the land, they were impressed with the ever-growing restaurant business. The business continued to bring in hordes of hungry, fried chicken–loving folks. Omaha couldn't get enough, and to think the restaurant was over forty years old! Rose Lodge was now employing fifty-plus people and bringing in about $500,000 a year. But in the summer of 1984 O'Connor and Ross got an offer they just couldn't refuse.

Selling Off Rose Lodge

In a kind of strange agreement (although I have heard of stranger) the three acres including Rose Lodge were purchased by Children's Hospital and traded to O'Daniel Olds-Honda for nearby land owned by O'Daniel. Mike O'Daniel already owned property at 7801 Dodge, and he wanted a separate agency for the Honda franchise. Evidently, he also owned two acres

36. The O'Daniel Honda business as it appears today
on Beverly Drive. Photo by author.

southeast of Farnam Street and Beverly Drive, which the hospital, in turn, wanted for its newly proposed day care center for children of Methodist and Children's Hospital employees. (It appears now to be the Children's Hospital's Carolyn Scott Rainbow House / the Ted E. Bear Hollow organization.)

By November 1984 the City Planning Board approved the rezoning propositions, and the *Omaha World-Herald* quietly announced the closing of Rose Lodge. O'Daniel Honda was built in 1986 at 123 Beverly Drive on 2.91 acres, which included Lots 2 and 3, and an "irregular part of creek." As you can imagine, this has been a very good Midtown location for O'Daniel.

A New Rose

Meanwhile, back in 1984 O'Connor and Ross held steadfast that they were looking for a new location for Rose Lodge. This never came to pass. Was it a dodge to keep those fried chicken lovers from rioting in the streets? We don't know for sure, but I do know that sometimes life gets in between one's plans for the future. And honestly, between you and me, I do not remember Rose Lodge's closing or any of this piffle. I was too busy investigating the back alleys of downtown Omaha in those days.

Magically, in November 1987, the Rose opened on Highway 92 in Treynor, Iowa. Now I never knew about this savory spot, but apparently, it was well loved and quite popular. Judy and Don Harwick owned the Rose. They say Judy's mother was a cook at the original Rose Lodge for forty-seven years, and Judy had also worked there for thirteen years. Can you believe that? Did one of these gals serve Bill Gonzalez those fabulous gizzards he's still raving about? Sadly I discovered at the Rose Restaurant Facebook page that it, too, closed in August 2013. I wish I could have gone there!

Our Rose Rose

I found our enigmatic Rose Rose died of natural causes in 1989 at the age of ninety-four. Although she resided in Florida, Rose is buried in one of my favorite all-time Omaha places to rattle around, the Bohemian Cemetery at Fifty-Second and Center.

Woefully, I never got the true account of Rose Rose, and there was so much more I wanted to know. For example, was she the workhorse she appeared to be? What amused her? Did she yell out anything fantastically colorful while she grabbed at that policeman holding a gun on her husband? How did she dress? You have to know by now that these things keep me up at night. What I can imagine is that she was a very strong woman, a characteristic I much admire in my women. Rose Rose would surely enter a room of strangers with the confidence that she was just as good as any of them, no matter what titles they came up with. And I am not a seer, but I sensed her fried chicken recipe was only one of many, many secrets. I imagine I will stay on the case, as I have found a case is never really closed, detective friends.

CHAPTER 4

The Secret of the House That Moved

I did not have to wait for long. After all, sometimes a mystery just falls into one's lap. Soon after the summer publication of my article on the "Tree Swings of Dundee," I received a delightful message from Gretchen J. about one of the homes featured in the story. In her words: "Rumor has it that the house at 403 North Happy Hollow Boulevard was moved to its current site sometime in the 1970s. I was told that it used to sit on one of the lots that were purchased to build the A. V. Sorenson Library and Community Center. I grew up near the home and as children, I remember the summer we spent sliding down the dirt pile that was made when they excavated the new basement for 403 until an adult of some sort told us to stop. What I can't recall is whether the dirt mound was on the property, or across Happy Hollow Boulevard in front of the ravine?"

This exciting complication of details sent my mind whirring. I similarly paced about in my detective's study, Virginia creeper peering in through the windows as I fixated. I distinctly remembered the warm 403 Colonial Revival and its solid construction when I was working on a kiddie swing story, noted for its unusual, angled placement on the small lot—atypical of the proud boulevard. It instantly seemed plausible that this house had been relocated. And to think I had always found 403 perfectly snuggled into its corner lot in all of my years of strolling by on foot. Could this rumor be true, and why had the home been moved? It was just the kind of Hidden in Plain View Mystery that Miss Cassette lives for.

Now I suppose I should let you in on a little secret. Since my very early formative memories, probably from my Ak-Sar-Ben Coronation Ball days, which Mr. Cassette teasingly has referenced as Her Days on the Ball Circuit, I had acquired a taste for Happy Hollow Boulevard and crab cakes. Or was it shrimp cocktail? Oh yes, the crab cakes would be unveiled much later at a decadent dinner at the Café de Paris down on Sixth Street in the early 1990s. One must never forget these pleasurably proceedings, and here I am getting turned all around. Regardless, my child's eye observed the Happy Hollow Boulevard homes, and those of Woolworth Avenue offered the very best in pre- and post-ball parties, including the best hostesses, the best interiors, the best appetizers (peeled shrimp on crushed ice in a cocktail glass corrupted our grade school set), and I took all of that into account when I surmised those who had passed their days within these ivy-covered abodes quite possibly had the best lives. To this day the very string of words *Happy-Hollow-Boulevard* sends me down that cool, winding, tree-lined road of my imagination to knock firmly on the dark, arched doorway of childhood and indeed has never left me. For I have dreamed of these auspicious environs ever since.

It didn't take long to begin searching, looking for general clues about this purported house that had moved, but alas, I could find nothing. Eventually, I would make contact with the current owners, and Mr. and Mrs. Homeowner (names have been withheld to protect their privacy) verified that their house at 403 North Happy Hollow Boulevard had indeed been moved to its current location. They were able to provide me with the previous address, 4814 Cass Street, but they did not know much about the history except for that bit about the library. With the old address in hand, I was better able to root out the hidden clues. I could hear the dark, arched door of shaded Happy Hollow Boulevard open to a pleasurable swoosh. Oh, that we could step over the sill together and you could see for yourself.

DUNDEE CLUES

After reviewing the *Dundee and Twin Ridge / Morton Meadows Neighborhoods Nebraska Historic Building Survey* of 2004, created by the City of Omaha and the Nebraska State Historical Society, I discovered that Dundee had sprung up to the east of John Nelson Hayes Patrick's estate, pleasingly named Happy Hollow. The Patrick family and their large eight hundred–acre estate were favorably mentioned in Margaret Patricia Kil-

37. Brownell Hall at 400 North Happy Hollow Boulevard. The old Patrick
mansion. The couple in the open-top car is Mr. and Mrs. Charles Drew. From
the KM3TV/Bostwick-Frohardt Photograph Collection at the Durham Museum.

lian's book, *Born Rich: A Historical Book of Omaha*, and were a frequent
focus in my investigations, primarily because it would later become the
first Happy Hollow Club (then a public golf course and later Memorial
Park), and in 1922 the Patrick home would transform into the third variation of Brownell Hall / Brownell Talbot School, located at 400 North
Happy Hollow Boulevard. Fellow sleuths, I will tell you now, the Patrick
story deserves its own book, and someday I hope to attend to just that . . .

From my digging I found that the Patrick Land Company began to
develop the large Patrick property into Dundee Place subdivision in 1887.
The meager building permits began trickling into the public record the
summer of 1888. But it wasn't until 1893, when additional land would be
acquired and eventually augmented to Dundee Place, that the development truly began in full. Dundee was incorporated into its own village;

later Douglas County Omaha annexed Dundee in 1915 and, by all accounts, became the first western streetcar suburb. Early planning developed the Dundee hard-lined street grid of the traditional city neighborhoods of this time period. Later Omaha would be introduced to the curvilinear garden suburbs of Happy Hollow, Minne Lusa, Fairacres, and the Country Club neighborhoods. Dundee claims as its perimeters Hamilton Street on the north, Forty-Sixth Street on the east, Leavenworth partitions the south, and the meandering Happy Hollow Boulevard borders the western side. Although I could not find the relocated house mentioned in the *Historic Building Survey* or in *Born Rich*, both books made a focal point of the impressive, varied architectural styles found in Dundee—a point of distinction influenced by individual owners hiring architects to custom-design each home. And so Dundee was built up into something quite unique, parcel by parcel. For those interested in a further study of the Dundee neighborhood, may I suggest Dan Rock's fantastic book, *Dundee Neb.: A Pictorial History*.

HIDDEN COVENANTS

Let us not turn a blind eye to the racially restrictive covenants of Omaha's early suburbs. These beautiful houses and well-designed neighborhoods of Midtown came at a cost, by segregating local families along racial divides. Author Richard Rothstein's book *The Color of Law*, examined this federally approved racial segregation found in housing across America. The United States Supreme Court validated the use of racial deed restrictions in 1926, and the practice became commonplace after that. This lawful act specifically targeted African Americans, to keep them from moving into well-to-do or "better" neighborhoods, but also could prohibit the sale or rental of property to Jews and Asian Americans. A racially restrictive covenant might read, "This lot shall be owned and occupied by people of the Caucasian race only" or simply "Whites Only." This systematic form of segregation ensured not only mutual agreements between property owners in a neighborhood but also real estate boards and neighborhood associations. The Federal Housing Administration, Rothstein wrote, "furthered the segregation efforts by refusing to insure mortgages in and near African-American neighborhoods—a policy known as 'redlining.'" Redlining practices of Old Omaha continue to affect our community to this very day.

By 1948 the Supreme Court declared that these racial restrictions were no longer "enforceable," although realtors and property owners could and would continue to discriminate at will on the basis of race. "In 1968 Congress passed the Housing Rights Act, finally outlawing discrimination on the basis of race or ethnicity in the sale or rental of housing. Since then it has been illegal to act on the race restrictions that are embedded in so many deeds."

I had reached out through social media to *My Omaha Obsession* readers living in pre-1920s Dundee–Happy Hollow homes but did not unearth a single racially restrictive deed from this time period. Maybe there are truly none out there, or maybe there is one to be found in an abstract, in someone's Everything Kitchen Drawer. Most likely, it was assumed back in the early days of Dundee Place that a Jewish person or an African American family would never attempt or could never acquire land in this development. I did find evidence that these racially motivated restrictions were customarily written into deeds of housing from the 1930 and 1940s in neighboring Midtown subdivisions.

CASS STREET

I have always held a fondness for Cass Street. I can still remember the Peony Park amusement advertisements mentioning the name Cass Street, and I had favored it early on. It held a perceived crisp chicness that seemed so foreign to my life in Benson. According to the exhaustive, brilliant research of H. Ben Brick, in his tome *The Streets of Omaha: Their Origins and Changes*, Cass Street was named in honor of Lewis Cass, secretary of state to President Buchanan. This east-west-running street, on the traditional grid, is a staple of downtown and midtown Omaha, but at about Eighty-Sixth Street it discreetly merges into West Dodge Road, never to be heard from again. Brick cites that Cass at that juncture was originally a country road, later adapted as West Dodge Road, according to the city atlas. Of course, there is always the opportunity for Cass Street to reemerge on, say, Two Hundredth Street, and I just might never be privy to this phenomenon. Although I have often wondered in the wee hours if Cass peeks its head out in some extra-solar location, I will have to trust those of you who live beyond the yonder.

Cass Street, in this swath of Dundee, is a quiet lane, bookended by Forty-Eighth Street to the east and Forty-Ninth Street on the west. Cass meets a *T* in the road at Forty-Eighth Street, perhaps making this expanse of Cass more of a destination block, which appears to be a-okay with its neighbors. I found 4814 Cass on the north side of the street, now actively serving as a parking lot to the A. V. Sorensen Library, to its east. On the same side of the street, to the west of the proud parking lot, were three lots, all operating as midcentury modern apartment buildings. Conspicuously nestled into the last lot on the Forty-Ninth Street corner, an older home shared tight quarters with one of these apartment buildings. My detective's mind envisioned other pre-1920s homes on the block, all razed for the 1950s apartments or conceptualized a very sparse block, architecturally speaking, with large glorious gardens for the few homes it supported. Either way, I was struck with its peacefulness.

EARLY SEARCH

The Douglas County Assessor's site gave lead that 4814 Cass was constructed in 1919, but I have learned that this valuable source is not always accurate. My true search began at the W. Dale Clark downtown library, a favorite haunt, when I began poring over the Omaha City Directories. I chose the year 1915, cracked open the large, library-scented book, and looked up 4814 Cass. There was no address. In fact, the only addresses on the block in 1915 were 4811 and 4819 Cass Street. Happily, 4811 and 4819 are still extant and can be spied upon at your earliest convenience. The house at 4811 was built in 1903 and was split up into apartments long ago but still has the dignified look of a single-family frame house. I adore it. The Assessor's site has 4819 recorded as having been built in 1917, but we know from the city directory that it was standing by 1915. I am not here to squabble over these life-or-death matters. Interestingly, there was still no address for 4814 Cass by 1920, and I was getting nervous. By 1921 the name W. J. Miller appeared as the first listing of the address, and I was intrigued with the initial bit of human contact. I excitedly jotted the name in my notebook. I believe this might be a proper time to direct you fine readers to obtain your own pen and notepad, as this will begin to compound much like a Russian novel.

According to the Douglas County Register of Deeds Office, Maggie L. Peters and husband sold the original empty parcel at 4814 Cass Street to Eleanor Miller in May 1919. The War to End All Wars had officially come to a halt in 1918, and these must have been happy years in Midtown. As I paged through the large Dundee Place addition, I learned that Maggie Peters owned a good deal of property in the Dundee area. Another property owner in the vicinity I happened upon was named R. C. Peters and made an additional note in my clever little detective's book. Yet another landowner of abundant property was a name I knew I recognized, Mr. George A. Hoagland. But more on him later . . .

R. C. PETERS

My digging began with Maggie L. Peters, which, truth be told, did not get me very far. Although green to this sleuthing business, I had learned that searching for a woman's name back in the early 1900s does not often detail more than a superficial glance. Ms. Maggie owned many, many properties, although there was next to nothing explaining how she had acquired this bountiful grouping of parcels all over town. Woefully, there was nothing more. Was R. C. Peters perhaps a relative?

My first *Omaha World-Herald* search for R. C. Peters revealed the man had been made "First Vice President" of the Farm Mortgage Bankers' Association of America in Kansas City, Missouri, back in September 1918. This was a good start. *Omaha Memories: Recollections of Events, Men and Affairs in Omaha, Nebraska from 1879 to 1917* by Edward F. Morearty included the somewhat hazy-named R. C. Peters among his short list of Those Prominently Connected with Omaha's Upbuild. If you have not pried open this odd little book, may I recommend a punctual review? Fascinating. Incidentally, why were so many men of yesteryear identified by their initials?

Through volume 2 of Arthur Cooper Wakeley's *Omaha: The Gate City, and Douglas County, Nebraska*, I finally learned R. C. Peters's proper name: Richard Calvin Peters. As a sidenote, I often wonder if Wakeley Street, which runs by Indian Creek Nursery, is named after this Arthur Cooper fellow? Peters allegedly moved to Westpoint, Nebraska, from Michigan in 1886. Once in Nebraska, he established a real estate and loan business. After eleven years Peters pulled up stakes, forging on to Omaha in hopes of yet more opportunity. Here he organized the R. C. Peters & Company, a mortgage loan and investment business. I might be making assumptions, but this would appear to explain Ms. Maggie's acquisition of the aforementioned inexhaustible list of properties. The *Omaha Daily Bee*, Sunday edition, on February 16, 1902, exposed that the R. C. Peters & Company was housed at the Bee Building at 1702 Farnam Street.

Later his most well-known venture, the Peters Trust Company, would establish R.C. as a prominent Omaha businessman. Peters was the president and chief executive officer; additionally, he held a position as one of the Farm Mortgage Bankers' Association directors. Wakeley wrote of R. C. Peters in 1917, "There is perhaps no one in Omaha better informed concerning farm properties and values." Maggie Peters, R. C.'s wife, started life as Miss Margaret L. Reed. The couple married in 1887 in Illinois and would raise four children in Nebraska.

Together the Peters had amassed a great amount of realty in Omaha and surrounding areas, particularly in Dundee and the nearby Field Club area. From the amazing *National Register of Historic Places Registration Form: Field Club Historic District*, compiled and prepared by Melissa Dirr and Jill Ebers in 2000, I discovered that the Peters real estate moguls owned a number of mysterious lots in the Field Club neighborhood, including 1301, 1302, 1319, and 1323, all on South Thirty-Fifth Street and all reportedly built in 1907. Meanwhile, the Nebraska State Historical Society displayed that 1305 South Thirty-Fifth was designed for the Peters Trust Company in 1907 by none other than our old friend architect Frederick A. Henninger. This led me to believe that the Peters Trust bought and built many great homes in Omaha with strong pointers to a Peters-Henninger professional relationship. And as you sly ones might have anticipated, this fine architect would figure into the mystery of 4814 Cass a bit later.

Maggie and R. C. Peters owned other lots in the 121 block in Dundee. Additional lots on numerous blocks around Dundee Place were held under R.C.'s name and were sold to, no doubt, eager buyers by 1904. It would appear that the 4814 Cass transaction from Ms. Maggie to Eleanor Miller in May 1919 included an additional empty lot, number "16," I assumed to the east of the property. I have since gone back and now know that Lot 16 is to west of the original 4814 Cass parcel. Standing on the lot is a large brick apartment building of a solid, nondescript 1951 design. You know the kind of which I speak—no frills but hard workers nonetheless.

FREDERICK A. HENNINGER

According to Nebraska State Historical Society historical records, Frederick A. Henninger designed 4814 Cass Street. I contacted Trina Westman, city planner—Urban Design and Historic Preservation with the Omaha City Planning Department—to verify this fact, and she located a tidbit of a confirmation as well. This discovery, I will confide, gave my detective's slink an additional air of confidence, as I knew this highly regarded architect from my past investigations. In fitting with the trend of the day, the architect was often referred to as "F. A. Henninger," having blown into town after study at the Chicago Art Institute. As my friend Randall Smith educated me early on in my sleuthing, the architect had earned the name "House-a-Day Henninger" for his exhaustive output in architectural design. From *A Comprehensive Program for Historic Preservation in Omaha* compiled by the Landmarks Heritage Preservation Commission and the Omaha City Planning Department, I was reminded of Henninger's prominence as a Period Revival architect, noted for his works in residential Midtown—the Field Club, the Country Club; additionally, Henninger is credited with having built over thirty homes in the Dundee–Happy Hollow historic district. From the Landmarks book, Henninger was said to have distinguished himself by "designing homes for the city's wealthiest residents in the years between 1910 and 1930." In the early 1930s F. A. Henninger would be joined by son, Fred Jr., and establish a new firm, F. A. Henninger & Son. Father Henninger (I like the sounds of that) would later retire in California, leaving his son to continue his practice as the sole designer.

With the Peters-Henninger collaboration tip, I questioned whether the Peters or the Millers actually built the soon-to-be Colonial-fashioned home at 4814 Cass. As mentioned earlier, the Douglas County Assessor's Office had recorded that 4814 Cass was erected in 1919. This matched what I found at the Douglas County Register of Deeds, although the actual address wasn't cataloged in the city directory until 1921. As you by now know through my adventures, the city directory isn't altogether error free, and often my own PI path has been strewn with discrepancies, despite my best efforts at Tidy Mystery Solving.

THE COLONIAL REVIVAL

Through *A Field Guide to American Houses* by Virginia Savage McAlester, a bible of sorts, I sharpened my skills in a fully obsessive Colonial study. Here are the fine points. The Colonial Revival rose to fame in America from about 1880 to 1955. Considered the most favored Renaissance Classical style, the Colonial Revival dominated 40 percent of new buildings from 1910 through 1930. This long-lived American house drew upon the architectural characteristics of the American Georgian and Federal styles.

The Colonial Revival conveys a proud, upstanding look, due in large part to the obsession with symmetry, seen in the balanced windows and emphasis on the well-centered entry porch with pediment framing. In studying the Henninger home of our focus, now situated at 403 North Happy Hollow Boulevard, the beautiful portico entry has a center gabled roof, complete with a friendly curved underside. Slender but stately columns uphold this crown; its pilasters are visible from the sidewalk, flanking the door. These essential, classic details aid in conveying visual harmony and give homes of the past such a strong structural point of view. The perfect details are often missing or misappropriated in contemporary homes. Sigh.

I am in love with its steep pitch roof, not commonly found in the Colonial Revival. The fact that her harlequin diamond–patterned, original

38. Western elevation of the house at 403 North Happy
Hollow Boulevard. Photo by author.

slate roof has been lovingly maintained is only icing on the cake from
my perspective. Long live original slate, a true work of art. These lifetime roofs fight the good fight, and for those homeowners lucky enough
to still maintain theirs, they well know the dance of the unscrupulous
roofing contractors who want to wrongfully condemn these beauties.

McAlester estimated that 30 percent of Colonial Revivals are thought
to be two-story rectangular shaped blocks with a side-gabled roof. The
visible left wing—or dependency, as it is called—of 403 North Happy
Hollow Boulevard, is flat-roofed, which is usual, another giveaway to a
Revival style from this period. This addition has some exceptional detailing, including well-crafted pilasters and entablature, accentuated by the
attractive painted trim. The windows stand alone as single units, double-
hung, six over one. The triple windows on the left wing and the trio visible on the build-out to the south, no doubt a dining room, further signify

that this is a Revival rather than an original. Vernacular examples of the Colonial Revival were commonly constructed of wood before 1920, with masonry techniques developing and soon dominating the mainstream soon after. This was absolutely in following with our 4814 Cass Street Colonial timeline previous to its Happy Hollow relocation.

There are three things I love about this house, above all other things I love about this house. There is a slight, shy overhang, and if you look carefully, it is decorated with dentils. The under dentil trim or moldings are peeking at you from under the eaves. Another point of my pleasant neurosis—the shutters. Exceptional. Functional or doing a fine job of impersonation. Please heed that these real wood shutters are not nailed to the house. They fit the window size and are hung by authentic hinges. The shutters are teetering in different states of "openness" due to the genuine shutter dogs at their base. This is how historic homes look. Lived-in perfection. Another feature I adore has nothing to do with the original architecture but, rather, an addition when the home was moved to Happy Hollow. I add it here because it seems to make sense. Upon your next visit, notice the informal sidewalk that leads from the public sidewalk on the south up to the house. This path leads across the front to the driveway, down to the public sidewalk on the north side. It's a detail that conveys warmth and attention to community. And I'm sure the neighborhood postal worker is appreciative.

THE CASS STREET NEIGHBOR

Ceremonious consideration should be given to the grand estate directly to the east of the original 4814 Cass address. This large home had been famously moved across town after being cut in two, a widespread story shared in Margaret P. Killian's book, *Born Rich: A Historical Book of Omaha*. Killian stated the Hoagland House was originally on the northwest corner of Sixteenth and Howard and was later moved to Forty-Eighth and Cass. I had come across this exciting tale while investigating the Hill Hotel for another article earlier this year. I tracked its ownership to one George Appleton Hoagland, an interesting early Omaha character, known initially for his affiliation with his father's wholesale and retail

39. The Hoagland family home at 4802 Cass Street, which was moved from Sixteenth and Howard Streets. Two men are working in the yard, ca. 1906. From the KM3TV/Bostwick-Frohardt Photograph Collection at the Durham Museum.

lumber business, Geo. T. Hoagland & Company, aptly named for George Tunis Hoagland. George A. would later purchase his father's interest in the business in 1874 and go it alone, to great success.

I found the Hoaglands and their moving house had already been established in Dundee by 1904, as asserted by the *Omaha World-Herald*. Hoagland saw fit to cut his large 1880 Victorian Queen Anne in half and have it moved "due to the growth of the business district" from Sixteenth and Howard. In 1905 the district attracted the Orchard & Wilhelm Company, a furniture store, to the very site of the previous Hoagland estate, adopting the address 414 South Sixteenth. This well-liked furnishings retailer would maintain its popular downtown habitation until closing in the summer of 1971.

Meanwhile, the Hoagland's new address, non-extant, was 510 North Forty-Eighth Street and at other times, curiously, assigned the cross-street address of 4802 Cass Street. These were in fact the exact same large corner lot, purportedly almost an acre. In August 1905 Mrs. George A. Hoagland was advertising for a "Cook or Competent Girl for general housework in our large home at Forty-eighth and Cass, Dundee." Within that year Mrs. Hoagland would look for a nurse and a second girl to round out the full staff. I would soon learn why the Mrs. needed so much domestic help. Through the *History of the City of Omaha, Nebraska* by James Woodruff Savage and John Thomas Bell, I found Mrs. Hoagland was originally Ianthe C. Wyman, daughter of a prominent local journalist. By the bye, I found her name spelled *Iantha* in Wakeley's *Omaha: The Gate City* volume. I cannot be sure which she preferred. Mrs. Hoagland had been bred into the elite of Omaha and was often featured in the news for her many contributions to the beau monde. Her prestigious houseguests were announced with regularity throughout 1905–12. Ianthe and George had seven children, including William Wyman Hoagland, who would make his presence known later in the investigation. William and his family lived down the way, at Fifty-First and Cass Streets. Reviewing my detective notes from the Register of Deeds Office, I could see that father George had sold or moved a large amount of his Dundee parcels into son William's name in and around 1907.

THE ELEANOR AND W. J. MILLER FILE

The deed gave inkling to the Miller name. As stated previously, Eleanor Miller purchased the land in May 1919. Although I wouldn't find the property in the city directory until 1921 under the name of one W. J. Miller, I did find an advertisement from 1919 soliciting a "competent maid" for a "two in family" household at 4814 Cass Street.

As you can imagine, I had a good deal of fun traipsing through the histories of numerous colorful W. J. Millers, all over the country, a name as vague as our R. C. Peters. But when I finally discerned the trail of W. J. Miller, our Omaha W. J. Miller, I discovered he was yet another well-known Omaha lumberman—in fact, a close friend of George A. Hoagland. I found evidence that W.J. had originally come to town from Hastings, Nebraska, in the late 1800s and began his Omaha journey with a stay at the Iler Grand in downtown Omaha. A visit from Mr. and Mrs. George

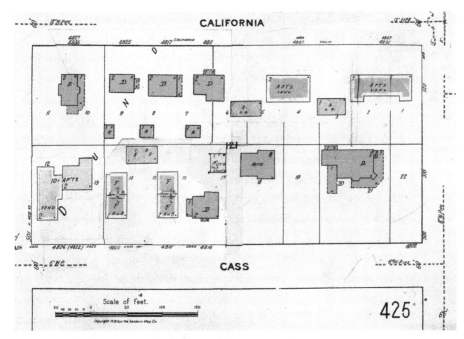

40. The Sanborn map of 1960 reveals the footprint of homes on Cass Street. The house at 4802 Cass is shown holding its ground on three lots in the lower right corner. Lot 18 shows the carriage house in 1960, labeled "auto." The property at 4814 Cass, to the west, also has a garage labeled "auto," additionally "tile stucc'd." Sanborn map courtesy of the Omaha City Planning Department.

Kribly of Galva, Illinois, to their daughter's home gave indication that Eleanor Kribly Miller and W. J. Miller had officially moved to Omaha by 1902. The couple bought an earlier home from a G. E. Miller in South Omaha in 1905, which I later came to find was in the area of Fifteenth and N Streets. Unfortunately, the sudden death of the couple's five-year-old son in March 1907 is what permitted me to find their South Omaha address. The couple never had another child, hence the "two in family" explanation in all further advertisements for servants from that day forward.

The *Omaha World-Herald* archives indicated W. J. Miller wore many hats as secretary, treasurer, director, and manager of the Updike Lumber and Coal Company, a company that boasted twenty-five lumber and coal yards along the North Western railroad throughout Nebraska in 1906.

Omaha was the supply and general office point. Additionally, Updike had operated as a grain company. All ventures appeared to be quite profitable. By 1917 a division of Updike Lumber and Coal was located at Forty-Sixth and Dodge.

The Millers were customarily included in the Who's Who of Omaha Society right alongside the Mercers, Millards, Pratts, Spragues, Boyds, Kinslers, Redicks, and Beatons. In one "Theater Parties" announcement, W. J. Miller was entertaining on a Monday night at a "box party" within the Brandeis Theater, in celebration of the Henry Miller and Ruther Chatterton show *A Marriage of Convenience*. The year was 1919. Between you and I, I am not sure how these society people found time to entertain so much. Not only did they socialize throughout their week; they apparently were up all hours of the night. What is even more perplexing— these moneyed men were often running multiple businesses, were on local boards, and held political offices to boot.

Eleanor Kribly Miller was spoken well of, mentioned often in the papers as a gracious, fun-loving hostess. This high-styled society clue was made a bit clearer when I read a report of Mrs. Eleanor Miller suing the Pullman Company for one thousand dollars in 1910 (worth roughly twenty-five thousand dollars in 2017). Founded by George Pullman, the "Pullman" referred to a railroad sleeping car, operating on the U.S. railroads system. Mrs. Miller proclaimed she had been robbed while traveling from Salt Lake City to Portland, the bandits making off with a solitaire ruby in a Tiffany setting, two solitaire diamonds both in Tiffany settings, an emerald set in two diamonds, and an opal set in ten diamonds. The importance of the "Tiffany setting" name drop was the distinguishing character of the Tiffany & Co. design, known for its high-quality insistence of a special number of prongs and particular collet. All of these jewels, Mrs. Miller claimed, she was wearing in a concealed chamois skin bag on her person. My goodness gracious . . . quite the snaffling.

In June 1913, I discovered, the W. J. Miller and R. C. Peters families were not only buyer and seller but also very close friends. The two families embarked on the steamer *North American* for a Great Lakes trip destined for a "vacation period in Hollingwood, Ontario."

NEW DEVELOPMENTS

Months into the investigation I came across an article announcing that Mrs. George A. Hoagland had died suddenly in her ornate Queen Anne at 510 North Forty-Eighth Street in February 1919. This meant that George A. Hoagland was living next door to the Millers as a widower in the years that they occupied the Colonial.

March 10, 1921, an *Omaha World-Herald* article notified the public that W. J. Miller, treasurer and general manager of the Updike Lumber and Coal Company, had resigned on account of ill health. The Omaha City Directory of 1923 listed W. J. Miller as the homeowner of 4814 Cass, but curiously, a brief snippet in the *Omaha World-Herald* dated February 11, 1923, made mention that "Mr. and Mrs. E. M. Syfert who have been living at the Hotel Sanford, have taken a home at 4814 Cass Street for two months."

That summer, on July 22, 1923, the Millers had listed their home for sale. "The beautiful colonial home of W. J. Miller is now offered for the first time. Ideally situated in a proper colonial setting, this Home will please the most fastidious." Don't you love it? But what did a "proper colonial setting" mean?

Another discovery from 1923 enabled me to learn of George A. Hoagland's death at age eighty years old. The pallbearers were chosen from Hoagland's former business associates, his close friends. Mr. W. J. Miller was one of the chosen shortlist. The aerial view of the Forty-Eighth and Cass area (from 1941 DOGIS surveillance photos) showed how very close and exclusive this beautiful corner shared by the Miller-Hoagland families must have been. One can see what must have been the large coach house behind the Hoagland home. To the west is the original setting of the 4814 Cass house.

MARY B. GLOVER

By searching the Omaha Deeds Office, I found "Mary B. Glover and husband" bought 4814 Cass from the Millers in December 1923. My favorite clue, which came very late in the exploration, was a 1923 article announc-

41. "Two residences valued at $48,000, sold by C. B. Stuht in a week,"
December 9, 1923. There it is, our Colonial. It looks exactly the same
today, I exclaimed. Is that a beautiful garage up the drive and to the right?
What a cunning little drive that must have been, bordering the Hoagland
shrubs and trees to the east. I delighted in the photo, a treasured glimpse
of the past. Reprinted with permission from the *Omaha World-Herald*.

ing the curious house swap of two families. The Dean and Mary Glover
home at 307 North Fifty-Fourth Street, valued at thirty-three thousand
dollars, was sold to W. J. Miller, and the Glovers in turn bought the Millers' home. The 307 North Fifty-Fourth Street home was noted for being
but a year and a half old, boasting eleven rooms. 4814 Cass was quoted
at seven rooms and sold for fifteen thousand dollars.

Cyrus Dean Glover made news as a curious four-year-old for reportedly
burning down his family's barn and contents out in Long Pine, Nebraska,
in order to experience what he called a "bon fire." As an eleven-year-old,
the young fellow, by then called Dean, accidentally fell against the "hand
car" machinery he was riding. Someone in the audience will have to let
me know what a hand car meant in 1897. He walked away with a semi-
circular scalp wound, but I was beginning to see a familiar pattern. If

you have ever happened across an adventurous child such as this, you can understand why I was shilly-shallying about digging further. But we must be brave in these wavering times, and it was all okay. By 1908 the Dean Glover family had moved to Omaha and were residing in the Bemis Park area.

By October 1909 the *Omaha World-Herald* Weddings section announced the engagement of Miss Mary Bingham Fenn to Mr. Cyrus Dean Glover, son of Mr. and Mrs. Charles Robert Glover. I inferred from the lengthy wedding description that year that the Fenns and/or the Glovers were a well-heeled society family. Every nuptial detail was fussed about and labored over by the social desk reporter, so one must assuredly assume I was luxuriating in the narrative. I won't bore you with the details, but you might like to know the bride was described as "a dainty brunette" whose pearls and white veil were thought to be an attractive contrast with her dark hair.

Mr. and Mrs. Dean Glover were found regularly on the Social Whirl pages, entertaining extensively, attending the Orpheum, dining at the Happy Hollow Club, hosting home luncheons and tea service, and enjoying supper-dances in the best of hotels and homes. It seemed every time Mrs. Glover left town, which was frequently, the press was there to report on it, and the Glovers gave the appearance of entertaining more out of town guests than any family I'd ever researched before. It was frankly dizzying, and I wasn't even there. I would find only later that Dean's sisters were the semi-famous Miriam and Maziebell Glover, beauties of the New York stage, known for their extensive musical training in violin and, perhaps, dalliance into vaudeville by way of a colorful manager. The Glovers' young son, Robert, would later make headlines in 1925 for helping to pitch an exact replica of the tepee residence of Chief Dull Knife of the Cheyenne Tribe, along with other fellow Boy Scouts, down on Twentieth and Farnam.

Following the breadcrumbs, I was soon to learn that Dean Glover was yet another real estate mogul, operating under the name of Glover Realty Company. Quoted as "the astute and successful young realtor," Glover was also a well-spoken member of the Real Estate Exchange Committee.

THE SECRET OF THE HOUSE THAT MOVED

At least he was the one they sent to be interviewed by the press most regularly. Years later W. G. Spain bought half-interest in the Glover Realty Syndicate (I love when they use that word) and formed a new firm—the Glover-Spain Realty Company.

THE GLOVERS MOVE ON

Ida E. Cummins bought the house from Mary B. Glover in May 1927. The real estate transaction between the Glovers and Mrs. Ida E. Cummins for fifteen thousand dollars was distinguished as the largest Omaha sale that week. I was excited to peer into the life of Ida Cummins, but first I would need to see the Glovers off.

As my investigation eventually turned up, the darlings of the Omaha press, Dean and Mary Glover, had decided to relocate to fashionable Los Angeles. Son Robert Dean Glover's nuptials in November 1937 unveiled the news.

THE HOAGLAND EASEMENT

By letter of the deed, William Wyman Hoagland made some alteration or claim to the "eastern ½ and E 27.1" portion of Ida Cummins's 4814 Cass parcel in 1925. I would learn much later that son William moved into his parents' large, park-like property following George Appleton Hoagland's death in 1923.

A BIT MORE ABOUT R. C. PETERS

Forgive me, but I must step back and catch us up on Mr. Peters because this, fellow snoops, is interesting. The Peters National Bank faced a merger with the Omaha National Bank in November 1929. The *World-Herald* article did not mention the Wall Street crash from October 1929, but one could speculate this merger was a result of that economic decline. One million dollars in securities, sixteen employees, and several officers moved into the Omaha offices. The Omaha National Bank Building was located at 1650 Farnam Street, originally the New York Life Insurance Company. This proud 1888 building stands as one of Omaha's greatest Italian Renaissance showpieces and has greeted us over and over again

42. "Friends Give Farewell Dinner for C. Dean Glover," July 24, 1937. Cyrus
Dean Glover with some friends gathered for a toast at the Omaha Athletic Club,
where he was presented with a goodbye wristwatch. The Omaha Athletic Club,
located at 1714 Douglas Street, was a private social club and a John Latenser
& Sons design. Reprinted with permission from the *Omaha World-Herald*.

in my various sleuthing missions. Today it is home to Kutak Rock Law
firm and has been renamed the Omaha Building.

Significant to this story, R. C. Peters and W. J. Miller, along with friend
H. H. Fish, bought up huge swaths of land in 1914 as an investment of
what would later be developed into Fairacres. By 1931 their lushly land-
scaped property was primed for subdivision into home sites by the Stuht-
Bedford Company. Thought to be the "highest knoll in the district," the
shared land offered more than one thousand trees and shrubs imported
from Japan, Italy, and other countries, bounded by Underwood Avenue,
Fairacres Road, Prairie Avenue, and "on the west by the Crofoot estates."
The Crofoots had made an appearance in my Burt Street investigation.
By the early 1930s water, sewer, gas, electricity, and hard-surfaced road-
ways were practically complete, according to the developers. Some eighty
fine fruit trees were removed by way of dynamite in order to make way

for the soon-to-be homes. The Peters, Miller, Fish development offered lots from one-half acre up "outside the city limits," and you can bet they went for a pretty penny. W. J. Miller died in his Fifty-Fourth Street home subsequent to a stroke only two years later.

R. C. Peters would pass away while traveling with family in Texas in the year 1936. Within this obituary I learned the primary Peters family home was at 4822 Cass Street. I about jumped out of my gumshoes as this address was at the opposite end of the block, same north side of the street, in what would have been a consecutive line from Hoagland estate to the Millers' property to the Peters on the other corner. Now that is what I would call a tidy mystery. This shed light on the Peters multiple parcels in this area as well as the grand, mysterious home we had noted while on a Cass Street stakeout. The house at 4822 is a home I have long churned over since that fateful night. Mr. Cassette is obsessed with its glorious, curved copper awnings, and I don't take that lightly, as he rarely gets excited about human creations, let alone architecture that isn't hidden deep in the earth and covered by a living, mossy roof. (Case in point, his agreement to join me on this sleuthing expedition was rare.) To the contrary, this gorgeous home and its large corner lot appear to have been later flanked by some too-close-for-comfort-apartment additions, presumably an attempt to make some extra money during the following decades. The parcel now carries the address 4824 Cass, including an apartment building adjoining the original home at 4822. I would later find clear indication that the Peters's house had been on that corner since 1906. This estate is a story begging to be told, and I know just the detective to cover the beat. Much later.

THE IDA CUMMINS FILE

I had a good time following the footprints along the Ida Cummins's family path. Ida E. Pratt was born on a farm in Wenona, Illinois, in 1853. She married Wilson B. Cummins, a grain merchant in Streator, Illinois, and the couple had one child, Isabelle, in 1875. Wilson died in 1910 at the age of fifty-nine. Ida would continue to live in that community until moving to Omaha in 1926 to be closer to her only child. In May 1927,

43. 4822 Cass Street. The Peters family estate, now cushioned
by apartment buildings. Photo by author.

at age seventy-four, Ida E. Cummins bought 4814 Cass Street, a home
shared with her daughter's family. Daughter Isabelle (Belle) had married a much older man, Edward Hildreth Robinson in Streator, Illinois,
in 1908. Edward was originally from Michigan and was only two years
younger than her mother, Ida. Edward worked as a clerk in 1929, according to the Omaha City Directory. A part of me questioned a man of that
age still working in those days, but I shrugged off my doubts as being
ageist. Unusual at the least, I concluded. The city directory persisted in
listing Edward H. Robinson as the homeowner, but I suppose that was
telling of the times.

Much time had passed by the arrival of another clue—Miss Belle had
been married at age twenty-one to another older gentleman, eleven years
her senior, named Frank Mears up in Chicago. By age twenty-six she was
back living with her parents, previous to her father's death.

CASS NEIGHBORHOOD FROM 1930 TO 1940

The 1930 U.S. Census displayed Edward, Isabelle, and Ida living in 4814 Cass together. There were no live-in maids. Richard and Margaret Peters at 4822 Cass shared quarters with their twenty-four-year-old daughter, another Margaret. A young Swedish servant, Charlotte Schonberg, waited on the Peters family. William W. and Florence Hoagland, to the east at 510 North Forty-Eighth Street, resided with their twenty-three-year-old son, William B. Hoagland. They retained two live-in domestics for the large home—Irish natives, sisters Ann and Agnes Melvin.

In December 1931 William W. Hoagland died at the young age of sixty-one. The funeral was held in the family's Queen Anne home. His wife, Florence, her mother, and various family members would continue to live in the large home on the corner lot. Subsequently, the 1940 U.S. Census divulged the Peters had moved from the Cass block, most likely after the death of R. C. Peters. Edward, Isabelle, and Ida remained at the 4814 Cass Colonial. Florence Hoagland now was living with her daughter, Emma; Emma's husband, Jay Gibbs; and their little daughter, Ithana. Son William B. continued to live in the house, age thirty-three.

THE FASHIONABLE MRS. EDWARD H. ROBINSON

The *Omaha World-Herald* ran a consuming story in February 24, 1932. The Browning-King store, Brandeis department store, Nebraska Clothing Company, Natelson's, and Hayden's, to name but a few, honored the Anniversary of Omaha in their winter window displays. I found that a number of Omaha women lent the window designers their vintage clothing from the 1800s to illustrate what appropriate period attire had been. Mrs. Edward H. Robinson (our Belle Cummins) of 4814 Cass Street was one such lady and had thoughtfully loaned hats and dresses to the Thomas Kilpatrick & Company. A woman who had clothes from the 1800s in 1932? I dreamed she might have been a like-minded sister after my antique heart. Were these Belle or Ida Pratt Cummins's vintage pieces? Regarding the Thomas Kilpatrick Company—I traced this downtown department store to its 1509 Douglas Street location. When I was a very young girl, Younkers-Kilpatrick's, as it was later named, could be found at the Westroads mall, but I recall Mother of Miss Cassette calling it Kilpat's, as all mothers did back then.

DEATH OF EDWARD ROBINSON

March 9, 1943, Edward H. Robinson, age eighty-six, passed away. His death certificate exposed that he died at his 4814 Cass Street home. Curiously, a mystery daughter was listed as Mrs. H. M. Waters, with two grandchildren from Sails Point Hassock, which I tracked to Queens County, New York. I would be willing to put money on this daughter having been from a previous marriage. I could find no indication that Belle ever had a child. Edward's only sibling, brother Charles, was recorded as living in Omaha. The obit read: "Strictly private funeral. Please omit flowers," which always makes me pause. Later still, the 1870 U.S. Census also showed Edward Robinson had a sister younger named Ida. Because of her disappearance from genealogy records, I became overly obsessed that his missing sister was Ida Cummins. I assured myself everyone was named Ida back then.

THE SECRET LIFE OF IDA E. CUMMINS

Friends, this is where things got a bit more complicated, as if they were not already complicated enough. When perusing the Omaha City Directory of 1946, I decided to look up the name Ida E. Cummins rather than just look up the address. Just so you can steady yourself, under the address 4814 Cass I found the name "Ida E. Cummins (2)," signifying that two people resided there. All is well. But in looking up her name in cross-reference, I found an unexpected hint. I unearthed "Charles D. and Ida E. Cummins real estate h. 524 South 41 Street." This was once a very nice house, in the area that is now consumed by the ever-expanding University of Nebraska Medical Center campus. In my perplexed state, I at first imagined that this was Charles Robinson, Edward's brother, and they were simply cohabitating. Finding that Ida potentially had a real estate career that I hadn't caught wind of, coinciding with the previous owners of 4814's real estate connections was beyond my comprehension.

That, coupled with the article from December 1946, announcing that Ida E. Cummins had just celebrated her ninety-third birthday and was "very spry for her age," seemed preposterous, no matter how spry. Was I wrong in thinking that Ida E. Cummins was a fairly unusual name? I would stay up late on more than one occasion staring into the coal black ceiling about this conundrum.

Tracking Charles D. Cummins was easier than I thought, and thanks to volume 2 of Arthur Cooper Wakeley's *Omaha: The Gate City, and Douglas County, Nebraska*, I discovered Charles was indeed a well-established Omaha real estate man. Cummins was founder of the Omaha Realty Company and the C&C Bonded Collection Company. Is it happenstance that Charles had previously been a lumberman alongside his father at J. C. Cummins & Son? In addition to the abundance of Idas, this detective's trail seemed to be made up of characters employed in real estate and lumber. I enjoyed the serendipitous path. Ultimately, I could find no trace that Charles Cummins had been related to Wilson, Ida's husband, nor was Charles from Illinois, where the Cummins brood had lived. It would be much later that I established Charles D. Cummins had married one Ida Eliza Cummins in 1884, earning her full right to the name "Ida E. Cummins." This Ida E. would have five children. So, although my imagination took our ninety-four-year-old Ida Pratt Cummins on a moonlighting real estate venture, it was not to be.

THE 1950S CASS STREET FOLDER

In May 1948 the Omaha Register of Deeds Office revealed that Ida Cummins had made an addition to the 4814 deed into the name "Ida Cummins et al." This is commonly found on deeds to expand ownership to family members. Perhaps this was in preparation for her death. Ida Cummins, at that time, held the high honor of being one of Omaha's oldest persons. There was a grand celebration at 4814 Cass on the occasion of Ida's one hundredth birthday. Additionally, I targeted the reshaping of the large homes on the south side of Cass into amended apartments in the 1950s. This was a common trend, especially in the West Farnam–Gold Coast area, as large, single-family homes became difficult to afford and maintain. During this time it appeared that Ida Cummins sold her Lot 16, to the west of 4814 Cass, to Dorothy and R. Nile Booth. I estimated the Booths probably built the 1950s apartment buildings at 4816, 4820, and 4824 Cass, as all were constructed between 1951 and 1956. Toward the end of my investigation, I would find solid confirmation at the library that these 1950s apartments were indeed built by the Booths; the 4816 and 4820 Cass buildings were named Booth Court Apartments. As previously mentioned, the Peters home at 4822 Cass can still be found pinched between these newcomers, sharing Lot 13 with the apartment building at 4824. These were aptly named the Booth Corner Apartments.

DEATH OF MOTHER AND DAUGHTER

It was not long until I found Mrs. Cummins had died in June 3, 1955. She passed away in her 4814 Cass Street home at the impressive age of 101, Omaha's eldest resident. Other than her daughter, Isabelle Cummins Robinson, "there are no other survivors." She was to be buried in Streator, Illinois, with her husband.

Five years later, in July 1960, I came across the obituary of Isabelle Robinson. She died at the age of eighty-seven. I was touched to read: "No living relatives. Survived by Nurse Fay(e) Schlueter." Isabelle was to be buried in Streator, Illinois, with her parents. Her husband, Edward Robinson, was interned at Forest Lawn Cemetery here in Omaha.

THE NURSE

Ida and Isabelle in their later years were cared for by a very special nurse-caretaker, Mrs. Faye Schlueter. I could not be sure when exactly she began living in 4814 Cass and working for the family, but there is evidence that Ida E. Cummins's deed inclusion of "et al." was extended to Nurse Faye. If this account is not telling of a lovely woman, then I don't know what is. Nurse Faye made the news in March 1958 for a lasting female pen friendship with a woman she had never met, all established because of her delicious banana cake recipe. When Nurse Faye's son, Glen Schlueter, was sent overseas during World War II, she "spent sleepless nights worrying about him," as she did not know where he was stationed. While assigned to Nome, Alaska, Glen met Mrs. Carrie McLain and got to bragging about his mother's incredible banana cake. Mrs. McLain was slyly able to mail an uncensored civilian letter to Nurse Faye, asking for her highly regarded recipe, meanwhile consoling the worried sick mother about her boy. The recipe exchange led to a sixteen-year pen pal relationship. The two were photographed eating that fine banana cake at the 4814 Cass Street home.

I found evidence of Nurse Faye Schlueter living in the 4814 Cass Street Colonial from 1958 through 1961. So, while mother and daughter had passed on, the Omaha City Directory listed Mrs. Faye Schlueter as the occupant, even though her name was not on the deed.

THE CUMMINS-ROBINSON ESTATE

A pleading but beautifully written advertisement appeared on September 11, 1960. This was the first indication I had as to the interior of the home at 4814 Cass, and I was chomping at the proverbial bit. It read: "4814 Cass. Gracious old colonial must be sold to SETTLE ESTATE! 7-room plan with central hall, beautiful staircase. Large living room, fireplace, sunroom, dining room, kitchen down (stairs?); 3 bedrooms (2 are master-size). 2½ baths up. Cabinet GAS heat. Full basement. 2-car detached garage. A truly large plan and perfect. Colonial center hall style. Priced in the $17,000's. For showing call Bill Loring, 451–5683." I was keen to know more about the need to settle the estate.

THINGS GET HINKY

The advertisements would run until October 1960 and then disappeared. Quite literally, there was not a peep about 4814 Cass in the *World-Herald* archives from October 1960 until 1976. The dreamy girl sleuth in me hoped the home had been willed to Nurse Faye and that she had continued to live there. But if so, why had 4814 Cass been put up for sale to settle the estate? In retrospect my daydreaming about Nurse Faye had led my architectural detecting astray. The last city directory notes I had taken in my little black book were that of Mrs. Faye Schlueter in 1961.

Why had I stopped fervently digging with that year? I would pay for it later with subsequent late-night missions to the library.

The deed displayed First National Bank entered into the picture as grantor with an "Ext" written behind the bank name on November 1960. The grantee was shown to be "Fred A. Cuva and wife." The character of instrument was noted "Ext D." The sold portion was "w 22.9." Or was this really a sale? Honestly, sometimes the curlicues and loop-de-loops of the past Douglas County Register of Deeds workers escape me. Did this cursive stand for "extension of deed agreement" or "extended" or "exempt"? After probing for deed coding, I found a bit of proof this was some type of Extension of Deed of Trust or Mortgage by Owner of Indebtedness. I would ultimately accept that our Ida E. Cummins, perhaps, didn't fully own the house or had fallen into arrears. I wondered if the Cuva family bought and lived in the home or if it was a rental investment. Or was this just a sale of a portion of the western easement of 4814 Cass? On the same exact date, Fred A. Cuva and wife had an identical character of instrument entered in on Lot 16 (the previously owned empty lot to the west of 4814) but specifying the eastern portion. Were the Cuvas in business with the Booths and had decided to widen Lot 16? If I had a widow's walk atop our home, I surely would have paced about over this Cuva conundrum. Instead, I headed back to the library to inspect the unturned rocks.

THE FRED A. CUVA KEY

Very soon, my friends, we shall get into the definite material, the facts of my discovery. You know how I like to dawdle my hints about. But before . . . before I reveal these clues, allow me to show you what I found early on about young Fred Cuva.

Jump to November 1960: I was able to confirm Fred Cuva did purchase 4814 Cass Street from the First National Bank. He was by then married to Arlene G. Cuva. The couple had five children during their marriage, Mary Beth, Cathy, Nancy, Mark, and Fred, and maybe one of them in time will shed further light on their parents' real estate ventures. It would appear that Fred Cuva allowed Nurse Faye to stay on in

A Business Man...

44. A young Fred Cuva is shown shining shoes, as downtown youngsters
are a vital part of the family budget, handing over their nickels and dimes
to hard-pressed parents. The 1938 article revealed that Fred was "kept off
the streets" thanks to YMCA recreational classes. According to the 1940 U.S.
Census, Fred A. Cuva was fifteen years of age. He lived at home with his
parents, Joseph and Nettie Cuva, and siblings Louise, Sam, Carmelina, Joseph,
and Angelo. Reprinted with permission from the *Omaha World-Herald*.

the home, at least for a while. The Cuvas at that time were living at 3606
Lincoln Boulevard. This Bemis Park home was built in 1900, and at that
point I knew this family had exceptional taste. Do not hesitate to stroll
by this lovely house. By 1962 the Cuvas were occupying 4814 Cass, as
found in the Omaha City Directory. It brought a smile to imagine the
home filled with all of those kids. Mr. Cuva worked as a rate clerk with
the Union Pacific Railroad in those years, compiling data and charges
and preparing invoices for billing purposes. By 1966 Cuva would jump

ship for the Kellogg Company's Omaha plant as assistant to the traffic manager. The Kellogg Company had been in Omaha since the 1940s, and its current plant at 9601 F Street dates to 1965, when Fred Cuva was in its employ.

Notably, the Fred Cuva family took up residence at 4902 Cass in the year 1977. I penned this detail into my little notebook, for this house was right down the street from 4814. You must go have a peek at this glorious home the minute you put down this book. The house at 4902 Cass is on the same (north) side of Cass but a jaunt across Forty-Ninth. This fine brick home has a heavier Georgian influence to its Colonial style and is outlined by a low iron fence. I am particularly enamored with its proud stairs and voussoirs above the first-floor windows. Originally, this home would have been within view of the Peters house. A police report of a stolen ladder gave a hint that the Cuvas would call this corner parcel home into the 1990s. We detectives must take our clues where we can find them.

THE WRITING ON THE WALL: 1965

Let us revisit the death of Florence Hoagland, wife of William Wyman Hoagland. Now that I have unraveled enough of this secret silken skein, I have surmised this is the exact point at which the plot thickened. After Florence's passing, William B. Hoagland, son of Florence and William W., sold the three-story Victorian at 510 North Forty-Eighth to a company with intentions to demolish it. "The disappearing example of a Victorian," as it was called, was purchased by none other than the Allou Corporation. The then eighty-five-year-old house would be razed, although "plans for the site are indefinite," sidestepped Edward Shafton, secretary of Allou. Arrangements were being made with Joslyn Art Museum to remove parts of the historic interior. Someone better connected than I might know if this ever transpired or if portions of salvage are still within Joslyn's possession.

The 1965 entry into the 4814 Cass deed confused me. "William B. Hoagland TR Deed." I found that a deed of trust, or trust deed, is a legal transfer of property to a trustee, which holds it as security for a loan (debt) between a borrower and lender. I would come to believe this portion of the 4814 Cass land, held in William W. Hoagland's name, was transferred to his son, William B., including his family home, then was sold to the Allou Corporation. Weeks later my patience was rewarded when I found out more about the elusive Allou Corporation.

THE SHROUDED ALLOU CLUES

From the deed I could work out that in May 1974 the Allou Corporation sold the Hoagland portion of land to Alexander V. Sorensen. Yes, the former mayor Alexander V. Sorensen. From his *New York Times* obituary in 1982, Mayor Sorensen "was credited with restoring integrity to a city government racked by scandal in the mid-1960s and for helping initiate downtown redevelopment." I was curious to find out more about this Allou Corporation. From a 1971 Omaha Public Power District advertisement for its new (almost 72 percent built) nuclear power plant, I learned that A. V. Sorensen was secretary of the OPPD Board of Directors and president of the Allou Corporation. The only other mention of Allou Corporation was from a November 15, 1969, *Omaha World-Herald* article upon Sorensen's retirement as mayor. The Allou Corporation title was derived from a combination of Sorensen and his wife's names. The business apparently handled his investments and managed his real estate holdings, a solely owned corporation.

The deed's entry of May 1974 unveiled that Sorensen and his wife sold the "E ½" of the original Colonial Revival property to the City of Omaha. The Allou Corporation later sold the "E 27.1 portion" to the City of Omaha in July 1974. From the A. V. Sorensen Library and Community Center website, I read: "The former Mayor A.V. Sorensen agreed to donate an acre of land at 48th and Cass Streets for a multi-use facility, under the provision that it would be built within the next three years, or be transferred back to Sorensen." A city plan was drawn up to turn the Hoagland corner lot into the Dundee neighborhood library. The original 4814 Cass Colonial Revival home was scheduled to be torn down, absorbed in expansion plans of the proposed library. The library needed a parking lot, a familiar Omaha story.

45. Tom Werner, Mrs. Dennis Buckley, and Mr. Buckley at St. Cecilia's Green
Thumb booth at the Oktoberfest celebration of 1975. I found numerous tips
leading me to surmise that the Buckleys were members of the St. Cecilia
Cathedral parish. Reprinted with permission from the *Omaha World-Herald*.

THE DENNIS J. BUCKLEY DOSSIER

In May 1976 Fred Cuva and wife then sold the portion of the parcel with
the actual Colonial settled on it to Dennis J. Buckley and wife. (Sadly,
Arlene Cuva passed away just two years after this sale. Fred Cuva died in
2003.) By the summer of 1976 all of Omaha could read of the Buckleys'
honorable intentions in buying the home, when quoted in the paper:
"You shouldn't knock a good house down." The Buckleys laid out their
high-minded design to rescue the home at 4814 Cass and move it down

the street and around the corner to 403 North Happy Hollow Boulevard. The sainted Buckleys, I dare say. Where did these brilliant citizens come from, and why can't there be more folks like them?

From what I could trace, Dennis and Catherine A. Buckley lived at 4912 California when they hatched their remotion scheme. The house at 4912 California remains a classic Midtown Foursquare just a hop, a skip, and half a jump away. The couple had four children from what I could find. In 1964 the Van Horne Investments group employed Dennis. Buckley advanced to become the vice president–treasurer at Van Horne. John E. Van Horne Sr. and his father, Edwin N. Van Horne, went into business in 1959 as Van Horne Investments, establishing themselves in the historic Farm Credit Building at 206 South Nineteenth Street. As a sidenote, have you seen the renovation in this building? A hip new apartment concept being called the Bank Apartments. The Van Hornes could proudly trace their Nebraska banking and financial roots to the 1880s. Son John E. Van Horne would sell the family business in 1977. That might explain why in 1977 Mr. Buckley had taken a position as credit manager at the Union Pacific Railroad Credit Union. By 1980 he was listed as controller for Anderson Fire Equipment.

THE PLAN AND THE HISTORY

This amateur detective cannot be absolutely sure how the Buckleys made their decision as to where to situate the Colonial home, but Miss Cassette does conclude it was an impeccable solution. The address 403 North Happy Hollow Boulevard is assigned to city Lot 9 of Block 3, previous to 1976 an empty lot. But why was there an empty lot on this gorgeous, well-designed road to begin with?

From there I backtracked. The history books show Charles C. George of the George & Company buying up a considerable number of parcels to the east along Happy Hollow Boulevard in 1910. As you might remember, this fine boulevard was named for the Patrick estate, Happy Hollow. Charles C. George owned many properties in town and was a well-known real estate developer. He operated his profitable business down on 1601 Farnam Street. George obviously had a nose for real estate, and the beautiful lots along Happy Hollow Boulevard were right in line with his taste. That, and any realtor from 1910 could have seen that empty lots in Dundee were a sure bet.

Now this part of the exhuming went awry at times, I will confide. Again, my assumptions about the placement on the lot led me astray in directions now blush making. From what I have pieced together, the empty parcel where our Colonial is now located, Lot 9, originally included the home to the north. Built in 1939, 409 North Happy Hollow is a beautiful home. The deed gave proof that this assumption might be correct in revealing Lot 9 was split into at least two parts that year. Coincidentally, Lot 8 on Block 3 (one house to the north, at 411 North Happy Hollow Boulevard) also had a division of its lot in the year 1939. The house at 411 is also presumed, by the Deed's Office, to have been built in 1939. So Miss Cassette is putting forth that this whole endcap along Happy Hollow, between Cass and Chicago, sat as an open expanse for decades. These relatively young houses along the stretch might have been sold off as parts of the tracts directly to their east, at 5225 Cass Street and 5218 Chicago Street.

With notation of the two Colonials at 411 and 409 on Happy Hollow Boulevard having been constructed in 1939, I pored over the 1961 Omaha City Directory to verify what might have stood on the 403 lot. The only addresses on the block were Brownell Talbot Hall School at 400 North Happy Hollow, 409 belonging to a Mrs. Laura Braden, and 411, where the Eugene Miller family resided.

THE WILLIAM AND LAURA BRADEN MYSTERY

It was a cinch to find Mrs. Laura Braden's name attached to 409 North Happy Hollow Boulevard, but the clues became more difficult after that. I had discovered she was originally Miss Laura Walsh of Louisiana. Laura and William lived in Lake Charles, Louisiana, until Mr. Braden moved the family to Omaha, after attaining employment with the Woodmen of the World Insurance Company in 1934. The 1940 U.S. Census showed the Braden family also included children William C. Jr. and Mary Laura. William C. Jr. would go on to graduate from Vanderbilt

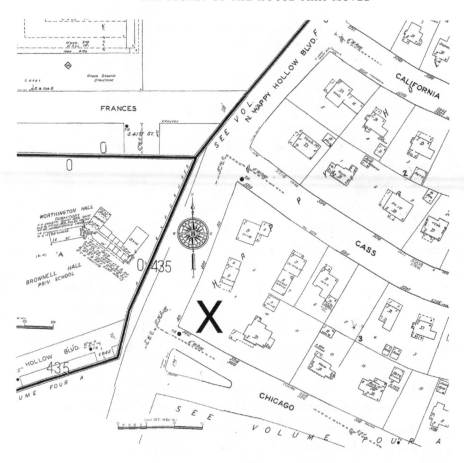

46. Sanborn map of North Happy Hollow Boulevard stretch, 1960.
X marks the empty lot where the 4814 Cass Street house would be
relocated. Courtesy of the Omaha City Planning Department.

University and study law at Yale University, before joining the navy. After
fifteen months' duty aboard a PC boat in the South Pacific in 1944, the
young navy lieutenant would return to Omaha to marry Dorothy Jane
Reed. A beautiful sorority girl, Dorothy Reed was featured in the "What
She Wore" section of the paper. Another society girl often highlighted in
the news, Miss Mary Laura Braden would graduate from Brownell Hall
and attend Northwestern University. If my publisher permits, you will
see a photo of the gorgeous brunette. Stunning. Later she would marry

47. The 5218 Chicago Street house, one door east of 403 North Happy
Hollow Boulevard. Green Spanish tile roof perfection and porte
cochere. Thunderous beauty never ceases! Photo by author.

Lt. Malcolm D. Young, an officer with the U.S. Army in 1943. Malcolm
Young would later become an Omaha attorney and a board member of
the Metropolitan Utilities District. The Youngs would have nine children. I had assumed that the Braden clan lived at 409 in all of those
years, until I found William C. Braden Sr.'s obituary from August 1954,
which made clear the Bradens, at least parents William and Laura, lived
at 5218 Chicago. This is a most glorious house, directly to the east of 403
North Happy Hollow Boulevard.

Over the years mother Laura would have either son William or son-in-
law Malcolm holding the deed for the smaller 409 house facing Happy
Hollow, a fanciful version of the mother-in-law cottage. The Braden
parents and adult children lived together on these three lots at the corner of Happy Hollow and Chicago from 1939 until 1971. By then there
were eight grandchildren inhabiting the homes as well. Daughter Mary

48. *Omaha Sun* (RIP) photo of house inching down Underwood Avenue, 1976.

Laura would clarify what I suspected in a news article from the 1980s: "For 27 years, we lived in a house purchased by my parents, William and Laura Braden, on Happy Hollow Boulevard near Chicago Street." Are we getting confused yet? Unless I am mistaken, 409 North Happy Hollow was then sold to another family. Since 1973, 409 has been continuously owned by one family and happily still is to this very day.

MOVING DAY

As the story goes, Buckley would hire Clyde Peterson of Ace Building Movers, after having driven him by the 4814 Cass house and the proposed site. Peterson said simply, "There would be no problems whatsoever." At the Register of Deeds' Office I found son William C. Braden Jr. and wife sold their empty corner lot to Dennis Buckley in April 1976. The new Sorensen Library and Community Center opened on August 2 of that year. A building permit from May 12, 1975, showed the 4808 Cass Street library (its new address) cost $750,00. The split-level facility offered a recreation center on the first floor and a library on the second. Miss Cassette and many local children would spend summer days here in Sorensen's early years, skipping into its modern environ without any knowledge of what had transpired. I have nothing but warm memories of this quiet branch.

According to a wonderful article by the now defunct *Sun* newspaper from September 2, 1976, the Colonial house was moved on August 18 and 19, 1976. The route appeared to include a passage down Underwood Avenue, the main street of old downtown Dundee. Can you imagine the spectacle? When describing the Ace Building Movers' expertise and technique years later, Clyde Peterson's son Merlin told a story of moving a full house that still had a glass on the kitchen table when they set the house down in its new location. Of interest the Buckleys had a new basement excavated and foundation laid for their Henninger Colonial, evoking Gretchen J.'s childhood summer memory of sliding down the fantastic dirt pile. For their part Mr. and Mrs. Homeowner shared that they do not fret over an old, stale, rainwater-scented, leaky basement like the rest of us hand-wringing old house lovers, no doubt due to their "brand-new" excavated basement from 1976. I say this is possibly the best of both worlds. On August 28 Dennis Buckley sold the remainder of the 4814 Cass lot to the City of Omaha, and it was later developed into a parking lot for the Sorensen Library. As of the September 2 *Sun* article, the Buckley family was still waiting for the house to be "placed" over the new basement and utilities to be hooked up before moving into their new home.

DIRECTORY OBSESSION

The library address at 4808 Cass entered the Omaha City Directory for the first time in 1977. The 510 North Forty-Eighth Street Hoagland address had officially fallen off the books. To this day 4814 Cass is listed as a separate parcel with the Register of Deeds, but as we know, it is a parking lot. The proud Colonial must have served the Buckleys well, for they lived on this beautiful corner until 2003, only then to sell their rescue home to an all-new family. I do believe the Buckleys deserve some sort of *My Omaha Obsession* Award, but perhaps this knotty tangle of an investigation will suffice for now.

In studying the city directory inhabitants dotting Happy Hollow in 1977, I came across a true delight of research wonderment. Along with buildings Brownell-Talbot School across the street at 400 North Happy

Hollow and Geoffrey Lieben at 409 North Happy Hollow, Miss Margaret Killian was listed as residing at 411 North Happy Hollow—Margaret Patricia Killian of the infamous Killian sisters and my favorite author of *Born Rich: A Historical Book of Omaha*. I was overjoyed to have tripped over her home. What a fantastic clue of Omaha happenstance, I thought. I began to obsess about tracking her movements and envisioning all of her possible homes—and here I had promised Mr. Cassette I was coming home soon, and after all, we did have plans at the movie theater. My land, but that tempting tree-lined Happy Hollow Boulevard was calling to me again. Much like my girl Nancy Drew, Mr. Cassette understood that mystery and I were never far apart.

CHAPTER 5

The Clue to Bircheknolle

My cluttered little 1940s office was always a good place to mull over new adventures. If only I smoked a detective's pipe, I sighed, then I would have clenched the bit in my mouth as I gracefully eased back into my popie's old Frieze club chair. Not a habit I ever picked up, although there was still plenty of Popie's decades-long cigarette smoke subsumed within the chair's scratchy, metallic design to intoxicate my many night wanderings. The inelegant truth was that the chalkware fish lamps flickered when I plunked down particularly hard, and strange shadows were cast on the ceiling from their wobbling, tiered, fiberglass shades. Bark cloth curtains shielded against the howling wind and fall rain lashing the windows, their bright tropical leaves a raffish reminder that Nebraska was seldom balmy. But I suppose it was all rather artistic and staged and it felt like quite another time altogether, which is exactly how I like things around here. I turned a small handwritten note over and over in my hand as Billie Holiday pleaded softly from a dark corner. It is in these moments that I can go into an Absolute Spell.

It all began when I was gathering mysterious photos for my website's new design. After stumbling across a haunted mansion of sorts in the Durham Museum collection, I began obsessing. I cannot be unequivocally precise in my perception of this particular hazy black-and-white photograph, but I reserve the right to make these bald-faced assumptions now and again, and I have been known to name inanimate objects. And make up stories. In studying the image, maybe Haunted by Spirits was not quite the right interpretation as much as Tormented with Memories. The actual photo description read: "Bircheknolle Sanitarium at 2211 St. Mary's Ave in the former Judge James Woolworth's mansion. Surrounded

49. Bircheknolle, 1910. From the KM3TV/Bostwick-Frohardt
Photograph Collection at the Durham Museum.

by many large trees." Aren't those words just a delicious fright? You surely
know me well enough by now to have guessed that I penciled the words
Bircheknolle Sanitarium into my small Pinkerton Pocket Pad.

I turned the ruffle-edged note over and over, allowing myself to wander
and dream about Bircheknolle, such a pretty-sounding place, and about
the meaning of the word *sanitarium*. Was Bircheknolle truly a sanatorium,
a sanitorium, or a sanitarium? I had already looked up the discerning
qualities and selfishly fancied Bircheknolle a mental asylum or a health
resort rather than the tuberculosis quarantine wing or a measly hospital.
But then again, wouldn't that be an interesting discovery in a troubled
mansion? I didn't know the history of Judge James Woolworth, but I was
quite familiar with the surname, as Woolworth Avenue had long ago
made my top ten favorite local street names. Happy Hollow Boulevard
was certainly first string in my book of names, but Woolworth Avenue,

with its silver spoon charm, ranked not far behind. Why had Woolworth's estate become a sanitarium? Here I must pause for a moment to record, if I might, the recollection of my mind thrumming along on that night as the wind shook these old house windows. My systematic library of Omaha history books was soon in teetering heaps on the floor by my own neurotic hand. Suddenly one of our fur friends appeared and just glared at my madness from the doorway, then turned, almost shaking his head, as he passed quietly down the hall. I longed to find every last peculiar detail of the Bircheknolle Sanitarium. Little did I know that Bircheknolle was but a sliver of the story.

JAMES MILLS WOOLWORTH

Our investigation really begins with James M. Woolworth. I paid a visit to the reference desk of the W. Dale Clark Library in downtown Omaha. Librarian-Detective Martha was able to cart out a whole slew of clippings and books to aid me in this venture. The early information I share about Woolworth is from those uncovered findings on that day. James Mills Woolworth was born in Onondaga Valley, New York, in 1829, very near Syracuse. Many years later Omaha would come to know Woolworth as its first city attorney, a judge, a politician, a wealthy venture capitalist, and a real estate mogul. He was considered a pioneer of early Omaha.

James married Helen Marie (sometimes spelled *Maria*) Beggs. She was born in Syracuse, New York, in 1829. The couple married in 1854, and James was admitted to the bar in New York the same year. He would begin a law practice in Syracuse. The Woolworth family can be traced back to England. Early in his law career, James Woolworth would leave his Presbyterian upbringing and convert to the Episcopalian faith, about sixty some years after the Episcopal Church had separated from the Church of England, after the American Revolution. His Episcopal faith and church involvement became a defining factor throughout Woolworth's life, the church in fact now headquartered in his birth state of New York.

Helen gave birth to Charles Peck Woolworth in 1855. The young family moved to Omaha in 1856, this purportedly just two years after the construction of the first house ever built in the city—we must assume they mean by a Caucasian settler. Incidentally, 1856 was the very year James's father, Dr. Samuel Buell Woolworth, became secretary and treasurer of the Board of Regents of the University of New York. I beg your forgiveness as I spin into my name obsessions. Sometimes Samuel's name was spelled *Buel*. The *History of the Buell Family in England* certainly made this discrepancy clear as mud by asserting there are apparently fifty different spelling conventions of *Buell* in place along the Celtic fringe of Europe since Roman times. Dr. Woolworth was first written about as principal of the Onondaga Academy, later principal of the Cortlandt Academy in Homer, New York. Put this Cortlandt name up your sleeve. In 1852 the senior Woolworth would relocate to Albany to become the principal of the state normal school. I gathered from these and other clues that the American Woolworths were an educated, prominent family.

A NEW TOWN

Although I cannot say definitively what brought the young Woolworths to Omaha, one could guess that the newly opened territory held great promise for a driven, educated man such as James Woolworth. Upon setting foot in Omaha, James became the very first attorney in the city. It would appear that Woolworth immediately began venturing into real estate and later became an early investor in the Union Stockyards Company in South Omaha, developed by 1883. I discovered through the *American Guide Series Omaha: A Guide to the City and Environs* that within his first year in town Woolworth penned a book, simply entitled *Nebraska in 1857*, which I have yet to lay my hands on. However, *Anecdotes of Omaha*, compiled by Mrs. Mary B. Newton in 1891, includes chapters from Woolworth's book. She identified him as an "attorney, and a counselor-at-law and general land agent." One humorous account, which Mrs. Newton named "Lesson 13," is Woolworth's minute detail-by-detail elucidation of how to get from New York to Omaha, Nebraska. (And some in the audience thought *I* was a bit wordy.) With certainty I presume Woolworth was not aiming for humor. It is a quite wonderful description. It would appear he published another book in that year: *Omaha City, the*

Capital of Nebraska: Its History, Growth Commercial, and Other Advantages and Future Prospects.

I am sure it is by no coincidence that Omaha was incorporated in 1857.

THE EXPANSION OF OMAHA

Important to early Omaha, by 1861 the Western Union Telegraph Company connected Omaha to the Pacific and Atlantic Coasts by suspending telegraph wires from one side of town to the other. The Civil War began that year, and in 1862 Abraham Lincoln chose Omaha as the eastern terminus for the Union Pacific Railroad, securing its position in the transcontinental system. The very same year the president made his Emancipation Proclamation speech, laying the early groundwork for freeing of the slaves in January 1863, although many African Americans would not experience this freedom. President Andrew Johnson in 1867 declared Nebraska admitted into the Union as an official state. Between 1860 and 1870 the population of Omaha reportedly quadrupled, becoming Nebraska's largest city. An act of the legislature declared Omaha to be a city of the first class in 1869. Nebraska doubled its population between 1880 and 1890, with Omaha expanding even further.

The Woolworth family lived in downtown Omaha, as most early Caucasian settlers did. In this well-organized, traditional city grid, families lived near their work, commerce was held within mere blocks, and all were positioned close to the banks of the Missouri River. As I have mentioned in other stories, prominent pioneer families were prophesied to have established their homes in the hills of Child's Point, immediately south of downtown Omaha. Instead, as working-class homes were built up just north and south of the downtown, because of their proximity to gainful employment, the wealthy families in turn constructed their homes west of the business district. Omaha had extended its bounds to Thirty-Sixth Street by 1870. *The Reconnaissance Survey of Selected Neighborhoods in Central Omaha*, prepared by Mead & Hunt, Inc., in 2003, established the boundaries of the well-to-do business leaders from this time "between Capitol Hill on the north and Jackson and Howard Streets in the south." From *American Guide Series Omaha: A Guide to the City and*

Environs, written and compiled by the Federal Writers' Project Works Progress Administration, I had previously gathered that Howard Street at Nineteenth was "one of the finest residential streets of Omaha" in the late 1800s. "Here lived such prominent citizens as George Hoagland, James Woolworth, Charles Turner and Herman Kountze."

JEANIE WOOLWORTH

Although not listed in many genealogy sites, daughter Jeanie (Jean, Jeanne, or Jennie in other places) was born in Omaha in 1859. Based on multiple sources, I assumed early on that Helen and James Woolworth had only two children, Charles and Jeanie. From the United States Births and Christenings records, I found Jeanie Woolworth was christened on May 16, 1859, at Trinity Cathedral Episcopal Church in Omaha. Omaha's first settlers founded the Episcopal church in 1856. During his time as bishop, Robert Harper Clarkson was credited with building Trinity Cathedral, a Late Gothic Revival structure. I was pleased to read that the Eighteenth and Capitol Street church was built in 1883, making Trinity Cathedral the oldest church building in Nebraska still in use, quite a feat considering the ever-swinging wrecking ball on older buildings in downtown Omaha. Very nearby, B'nai Israel Synagogue on Eighteenth and Chicago was not so lucky, having been demolished in the early 1950s to make way for the Omaha Civic Auditorium. In Omaha's absurdly sportive manner, the Civic was in turn razed in 2017; a large dirt pit now sits across from Trinity Cathedral. If that building could talk. The 1860 United States Census disclosed the Woolworths living in Omaha City's First Ward, Nebraska Territory: James M. Woolworth, age thirty; wife Helen M., twenty-nine; Charles P., five; and Jeanie Woolworth, one year of age.

A MYSTERIOUS YEAR

I found the couple had other children, but I wouldn't find these indicators until later. Daughter Sophia Woolworth was born in 1858, a year before Jeanie. Daughter Mary Buell Woolworth was born in 1860 (listed as 1863 elsewhere). Yet another daughter, Leonora Beggs Woolworth, was born on February 21, 1865; surprisingly, little Leonora died on May

3, 1867, at the age of two. Her headstone at Prospect Hill Cemetery reads, "Leonora Youngest Child of James M. and Helen Woolworth." Sadly, her mother, Helen Beggs Woolworth, died months later, in October 1867, and is also buried at Prospect Hill. Helen's headstone reads, "The First Wife of James M. Woolworth," and I had to wonder, at what point was that engraved? Surely the headstone was engraved much later, after remarriage, or would a fella like James assume when one wife died that of course he would remarry? Just things I ruminate on late at night. To make matters much worse, daughter Mary Buell Woolworth died in December 1867 at age four. Sophia Woolworth's death at age nine was similarly listed in December 1867. Notably, Sophia's tombstone reads, "Sophia Eldest Daughter of James M. and Helen Woolworth." Was there an accident in 1867? It certainly was suggestive of a disturbing turn of events. As hard as I dug, I could not find any articles about the girls or the death of their mother in the Omaha papers, this at a time when macabre details were commonplace in the press. In fact, the first Mrs. Woolworth was never even mentioned in any papers that I could unearth. Believe when I say, I nearly went mad searching. All of the Omaha history books I could track down chronicled that James had only two children with his first wife.

Obviously, life expectancy was shorter in those days (adults were doing well to see age thirty-nine), and the survival rate through childhood was slim. In any time period, no matter what the mortality rate, it would be difficult to fathom the pain of losing three young daughters and a wife within one year. I would find this sorrowful theme reflected in the music of the day. "Cradle's Empty, Baby's Gone" by Harry Kennedy gloomily described this frequent phenomenon in his painful lyrics. Coincidentally, his other big hit was "A Flower from Mother's Grave."

In trying to find out more about the curious deaths of these daughters, I did locate some clues to Woolworth's children's names. From volume 9 of the *Magazine of Western History*, I would learn that Mary Buell Woolworth was the name of James's paternal grandmother. James would name his third daughter after this grandmother. *The History of the Buell Family in England* revealed that Grandmother Mary was originally from East Hampton, Long Island. James's father, Dr. Samuel Buell Woolworth, was born in Bridgehampton, Long Island. Dr. Samuel would marry Sophia Mickles, James's mother, in 1825. Word on the street was that Sophia Mickles's family had emigrated from Scotland and that Sophia was a great beauty. James would name his first daughter after his beloved mother. To further complicate all matters of genealogy, James's oldest brother was also named Samuel Buell Woolworth, and his only sister was also named Sophia Mickles Woolworth. Dr. Samuel would later marry Betsey Brewster one year after the sudden death of his wife Sophia, just one year after the birth of their youngest child, James's brother, Charles Dorwin Woolworth. James's first child is named after this brother. With regard to Charles's middle name, Peck—there was an early Omaha pioneer, a real society man named Dr. J. P. Peck—could it be that son Charles Peck Woolworth was named after him?

According to the 1870 United States Federal Census, the Woolworth house number was 307 of a mystery street name I never did find. James Woolworth was then forty-two, his occupation given as "lawyer." Living in the home were Charley, age fourteen, and Jeanie, age eleven. Annie McBride was their twenty-year-old housekeeper, born in Austria. John McBride, Annie's husband, was twenty-five years old, from Scotland. He was listed as the house "laborer." The next year Woolworth would become a member of the legislature for one term and a member of the First Constitutional Convention.

NEW FAMILY

James's second wife was Elizabeth Stanton Butterfield Woolworth, born in 1836 in Homer, Cortland County, New York. The couple would marry in 1871. Her parents were Moses Bradford Butterfield and Mellona Dorcas Butterfield—don't you just love it? According to Michael J. Tan Creti's thorough book *The Great Crowd*, chock-full of amazing details of early Omaha, James Woolworth was a very devout, spiritual man. Likewise, his second wife, Elizabeth, was "dedicated to church work." Creti reported that wife Elizabeth came to Omaha "to serve as head mistress of Brownell Hall." As previously mentioned, Woolworth was a faithful member of the Trinity Cathedral Episcopal Church, and there he possibly befriended, but at the very least respected, Robert Harper Clarkson, a consecrated missionary Episcopal bishop of Nebraska. Bishop Clarkson's wife was named Meliora. The reason I am blathering on and on about the Clarksons will become clear. Elizabeth and James Woolworth would have two children, Meliora Clarkson Woolworth, born in 1873, and Robert Harper Clarkson Woolworth, born the following year. Now I may be overstepping and making connections that I do not have evidence for, but I suspect these two children were named after the bishop and his wife.

DEATH OF ROBERT HARPER
CLARKSON WOOLWORTH

James and Elizabeth's second child, Robert, died in March 1879. I am not exactly sure of the cause of death. "On Monday March 31, Robert Harper Clarkson Woolworth, beloved child of James M. and Elizabeth S. Woolworth, age 4 years, 6 months, 17 days." He is buried at Prospect Hill. From volume 1 of the *Illustrated History of Nebraska* by Julius Sterling Morton, I would receive confirmation of Woolworth's family, where he spelled out that "his three children survived"—further proof that I was on the correct path.

DOWNTOWN MOVES AND THE
HOWARD STREET CLUE

From 1878 through 1879 James Woolworth was immersed in Woolworth & Munger, attorneys at law, at 463 Twelfth Street with his partner, William H. Munger. The Woolworth family home was situated at 186 Howard Street. Was that directly right off of the river, or was this an early address that would change over time? The 1879–80 city directory revealed that James Mills Woolworth had ventured out on his own, his office at 310 South Thirteenth Street. The Woolworth home had migrated also, or the address had been changed, which is more common than I ever would have guessed when I started these investigations. The new home was at 1218 Howard Street. This is right in the heart of what is now the Old Market, at about Omaha Healing Arts Center (OM) and Imaginarium Antiques. A month later I would read of Rasmus Petersen, former president of the Gate City Malt Company of South Omaha, who, along with his wife, turned the "old Woolworth home at Twelfth and Howard" into a large, profitable boardinghouse. So, although I was not able to gather much more detail on the building, the early Woolworth home must have been of good size. The 1880 United States Federal Census told of the familial inhabitants:

James M. Woolworth, 50

Elisabeth Woolworth, 43

Jeanie Woolworth, 21

Meliora Woolworth, 7

Gustave Larsen, 26, servant from Denmark

Christine Ehrnholm, 27, from Sweden

Anna Anderson, 35, from Sweden

James Woolworth was called home to New York in July 1880, when notified of his father's grave illness. Dr. Samuel Buell Woolworth died in the home of his son Calvin C. Woolworth, in Brooklyn, New York. James and other family members were able to make the trip before Dr. Samuel's death.

VISIT TO THE DEEDS OFFICE

In trying to track the history of ownership, I paid a visit to the Douglas County Register of Deeds Office with my St. Mary's address in my notepad. Unfortunately, I would not be working in the handwritten ledgers that I love to pore over. I was told that this property was in "Lands"—in other words, the property was never platted and came from a section township and range legal description. Good grief, what did all of that mean? Section Township Range is a survey system for specifically delineating a property's boundaries. *Specifically*, I would come to find, was relative, like the phrase *more or less*. I learned many lessons on that day, and the Deeds Office staff was as helpful as could be, just short of doing my detective work for me. Truthfully, it was a self-imposed, harried mess but thoroughly worth it. Diane, manager of

the office, showed me our 2211 St. Mary's Avenue address was legally
described as follows:

> Beginning at the intersection of present South line of St. Mary's
> Avenue and West line of 22nd Street; thence South along West line of
> 22nd Street 170.8 feet more or less, to a point 130 feet North of Jones
> Street; thence West along a line 130 feet to North of and parallel to
> the North line of Jones Street 246 feet more or less, to a point on
> the East line of Hillcrest Addition in Section 22, Township 15 North,
> Range 13 East; thence North along East line of Hillcrest Addition
> 148.5 feet more or less, to present South line of St. Mary's Avenue;
> thence Northeasterly along present South line of St. Mary's Avenue
> 247.1 feet more or less, to the point of beginning.

Did you catch all of that? My goodness. All of the *thences* reminded me
that I, too, would like to start employing the word more liberally. Thence,
thence, thence.

With Section 22, Township 14, and Range 13 jotted down, I was able
to move to the Lands archives. Just as in my 2226 Howard Street story,
I found that Sarah A. Johnson, mother of Harrison Johnson, had bought
large swaths of land around the area of Twenty-Second to Twenty-Fourth
along St. Mary's Avenue from none other than the United States government. *American Guide Series Omaha: A Guide to the City and Environs*
called Harrison Johnson "an early settler." Purportedly, Johnson carved
the trail, later a country road to downtown. As the city grew, additions
were platted along the road, and it became a St. Mary's Avenue. According
to clues found later, the Johnson family paid forty dollars for this original tract of land at 2211 St. Mary's Avenue. If my tracking was correct,
Sarah A. Johnson then sold the Twenty-Second and St. Mary's Avenue
corner to C. Briggs and J. I. Redick in October 1869. John I. Redick, an
attorney, owned large quantities of land downtown. Jumping ahead, I
found Rose D. Coffman and husband then sold the property to James M.
Woolworth. Other clues would point to W. J. Connell selling the land to
James Woolworth in 1878. My 2226 Howard Street story made mention

of the Oscar F. Davis map, detailing the area. The name H. Johnson is found on the middle left-hand side very near the Howard Street property, along what would become St. Mary's Avenue.

THE AREA

Earlier I had consulted with H. Ben Brick's fantastic book *The Streets of Omaha: Their Origins and Changes* to find that St. Mary's Avenue was "so named because St. Mary's Convent was situated at the top of the hill." The convent was located just north of about Twenty-Fourth and St. Mary's Avenue, leading this subdivision to be named Convent Place. The Sisters of Mercy, comprised of seven young New England women who arrived in October 1864, would open the first Catholic convent in Nebraska. Some time ago I rented an apartment in a row of duplexes off of St. Mary's Avenue not far from the focus of our investigation, as I had always taken great interest in the area. I knew these streets like the back of my hand, though its colorful cast of characters had long ago left the garish stage for parts unknown. There are three things I continue to adore most about St. Mary's Avenue. The first is its limited edition quality. It has a short but solid run from about Sixteenth Street to Thirty-First Street. The businesses, homes, and people walking the street give me so much pleasure that to this day I sometimes have to pull the car over and investigate on foot. The cherry topping is its meandering stroll, unlike the strict grid observed in most of downtown Omaha.

The Reconnaissance Survey of Downtown and Columbus Park Omaha report of 2011 revealed more of St. Mary's Avenue. By 1889 horse-drawn streetcar service routes, courtesy of the Omaha Street Railway, had been carved out along Farnam, Leavenworth, and St. Mary's. By 1926 the electric lines of the streetcar system had arrived in full, after a consolidation by a number of motor railways into the large Omaha & Council Bluffs Company. St. Mary's Avenue was one of the major thoroughfares on this streetcar line. St. Mary's Avenue hill was very steep in the early years; passengers of the horse-drawn streetcars frequently had to get off and walk until the cars reached the summit. The hill was graded and cut down in the late 1880s. Other streets included in the grading project

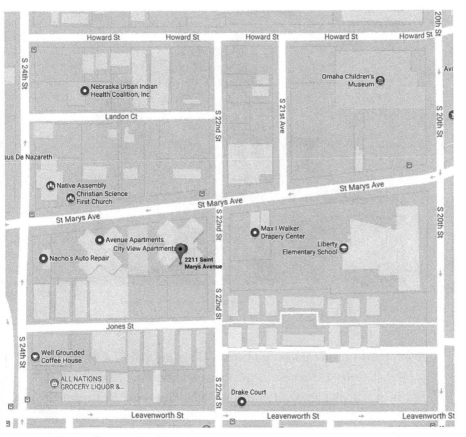

50. Google Map of Twenty-Second Street and St.
Mary's Avenue and surrounding areas, 2017.

were Dodge, Douglas, Farnam, and Harney. This huge undertaking, with emphasis on the higher-elevated west side of downtown, was thought to make the downtown core more accessible and improve travel, thus increasing Omaha's commercial potential. There would be another massive regrade and lowering of St. Mary's Avenue by 1921.

THE ARRIVAL OF THE WOOLWORTH ESTATE

The house at 2211 St. Mary's Avenue is located just south of what is now referred to as the Park East area. The large southwest corner lot sat facing east on what is now called Twenty-Second Street, originally South

51. Image of 2211 St. Mary's Avenue in 1880. *Omaha Daily Bee*, January 1, 1881, morning edition.

Avenue; its northernmost border ran along St. Mary's Avenue. This plat is between what is now the Hillcrest Addition and Cortlandt Place addition. A book published in 1888, *Omaha Illustrated*, christened the Woolworth Mansion "one of the most handsome residences in Omaha." The Woolworth home was erected in 1880, according to the *Omaha Daily Bee*, January 1, 1881, morning edition. I was pleased to find the home of our focus listed for the first time in the 1880–81 Omaha City Directory. James Woolworth's office was found at 310 South Thirteenth, but his residence was not yet given a formal postal address, instead reading "res: s w c St. Mary's Avenue and South Ave." This most likely meant "southwest corner," but I am sure you detectives figured that out. I was interested to find this simple description would continue for at least a few years.

On November 8, 1887, the *Omaha World-Herald* ran a long article entitled "Some Omaha Residences," an architectural detective's dream story, filled with just the kind of tantalizing house descriptions to keep one humming for days. Here it is in full:

"Courtland," the residence of James M. Woolworth, is named after the former home of Mr. and Mrs. Woolworth in New York. It embraces one and one third acres facing on St. Mary's Avenue and on South Avenue. A terracing of the level on which the house stands and a gentle slope to the street diversify the lawn, which is thickly grown with forest trees. The dwelling is built after an English domestic gothic design by the architect who planned Trinity Cathedral in this city and Stewart Memorial Cathedral at Garden City, Long Island. Verandas, twelve feet in width and 100 feet long, flank the house on three sides and from them a view of the valley beyond is obtainable for a distance of thirty miles in clear weather. The parlor, library, hall, and dining room, occupying the main portion of the first floor, are so arranged that they open together, and a person standing at almost any point can look into all of them. They thus constitute a delightful suite. The partition walls are broken with angles into a pleasing irregularity. In the dining room two handsome china cabinets are noteworthy objects and a number of paintings by distinguished artists are also among the treasures of the house. The south hall, which opens from the carriage porch, is so planned that guests coming or going can reach and leave the dressing rooms without passing through the main hall. The conservatory opens out of the parlor and the library to the south. The house stands fifteen feet above the street and well removed from the noise and dust of travel. It was completed in 1881 and comprises sixteen rooms.

THE ARCHITECT

The clue to the architect was a welcome find. I squealed to myself and soon burned a hot path after the name of the person who designed Trinity Cathedral, previously mentioned as the original church of the Woolworth family down on Eighteenth and Douglas. This beautiful little church was attributed to noted English architect Henry G. Harrison. I discovered Trinity Cathedral was added to the National Register of Historic Places in 1974, which might answer my previous pondering of how it had missed the Omaha wrecking ball, although that does not always do the trick. Henry G. Harrison (1813–95) became known in America for his Gothic Revival designs in New York from 1853 to 1891. He is featured in *Long Island Country Houses and Their Architects: 1860–1940*. A number of his works from this time period are listed on the U.S. National Register of Historic Places. It is likely that the Woolworth family knew of Harrison's work from their contacts back east, perhaps establishing the connection for the design of Trinity.

ARCHITECTURAL STYLE

Considered a showplace in its day, 2211 St. Mary's Avenue was the first home in Omaha to have electricity. Power to the house was first supplied by a private generator, according to E. A. Baird, president of the Conservative Saving and Loan Association. Later the mansion obtained its power from the street railway system. The Victorian home featured a number of gables with a steeply pitched roof, all of a rectangular nature. Looking at the photos acquired in my search, the emphasis was clearly on decoration. Mystery house, I say! The colorful bands of multicolored slate tiles of varying shapes were patterned much like a candy house in a storybook. And all of those chimneys with their clever, multiple chimney pots. The Victorian chimney pots of terra-cotta, or baked clay, were thought to improve the chimney's draft by extending the length of the chimney. The multiple pots placed atop a chimney indicated there was more than one fireplace on different floors sharing the chimney. The divine woodwork evident in the multitude of ornate dormer trusses and elaborations, the intricate stickwork of the porte cochere, overhanging eaves, exposed rafter ends and emphasis on wooden wall cladding, the glorious wraparound porch, all led me to believe that the "Gothic Revival" house that contemporaries of Woolworth had hinted at was actually a Stick style house. In her fine book *A Field Guide to American Houses*, Virginia Savage McAlester wrote that the Stick style was a transitional architectural link "between the preceding Gothic Revival with the subsequent Queen Anne" styles. She concluded that all three styles were adaptations of Medieval English building traditions. According to *The Visual Dictio-*

nary of American Domestic Architecture by Rachel Carley, the Stick style was thought to have taken influence from Late Medieval rustic country architecture, an example being the gingerbread-ornamental chalets of the Alps. This Stick style branch of the Victorian architectural family rose to popularity in America from 1860 to 1890. Of note, it was not called the Stick style during the era in which it was built. Somehow this comforted me regarding my research and the incongruence in 1880 reporting.

The home was encircled in a stone fence with impressive iron gate work. I could see from early fire insurance maps, or Sanborn maps, shared by the City Planning Department that Woolworth also had a very large carriage house–livery stable built to the west of the house. Most likely two floors, this carriage house appeared to have the footprint of at least half the size of the main house. Impressive. Large oak trees, numerous fruit trees, and spirea shrubs were evident in the 1910 photo, but back in the early days of the Woolworth estate, the grounds were said to be densely wooded. Could the family hear the trees from those long dormer windows or the plodding of horses up St. Mary's? Clematis and honeysuckle vines climbed and cooled the expansive, wraparound porch. I liked to imagine that hummingbirds came for frequent visits as the family sat out on their summer porch. The Victorian era brought in the idea of the American porch as an extension of the home, a place to relax or entertain. Did the women fan themselves as they rocked in a chair or luxuriated in a delicate weaved wicker? This picture, a perpetual delight. I would have liked to wander 'round the garden and meet a man like Mr. Cassette watering the flowers.

SOCIETY PEOPLE AND CULTURAL HINTS

The *Illustrated History of Nebraska Volume One* by Julius Sterling Morton of Nebraska City fame is a real adventure. The book revealed the friendship of Morton and Woolworth, although you wouldn't know it by his cryptic words summarizing the Honorable Woolworth: "His large practice and engrossing cares never debarred him from the enjoyment of cultured society." A Woolworth party was not one to miss. Mrs. Woolworth frequently gave afternoon teas at her home. The Victorian era ladies'

52. 2211 St. Mary's Avenue, 1910. From the KM3TV/Bostwick-
Frohardt Photograph Collection at the Durham Museum.

tea was a must, with the "afternoon pause," a fashionable social event.
Upper-class and society women would change into long gowns, gloves,
and glorious hats for their afternoon tea, served at home in the drawing
room between four and five o'clock. One can just imagine the modern
drawing room newly crowded with the large-bustle and blooming, wider-
shouldered tea sippers. There would be dances and holiday celebrations.

Early December 1881showcased one such an event in the local news:
"'Woolworth Party among the most charming of hosts.' Mr. and Mrs.
J. M. Woolworth entertained a large number of guests at a reception
given in their residence 'Cortlandt Place.'" As the story goes, there was
dancing, a live band, and much merriment into the wee hours. Music
of the time was largely focused on two social causes: temperance and
woman suffrage. Neither sounded much like party music to my ears.
Aside from such warm themes as early death of children and Ameri-

can disasters, the likes of big California earthquakes and Chicago fires, most likely the Woolworth parties were filled with classical music. A big hit from 1880 was "Lardy Dah," featuring a man of good cheer living in high style.

But what was this about Cortlandt Place? Miss Cassette does love it when wealthy families name their estates. It is all so dreamy. I began digging. There was a Cortlandt, New York. There was a Cortlandt Place addition, a development here in Omaha. I tiptoed across the selling of many plats at Cortlandt Place in the 1800s. And of course there was a Palmer Cortlandt character from the *All My Children* soap opera of my youth. I began to think about James Woolworth and Cortlandt, New York. It seems appropriate that you might pull that clue out from your sleeve now.

THE CORTLANDT CONNECTION

I delved into this possible connection. The journalist had suggested that the Woolworths named their estate after their home in New York. Of course I obsessed. There is a town of Cortlandt in northern Westchester County, New York. Nestled between Peekskill, Croton-on-Hudson, Crugers, and Montrose is the hamlet of Cortlandt Manor. Largely a residential area, Cortlandt Estates is also within these bounds. Both Cortlandt Manor and Estates were designated such after Dutchman Stephanus Van Cortlandt. Van Cortlandt was known as a colonial aristocrat who possessed almost all of northern Westchester County in the late seventeenth century, after being granted this tract by Royal Charter of King William III. To this day the Van Cortlandt Upper Manor House can be found in Cortlandt, originally part of a rolling 86,000-acre estate from the Hudson River on the west, the Province of New York, and the Colony of Connecticut on the east. The Manor of Cortlandt also included additional holdings, thought to have been acquired from the American Indians native to the area. During its salad days Cortlandt Manor operated as a fully self-sustaining community (able to retain an apple orchard, dairy farm, bee house, kiln, tavern, and carpenter and blacksmith shops) while the Van Cortlandt family inhabited the estate. Key to the investigation was the clue that Van Cortlandt Manor was thought "an essential stop on the route from New York to Albany." Dr. Woolworth was also principal of Cortlandt Academy, soundly connecting the family to this historic environ.

SIDENOTE: THE WOOLWORTH FIVE
AND DIME CONNECTION

If you are a Prying Pamela like Miss Cassette, you might have wondered if the James Woolworth family had a connection to the Woolworth Department Store fame. The F. W. Woolworth Five and Ten Cent Stores began in New York with Frank Woolworth. I could find no direct relation, which doesn't necessarily mean a thing. There were many English Woolworths living in New York, and one could assume they were all related in one way or another. Perhaps we detectives will hear from a long lost Woolworth family member from New England with the direct link. Agreeably, the Woolworths' store clan also had a branch of Pecks in their family, perhaps giving credence to the familial link of Charles Peck Woolworth. I couldn't be sure.

CAREER MOVES

From 1881 to 1882 the Omaha City Directory showed James M. Woolworth's attorney at law office located at 310 South Thirteenth Street. Son Charles and daughter Jeanie lived in the home. Woolworth was then attorney for the CB&Q Railroad. Gathered from clippings held at the reference desk of the library, James was on the Board of Directors of the Nebraska National Bank in 1884. The Nebraska State Census of 1885 showed that Jeanie had left the home, as had her brother, Charles. I assumed they had perhaps married. According to the census taker's notes, James was fifty-four, Elizabeth was forty-eight, and Meliora was twelve. Cline Graham, servant, was thirty-two, and Etta Frederick, servant, was twenty-four. Woolworth's attorney practice was located at "24 and 25 Paxton Building" by 1887. His home was registered as "Cortland Place" that year, a spin on *Cortlandt*, a word, I was soon to find, that lent itself to variant (mis)spellings.

CORTLANDT PLACE CONFUSION

Along with casual misspellings of *Cortlandt*, Woolworth's home, there was also a city neighborhood addition just north of the Woolworth estate that I believe James must have owned and developed. The first mention I found of Cortlandt Place addition was in 1887. From what I could uncover, the lots began selling in the *Omaha Daily-World* on February 8, 1887. In a July advertisement from the same year, a seven-room cottage was described at Cortlandt Place, "east of Twenty-Fourth Street, near St. Mary's Avenue." The historic Howard Street Apartment District and the fantastic buildings therein all land within Cortlandt Place; however, the old building permit copies I hold in my hand all say "Courtland Place." Spellings do get muddled around here, as you well know.

HIGH-STYLE DETAILS

Listen! There was a silence on the steep hill of Twenty-Second Street and St. Mary's Avenue. I would dream of lying in a second-story bedroom at the Woolworth Mansion, a thin layer of lace pulled over the tall window view, a heavier, rich material secured with cord and tassels and puddled on the floor. There I would listen for the sounds of the tree leaves, the horses sighing and snorting in their stalls from the carriage house, a rustling of the honeysuckle vines wrapped tightly around the porch, faint voices on the street below. If I held my breath and attended to every commotion, would I be able to hear the sounds of downtown Omaha, the horses' hooves trotting, a train, and a large riverboat?

Behind the reference desk of the W. Dale Clark Library was hidden the best little book of all time. A high-society social register of sorts: the *Excelsior Address Book and Family Directory of Omaha, Season of 1888–89.* The font was magnificent and clean. In its pages I was shown a listing for Woolworth, James M. "Cortlandt," 2211 St. Mary's Avenue. Also listed was Miss Meliora C. Woolworth, whom I would learn later was James's daughter. The 1888 book *Magazine of Western History Illustrated*, vol. 9: *November 1888–April 1889*, published in New York, coincidentally enough at 32 Cortlandt Street, recorded that "in his elegant residence on St.

53. Cortlandt Place viewed from southeastern angle. Omaha public librarian (and detective) Martha Grenzeback discovered the Woolworth Mansion in the pages of *Art Work of Omaha*, an incredible book by W. H. Parish Publishing Company, Chicago, published in 1896.

Mary's Avenue he has long exercised and still indulges a refined hospitality, which is alike alluring to the transient guest and to those who enjoy the privilege of his constant companionship. He enjoys early history of Nebraska. In the hall of his residence is a large mantel made of brick, stone and wood taken from public buildings, all long since extant, which were built before or shortly after the territory was organized." But by the 1890s an economic slowdown hindered nationwide architectural development, and Omaha was no different. Prosperity would return to Omaha, and new development was found once again in the Gold Coast–Joslyn Castle area starting around 1900, as the upper class moved ever westward.

PROFESSIONAL LIFE

Woolworth had been elected as chief justice of the state supreme court in 1873. He later became president of the American Bar Association, in

1896. He was the first Omahan chosen for the national organization. Later, in 1899, a second Omahan was chosen as president: C. Manderson. I began to think I would soon learn the origin of every Omaha street name. It was fascinating. Through the Alfred Rasmus Sorenson book *History of Omaha from the Pioneer Days to the Present Time*, I was astounded to learn that Charles F. Manderson was not only an Omaha attorney but also president of the Omaha Savings Bank and a state senator, proving once again that I simply wasn't doing enough with my free time. Mr. Woolworth was also one of the busiest men I have ever researched. He was closely identified with the growth and progress of Omaha and an early advocate for the public school system. A large investor in business property and real estate, *Omaha Illustrated* noted that Woolworth was an original trustee of the South Omaha Land Syndicate and was director of the South Omaha Land Company, in addition to being director of the First National Bank and chancellor of the Episcopal diocese of Nebraska. Atop all of those accomplishments, Woolworth was said to be a "large-hearted, high minded, Christian gentleman of deep learning and profound knowledge of the law."

THE LARSEN MYSTERY

I found an odd announcement, which later began to consume me. The September 10, 1897, morning edition of the *World-Herald* notified: "Larsen, Andy, aged 6 years, 11 months and 6 days, infant son of Mr. and Mrs. Anton Larsen, September 9, 1897. Funeral Friday afternoon at 3 o'clock from the premises of J. M. Wolworth [sic], 2211 St. Mary's Avenue. Interment at Mount Hope cemetery. Funeral private." I could find no familial connection of the Larsens to the Woolworths. I wondered if Mr. and Mrs. Anton Larsen had perhaps been servants of the Woolworth family. That would explain why their son was buried at Mount Hope and not Prospect Hill. I began to churn about who Andy Larsen was. I found a United States Census from 1920. Anton P. Larsen, age fifty-four, lived in Omaha Ward 2, Douglas County, and was head of the household. His birth year was estimated at 1866. His birthplace was Denmark, and he emigrated in the year 1887. His German-born wife, Margaret, was also fifty-four. Their daughter, Palma Larsen, lived in the home at age twenty-five. The Larsens had a roomer living with them, Iowan Fred Shaw, who was twenty-nine. If their son, Andy, had lived, he would have been twenty-nine years old at the counting of the 1920 Census. But I could not be sure of this relation, adding it to the mounting pile of clues in hopes that it would all make sense later.

DEATH IN THE FAMILY

Without much of a whisper, it would come to light that Mrs. Elizabeth Butterfield Woolworth died in 1897. I could find no details of her passing, and it was slowly whipping me to a frenzy. One thing I did know for certain: after losing two wives, James Woolworth would not remarry.

An 1898 article about a visit from Miss Jeanie, by then called Mrs. Guy C. Howard, gave premonition of changes to come. "Mrs. Guy C. Howard of Burlington, Vermont, who with her father Judge Woolworth of Cortlandt, Mr. Charles Woolworth of Chicago, a brother of Judge Woolworth had a fine gathering in the home." Calvin C. Woolworth, James's other brother, lived most of his life in New York. As one can see, *Cortlandt* stood up quite properly on its own in Omaha, almost mentioned as its own town. Confusing as it was, the Woolworth estate was also called Cortlandt Place off and on by the In Society page writer.

Both the 1899 Omaha City Directory and the 1900 United States Federal Census displayed some changes. James M. Woolworth was then head of his firm Woolworth, McHugh & Carroll, attorneys at law, located in a suite of offices: 410 to 414 First National Bank Building. His residence remained at 2211 St. Mary's Avenue. By 1900 Woolworth was seventy-one, and I finally received clarification that he was indeed widowed. I never did find out how Elizabeth died. Meliora Woolworth lived at home at age twenty-seven and was listed as single. Jeanie Howard was forty-one and surprisingly widowed also. Presumably, her children Helen Howard, sixteen, and Otis W. Howard, thirteen, also resided in the home. The household domestics were Bessie Grauson, twenty-six years, from Sweden; Hilda Carlson, twenty-eight, from Sweden; and Kate Kruss, twenty-seven-year-old servant from Ireland.

In 1908 Oliver Otis Howard published *Autobiography of Oliver Otis Howard, Major General, United States Army*. I later unraveled that General Howard had commanded Fort Omaha and was the man for whom Howard Street is named. He wrote: "On February 14, 1884, my son Guy married Jeanie, daughter of Hon. James M. Woolworth, of Omaha. They have had two children, Helen and Otis Woolworth Howard." Helen must have been named after Jeanie's beloved mother, and Otis, I assumed, was named for Guy's father. I uncovered the 1884 Nebraska marriage license showing Guy Howard was then twenty-four and "Jeannie [sic] Woolworth" was twenty-three. I discovered another interesting book from 1908, *The Prominent Families of the United States of America*. In it Arthur Meredyth Burke reported Guy Howard, lieutenant colonel, U.S. Army, was killed in action in the Philippine Islands on October 22, 1899. The Howards had been a military family. Sadly, I then understood why Jeanie and her children had relocated to her father's home. Jeanie did not remarry that I could find and was called the "widow of Guy Howard" the rest of her life. I imagined the Woolworths living together again in that large home and hoped they comforted one another, as Mrs. Woolworth had died just two years earlier.

CHARLES PECK WOOLWORTH CLUES

The *Omaha Daily News* from February 1, 1904, revealed an obituary for the son of James M. Woolworth, Charles Peck Woolworth, who died at age forty-seven in Altuna, California. (I also found a spelling for Altunia, California.) This was James's only son. He was buried in Prospect Hill. Interestingly, the *Omaha World-Herald* reported Charles died in San Rafael, California, and was forty-eight at the time of his death.

I tracked Charles Peck Woolworth's name to a 1902 fraternal organization booklet, *Sixth Decennial Catalogue*. He was a fraternal brother, having graduated from Hamilton College, like his father, with the class of 1877. His occupation in 1902 was listed as "insurance and steamship agent." He lived at 326 King Street in Santa Cruz, California, and he kept an office at 4 Cooper Street. Interestingly, the catalog made mention of Charles's "one year in college; admitted to the bar but never practiced." He would become the proprietor of the Loup Stock Ranch in Fullerton, Nebraska, in 1886. He later moved to Japan and went into the mercantile business from 1888 to 1890. After relocating to Castleton, New York, it is unclear what venture if any Charles was a part of from 1890 through 1897. He became an insurance and steamship agent in Santa Cruz in 1897 and remained in that job up till the writing of the catalog's publishing date in 1902.

THE MELIORA CLARKSON
WOOLWORTH FAIRFIELD HOME

Daughter Meliora Clarkson Woolworth was famously the first Queen of Quivera at the original Ak-Sar-Ben Coronation Ball, paired with King E. M. Bartlett. E. M. Bartlett was a well-known attorney in town, at Bartlett, Baldrige & DeBord. Beginning in 1895, the Coronation Ball Committee aimed to recognize individuals in the region for their civic endeavors. Every year a King and Queen were crowned in the magical Kingdom of Quivera, the pomp and mirrors growing more and more elaborate as the decades rolled by. I suppose all of that sounds very odd to someone not from Omaha or even if from these parts.

Through persistence (or was it fixation?) I finally found the marriage license announcement for Edward M. Fairfield and Meliora Clarkson Woolworth from December 4, 1900. (I would find his name spelled Edward and Edmund throughout my search. I would come to believe it was truly Edmund.) Edmund Minor Fairfield was general manager of the Omaha Water Company and son of Edmund B. Fairfield, a prominent Congregational minister and chancellor of the Nebraska State University, according to volume 2 of Julius Sterling Morton's tome *Illustrated History of Nebraska: A History of Nebraska*. Regarding Julius Sterling Morton, he was considered a friend of Woolworth, having moved to the Nebraska Territory in the fall 1854. The Mortons famously settled in Nebraska City, their original 160 acres now a tourist location. Morton would become the editor of the local newspaper and later largely served in politics. His son, Joy Sterling Morton was also a lifelong friend of the Woolworths.

But where was I? Meliora Woolworth Fairfield. I found an indication that by 1902 Meliora was looking for a "good plain cook" for the new

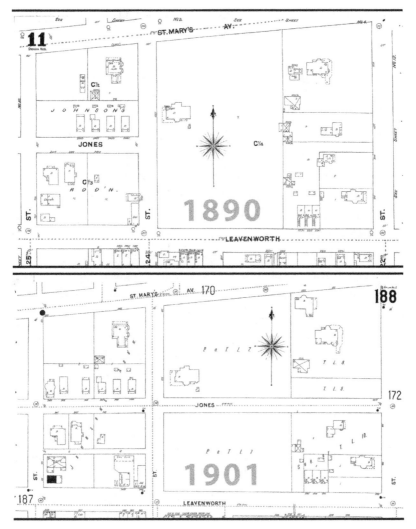

54. Sanborn maps of 2211 and 2219 St. Mary's Avenue, 1890 and
1901. Courtesy of the Omaha City Planning Department.

couple. This was my first clue to 2219 St. Mary's Avenue. James Woolworth would have the huge Tudor style home built for his daughter and
son-in-law on the western most part of his grounds. Their front door
opened onto the St. Mary's Avenue side. Thanks to Trina Westman of the
Omaha City Planning Department having shared the city's early maps, I

could see that 2219 St. Mary's Avenue had been added to the large plat of land by 1901.

THE ARCHITECT'S MYSTERY

James Woolworth's wedding gift to his daughter, Meliora, was a fantastic, fairytale-like Tudor of large proportion, featuring rare full timbering, except for the lower (basement?) level on the north side. I could find no proof that Henry Harrison had designed the home or an indication of any other architect for that matter. I thought I might go daffy trying to unravel this clue. Did soon-to-be neighbor Thomas Rogers Kimball, also an architect, have a hand in all this magic? The glorious home at 2219 St. Mary's Avenue appeared to be a true eclectic mix of Queen Anne and Tudor styles of architecture. The steeper-than-steep pitched, irregular roof; the asymmetrical facade, different on all four sides; the rounded tower on the north elevation; the conical roof; its copper finial ornament; and that unique window protruding from said roof looked so very Disney-like. The Fairfield home appeared to have four full floors, with what appears to be a basement level visible from the St. Mary's side. The multiple, one-story-high full porches would be screened-in decades later. Extraordinary, dominant chimneys complete with varying chimney pots, along with the other remarkable features, had me guessing this wedding gift was a decorative timbered Queen Anne. It is a rare Queen Anne house that features (of those still extant) half-timbering in their gables and upper-story walls. Atypical, the Fairfield home featured full first-story timbering, a distinguishing characteristic for a Tudor or a timbered Queen Anne, giving the impression of a striking, wide-striped suit. The groupings of lines of windows, heavy porch supports, and the solid brackets almost with a whimsical, curved gnomelike quality, were astounding. In one image that I obtained, I can spy tiny, irregular third-story storybook windows with shutters. My review of early American Tudor homes revealed that initial designs offered upper stories and gables that overhung the lower stories. These often featured a stronger, heavier timber skeleton than successors. The Tudor typically was a loose, imprecise nod to English architecture, based on Late Medieval and Early Renaissance styles. I came to believe that this home was a very well-designed, eclectic work of a strong, experienced architect. The curious, inventive nature of the positioning on the grounds held my attention as well. It is said that this home opened out onto St. Mary's Avenue, the north side, but I can see from other photos that it actually had another, more stately front door that faced east. There was an entry point on the north side of the stone fence for those guests arriving on the St. Mary's border. The Fairfields most likely shared the carriage house with the Woolworth house and possibly entered through yet another formal wraparound porch on the south. The Fairfield grounds were adorned with a beautiful, impressive mixture of walnut, silver maple, and cottonwood trees. I can say I have never seen another like it.

A PARTY FOR JEANIE'S DAUGHTER

The November 1, 1903, article from In Society of the *Omaha World-Herald* described in flattering detail a special coming-out party for Miss Helen Howard, Jeanie's daughter. I include it in full here, as it gives an exquisite view into the Woolworth family and their friends:

The largest and one of the most beautiful social functions of the season was the afternoon tea given by Mrs. Guy Howard Thursday afternoon from four to six at Cortland, the home of her father, to formally introduce her daughter. The prominence of the families and the perfection of the appointments made the event a notable one in many respects. In two, it departed from the usual coming out reception of a debutante. Miss Howard who stood with her mother instead of wearing a customary white was gowned in pink voile and carried pink chrysanthemums. Mrs. Howard wore black liberty satin inset with guipure lace. The presence of men was also an innovation.

The spacious rooms of the Woolworth home were probably never more beautifully decorated and the fact that the flowers were the gifts of friends made them all the more beautiful. The prevailing colors in the dining room were green and white, a mound of white

carnations and green ferns forming the centerpiece while candles
with jeweled green shades shed a soft light. Throughout the room
candlelight was used, the only exception being in the dining room
where an electric light had been dropped into a fern globe. Mrs.
Chase had charge of the dining room. Assisting her were Mesdames
Bourke, Ringwalt, Charles K. Kountze, Offutt, E. P. Peck, Hitchcock,
McClernand and Connell.

The punch bowl in the library was in the charge of Misses Coff-
man, Jane Orcutt, Woolworth, Hitchcock and Susan Holdrege.
Awaiting throughout the rooms were Mrs. Fairfield and Misses
Mary Hamilton, Gretchen and Marie Crounse, Kilpatrick, Peck,
Mary Holdrege, Jean Merton of Chicago, Butterfield and Mrs. Vic-
tor Caldwell. Over 600 cards were issued.

This matter of six hundred cards being "issued" was recorded for a very
important reason, and anyone reading the article in 1903 would have
understood. A society woman's calling card was acknowledged as a payment of social debt, a carryover from the English nobility. A calling card
had numerous social purposes and was accepted under strict etiquette
guidelines, such as notices of arrival or departure or as a means of intro-
duction, and should follow specific expectations in terms of size (2.75
to 3.5 inches wide by 2 to 2.75 inches high for a woman), simplicity or
elegance of design (engraved), manner of delivery (by a servant while
the bearer waited in a carriage), and appropriate, timely response (a
return card in a few days, inviting an in-person visit, if the receiver was
interested). In the case of an aspiring socialite, such as Miss Helen Howard, these six hundred simple but significant cards no doubt expressed
congratulations from friends, family members, and potential admirers.

THE DEATH OF JAMES WOOLWORTH

As I moved through the years of the Omaha City Directory on my W.
Dale Clark Library venture, I found the 1906 listing much like those of
the previous years. The house at 2211 St. Mary's Avenue was registered
to James Woolworth. I backtracked under the Howard name and found

"Jeanie Howard (widow Guy)" at 2211 St. Mary's Avenue additionally. I found it strange that they did not mention her under the street address record or Woolworth name, as was customary.

On June 18, 1906, the Omaha papers announced the death of James Mills Woolworth. The *Omaha World-Herald* spoke of the "simple, solemn and dignified service" at Trinity Cathedral, which was apparently overflowing with those who came to pay their respects "to the most eminent Nebraska pioneer and lawyer." Atop his black casket was a "great cross of red rambler roses, picked from the vines at the Woolworth home." The entire body of clergy of the Episcopal churches of Omaha was present as well as a large delegation from the Douglas County Bar Association and members of the Omaha Water Company, of which Judge Woolworth was vice president. Only the members of the family and very close friends followed the body to Prospect Hill, where the burial was "strictly private." The saddest line I was to read also shared a tremendous clue: "At the grave the brief Episcopal service was read. Anton Larson, who had been in the employ of Judge Woolworth for a quarter of a century, performed the service of lowering the casket into the grave, the same service he had performed for Mrs. Woolworth years ago." Although the surname was spelled differently than the previous 1897 announcement of the death of young Andy Larsen, I finally understood the alliance between Mr. Larson and Judge Woolworth. A trusted domestic servant even in death.

PUZZLING OCCUPANT

Just two short months after the death of Judge Woolworth, I read of a young man who took up the lease of our mansion on the hill. The morning edition of the *World-Herald* of August 21, 1906, publicized a short article about John N. Baldwin having regained his health after a mystery ailment and a good rest at his parent's estate up in Watertown, New York. Baldwin had been a general solicitor of the Union Pacific Railroad. Revitalized, he returned to Omaha and promptly leased the Woolworth home at Twenty-Second and St. Mary's Avenue. This was my first indication that Jeanie Woolworth Howard and her children had moved out of the large home. But the article made plain Baldwin was leasing and did not buy the

55. Lawyer and judge James M. Woolworth sits on a bench
in front of a porch. From the KM3TV/Bostwick-Frohardt
Photograph Collection at the Durham Museum.

estate, leaving me to believe that one or both of the Woolworth daughters had maintained family ownership. As it turned out, both homes were willed to Meliora at the time of Judge Woolworth's death. The Fairfields continued to live at the property, next door at 2219 St. Mary's Avenue. I would find evidence through the *National Improvement Bulletin* of 1908 that "Mrs. Jeanne [sic] Woolworth Howard" obtained a "building permit and will have the warehouse at 12th and Howard Streets remodeled and made modern." Jeanie, like her father, would become a real estate owner.

A FASCINATING RABBIT HOLE

Joy Sterling Morton, son of Julius Sterling Morton from Nebraska City, shared a fascinating story with the newsmen involving the Woolworths, and I found myself frozen at the library. The story follows the tracing of the death mask of Napoleon, one of five made in 1821, upon Bonaparte's death, by French doctor François Antomarchi. Two of the masks were at the Louvre, one in a British museum, and one owned by Lawrence Hutton. Antomarchi kept one mask for himself, which he transported, apparently, on various travels. Odd and wonderful. While exploring in Mexico, Antomarchi fell and died, having left his box of treasures at a friend's home. The mask was gifted to Guy Howard in 1892, who as we know died as a colonel in the Philippines in 1894. Jeanie Woolworth Howard would later bring the Napoleon death mask to her father's home on St. Mary's, where, so it seems, James Woolworth enjoyed quite a varied art and historical relic collection. Jeanie would then escort the death mask on her move to Connecticut years later. I am not entirely sure how Joy Morton came to own the mask, but his family friendship with Jeanie Woolworth Howard most likely endured their various relocations across the country. Morton would move to Illinois and go on to found Morton Salt. He is rumored to have presented the missing fifth death mask of Napoleon to the Chicago Historical Society in 1924.

THE MARY ROGERS KIMBALL ESTATE

The Mary Rogers Kimball house is one of Miss Cassette's Infatuation Homes, located at 2236 St. Mary's Avenue. This glorious abode was designed by renowned Omaha architect Thomas Rogers Kimball for his mother and sister. I had not known until the research of this story that the sister's name was Arabel M. Kimball, or "Miss Kimball," until her death in 1949. This mansion was rumored to have been built in 1905 and was crowned an official Omaha City Landmark and is listed with the National Register of Historic Places. One gander at its tile-covered entry gate stairs along St. Mary's will leave you breathless. (Kimball also built my favorite downtown Omaha Public Library branch, at 1823 Harney Street.)

In my research at the Deeds Office, I found out that 2236 St. Mary's in the "Convent Place" addition, Lot 17, was sold by Rt. Rev. Richard Scannell to Mary Porter Rogers Kimball in June 1908. Thomas Lord Kimball, her husband, had apparently died in 1899. So the Kimball home couldn't have been built by 1905, unless by some odd deed arrangement. After further digging, I unearthed that the Convent Place addition was most likely named for the site of St. Mary's Convent and Academy, originally the plat of 2236 St. Mary's Avenue. Rt. Rev. James M. O'Gorman purchased the land in 1863 for the Sisters of Mercy academy. When the seven New England nuns arrived, they were asked to climb one hundred steps to reach the new, three-story brick building, barely finished. Carpenter's tools and wood shavings were said to have still been scattered across the floors upon their auspicious arrival. By 1870 the Sisters had founded the St. James Orphanage. Mysteriously, within sixteen years the convent property was sold, and the buildings were razed. I have long wanted to investigate the St. James Orphanage of Benson, a childhood obsession. Was this the same institution? My sleuthing heels clicked at this mystery potential.

THE THOMAS ROGERS KIMBALL ESTATE

I did find evidence pointing to Thomas Rogers Kimball's home having been constructed in 1905. My first indication was the announcement of a worker having been killed on Kimball's construction site due to a building accident, complete with a darkened foreboding of the casualties to expect in the buildup and potentially deadly expansion of our city. This grand estate was farther west than his mother's home, across Twenty-Fourth Street, on the north side at 2450 St. Mary's Avenue, and was thought to have been completed in 1907 for forty thousand dollars. The estate was on a large lot; it has since been divided and now carries the addresses of 2448 and 2450 St. Mary's Avenue.

Rumored in its days to have been encircled in an iron fence, the castle-like mansion had twenty rooms or more. A proper wine cellar, a large cooking room with a fireplace big enough for a whole steer, a complete library, and the third-floor recreation room descriptions had Miss Cassette wanting to jump ship into this new cloaked mystery adventure. "Four Gothic pillars stood ahead of the front door. It is said they were covered with nineteen coats of hand-rubbed white enamel." The stately home, boasting three floors and seven fireplaces, was razed after Kimball's death, as declared by the Town Tattler in December 1940.

Digging further, I found that Safeway Grocers had bought the property, desiring an anchor along the fast-growing commercial district of St. Mary's Avenue. Safeway made noble attempts to sell and have the mansion removed from the site; Red Cross showed interest, but ultimately no local movers could pull off the large endeavor. Woe is me, there were no other takers, and Safeway Grocers replaced the flattened parklike environ of Kimball's original corner lot. Air Conditioning Utilities, Inc., a local contractor, now calls this address home, and my detective's trail revealed some semblance of air-conditioning business has been at this location since the 1950s. The site to the east of Thomas Kimball's, at 2412 St. Mary's Avenue, had been farmland and later another large residence. I am not absolutely sure of what local grocery store originally constructed the later building, but I found solid leads that it was a Hinky Dinky Store in the 1940s. The original Hinky Dinky grocery building now houses CASA for Douglas County—Court Appointed Special Advocate programs for children—maintaining the same address at 2412 St. Mary's Avenue.

By 1909 I could find no Woolworths listed in the Omaha City Directory. Only the Woolworth Company, the notions store, was found registered at 114–18 South Sixteenth Street, peculiarly just blocks from James Woolworth's original downtown home.

THE BIRCHEKNOLLE INN CLUES

A curious article heralding the most significant of seasonal society parties made first mention of "Birch Knolle." Miss Cassette loves to read about the formal parties from this era. The evening edition of the December 30, 1909, *World-Herald* declared, "Mr. Theron C. Bennett entertained at dinner at Birch Knolle Tuesday evening for Mr. T. C. White of Denver, Colorado." I counted no less than twelve covers laid for the Messrs.—no Misses or Mesdames.

In the Omaha City Directory of 1910, I found the name Birch Knoll Inn under the 2211 St. Mary's Avenue address. What had become of Cortlandt? From a lead I gathered later about the proprietor's name, I was able to delve back in that year and find the "Mrs. Georgia B. Chadd Hotel" residence and business listed as 2211 St. Mary's. Georgia must have been an industrious young woman. According to genealogy sites, Chadd was originally from Kansas. In 1910, at age thirty-two, Georgia was single and operating an apartment hotel out of the Woolworth home. Regardless, the city directory had labeled her a "Mrs." This sent me back to the city directories of 1908 and 1909, where I discovered Georgia B. Chadd was running the Shelton Hotel in those days. Her residence was listed at 101 South Twenty-Fifth Street. Was her home the Shelton Hotel? Through my many investigations I have learned that running a boardinghouse was a respected business venture for single and older women alike—an early means of income for women. The Census of 1910 displayed twelve boarders (I am not sure if they were travelers or long-term renters) and four servants helping Chadd run the large Bircheknolle Inn property. But all I longed to know was, did Georgia B. Chadd name the Woolworth Mansion Bircheknolle and why? Chadd would head the Bircheknolle Inn until 1912.

A SIDENOTE FOR THE PRICKLY
PATTIES IN THE AUDIENCE

If you are a stickler for details like Miss Cassette, you are most likely already annoyed by the variant spellings of B-I-R-C-H-K-N-O-L-L you have found herein. Friends, this is what I have uncovered. A 1910 photo of 2211

St. Mary's reveals a small, hand-painted sign on the stone fencing of the property that reads BIRCHEKNOLLE. If the historic sign painter is to be trusted and not taking liberties as sign painters sometimes do, this was the first intentional spelling of the enterprise. As we have already seen, the *World-Herald* originally spelled the home *Birch Knolle*. Later medical advertisements would spell it *Birch Knoll*. When these changes or misspellings occurred across countless clues, I copied it exactly as I found it.

THE APARTMENT HOTEL CONCEPT

Capt. and Mrs. W. T. Wilder made the news in the late summer of 1910 for having "taken apartments at Birch Knoll Inn for the winter." I pondered exactly how many apartments they needed. I would find other names listed moving in and out of the gorgeous home. Although I knew the Blackstone and Colonial Hotels to be apartment hotels, I would have some investigating to do. The American apartment hotel became an option following the Civil War but didn't appear to rise to popularity among members of the upper class until the late 1890s and early 1900s. It should be noted that there appeared to be apartment hotels at all differing price levels. The flexibility that the apartment hotel offered, sans fixed contracts and agreements, satisfied the migratory nature of modern city dwellers. Accommodations could be secured for a few day, months, or years. Individual guestrooms or rental family wings could be requested under the direction of a resident manager, often living in the home also. The apartments were fully outfitted with furniture, towels, linens, and such. Another advantage was the inexpensively shared services such as heat, lighting, and hot water, considered posh amenities in those days. The common dining room, home-cooked meals, as well as a full staff of domestics would be shared by different families, a distinct contrast from apartment house living.

NEIGHBORS

The United States Census of 1910 showed the Fairfields living at 2219 St. Mary's Avenue: Edmund M. Fairfield was then forty-six and gave the hint that he had been born in Michigan. Meliora W. Fairfield was thirty-five.

The couple had two children: Elizabeth Fairfield, eight (no doubt named after Meliora's mother), and their youngest, Mary W. Fairfield, seven. A prominent newcomer to the block soon entered the picture. First Church of Christ Scientist at 2324 St. Mary's Avenue, on the northeast corner of Twenty-Fourth and St. Mary's Avenue, was erected in 1911. The church was first organized in 1893.

THE REIGN OF ST. MARY'S AVENUE

A jaunt west on St. Mary's Avenue these days does not give much indication of its golden past. There were hints tucked away all along. I had always wondered about the glorious Mary Rogers Kimball home (2236 St. Mary's Avenue) and the solid beauty of the First Church of Christ Scientist (Twenty-Fourth and St. Mary's) plopped right in the middle of this dense, colorful route. Everyone within earshot knows I am obsessed with the Howard Street Apartment District to the north, the Drake Court Apartments, the Drake Court Walk, and the covert Jones Street annex apartments to the south have given me many nights' delight tiptoeing about. But who knew it was once the center of Omaha's Social Whirl? From old city maps and DOGIS aerial photos, I could make out proof that the wandering St. Mary's Avenue was once lined with the spacious properties I was soon to read about. The well-known, large brick Hellman Mansion was once across the street and down the way from the Thomas Rogers Kimball's estate. On the southeast side of Twenty-Fourth, the W. J. Connell home was established. Connell was once the city attorney. The Woolworth home would come to be known as the center of a great many of Omaha's leading social events. The In Society section of the *World-Herald* entertained the common folks as well as the comfortable set with tantalizing descriptions of high society parties on and around St. Mary's Avenue. Across the street to the north of the Woolworth's was once a great stone mansion built by Frank Murphy, an Omaha banker, street railway president, gas company executive, and philanthropist. During James Woolworth's days on St. Mary's, a Mrs. Margaret Cuming lived in the Murphy residence. This massive home is long gone, like most on this street, although the address remains. The structure at 2204 St. Mary's Avenue is now a flat, midcentury, nondescript building, having been morphed from one venture to another over the years. The one-floor building was constructed in 1953 and currently is registered under 2202 and 2204 St. Mary's—most recently operating as Woody's Classic Barbering Services and Midwest Hair Replacement Center. It has looked quietly abandoned for as long as I can remember, making it all the more intriguing to Miss Cassette! I will tell you, this property has the last of the authentic 1950s billboard signs sitting on a slight incline to the west. If you can, pull over and inspect the lights on these signs and the backside construction. A rarity these days.

The homes on St. Mary's Avenue were admired as they set back from the street with beautifully manicured, sloping lawns, gorgeous wrought iron fence work, and elaborately designed paths and gardens. Mrs. Margaret Cuming had charmingly lived alone in her large estate directly to the north of the Woolworth Mansion, at 2204 St. Mary's Avenue. Widow of Thomas B. Cuming, past governor of the territory who later filled the position of secretary of state from 1854 to 1858, Margaret Cuming was the Social Leader of Omaha in her day. Mrs. Cuming was referred to as "elderly" in 1901 and, without reservation, one of the True Omaha Old Guard. Of course, who could have questioned her at that point? In a fantastic news article she educated that Omaha society truly began in 1857, when the beau monde began holding little gatherings and balls, although "we were isolated from the rest of the world," and because steamers were not delivering the "latest patterns promptly to us," the Omaha fashions were behind the times. This could be said of Omaha up until the 2000s, and some of our coastal friends might still say it. As a sidenote, I understand that Mr. and Mrs. Julius Sterling Morton of Nebraska City were so charming and immersed in the Omaha set that "no one ever thought of giving a ball without inviting them," and likewise, it would appear no gathering was complete without one Mrs. Margaret Cuming.

MUSIKVEREIN SOCIETY

A most curious article popped up along the trail for the call of subscriptions to the Musikverein Society to purchase the Woolworth mansion in May 1912. This musical society was made up of Omahans of German descent, both for the love of singing and the appreciation of music. "G. E. Shukert opened the subscription for the Musikverein to buy the Woolworth home at Twenty-Second and St. Mary's Avenue and build a music concert hall for $1,000." In my digging I soon discovered the well-known Wiener Musikverein concert hall is located in Vienna, Austria, having been erected in 1890. Considered one of the finest concert halls in the world, this Musikverein was surely known to the German American society of singers. An article from 1911 hinted that previous German musical societies had been made up of three separate groups, the Mannerchor, Concordia, and Orpheus. The singers would steel themselves as allies and become Saengerest. This name was short-lived, however, and after a bit of quarreling, the singers thought better of the Musikverein title. There was even a Ladies Musikverein. By the way the glorious Musikverein of Austria was an architectural influence on designers of the Holland Performing Arts Center on Douglas Street.

But getting back to the Musikverein plot to buy the Woolworth Mansion. A number of big German names in town were busy raising funds for this new concert hall, with dreams of seating fifteen hundred for their full-capacity concerts. Who knew? The news article led one to believe that the singers were taking possession the very next month. But that was not to happen. A pitiful little article from June 1912 reported that the music club had not raised enough funds, even with the option on the building having been extended. They were five thousand dollars short.

THE HOSPITAL

When I eagerly inspected the 1913 Omaha City Directory, I found the Bircheknolle name omitted. Instead, I found a Gertrude R. Smith logged at the address. The closest neighbors displayed in the city directory that year were:

2204 Mrs. M. C. Cuming
2211 Gertrude R. Smith
2219 E. M. Fairfield
2236 Mrs. M. R. Kimball

An intoxicating advertisement from April 1913 shared the news of the fresh Birch Knoll Sanitarium: "Those suffering from a nervous breakdown caused by the recent storm will find a quiet and restful place at the Birche Knolle Sanitorium. Gertrude R. Smith, Graduate Nurse, Superintendent. 2211 St. Mary's Ave. Tel. D. 6808." So now we knew that the Gertrude R. Smith character was a nurse, I penciled into my notes. For the record, the storm that this advertisement most likely referred to was the March 23, 1913, Easter tornado that devastated our fair Omaha. The 200 miles per hour winds left 103 people dead and 350 injured and eight million dollars in damage, equivalent to about two hundred million dollars today. I cannot imagine the destruction and how this affected early Omaha, but this ad made Birche Knolle almost sound like a spa resort. (I should say that Birche Knolle became Birch Knoll after that advertisement.)

What a divine home in which to recover, I mused. I dreamed of looking out onto the rolling tree-filled grounds and the gorgeous woodwork flaunted inside the home interior. I again imagined that large wraparound porch covered in vines, this time filled with society women recovering their nerves. Of course, I could easily imagine finding comfort there, but maybe in my case more of a rousing. If I were to be a patient there, I would be digging through closets, running up and down the maids' stairs, looking for hidden passageways, and pulling up Turkish rugs to inspect inlaid wood designs. I might even whisper out in the hallways for lone ghosts. I surely would hide behind lace curtains when called for dinner, unless there was a fine chocolate dessert. Glory be, I might never be well enough to leave, I'd make sure of that! From what I gleaned about the clientele of the sanatorium, I was not the only person obsessed with being a patient at the rambling estate.

MISS GERTRUDE REID SMITH

The young Miss Gertrude Smith was a very busy bee as director of the Birch Knoll Sanitarium. Miss Smith had received her schooling at the Presbyterian Hospital in New York City, later a base hospital. From what I could find, Meliora Woolworth Fairfield was leasing her father's home to Miss Smith. Once directing Birch Knoll, she also headed up the Nurses'

Official Registry in Omaha. It was her opinion that Cupid had stolen 8 more nurses from the medical ranks after recent marriages, leaving the registry down to 108 nurses in 1913. Miss Smith also facilitated the Nurses' Central club—its meetings, alumnae, and state events—out of 2211 St. Mary's Avenue until 1915. I cannot be sure if Birch Knoll functioned in this manner, but the custom of these types of national clubs was that nurses would rent rooms to live in, eating meals together and supporting other young nurses in a safe environment, hence the focus on those marrying out of the field. Miss Smith had a whole staff of nurses, aides, and servants, including a Swedish cook, Miss Anna Charlotte Frederickson, newly made American citizen.

THE SANATORIUM VERSUS SANITARIUM

The Birch Knoll spelling of *sanatorium-sanitarium* would also prove to be complicated. I found *sanitarium* spelled differently in many listings. As with Birch Knoll, I worked to just copy the documents as I discovered them. It would appear that once it moved into the hospital business, *Birch Knoll* was the new simplified spelling. Here is what I learned. The term *sanatorium* refers to Edward Livingstone Trudeau's therapeutic movement out of the Adirondacks, intended to cure tuberculosis. Trudeau prescribed a rigorous regime of healthy eating and outdoor living that led to his own recovery of tuberculosis. The essential tenets of sanatorium healing required residents to spend daylight hours outside riding horseback, walking, or reclining on the broad porches on "Cure Cottages." Patients were prescribed several large meals a day, including at least three glasses of milk, and maintained a strict code of personal behavior that prohibited drinking, smoking, and cursing and enforced a dress code. By the way, Trudeau ultimately died from tuberculosis in 1916. *Sanatorium* also referred to a hospital used for a long-term illness.

A sanitarium, on the other hand, was considered an early health resort similar to that used for injured soldiers. I envisioned it as a spa with emphasis on physical rehabilitation. As the story goes, John Harvey Kellogg, director of the famous Battle Creek Sanitarium in Battle Creek, Michigan, claimed, "A change of two letters transformed 'sanatorium' to 'sanitarium,' and a new word was added to the English language." These resort getaways became destination places for the well-to-do and members of the middle class across America—those looking to relax, "calm the nerves," boost depressive states, and leave the stresses of their own personal lives. Most major cities offered these services in a homelike or palatial setting. Kellogg's sanitarium, like others in the county, focused on avant-garde treatments of the day such as electrotherapy, hydrotherapy, a specialized diet plan, phototherapy, exercise, thermotherapy, and cold-air cure. Hydrotherapy involved the cold water cure, being fully submerged in a bath, as well as healing hot water. Enemas, douches, sitz baths, cold mitten frictions, salt glows, towel rubs, wet sheet rubs, wet and dry packings, compresses, in combination with "electro-hydric baths," were thought to be relaxing treatments. Solar and electric light used during winter was seen to aid in depression as well as sun and open-air exposure for health and stimulation of the skin. Gymnastics, swimming, vibrotherapy, and calisthenics encouraged movement.

When I began to learn that Birch Knoll was given over "chiefly to the care of cases of nervous disorders, and is patronized by a wealthy class of patients," this amateur detective began to formulate what that might have looked like. I surmised Birch Knoll was more in fitting with a sanitarium the likes of Battle Creek rather than a tuberculosis wing. Of course, mental health was Birch Knoll's primary emphasis, but I assumed it might take on other medical issues or acute emergencies as well. I would savor my imaginings of the full and strange list of avant-garde therapies likely offered at Birch Knoll from my popie's club chair. I envisioned in Birch Knoll a sense of sanctuary for many.

MRS. MARGARET CUMING'S ESTATE

Neighbor lady Mrs. Margaret Cuming had planned large charitable gifts at the time of her death. February 1915 announced that St. John's Church on the Creighton campus would be doubled in size, the fulfilling the original design with Mrs. Cuming's forty thousand–dollar gift. St. Cecilia's Cathedral would get twenty-five hundred dollars from her estate, funding needed for the estimated sixty thousand–dollar new roof. St. James

Orphanage, my childhood obsession while growing up in Benson, was to receive another twenty-five hundred dollars. But what really intrigued me was the rescript of the "Old Cuming Residence to be Private Hospital" in March 1915. Miss Ellen Stewart, superintendent of Clarkson Hospital, was to take charge of the mansion–turned–maternity hospital. The Cumings' fine residence was being converted in what the newsmen asserted was a growing trend in the teens.

"Negotiations are on foot to turn another of Omaha's fine residences into a hospital," announced the *Omaha World-Herald*. "This is the former home of the late Mrs. Margaret Cuming at 22nd and St. Mary's Avenue. Miss Ellen Stewart, superintendent of the Clarkson Hosp is the promoter of the scheme, her idea being to open a first class maternity hospital. A number of prominent surgeons including Dr. C. W. Pollard, Dr. Palmer Findley and Dr. Elonzo Mack, will have their patients there. The old Woolworth residence near the Cuming Place is leased by Miss Gertrude Smith for a hospital for nervous diseases, called Birch Knoll Sanitarium. The old Poppleton home in the north part of the city was the Roselle Sanitarium and the old Turner home on Farnam is now being remodeled for a hospital." For a time the Stewart Maternity Ward and the Birch Knoll Sanitarium would operate across from one another.

DEATHS AND CLUES TO BIRCH KNOLL

As the word spread among Omaha's society people about their curative, healing experiences at Birch Knoll, all within a private, luxury mansion "from Omaha's former days," complete with carefully tended and natural grounds, there would be a waiting list to recuperate in such high style. Miss Gertrude Smith, director of the sanitarium, wisely kept a limited sixteen beds available. The well heeled took a liking to this restricted experience, no doubt creating a demand for the "peace and quietude and special care most likely to help troubles of a nervous nature." Imagine my surprise, what with all this inner circle hullabaloo, to discover that one such society woman of Logan, Iowa, hanged herself at the Birch Knoll Sanitarium. In January 1916 Mrs. Margaret Williams had been suffering with melancholia when her husband, Dr. David Williams, a prominent physician from Logan, checked her into the Birch Knoll. Head nurse, Marcia Prasser, found her. Apparently, Gertrude Reid Smith was out of town, and the staff respectfully declined to comment on Mrs. Williams's death. Poor Mrs. Williams left behind her husband and two teenage children. The news spread through the country as "Woman Hung Herself at Birch Knoll" made headlines. A few weeks earlier Mrs. W. O. Dimmock had also died at Birch Knoll, a vague quotation left to explain "her ill health extended over several years."

Another death in March 1916 indicated that Birch Knoll had expanded its medical care offerings. Mrs. Frances W. Sair, wife of Charles Sair, died at Birch Knoll Sanitarium, following a caesarian operation. She was but twenty-six years old. The newborn, a baby boy, was sent home with his father to Wahoo, Nebraska. As it turned out, Meliora Woolworth Fairfield and family had moved from 2219 St. Mary's Avenue, and their home was turned into a maternity ward, often called the Birch Knoll Maternity Cottage. Hardly a cottage! Gertrude Smith carried on as head of the sanitarium, and Eva Rennick, RN, was head nurse of the Maternity Cottage. "A good many maternity cases are taken at Birch Knoll, especially from Omaha's finest families. The hospital building was once one of the finest mansions in Omaha," according to the *Omaha World-Herald*.

BIRCH KNOLL IN THE PRESS

The two mansions-turned-hospitals would gain favorable attention not just with the wealthy class, when in May 1916, they were featured in an article entitled "Omaha Known for Its First Class Hospital Equipment." Volume 35 of the *Medical Herald*, from 1916, also had this to say: "The Birch Knoll Sanitarium, with 16 beds and valued at $25,000. Besides this score of institutions (in Omaha) are many private sanitariums for the treatment of certain diseases. This condition in a city so noted for its healthfulness as Omaha is due to a combination of causes." One of the causes was the abundance of highly trained medical staff. In 1917 volume 75 of the *American Journal of Obstetrics and Diseases of Women and Children* featured a case history of a twenty-four-year-old woman admitted to "Birch-Knoll Maternity of Omaha." Very interesting reading, indeed.

The 1917 Omaha City Directory was the last time I would find the Birch Knoll name. The familiar street addresses had transitioned:

2204 Stewart Maternity Hospital

2211 Birch Knoll Sanitarium

2219 Birch Knoll Maternity

2236 Mrs. M. R. Kimball

CITY HOMES FOR GIRLS

According to the clippings secured behind the reference desk of the W. Dale Clark Library, the Woolworth and Fairfield Mansions were officially sold in 1918. It was something of a jolt. A more descript article from the *Omaha World-Herald* in early January 1918 shed a murky light. The Omaha Association for the Betterment of Boys and Girls planned to erect a new Girls' Club on the southeast corner of the Woolworth home site. Surprisingly, John McDonald, architect, was drawing plans immediately. A name I knew well. "The promoters hope to have construction on the new $150,000 building start as soon as frost is out of the ground. The place will accommodate 200 girls." The next day the executive committee for the Protection of Boys and Girls met at the home of Mrs. George A. Joslyn. Joslyn Castle, to you and I. The fact that plans had been submitted by John McDonald for the building suddenly made perfect sense, as I knew from an earlier investigation that the Josylns were substantial patrons and friends to the McDonalds. The article made a point to say Birch Knoll Sanitarium would not be used in connection with the home and that the hospital would continue to operate at its location. Dr. Jennie Callfas, president of the organization, asserted that she already had fifteen applications for girls' rooms. Curiously, their focus would be on transient young women and had plans to hang signs "in the stations" directing the girls who came to the city as strangers.

Four months later, in a turn of events, the association had decided to immediately commence reconstruction of the Fairfield and Woolworth homes for a temporary Girls' Home with accommodations for fifty occupants: "An arcade will connect the two buildings." Dr. Jennie Calfass had

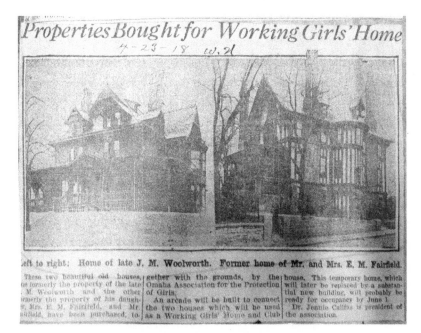

56. *Omaha World-Herald* article, including photos from the W. Dale
Clark Library reference desk clippings file, April 21, 1918.

recently purchased James Woolworth's tract and stated that the original
plans to build the new McDonald home were abandoned due to scarcity
of material and labor. Later I would find proof that Meliora Woolworth
Fairfield officially sold the 2211 and 2219 properties at this time. I would
learn much later where the Fairfields relocated. Dr. Calfass gave details
of the renovation, including converting porches into outdoor sleeping
rooms, and hoped the building would be ready by summer. Sarah Joslyn
remained on the planning committee.

THE FALLEN WOMEN HOME

Although Dr. Calfass and her team had bought the Woolworth and Fairfield residences for the Betterment of Boys and Girls, in a shocking
move just three months later, according to the *Omaha World-Herald*,
"an imperative demand came from the government to deal with fallen
women." Dr. Calfass and her committee willingly abandoned their plans

and entered into a new line of work. These young women "afflicted with social diseases" were to receive medical treatment by order of the federal government and under supervision of the city. The story became somewhat more disturbing, in large part due to societal attitudes toward women in general, certainly sex workers, and the general tone of journalism in 1918. Sadly, the doors of both mansions were bolted, and the gates of iron fences were chained and padlocked. No solution was offered for the societal issue of women infected with syphilis, "for the problem will endure as long as uncontrolled passions dominate and folly yields to temptation." The journalist found it sad to relate that among the young women locked up, "some do not appreciate the remarkable effort being made to restore them to health and decency." Although vague, I began to understand that most of the women were either sex workers, "cultured women who began with the drug habit," and/or "victims" of much older men. After the girls and young women were being rounded up in raids on dance halls and "questionable resorts" because "good American soldiers" were being infected, it is easy to imagine their terror of being locked into an old mansion, no matter how gorgeous the rooms were. Apparently, if the Omaha women escaped the Woolworth grounds, they would be arrested—this coming from the War Department of Washington, as it was called. The war measure was lightly extended to American soldiers, more of a slap on the wrist, it seemed. "Soldiers caught under suspicion are punished and also subject to treatment."

So what to make of all of this? Why were young women in Omaha being locked up due to military orders, paid in full by the federal government? My understanding, after looking into the history of syphilis, World War I, and the medical and societal views during this time period, is that the end goal was the speedy recovery of as many United States soldiers as possible back into the field. Venereal diseases were on the rise among all military personnel of the war, not only Americans. New and frequent sexual experiences overseas, the ease of anonymity and mobility factors, loss of familial and religious monitoring mechanisms, are thought to have led to the spread of sexually transmitted infections across all militaries. It would be years until Alexander Fleming discovered penicillin. So, although I am not absolutely certain, from my research I would assume that mercurial cream was being applied during this time period and/ or mercurous chloride tablets taken orally. The toxic mercury was thought to cure many different illnesses, but as we now know, it slowly poisoned those who used it.

The Woolworth and Fairfield mansions were thought to create a moral and social atmosphere for these misguided, ruinous women. Light, airy, and well appointed, with lovely furnishings "better than the average hospital," the mansions also featured a piano, and sheet music was available. There were medical books easily accessible "that inmates may study the nature of their awful plight." All of the women, ages sixteen to twenty, were attired in blue gingham dresses, and they sewed their own undergarments from two bolts of muslin. These were the key visual elements that allowed the few Omahans who even knew of the syphilis house to continue thinking this was a good, just cause. Head nurse Miss Alta Burger, assistant nurse Mrs. M. M. Duval, head of the public health department Dr. E. T. Manning, women's specialist Dr. Palmer Findley (a name you might recall from the early formation of Stewart Maternity Hospital), policemen, guards, cooks, and other staff were praised for their sacrifice and courage in working with these unfortunates, committed to what was called "war work." There were twenty-seven young girls and women in total under lock and key of the mansions. To that date, only four women had been cured of their venereal diseases. The "infected women" were also made to aid medical staff in the painful, toxic operating room procedures, as they held down fellow writhing inmates. I could not believe what I was reading. The saddest reality was that many of these young women were thought to be the victims of their parents, improper amusements, and indiscriminant companions—one being a known married Omaha man, the father of two children. Any girl or woman at this time "caught under suspicion" was subjected to examination and treatment.

Mysteriously, the 1918 Omaha City Directory had the former Woolworth estate's 2211 St. Mary's Avenue address listed as "vacant" in that year. Even more confounding, the Fairfield's 2219 St. Mary's address fell off the books. It was nonexistent. Another puzzle was a lone article that made mention of a birth at the Birch Knoll Maternity Cottage in August 1919. I could find no mention beyond 1918 of the hidden women's prison infirmary. I was convinced this might have been because World War I ended in November of that year. I would back away and take a deep breath.

THE BOARDINGHOUSE YEARS

The trail would grow cold throughout the investigation of the Woolworth and Fairfield residences as I tried to find clues for the missing years, denying that this fixation would involve my ruin. What a way to go, I convinced myself, if it was possible to be utterly consumed by a sleuthing mission. The Stewart Hospital, later Omaha Maternity Hospital, housed in the old Murphy-Cuming residence on the northwest corner of Twenty-Second and St. Mary's Avenue, continued to do well throughout the 1920s under the direction of Nellie Steward and head physician Dr. C. W. Pollard. After the disappearance of the syphilis infirmary, I could not find anyone occupying the Woolworth address at 2211 until the 1920 United States Federal Census. The city directory did not even carry the address. I tripped across Etta W. Powers renting the large home. Powers was a transplant from New York, born in about 1858. She was widowed in 1920 and at age sixty-two was head of a rooming house in the sprawling 2211 St. Mary's Avenue mansion. Those under her roof included Arthur R. Stone, Eva Emery, George A. Emery, Guy S. Williams, Hazel C. Williams, Alfred C. Blake, Birdie Meedham, Pearl Pranti, Elsie Pennington, Ella Clancy, Winnina Brownson, Hans P. Crause, Emma Hakely, Marie Hakel, Mabel Knudson, C. Charles Woolheter, Cass C. Camp, and Peter J. McLaughlin. Miss Knudson was the youngest, at age eighteen, and Mr. Emery was the oldest renter, at seventy. Meanwhile, an H. A. Snow was running a boardinghouse out of the Fairfield estate at 2219 St. Mary's Avenue. I tracked the name to Iowan Henry A. Snow. At fifty-two Mr. Snow was renting the large estate, living with his wife, Mary, fifty-three. The two were heading up the boardinghouse responsible for thirteen lodgers, all in their twenties, along with the Snow children: Bertha, twenty-seven; Elizabeth, nineteen; Herbert, seventeen; Lillian, fifteen;

57. Sandstone fencing clues left over from the once grand
Murphy residence, 2017. Photos by author.

and Fred, thirteen. I dreamed it was called the Snow House. I closed my
eyes to imagine the sounds of multitudinous feet on the stair runners.

Through the 1920s both mansions would change hands many times,
almost yearly. S. J. Galney, G. B. Collins, J. J. Hess, Howard Steinbaugh,
"Mrs. Cora Lamb furnished rooms," "Mrs. Anna Clearwater furnished
rooms," E. A. Delaney, Mrs. Maude Salsbery / J. W. Salsbery, "Mrs. P. A.
Finelli furnished rooms," V. H. Reed, Charles Lemon, and N. H. Strawn
were some of the rooming house proprietors. The first radio news broad-
casts would be transmitted in these years. I liked to think of the boarders
all gathered in the darkened parlor for a listen.

THE NEW ST. MARY'S AVENUE GRADE

The St. Mary's Avenue grading district between Sixteenth and Twenty-
Fourth was thought to look like a "new part of the city" by July 1921. A

58. Close up of sandstone fencing from the Murphy
residence, 2017. Photo by author.

sprinkling of large homes, along with the "old residence of Judge Woolworth and the Fairfield home, all on the south side of the street, are now
on a high embankment close to the edge of the new street." The opposite side of St. Mary's "where the late Frank Murphy's home, founder
of the Merchants National Bank, was on another large embankment." I
believe this lowering of the street also involved a widening of the avenue.

THE SALSBERY HOME

You have observed by now how my mind works, and you are most for-
giving. So you most likely understand that I would have desired to have
drilled down into the history of each and every one of these boardinghouse managers, but I couldn't do that to you, friends. (If you are reading
this still, you are surely the most patient person I will ever not know,
and truth be told, I could not do it to Mr. Cassette. You see, my fits of
fancy call me down to the library with such regularity that he is left

taking up all sorts of strange hobbies, such as self-hypnosis, quantum coherence, and the study of epigenetics.) But I did take up the trail of one John W. Salsbery because I could not stop myself. Salsbery operated his boardinghouse from 2211 St. Mary's Avenue in 1922 until 1937. So he deserved more than just a whisper for all of those committed years, I convinced myself. Besides those Great Depression years couldn't have been easy. In 1930 Mr. Salsbery was forty-two, and his wife, Maude M. Salsbery, was forty-one. The two had a daughter, Marion M., twelve years old. John's parents were from England, having immigrated to Nebraska by John's birth in 1888. Immersed in all matters of boarding services, John Salsbery was also employed by the Conant Hotel, previously called the Sanford, at 1913 Farnam. This historic building is now called City Pointe Apartments.

FAIRFIELD DOSSIER

Much later I would find the ultimate clue as to what happened in the transition of the 2211 and 2219 St. Mary's Avenue homes. Back in 1918 Edmund and Meliora Fairfield moved to New York City for a new life. The couple, surprisingly, divorced in 1922, and I believe that Edmund must have returned to Omaha at that point. When I last mentioned his career, Edmund was general manager of the Omaha Water Company before the Metropolitan Utilities District acquired it in 1912. At the time of his death on May 3, 1929, Edmund had been promoted to assistant to the vice president of the Burlington Railroad. He was interred with the Fairfield family in Wyuka Cemetery in Lincoln, Nebraska. The next year, 1930, brought the death of Mary Rogers Kimball, and her home would be left to her beloved daughter, Arabel M. Kimball, of Kimball Steele and Sandham Architects. Then in January 1956, Omaha's first Queen of Ak-Sar-Ben, Meliora Woolworth Fairfield, died in New York City. Her body was returned to Omaha, and her memorial service was held at Trinity Cathedral Church. Her obituary mentioned her daughters, Mrs. L. Gordon Campbell of New York City (this must have been Elizabeth), and Miss Wynne Fairfield of St. Paul, Minnesota. Daughter Mary W. must have gone by her middle name.

59. John Vachon photo from November 1938 entitled *Old House for Sale, Omaha, Nebraska.* Signs read: "Sleeping Room for Rent," "2211 St. Mary's Furnished Apts. Sleeping Rooms," and "For Sale [*not legible*]—Ft. on St. Mary's Ave. 120 Ft. on 22nd St. A Good Investment at Today's Low Price." Drake Court and Jones Street Annex apartments can be seen in the distance. From the Farm Security Administration—Office of War Information Photograph Collection, Library of Congress Prints and Photographs Division, LC-USF33-T01-001275-M2.

THE BEGINNING OF THE END

During the Great Depression the once sprawling stone mansion inhabited by the Stewart Hospital / Omaha Maternity at 2204 St. Mary's became the Phi Beta Pi Fraternity. This was a pattern across America, and this frat house phenomenon has shown up in my other investigations as well. Who else could afford to run such a large home in those days? I'm sure this must have been a lively crossroads, with two boardinghouses and a fraternity so close to one another. In 1937 David F. Hensley took run of the 2211 St. Mary's boardinghouse, at that time having fallen into disrepair.

60. Woolworth house at 2211 St. Mary's Avenue, 1938. From the KM3TV/
Bostwick-Frohardt Photograph Collection at the Durham Museum.

The once glorious Victorian mansion was still gorgeous by Miss Cassette's standards, but images of it reveal an abandoned, forlorn look, frequently seen in Depression era photos. Those dire years must have left
the various owners of the two mansions just aiming to keep the rooms
filled in hopes of warmth. The 1940 United States Census showed Hensley, a fifty-two-year-old, was managing the rooms. Along with wife Doxie
(Dixie?), forty-three, and their adult son, Taylor Hensley, age twenty-three,
the family had all made their way to Omaha from Tennessee. Hensley
also worked as a driver at YC&B Company, which I looked up and turned
out to be Yellow Cab and Baggage Company, located at 615–21 South
Twentieth Street. Violet Gardner, Emma Sleter, John Fotak, Wilbery
Stout, and Louise Gaghiolo were all lodgers in the home. In the next
decade Hensley was able to keep the house filled, usually with eighteen
to twenty-four lodgers. Dell Allen was operating his own boardinghouse
out of 2219 over the following ten years.

61. Meliora's house, the gorgeous Fairfield Residence at 2219
St. Mary's Avenue, 1938. From the KM3TV/Bostwick-Frohardt
Photograph Collection at the Durham Museum

A NEW ERA

In June 1950 a fatal announcement in the *Omaha World-Herald* proclaimed that the Woolworth and Fairfield houses would soon be razed by the Rorick Construction Company to make room for a "modern apartment building." Ernest Rorick's company had been in business since the early 1940s, from what I found, and had built a number of apartment complexes in town. The Woolworth mansion had been obscured by thick trees for almost a decade—the image would swirl in my mind. The old stone fence bordering the property on the east was rumored to have been there since 1888. The original Woolworth estate was then owned by T. H. Maenner, Inc., which had presumably been renting it to all of those boardingroom managers throughout the years. It made sense. The article described Woolworth's fireplace mantel again. The mantel, constructed of rare woods, had a curious pattern of inlaid tiles depicting the Sarpy

THE CLUE TO BIRCHEKNOLLE

Home in Bellevue, the first Territorial Capital, the Woolworth home, the second Territorial Capital, and the Trinity Cathedral. This mantelpiece was to be donated to the Nebraska Historical Society in Lincoln and developed as part of a Victorian age period room, following a preservation agreement that Meliora Woolworth Fairfield made with the historical society, if the house should ever be razed. Four years later the Woolworth fireplace was part of an ornate, plush-covered museum display in Lincoln, Nebraska. Is it still there? I wondered.

The 1951 Omaha City Directory did not yet have an address identified for the Rorick Apartments. Instead, it showed them "under construction s w corner" and spelled "Roerick Apartments." In time the Rorick Apartments would carry the address of 604 South Twenty-Second, and 2211 St. Mary's Avenue disappeared from the books. There was no longer a 2219 St. Mary's Avenue address listing either; instead, the somewhat awkward 2235 St. Mary's Cox Avenue Apartments filled in. The quieter, shorter, not-so-showy sister of the Rorick, the Avenue Apartments were actually built earlier. The Cox Avenue Apartments sought a building permit in December 1949 for the $800,000 project. These brick structures were simply called the Rorick and Avenue Apartments throughout my life. The similar post–World War II high-rise buildings both featured an eye-catching cross plan and were both built by Rorick construction, although they carried different names, as George Cox owned the avenue. The Avenue Apartments, designed by M. J. Lahr, opened in January 1951 with two floors of the six-story building already occupied. The simple layouts featured Murphy beds in the living rooms with Pullman kitchens and tile-walled bathrooms, boasting of electric wall heaters and shower-tub combos. The ground floor featured two lounges, a locker room, and laundry room. The Rorick, on the other hand, offered a superb entryway, one of my favorite rooftop signs in town, fantastic midcentury modern corner windows, and a great view. Both buildings shared a three-story parking garage. The Rorick emphasized amenities important to renters of this new era. A postcard from the very early 1950s had this to say of the Rorick Apartments: "236 units equipped with Electric Kitchens, Steam Heat, Free Parking, Heated Garages, Modern Laundry and Drying Room.

62. City View Apartments, 2017. Photo by author.

Lounge. Beauty and Gift Shop. Dry Cleaners. Sun Deck. Furnished and Unfurnished Apartments. Security Personnel."

By the 1990s the newspapers would describe the St. Mary's area as crime filled and risky, in spite of many efforts to rehabilitate the fantastic grouping of apartments and large homes for blocks around. Although I had been smitten with the Rorick since childhood, I was aware it carried a slippery ticket in many people's eyes. When speaking of the Rorick with a girlfriend at that time, Angel referred to the Rorick Apartments as a place that a potential tenant "would have to stab their way into" just to get to their doorstep. Angel's words never left me, and I suppose they were quite influential when I signed a rental agreement for a precarious duplex very near the Rorick years later. I would get the parlous adventure I desired in full within three short months, later breaking that lease due to a myriad of experiences, now good stories. Yet, it was all worth it.

The whole St. Mary's Avenue area and neighborhoods nearby are going through a hopeful rejuvenation of late. The current owners have since taken down the amazing red RORICK lighted sign atop the apartment building and put up a CITY VIEW sign with a large backward checkmark that forms the *V* in *View*. That fine foyer floor of the apartment building is still intact, with its proud inlaid *R* from 1952. And although the doorman and elevator operators have since dematerialized, the structure remembers what it once was. And so do I. To this day one can stand in front of the old Rorick building on Twenty-Second Street and easily view downtown Omaha, all the way to the hills of Council Bluffs, in much the same way that Judge Woolworth might have from his large, vine-covered wraparound porch.

CHAPTER 6

The Quest of Harkert's Holsum Hamburger

To my surprise, not everyone yearns to snoop around in drafty, old, semi-derelict mansions with a vintage RAYOVAC. My father is one such unfortunate person, not so much luckless as he is disinterested in architectural mystery. My childhood spying wasn't just about donning head-to-toe makeshift costumes; I was very curious and longed to live in such a glorious, obscured home. My father's indifferent position and his conclusion that a meandering manor house was all too ill fitting, too impractical, past its best in both matters of musty odor and sustainability, never made much sense to me. I have since learned it is commonplace for those who grew up in large, conspicuous houses to abandon said accommodations with fervor, once evinced of the Bright, Contemporary, Efficient models. I might never truly understand this.

While he did not share in my obsession for high adventure smack of secret city planning, hidden mansions, and building surveillance, Father of Miss Cassette did have a penchant for history of all types and story-telling, his favorite being shared (embellished) family history. Actually, both lines of his family enjoyed a good story. Of course, a plot was often helped along, naturally, by aid of our family's eccentric, opinionated, at times arrogant manner of communication. And the crowd measure of triumph? Intelligence, clever word election, and unflappable showman-ship. I clearly remember my grandmother's extended dining room table filled with the regular jovial cast, bordered in a deeply stained wainscoting with proper plate rail, beneath her parents' Moe Bridges–like frosted slip shade chandelier. The pinnacle was a complicated, well-woven comedic tale, followed by a higher-ordered rebuttal or a well-crafted quip from the gallery. The few quiet and meek among us were often trampled and

185

commonly excused ourselves to clear the dinner dishes, prepare coffee, or gather small dessert plates for the next round of table fireworks. Being an unheard member of such a roaring, festive group of chroniclers also allowed me the luxury to sit back, observe, and truly absorb. I only wish I could be back there again! I would have taken better notes.

Up at the large family home, I remember infrequent mentions of a place called Harkert's, a restaurant known for its exceptionally good split pea and bean soups, the checkerboard exterior with stretches of stainless steel and classic white porcelain interiors. As a marginal note, Father of Miss Cassette and Grandmother remain the only people I've known to rave about a good split pea soup. My father claims to have found an incredible bowl of it "just like Harkert's secret recipe" in the Chicago area. But there was more to the family tale than just the Harkert soups. As the story goes, my grandmother, grandfather, and great-uncle Jimmy were out for a night on the town many moons ago. They had just sat down in a nightclub for a round of cocktails, when purportedly a man came over and said, "Mr. Harkert would like to dance with this young lady." My grandparents were not yet married, and I suppose at this juncture I should mention my grandmother's petite figure, gorgeous shapely legs, and huge brown eyes rimmed with a curious smoky blue hue. Now Great-Uncle Jimmy was known far and wide for his good looks, tony style of dress, and great sense of humor but equally acclaimed for his bad Irish temper. They say Great-Uncle Jimmy told the innocent fellow, "If Harkert had any guts, he'd come over and get turned down in person instead of sending a flunky over." To make matters worse, Jimmy told the messenger, "Beat it back and tell your gutless boss the lady isn't ever going to be interested!"—or something to that effect. Now is that the God's honest truth? We will never know, and all parties involved have long ago passed away. Let me remind you that this particular side of the family was Irish, and they were known to put flesh on the bones of a story over time (even within twenty-four hours), but this narrative, for what it was worth, really got me wondering about Harkert and the "nothing-fancy but exceptionally good food" café my family couldn't seem to stop talking about.

OFF WITH A START

As with all good mystery pursuits, I started by ordering my tools into a backpack, including a rusting RAYOVAC flashlight, small favored pencils with moleskin notepad, a sturdy magnifying glass, a quick blonde wig, and a vintage silky scarf with equestrian motifs, because one can never be sure when one might need a speedy guise. I would practice my birdcall signals on the way down to the library that fine morning for a preliminary gathering of clues. Aah, I sighed, as the delicious work of salvage began. I do love a new mystery. It did not take long to find that the classic, easily identified, white-enameled, stainless steel "Harkert Houses" once dotted the Omaha streets with what I soon learned was the casual comfort and familiarity of a well-liked neighbor. My mind wheeled over the details. How did Omaha support these thirteen lunch counters (or was it twenty-one?), some within blocks of one another? Long before the enterprising Omaha pioneer of the Quick-Lunch, Dine-for-a-Dime, One on Every Corner concept became a well-known businessman, Walter Harkert's story actually began in a small town in Iowa.

FINDING WALTER ELMER HARKERT

Through an open door and down a long dusty corridor of the genealogy stacks, I would begin to track our Mr. Harkert. Walter "Walt" Elmer Harkert was born in 1889, the only son of Peter H. Harkert and Agnes Lemke (*Lembke* spelling also found). Father Peter was born in Holstein, Germany, to Claus and Anna Harkert. Mother Agnes was born in Davenport, Iowa, in 1868, although some background information determined she, too, was born in Germany. I did find evidence that mother Agnes's parents, Heward and Maria, were both born in Holstein as well. The Lemkes would later settle in Davenport, Iowa, according to the 1870 United States Census, among other new immigrant neighbors from Holstein, Prussia, and Ireland. Likewise, Davenport is where Peter and Agnes Harkert met and married. The Harkert couple also two daughters. Clara was born three years after Walter, and youngest Helen was born in 1898.

Not uncommon in those days, Walter only attained an eighth grade education. The older gentlemen I have known throughout my life with an eighth grade education often left school to help earn money for the family or work the family farm. And might I add, they had a better education than any of us. Harkert was a hard worker straightaway, a reputation that followed him throughout his life. In Davenport he worked in local retail and later, interestingly, ran a dance hall until age twenty-seven. This was the first intimation Harkert was notorious for his love of dance, adding a pinch more credence to Great-Uncle Jimmy's story. When the music began, in Walter's self-confession, he was first on the dance floor and last to leave. Did his affinity for dancing start in his early dance hall days with the waltz or the polka? I was off to a swell start, but as I was soon to learn, Walt would take my study on a wild goose chase. With one thousand dollars in his pocket (some stories say he saved this money, others say he borrowed), Walter Harkert moved on to the big-city lights of Council Bluffs, Iowa, to open a shoe store.

THE COUNCIL BLUFFS VENTURES

Like clockwork, this amateur gumshoe traced the ticktocks of Harkert's presumed landing at the Guarantee Clothing Company–Nebraska Shoe & Clothing House due to a fabulous advertisement from 1916. Once there, the twenty-seven-year-old Harkert sold the well-known, union-made Beacon Shoes, "the shoe that satisfies." Although this was a Nebraska Shoe & Clothing House operation, the advertisement pointed to a Council Bluffs location. In 1918 the *Nonpareil* announced the sudden death of youngest sibling, Helen Harkert, at age twenty. The funeral was held at Walter's apartment at Seventh and Broadway, likewise in Council Bluffs.

The United States had entered World War I in 1917. I could find no solid proof that our Walt had been in the service, as he never mentioned it throughout his diverse career, but future clues pointed to it. The Selective Service Act developed and required three registrations for American males through the duration of this particular war. Walter would have fallen into all three catchment age groupings during this time—the widest breadth was eighteen through forty-five years of age. Another point of suspicion is that Harkert disappeared from my chase for two years during the war.

I would explore a February 6, 1920, advertisement for a Babbe & Harkert: "The B. & H. Bootery" of 535 West Broadway. The now evacuated Daily Nonpareil Building, built in 1987, stands in this location in downtown Council Bluffs. The bootery would relocate to 521 West Broadway and rename the venture the Walter Harkert Store in the heart of the Bluffs business district. At this location Harkert peddled men's furnishings, largely silk shirts and socks. The popular Metzger's Café was situated next door, exactly where a man sat eating a meal back in 1921, when he happened to view three Omaha robbers enter Harkert's store by "unlocking the front door." Later this same eagle-eyed diner spied the trio emerge from the back door, carrying "three grips and a sack," get into an automobile bearing a Nebraska license, and start toward Omaha. How did he see all of that from the café window? is all this chary gumshoe wanted to know.

THE DEPRESSION OF 1920

Years later Walter Harkert himself would claim he "went broke" in the Depression of the early 1920s, shuttering his shop and moving to Omaha. This isn't exactly what the official record would reveal, but we'll keep these parallel stories afloat for now. Which reminds me to tip you off— some of you In The Know types will understand that taking notes during these adventures can be of service later. You might want to jot down the occasional memo as this mystery, like the others, can become muddled at times.

The Depression of 1920–21 was a brief recession period in the United States immediately following World War I's end. In retrospect it is presumed that the returning American troops flooded the civilian labor force, causing changes to the previous wartime economy, which further strained unrealistic price expectations America simply was not prepared for. The Roaring Twenties would soon bring economic prosperity, but Harkert had to downsize and reevaluate. My initial hint leading to an assumption about Harkert's business patterns arrived in a 1924 lead. This advertisement made plain Walter Harkert wanted to trade his "Boone, Iowa residence for property in Omaha or Council Bluffs." How curious, I thought. Furthermore I discovered he lived at 125 Nicholas Street, a wonderful little hillside Craftsman bungalow in Council Bluffs, not Omaha.

THE BIG MOVE

I pursued Walter Harkert to a new job in February 1924 with the Florsheim Men's Boot Shop at 315 South Sixteenth Street in Omaha, after selling his store. Apparently, for eight years he had conducted the Harkert Store for Men out of 521 West Broadway. There were other conflicting reports prior to his venture in Council Bluffs. Harkert was evidently connected with some of Omaha's most famous shoes stores and was well regarded in retail circles. Now Miss Cassette surely does not know the ins and outs of how all of that came together exactly, but one could assume that his Harkert Store for Men offered ample opportunity to fraternize with Omaha shoe merchants and well-heeled hobnobbers alike.

THE DOUBLE CAREYS MARRY

Mrs. Harriet Carey proudly announced the marriages of her two daughters on the same day. Upon further examination, it was Saturday March 2, 1924, that Miss Mercedes Carey married Walter E. Harkert at seven o'clock at night at Kountze Memorial Church. Kountze Memorial Lutheran Church has maintained its location at 2650 Farnam Street since 1906 and is thought to be the first Lutheran congregation organized west of the Missouri River. The church was founded by the renowned Omahan Augustus Kountze, designated in his beloved father's name, Christian Kountze. The five Kountze brothers shaped Nebraska banking, of First National Bank of Omaha fame, and one will find their distinguished surname engraved throughout Omaha corridors and lauded to this very day. At the time of the Carey girls' weddings, Kountze Memorial Church was credited as the largest Lutheran congregation in the United States. Another daughter, Miss Jane Carey, married Arthur H. Schwentker of Nebraska City at 9:00 p.m. at the very same church. Economically, Dr. O. D. Baltzly performed both ceremonies, leaving me to question if there was perhaps a wedding in between the sisters' nuptials? Mr. Harkert and his bride were to make their home in Omaha at 1039 Park Avenue, and the Schwentkers were presumed to live in Nebraska City.

THE EARLY SCHWENTKER FILE

I discovered that brother-in-law Arthur Schwentker was a reputed barber from a family of barbers: the Schwentker Brothers. Likewise, I found evidence that Arthur had a passion for music; he was a singer and later a choir director. I dreamed of the Schwentker Brothers commencing a barbershop quartet during their off-barbery hours, but I suppose this was wistful yearning on my part.

ENTER MERCEDES CAREY

Let us return to shine the large stage light on a wonderful, if not elusive, main character in our amateur inquiry: Mercedes "Mercy" Carey. Unfortunately, Miss Mercedes would remain a mysterious shadow being throughout most of my perilous journey, somehow managing to elude my meddlesome ways. Mercedes was born in Nebraska in 1891, the daughter of Charles Carey and Harriet Stanley. Her siblings were Helen, Florence, Charles, and Jane (also known as Jennie in some genealogy records). When the older children left the house, Mercedes and her sister Jane supported their widowed mother by working as stenographers in Omaha. The 1924 *World-Herald* marriage license announcement made known Mercedes was vaguely "over 21," but I estimated her age to actually be in the neighborhood of thirty-three. Walter was age thirty-five. It is intriguing to consider the couple's presumed maturity at their time of marriage in comparison to their peers.

Equally as riveting: I tripped across a short article from November 1923 in which I discovered Mercy was infamously struck by an automobile owned by Thomas C. Byrne, president of the Byrne-Hammer Company. The car, driven by one Frank Kersigo, was an employee of Byrne. Mercedes was asking a $10,000 damage suit in district court, a rarity in those days. Besides personal injury, "she claims her $3 hose were ruined, as well as an $18 hat." In 1923, $10,000 had the same buying power as approximately $142,860 in 2017. Did Mercy have extensive surgery or live with the lifelong effects of this automobile injury? The Inquiring Iris in me wondered what became of this settlement and if it helped Walter Harkert stabilize after his financial woes of the foregoing years.

THE BYRNE-HAMMER COMPANY

The Byrne-Hammer Company was a department store positioned at 425 South Ninth Street, essentially Ninth and Howard Streets. Originally founded in 1900 by George Hammer and "T. C." Byrne, the Byrne & Hammer Dry Goods Company began as a clothing factory producing work wear, the likes of hearty overalls, shirts, and men's pants, The factory was located at 1121–23 Howard Street, filled with one hundred sewing machines and more than as many hardworking women. Peter Iler, who seems to mysteriously work his way into many of my inquiries, would later erect a building for the firm's jobbing house at 1113, 1115, and 1117 Howard Street. As all good investigations seem to come full circle, this fine building is now called the Iler Building, located in the heart of the Old Market and serendipitously covered in one of my very first mysteries.

THE DARK HISTORY OF THE
BYRNE-HAMMER COMPANY

Be gently warned about the news that follows, for the Byrne-Hammer Company experienced what I would consider an unfortunate series of events. This is a bit of a side-winding bramble. For the record: A water pipe burst in the Byrne-Hammer Company factory at Twelfth and Jackson, causing much damage. One of the factory managers died of pneumonia. A heated argument ensued one night "over some trivial matter" whereby Pete Moore, salesman at the Byrne-Hammer Company, picked up a brick and threw it at P. J. Meehan, fracturing the unsuspecting man's jawbone. The garage of the Byrne-Hammer Company at Ninth and Howard was broken into, and two sample wooden cases of merchandise were stolen. After telling his wife he was going to fix water for her bath, August Maas, Byrne-Hammer Company employee, went to the basement of his home and hanged himself over the furnace pit. Leaving a note to his wife, directing her of where to find his body, Carl Burnett went into a vacant house at Thirty-Third and Leavenworth and slashed his throat from ear to ear with a butcher knife; she discovered his note when she returned from her work at the Byrne-Hammer Company. Edward Roth, twenty-year salesman (some accounts said ten years) in the ready-to-wear department of the Byrne-Hammer Company wholesale house, was questioned for his part in the alleged theft of what police were saying amounted to ten thousand dollars of stolen stock from this former employers' shelves. Roth originally gave his name as Edward Rothwell, along with a fake address. In reality the man lived in the Flomar Hotel. T. C. Byrne openly called Roth "a trusted employee." Later one charge of grand larceny and two charges of conspiracy with intent to commit felony were filed against Roth. He and two merchants were arrested after their age-old plot was discovered. Roth sold goods to the men, and when the shipment arrived at their places, there were more goods in the packages than had been charged to them. The wholesale house estimates its loss at about twelve thousand dollars. Later box car thieves dumped a large case of fur-lined coats from a freight train at 3:00 a.m. Theodore Peterson, whose land the box was found on, made the report to the police. He stated he saw three men open the wooden box and take out several coats, after which they set fire to the case and the rest of the merchandise. Seven partially fur-lined overcoats were found after the blaze was contained. It seems as though I had seen this crooked behavior in an old movie reel. The wooden box was consigned to the Byrne Hammer Company. Detectives, I feel a compulsion to further investigate the complete Byrne-Hammer Company history and comb for more mysterious details.

INSPIRATION

Just ten short months after the Harkert newlyweds had concluded their nuptials, their son Dale Wallace Harkert was born, on December 28, 1924. Unexpected medical bills, perhaps ongoing from Mercy's accident or the birth of their son, would plunge Walter Harkert into financial straits once again. Always an enterprising, hardworking man, Walter soon began looking for ways to supplement his income as a manager of a shoe department. He envisioned finding a place to sell cheap but tasty sandwiches during the American Legion Convention held in Omaha that September 1925. Unable to procure the perfect spot, the convention came and went. This was another common pattern I observed along the trail: Walter's inspiration came quickly, but his bankroll often could not match his ambition. On borrowed money Harkert impressively introduced Omaha to his first hamburger stand less than two months after his idea was hatched.

THE YEAR 1925

The 1925 Omaha City Directory identified Walter E. Harkert as a salesman with Florsheim Shoe Company. There were no other Harkerts found in the directory. Harkert called 1039 Park Avenue home, a handsome brick apartment building erected in 1910. I am happy to say this proud, mint chocolate chip six-plex is still prevailing down on Park Avenue. Go have a peek sometime when it is covered in a wintry snow. In March 1925 the World-Herald announced that Harkert would take charge of the brand-new men's shoe department at the Browning King Company, a local store of a national chain of twenty-four. A proud photo of Harkert was paraded in the press, a full moon–faced man. I had formerly come across this department store name in my other investigations.

THE FIRST HARKERT'S

It wasn't until late September 1925, I uncovered Walter Harkert's building permit for a "cement-block lunch room at 4633 South 24th Street" for a whopping one thousand dollars. This lunchroom venture is, unfortunately, no longer standing; I found this site currently an empty lot, adjacent to the ever-packed Jacobo's Grocery, where Mr. Cassette secures many a vat of divine, spicy tomatillo salsa for special nights at home. Walter would open his first Harkert House on November 11, 1925, as a five-stool hamburger joint called "U Eat a Hamburger." It really had a modern ring to it. I dreamed of making a T-shirt of the name. The menu simply offered hamburgers, coffee, and soda. The cheap, delicious meal was soon a huge success. Harkert would later expound on the economics of the budget meal. Hamburgers at that time cost sixteen cents a pound, and one pound could produce sixteen nickel hamburgers: one ounce, one cent. The bun likewise cost one cent. Pickles, mustard, and such came to half a cent. The materials cost 50 percent of the selling price, and the rest went for staff, overhead, rent, and profit. Later a ten-cent hamburger would be added—a bigger bun, featuring three ounces of meat. L Street ran just south of the dissolved lunchroom location, and I'm sure this busy corner made Harkert a fine profit. Each step of the way Harkert continued to plan, conserve, and cautiously grow his business as he retained his shoe store job. During this time he opened three more "hole-in-the-wall" lunch stops back in Council Bluffs. He was rumored to have managed the four stores "in his spare time, sometimes traveling fifty miles in a day by streetcar, working 16 to 18 hours a day." Meanwhile, the Harkert family home had moved across town to 2044 North Fiftieth Avenue, an adorable, well-shaded 1919 bungalow in the Metcalfe Park Neighborhood. I was beginning to see that Harkert had his own obsession—the dream of a local chain of counters.

THE EARLY DINERS

In the previous years American diners had evolved from a movable pull-cart or horse-drawn lunch wagon concept to the idea of the stationary lunch car. The lunch car, very much like a railway dining car, was designed and constructed by three American manufacturing companies and shipped to their new owners. In the early 1920s the diner car equipment and supplies were often included in the price of purchase and featured a sleek, narrow design—a long counter with few stools that enabled the diner car to be run as a one-man show. It was essentially a restaurant kit. The definitive history of diners is no better explained than in Richard Gutman's impressive book *American Diner: Then and Now*. I was soon to learn that true diner purists uphold a very strict combination of criteria in order to receive the favorable Diner Classification. One definition is that a diner must be factory built or prefabricated. Although the experts may dismiss me, for our purposes here, I do label Harkert's empire as a diner chain, if for no other reason than he consistently offered the public good food, a counter, stools, and an atmosphere of local camara-derie. Later evidence cropped up that Harkert's exteriors and interiors were possibly shipped and built on-site, albeit not barrel-roofed, isolated buildings. More on that later . . .

Harkert's U Eat a Hamburger was most likely a simple, local version of an East Coast diner, with apparently only five stools stationed by the counter. Let's assume it might have been an early hole-in-the-wall café, as booth service wasn't offered for years. This would mean that some custom-ers stood and ate their burgers out of a bag, while others might have eaten outside. In these days I found writing suggesting that women were slow to order and slow to eat, therefore deemed not good customers for the diner business, only leading me to suspect that eating quickly and getting out was encouraged. How else was a guy to make money off a nickel burger unless turnover was high? Additionally, it was assumed that most women did not feel comfortable sitting on a stool, at a counter, in a cramped envi-ronment, surrounded by men. The counter possibly served triple duty as customer table, storage, and workspace, with the backbar perhaps used as a gas-fueled flattop and sandwich board. As was popular at the time, the U Eat a Hamburger floor was probably covered in hexagonal white ceramic tiles, complete with white tile walls or a white metal ceiling. I longed to see a historic photo of this early Harkert's dinette incarnation.

MEMORIES OF HARKERT'S SOUTH LOCATION

Now it would be many years later, but a dear family friend, Carolyn, was able to draw a clearer picture of the first Harkert's, albeit from the 1940s. In her words:

> I grew up in North Omaha in the Miller Park / Minne Lusa area, and I do not remember any Harkert's in that part of Omaha. How-ever, during the summers of our grade school years, my sisters and I spent a lot of time at our grandparents' farm, which was just east of Papillion. Papillion was a very small town in the 1940s. When my grandparents went shopping, they went to South Omaha, mainly the Phillips Department Store on South 24th St., and those trips always

63. Harkert's at 4819 South Twenty-Fourth Street. A 1935 exterior view of
Harkert's, advertising HAMBURGERS and GOOD COFFEE. From the William
Wentworth Photograph Collection at the Durham Museum Photo Archives.

included lunch at the Harkert's on South 24th. Sometimes they ate
with us, other times they sent us off alone, but it was always a treat!
I remember Harkert's as a friendly, bright sunny, small place—a
counter and a few booths—and, by our standards, serving delicious
food. Although there must have been other items on the menu, we
always ordered the same thing: a hamburger and an orange Nesbitt.

Photographic evidence revealed that Harkert moved his southside
enterprise at least once. In October 23, 1936, I discovered Walt had built
a new storefront at 4819 South Twenty-Fourth Street for five hundred
dollars. William Wentworth captured the scene at 4819 South Twenty-
Fourth in 1935, although this photograph's date might have been logged
incorrectly. This location would have been about a two-block move into
downtown proper of South Omaha. This is most likely where Carolyn

experienced her lifelong impression of Harkert's hamburger and Nesbitt delight.

NEW DEVELOPMENTS

By the summer of 1926 Walter Harkert was striking up another swap. The notice read: "I want a nice 6-room bungalow, new or nearly new, west or south, $7,500 or less. I want to trade my 5-room bungalow at 2545 North 49th Street in on same or pay the difference. Walter Harkert, care of Browning, King & Company." I admired his forthright manner, but this discovery forced me to go back and scour my notes for his previous address, which had conflictingly been listed as 2044 North Fiftieth Avenue. These two homes are only blocks apart.

Early that fall Harkert became manager of the Harvey Brothers Store down on 317 South Sixteenth Street. A men's clothing store chain, Harvey Brothers was a seven-story Chicago clothing factory, known for its factory-direct woolen suits. Having since fallen off the books, this elusive street-level address originally housed the Murray & Company Meat Market, specializing in extra fancy bockwurst sausage, evidently a favorite of 1905 Omaha. At one point I mistakenly surmised Harvey Brothers must have been in the building demolished to make way for the Lerner Shops department store. Numerous retailers peddled their wares out of this slippery address, but it wasn't until the Walk-Over Boot Shop sharp marketing of 1914 nailed down the address to the "fifth door north of Harney, between Farnam and Harney," I guessed 317 must have been a street-level shop beneath the heavenly King Fong Café. I found the decadent Hanson's Beautiful Café was the original three-story restaurant, dating back to 1908. But it wasn't until I discovered a photo I had tucked deep into my cell phone years earlier that squarely identified the Harvey Brothers on the main floor of the King Fong Café. I do wish Mr. Cross would help me get my photo archives in order!

CALL NORTHSIDE

Mercy and Walter would have their second child, Jane Carey Harkert, on November 28, 1926. She joined older brother, Dale, completing the

Artistic English Type

This attractive home of English design at 2712 Martin avenue was sold last week to Walter Harkert for nine thousand dollars by the Joe Shaver company. Mr. Shaver is optimistic about business.

"We have more trouble finding desirable homes to sell than in finding purchasers," he said.

64. "Attractive home of English design at 2712 Martin Avenue sold to Walter Harkert," June 12, 1927. Reprinted with permission from the *Omaha World-Herald*.

family foursome. There is only so much we sleuths can determine from paper, but I was surprised to see Walter Harkert return to Browning King & Company after a few months' leave with the Harvey Brothers. He returned to his previous post as manager of the Browning King & Company shoe department. One might assume from these frequent flights that Harkert had a mercurial spirit, or perhaps he was a tough negotiator, holding out for better pay. Whatever the root cause, one thing was for sure. The Harkerts began moving in a new circle during this time period. The couple bought an "attractive home of English design at 2712 Martin Avenue" in June 1927. This 1926 Tudor style is a perfect Hansel and Gretel fairytale dream, featuring an attractive high-pitched roof, half-timbering, and a fantastic sloped garage. A variety of period homes could be found springing all over Omaha at that time. This fabulous three-bedroom home is still as pretty as can be and was built in the Minne Lusa neighborhood, one of Miss Cassette's favorite areas. Was Walter able to secure this cunning house trade?

THE ARTHUR SCHWENTKER CLUE

Corroboration from 1930 led me to follow certain breadcrumbs backward to 1927. Arthur and Jane Schwentker, Mercy's sister and brother-in-law, moved to Omaha and apparently took up the hamburger stand business in Council Bluffs. Coincidence? This stand was a real moneymaker. Was this Arthur's sole enterprise, or was this one of Walter's stands? From the city directory I would find Arthur and Jane, along with Arthur's mother, Mrs. Sarah Schwentker, residing at 2867 Martin Avenue, just a few paces from the Harkert home on Martin Avenue.

I could not be sure if Arthur had been an original member of Harkert's diner empire or if 1927 marked his move into the business. Most assuredly, the two brothers-in-law sought a building permit on March 1, 1928, for "Harkert & Schwentker, 2809 Sherman Avenue, metal and stucco lunch room, $1,000." Did his Council Bluffs stands follow the same simple model of burgers, coffee, and soda? The Walter Hartright Agency might have sussed out those hard facts.

THE BIG COMBO

Walter Harkert was later quoted as saying only when the four lunch counter locations were making a profit did he resign from his Browning King & Company job. I determined he must have given his resignation in the 1928 time period, as I never heard boo of the shoe peddling or the department stores again. Following his entrepreneurial spirit, it was in this bold resignation during the uncertain years of the stock market crash and impending Great Depression that Harkert's counters really began to take off.

NEW MENU ITEMS

Walter and Mercy concocted the first chili recipe served at Harkert House in their kitchen out of the Martin Avenue address. To be precise,

I should say Walter and "Mrs. Harkert" invented the recipe but without clarification of whom the *Mrs.* referred to. This is where Mrs. Agnes Harkert, Walter's mother, reenters our mystery. Agnes was known for her fine cooking and secret family recipes, many borrowed to great success at the diner. The Harkert family will hopefully enlighten us if their famous chili was Agnes's or Mercy's recipe. Astonishing as it may sound, apparently Mr. Harkert never cared for hamburgers. This must have been a godsend of sorts. Walter and Mercy would apparently make up large batches of chili at home and deliver it to the various stands in pails. This intensive chili operation soon became too much for the couple and their young children to maintain, so an official recipe had to be legitimized for all of the managers to create on-site at the various locations. I was amazed at how many local women asked other newspaper readers for the sumptuous Harkert House chili recipe throughout the years, long after the last diner was shuttered. Word is that the incredible pies served in the chain were also Mrs. Agnes Harkert's creation, which she offered to bake. I have my suspicions that she might have lived on Martin Avenue in Walter's house during that period. According to a *World-Herald* article, one day Agnes infamously remarked, "I might as well make some noodles and you can sell chicken noodle soup." Signs were soon printed up, "Chicken noodle soup with Mrs. Harkert's noodles." Apparently, some customers became leery of the homemade, all-in-the-family marketing of these incredible noodles. So, when Agnes became ill one time, Walter hung another sign: "Due to Mrs. Harkert's incapacity, our soup no longer contains Mrs. Harkert's noodles." The soup sales soared when Mrs. Harkert recovered and was back to making her noodles, the Harkert chain having earned a newfound respect for its homemade authenticity.

LOOSE CLUES

Typically, the city directories from this time period did not make mention of women unless they were widows. So, when I smoked out "Mrs. M. L. Harkert," also living at 2712 Martin Avenue with details that she was the "secretary" for the "Holmes-Wildhaber Grocery Company," I admittedly became confused. I initially thought this was Mrs. Agnes Harkert. But ultimately it was Mercedes who secured a job, working for the Holmes-Wildhaber business, a successful grocery wholesaler in operation throughout the 1920s. This organization was situated at 1112 Howard, in the heart of what is now known as the Old Market. The Niche/Habitat businesses, a contemporary furniture–home decor store, now occupy this location. Was this a functional plan to buy discounted food for the lunch counters? Was this job a way to bring extra money since Walter had left his full-time job? Either way, the connection made good sense.

CLUES TO THE STOCK MARKET CRASH

I was not sure how the Wall Street crash on October 24, 1929, had affected Harkert's chain. The only evidence I could possibly connect came from days later, in November 1929, in the form of another Harkert trade offer: "Sell two Chevrolets. One from 1928 for $20,000 or a 1929 for $7,000 to sell either or trade for coupe. Walter Harkert. 17 South Main in CB, IA or 1824 Dodge." I am no car expert, but the price on the 1928 Chevrolet seemed high. Perhaps a typo. The addresses mentioned did indicate other lunch counters. Another cryptic advertisement read: "HAMBURGER stand, now operating successfully. Will sell all or half. This is not one of my chain stands, but is owned by a friend of mine who is not able to take care of it. Phone Walter Harkert, after 6. KE 1989." Was Walter trying to unload this hamburger stand for his brother-in-law, Art? The phrasing was odd. Perhaps this was a lunch counter solely owned by Art, or did Walt not want the public to know one of his diners was not doing well? This clue would continue to stick in my craw.

Another strange clue from this uncertain time was found in the 1929 directory. The Schwentker & Harkert restaurant was stationed at 313 South Seventeenth Street. This site is no longer extant but appears to have been just east of the Douglas County Courthouse building, nestled between the (very uncomfortable) Farnam Plaza building at 1625 Farnam, built in 1973, and the classic Keeline Building at 319 South Seventeenth Street. The Keeline was completed in 1911, and for all I know, Schwentker & Harkert had been stationed in a street-level bay under this wayward address. The Keeline was the building where I once obtained shadowy employment as phone surveyor for the *This Old House* television show. Fascinating place to snoop around on one's cigarette break.

CLEVER MARKETING IN TOUGH TIMES

While most regular folks were struggling at a low point in American history, the Iowan with an eighth grade education was cleverly plotting his empire. As it turned out, the quick-lunch, dine-for-a-nickel or dime, one-man operation was the winning ticket during the Great Depression. Walter Harkert's cheap burgers and coffee served at the casual café were a comfort to the Every Man. The inexpensive digs were nothing to look at, as the infamous Harkert House look had not yet been developed, but this kept the meals low-cost and the overhead down. His wife and mother's chili, noodles, and variety of pies only solidified the wholesome family storyline in troubling times, but in my estimation what really sealed the deal early on for Harkert was location. Location, location, location. In the following years Walter Harkert would become an astute observer of Omaha real estate, his customers' tastes and national trends in the short-order café business.

THE PICKWICK CLINCH

My stalking of clues continued as I tracked the timeline in apple pie order. You see, Walter had not yet landed on a perfect franchise name. His lunch counter names varied greatly in the first ten years. Walter would test out another one of his schemes in 1930, after securing a sure-deal lease. The Pickwick Bus Depot at 1414 Douglas in downtown Omaha was in need of a lunch counter for its brand-new, soon-to-be highly populated terminal. (In "The Curse of the Clover Leaf Club" I will tell about the Pickwick Greyhound Lines freshly introduced to Omaha in June 1930.) Harkert would settle on the "Harkert's Hole-in-a-Role Hamburger Shop." I believe they meant a "roll," but that might be presumptuous on my part. From my understanding of the concept, the short-order cook would make a rounded indentation in a toasted bun or roll, pile the loose meat in the center, and call it good. Quite a gimmick. The ad revealed chili, tamales, soup, and pie were also in demand. Word on the street indicated this bus

Harkert's Hole-in-a-Role Hamburger Shop

Is the Swellest Little Place in Town to Eat

Listen to This:

We make a new style hamburger that is absolutely grease-less. It is loose and served in a toasted hole-in-a-role.

We make wonderful chili and tamales; our soup is the best you ever ate. The pies and pastries are very delicious. Our room is cool, clean and well ventilated. Come over tomorrow for breakfast, lunch or step in any evening.

We're Open Till 2 A. M.

Harkert's Hole-in-a-Role Hamburger Shop

Pickwick Bus Depot.   1414 Douglas St.

65. Harkert's Hole-in-a-Role Hamburger Shop, July 27, 1930. Other ads from this time would indicate local Robert's milk and cream was used as well as Coca-Cola products, Chokla malted milk, Graham's ice cream, W. L. Masterman coffee, and Central Market meats. This was the one and only occasion I could find the "Hole-in-a-Role Hamburger Shop" phrasing and advertising. Reprinted with permission from the *Omaha World-Herald*.

terminal diner did a steady business, staying open until 2:00 a.m. and up to the neck in hungry clientele.

MALES AT YOUR SERVICE

Although the early branding of the hole-in-a-role (and perhaps the unusual concept itself) would not pass the collective taste test, this great ad so simply illustrated the classic counter service of the 1930s diner, where clean, white-uniformed males stood at the ready. Diner employees were always male in those days. They wore all white, including a full apron or a white coat, often a bow tie and a crisp, white Garrison-type envelope cap atop their slickly cropped hair. If the lunch counter wasn't a one-man show, there may be one or two waiters in a small operation that stayed open 'round the clock. Years later the Harkert chain would include diners merely blocks from one another. Also note the inclusion of the new, modern female customers depicted in the illustration of Harkert's. Female customers began to frequent diners during this time. Booths would slowly be introduced, along with features such as attractive window treatments; open, welcoming doors; outdoor window boxes; and decorative touches. Wider restaurants were perceived to be more inviting to women, contrasted with the congestive counter and grill enterprise. Although women would spend money to dine at these small cafés, they would not have opportunity to gain employment therein until much later.

THE OMAHA ATHLETIC CLUB CONNECTION

The 1931 city directory logged only two Harkert's locations. The Harkert's at 1820 Dodge is no longer standing, but it is almost exactly where my friend's Bike Union / Mentoring Project is located in the fantastic *Jetsons*-like round bank building, originally designed by John Latenser & Sons in the 1960s. The second was the Pickwick Terminal, located at 1414 Douglas. That August a potential third new lunch counter was featured in the *World-Herald*'s "Highlights of Omaha Building during the Week"—"the building at 1718 Douglas Street is being remodeled into a lunchroom by W. E. Harkert. P. B. Puller is contractor." I believe this was one of those shifting addresses or simply a misprint, as I later followed the breadcrumbs to one of Omaha's most auspicious institutions.

The Omaha Athletic Club was once the ten-story social club of the upper crust, located at 1714 Douglas Street in downtown Omaha. Opened in 1918, John Latenser & Sons designed the mammoth members–only limestone building, with featured lounges, dining rooms, a ballroom, a bowling alley, billiards rooms, a rooftop garden, a two-story gymnasium, a nine-hole golf course in the basement, handball and squash courts, a swimming pool featuring women's-only hours, and rental quarters for members' out-of-town guests. There were about six rentable bays at street level for local businesses, and Harkert no doubt knew a good deal when he saw it. This was his big opportunity to introduce his delicious burgers to the in crowd. Harkert cleverly postponed his Athletic Club Harkert Stand opening until the night of the Ak-Sar-Ben Coronation Ball on October 9, 1931. The newly crowned King and Queen of Quivera "stopped by" for Mrs. Agnes Harkert's famous noodle soup. The very next day the wife of the new king, Mrs. George Brandeis, telephoned Mr. Harkert, thinking it might be fun to entertain fifteen out-of-town guests at his new hamburger place. Could he possibly close his Athletic Club location for the Brandeis private party? The publicity from this high-society soiree spread far and wide and put Harkert's on the map.

From all accounts the Athletic Club was the elite club of Omaha. Serving an all-white membership, the club was a central gathering spot for professionals, business and civic leaders, and at times visiting dignitaries. The Omaha Athletic Club was closed in 1970 and eventually torn down in 1992, as spectators braved February's temper to witness the stoic collapse. The vacant land was utilized as a parking lot until it became the site of the Roman L. Hruska Federal Courthouse.

THE DUNDEE LOCATION

In June 1932 Mr. Walter Harkert obtained a building permit for 4924 Dodge Street, where he had set intentions for "brick alterations to brick hamburger stand $300." After furtive exploration, I would deduce this move to the Dundee neighborhood was highly motivated by his success

66. Omaha Athletic Club at 1714 Douglas Street, April 26, 1945. Harkert's Holsum Hamburgers is shown on the corner. RICH THICK SOUPS. "Food for Thought and Good Coffee." FINE FOODS. Harkert House, Ross Florist, and Smith & Company were some of the companies at street level. The Fontenelle Hotel was located to the left. Although this photo was taken later, in 1945, it gives an idea of the Harkert look. From the KM3TV/ Bostwick-Frohardt Photograph Collection at the Durham Museum.

with the Omaha Athletic Club crowd. Turns out, Harkert was tiring of the simple lunch counter business and wanted to class it up a bit. Walter had his eye on the Dundee hotspot, but when he approached the owner about leasing the locale, Harkert was rudely educated, "People in Dundee won't eat hamburgers." Harkert informed the haughty owner, "People in Dundee are the same as people in South Omaha." The property owner later changed his tune and leased to Harkert—discovering that Dundee loved hamburgers. Soon after, Walt earned a new title and was informally crowned "the Omaha Hamburger King" by one local journalist. The Dundee location became Harkert's "Number One." He would number his locations from that point forward but was known to favor his Dundee diner. For whatever reason, Walter curiously stated after establishing Dundee that his "previous stands ceased to count."

A HARKERT'S DUNDEE MEMORY

Family friend Carolyn was so generous to share another glimpse of the Harkert House, this one from 1940s Dundee:

> The Harkert's in Dundee was on Dodge Street, next to the Dundee Theater. Our cousins lived on a farm far out in the country (at that time) on 144th and Dodge, and sometimes in the summer we would spend a few days with them. My aunt and uncle had friends who lived in the Dundee area, and I remember once they dropped the five of us off for a movie at the Dundee Theater while they spent the evening with their friends. They gave us money for hamburgers afterwards at the Harkert's next door, where they eventually picked us up. This was exciting for us since we were never out alone at that time of the night. I think perhaps because these Harkert locations were so far from our neighborhood in unfamiliar parts of Omaha, it made them more memorable.

A HUNCH

The 4924 Dodge address has since fallen off the books. Carolyn had remembered the Dundee Harkert's next to the Dundee Theater; a perusal

67. A 1938 view, looking east from Fiftieth and Dodge Streets in Dundee.
Included in the photo are Dundee Drug Company and the Dundee Theater.
From the William Wentworth Photograph Collection at the Durham Museum.

of Google Map pinpointed 4924 to Voila! Blooms and Decor, a great little boutique in the old Fenwick's soda shop location. Peculiarly, Voila!'s
actual address is 4922 Dodge. I estimated Voila!'s large parking lot was
unusual for 1932. That and the fact the Dark Horse Hair Salon and Spa,
the business to the west, is at 4950 Dodge led me to believe Harkerts
had once stood in that empty lot between the two buildings. It seems
to me that I had run across a photo of a filling station where the Dark
Horse now resides. Next to the Dark Horse Salon is the iconic Dundee
Theater, built in 1925. The old gal can rightfully claim to be the longest-
surviving neighborhood cinema in all of Omaha, at 4952 Dodge. I began
to wonder if Harkert's was in the bay that housed the Dundee Dell originally? The Dundee Dell claimed it was established in 1934. From my
digging I learned a series of hardware shops were initially based out of
4964 Dodge; eventually, William Herzoff migrated his Dundee Grocery
and Delicatessen on Fiftieth Street to the Dodge location in 1931, later
becoming a lounge. The Dundee Dell was officially renamed when the

Cohen family took ownership in 1940, bulking up their marketing of the bar as the hep place to be. 4964 Dodge would remain the beloved Dundee Dell home until its move to the heart of downtown Dundee on Underwood Avenue in 2000. So, unless all of these addresses have wandered and drifted—which, as any good detective will tell you, is not unheard of—I rest my belief that the Harkert House Dundee location was two doors to the east of the Dundee Theater. A month later I found the photographic proof.

THE CLEAN FOOD CALIBER

Aside from teaching the unnamed Dundee property owner a thing or two about the growing popularity of hamburgers, Harkert also learned a lesson from the man's harsh criticism, taking into account the stereotypes of sometimes-seedy diner food in those days. The more I studied up, I would become aware that during this time period, hamburger often contained "other ingredients" of a suspicious nature. Additionally, it was commonplace for people to become ill from restaurant food and certainly unclean diners, as there were not stringent regulations on food or the service industry. It wasn't until 1938 that the Food and Drug Administration was given the authority to issue food safety standards, previously an honor system. These benchmarks weren't truly imposed until the 1940s, 1950s, and 1960s. In gathering clues for this story, I found a wonderful collection of historic clippings (no doubt, a past librarian's 1950s hobbyhorse) housed at the reference desk of the W. Dale Clark Library. The short, prudent articles chronicled the history of dirty diners and frequent restaurant busts, due to not following FDA regulations, but most impressively, these fine specimens were cut by hand from the local newspapers, dates and data written in a beautiful cursive atop each compulsive clipping. I liked to imagine this librarian of the past as an Obsessive Sister of Sorts, slowly driven to neurosis by the persistent, systematic cataloging of unhygienic restaurant practices.

As for his own preoccupation, one might have thought Mr. Harkert a bit extreme, but no matter. Harkert wisely resolved to hire a testing laboratory to check his meat supply and prove the Harkert stands were above board to even the most skeptical and discriminating of tastes. One of his posted signs read: "Harkert's Holsum Hamburgers use only government inspected meats. Then to insure against the possibilities of any preservatives being added and further, to be certain of its freshness as well as it pureness, we have the Omaha Testing Laboratories call at our stands each and every day for a second and positive check. Avail yourself of this added protection. It is added value. The Harkert way is check and double check." Furthermore, the stands were thoroughly given the once-over every week. Hard to imagine, but a deep cleaning was a rarity in those days. In a curious, toxic execution, Walt related his precautionary exercise. Apparently, late at night they'd spray for flies and bugs. They'd turn all the lights out and let an electric sprayer run. Then they'd wipe the whole place down. This attention to self-imposed quality standards, safety, and cleanliness paid off in an uncertain time, and Harkert would continue to hang a daily certificate of purity in the door of every diner for many years to follow.

SPELLBOUND

Walter would eventually settle on a designation that had a bit more prominence than U Eat a Burger. No stranger to alliteration, the Harkert's Holsum Hamburgers epithet was formally entered by 1932. In this year Harkert also leased an office at 453 in the Brandeis Theatre Building. Restaurant locations were at 1820 Dodge, 4924 Dodge, and 1414 Douglas. A year later 1720 Douglas was added to the roster. March 4, 1933, marked the opening of Harkert's Fifteenth and Harney location, "Number Three," at 219 of the wonderful Sunderland Building. Harkert liked to point out that all of the banks were closed on that auspicious day, as Franklin Delano Roosevelt was inaugurated president. To no one in particular, this was also the same year Miss Ethel Waters first sang "Stormy Weather" at the Cotton Club nightclub, a torch favorite of mine.

October 6, 1933, marked the official grand opening of the Brandeis Theatre in downtown. This event had all the local eateries running ads of welcome and hoping to align with the theater. Brandeis Theatre was the new home for talking pictures and boasted of its RCA Victor photophone "high fidelity" sound system. As he was already leasing an office above, Harkert encouraged Brandeis patrons to treat themselves both "before and after the show" to his hamburger stand around the corner, at 1720 Douglas. During this time there was a national large-scale patriotic drive whereby many Omaha firms and small businesses signed the "NRA pledge," backing President Roosevelt's "progressive measures" in support of the National Recovery Administration. This formal pledge entitled business members to display the blue NRA eagle with the "We Do Our Part" motto in their business and in advertisements. Love the "check and double check" featured in Walter's diner ads, another infamous motto of his, or so I thought, this one signifying his volitional standards of cleanliness. I would learn later that *Check and Double Check* was a 1930 comedy film based on the top-rated *Amos 'n' Andy* radio show. This was actually a popular catchphrase from the show. An *Amos 'n' Andy* connection would materialize further on the meandering footpath.

In December 1933 Walter hired P. B. Buller as contractor to remodel yet another Harkert's Holsum Hamburger storefront at 101 South Sixteenth Street, essentially Sixteenth and Dodge. The Fox Universal Terrazzo & Tile Company laid the striking new flooring by March 1934. Observe the sign: "This is Ben Bernie Week. Two leaders: Holsum Hambergers [sic] and Blue Ribbon Beer."

THE ILER BUILDING

Walter's ever-expanding business was reaching new heights, at a period in the Great Depression when many restaurants were having a tough go of it. In December 1934 the business announced yet another formal opening, this time at the "modernly equipped shop" at Sixteenth and Jackson Streets. This location was moored soundly street level in the Iler Grand Hotel (featured in my "Cave under the Hill Hotel" query). This location would ensure constant foot traffic due to dependable boarders housed on the floors above. "A man's gotta eat," as Father of Miss Cassette always said. The four corners of Sixteenth and Jackson currently house the Union Plaza, the Greyhound Bus Station (or Trailways), and parking lots for the Magnolia Hotel and Omaha Fire Department station.

68. Fox Universal Terrazzo & Tile Company's new flooring in the Harkert's Holsum Hamburger diner at Sixteenth and Dodge Streets, 1934. From the KM3TV/Bostwick-Frohardt Photograph Collection at the Durham Museum.

A photograph from September 1937 exposed an attractive, mysterious corner with the proper striped corner awnings of the Riding Apparel Center. "The House of Good Habits" also peddled army officers' uniforms and accessories in addition to ladies' and men's riding breeches and jodhpurs. Furthermore, the Harkert House, Travelers Trunk Com-

69. The Iler Grand Annex Block in 1937, located on the northwest corner of Sixteenth and Jackson Streets. Various store signs read: RIDING APPAREL, HARKERT'S, and DIAMOND CIGAR STORE. From the KM3TV/ Bostwick-Frohardt Photograph Collection at the Durham Museum.

pany, United Rapid Shoe Repair Company (where a hat could be cleaned and blocked for only thirty-five cents), and the Diamond Cigar Store are shown in the photo. Yes, the Diamond Cigar Store of mythology—-where men offered beer, liquor, and the latest returns on all sporting events in Omaha's renowned bookie joint.

SWEET SMELL OF SUCCESS

Based on his triumph with the Iler Grand, Walt then set eyes on the corner of Eighteenth and Farnam. The handsome-looking Farnam Hotel Building must have made a good home for another Harkert's Holsum Hamburger counter. On January 12, 1935, another building permit was filed for a porcelain and steel hamburger stand for twenty-five hundred dollars.

Aside from naming his locations by number, these location nicknames were christened around this period:

214

70. A covetous interior view of the Harkert House at 1821 Farnam Street in 1935, street level of the Farnam Hotel Building. From the William Wentworth Photograph Collection at the Durham Museum.

Post Office Stand: Sixteenth and Dodge
Pickwick Stand: 1414 Douglas
Orpheum Stand: Fifteenth and Harney
Athletic Club Stand: 1720 Douglas
Dundee Stand: 4924 Dodge
Rome Stand: Sixteenth and Jackson Streets (for the Rome Hotel)
Farnam Stand: Nineteenth and Farnam Streets
2302 North Fifty-Fifth Street

April 12, 1936, announced a big move: "The Walter E. Harkert home at 2712 Martin Ave. has been sold to Dr. George H. Boetel, in a deal arranged by the Lippold Realty Co." The Martin address purportedly offered "air conditioning equipment," a modern water softening plant, and a recreation room. By August 1936 Schroeder Realty Company was wrapping up the finishing details of a new home at Fifty-Fifth and Grant, constructed to the specifications of one W. E. Harkert. Both the collaborative design between the new owner and the Schroeder group as well as the cultural significance of this move to the enviable Country Club neighborhood heralded a new era for the Harkert family. Harkert's Holsum Hamburgers was now generating a solid return and had become an Omaha staple. This afforded Walter and Mercedes new social opportunities, and my detective's sixth sense believed the move to 2302 North Fifty-Fifth in Country Club symbolized the new societal ingress. The U.S. Censuses throughout the following years showed another change: the family would employ a full-time servant.

Theodore Metcalfe had begun developing the Country Club neighborhood in the late 1920s, focused on creating a beautiful community environment, with tree-lined streets, decorative streetlights, and picturesque homes. The larger corner lot, at 2302 North Fifty-Fifth, crossed over by the curvilinear Grant Street, remains a gorgeous to-die-for property to this day. An eclectic mix of European period styles, I would wager it falls predominantly in the Tudor style. Its prominent chimney complete with glorious pots, solid masonry proudly announcing the front door, offsetting its informal patterned brickwork, steeply pitched roof, and that perfect spying window seen from the asymmetrical front gable handily won my adoration upon first viewing. The house at 2302 North Fifty-Fifth Street can also be found proudly listed in the *National Register of Historic Places Registration Form*, a 2004 report prepared by Lynn Meyer, Omaha Preservation administrator. According to Meyer's research, the George Schroeder business was rooted in real estate development and, along with Metcalfe, was responsible for the majority of original homes in the neighborhood. Early on, Schroeder did not use architects, although later he would employ John Hyde Jr. for seven homes, and Reinholdt Hennig, my architect crush, for one home. The record shows that the Schroeder Investment Company, most likely without the bearing of an architect, designed the Harkert home.

For those who want to bore in a bit more, I found this salacious description upon completion of 2302 North Fifty-Fifth Street from the *Omaha World-Herald*:

71. "Harkert Home Featured by a Porcelain Kitchen" claimed to be "the most complete home in Omaha," phrasing that delighted me, although I did not understand what that could possibly mean. But after poring over the description, it appeared there were a number of features unique to the new house at 2302 North Fifty-Fifth Street, especially considering the financial downturn of most of America in 1936. "One of the features is the kitchen, finished in white porcelain and stainless metal. The porcelain manufacturers say there is no other like it in a private home anywhere. Another is the smooth terrazzo floor in the amusement room in the basement. Both of these ideas were borrowed from the chain of restaurants operated by Mr. Harkert. The stainless kitchen sink is seven feet long. Marble steps, once in another building, lead to the basement from the first floor." I was quite impressed with the fortuitous repurposing of those marble steps and couldn't help but wonder what building they were from originally. Reprinted with permission from the *Omaha World-Herald*.

The house includes ten rooms, four and one half baths. One fireplace is in the basement, another in the living room and a third in the sitting room on the second floor. Downstairs walls are done white and the gum woodwork is stained a chestnut shade, with which carpets and drapes are in harmony. The living room is illuminated solely by sidelights. The main bathroom, orchid and tan, is finished in colored tiles with fixtures to match. The bedroom of

Dale, 12, is decorated in a transportation theme, that of Jane, 10, has a ceiling of stars. The house has a circulating water softener. All concealed piping is of copper. The insulation is accomplished with 4,400 square feet of four-inch rock wool. It is air-conditioned and has a gas furnace. To meet any possible future demand, extra heavy wiring is used in the electrical system. There are no unfinished places in the house. The garage is a foot wider and a foot longer than the average.

My oath, Sherlock! This sounded more than acceptable, in any decade.

THE OFFICE ARRIVES

Another telltale indicator of Harkert's new reach was the leasing of one of Omaha's historical gems, the Goodrich Building, erected in 1868. From an earlier investigation I knew this fine building had initially quartered the flagship C. S. Goodrich and Company. Wonderfully extant, this is one of Omaha's oldest buildings. The August 1936 quotation from the *World-Herald* revealed: "Harkert leased entire three-story building at 1415 Farnam for his ninth Omaha Harkert House. He plans to remodel the building for occupancy about October 1st. A recreation room for his employees will be on the second floor." The building permit went into the record the next day with a storefront facade cost of five hundred dollars. This location had previously accommodated the Comisar Club, famous for its steaks and seafood, "where Omaha dines and dances. From cocktail to dessert, 60 cents and up." As it turns out, this sixty-cent meal was a big thing in Omaha. Other popular downtown restaurants offering this sixty-cent complete meal concept, "from cocktail to dessert," were the Lido Café at Twenty-Fourth and Harney, the Ambassador Café at Twenty-Fifth and Farnam, the Virginia Café at 1413 Douglas, and the Chat 'n' Nibble at Nineteenth and Farnam. Unlike the simple Harkert House model, these local eateries were of a fancier strain, with a tablecloth and cloth napkins, serving up a steak dinner and multiple courses for under a buck.

72. Although years later, in 1940, this perfect photograph gives the feel of the
1415 Farnam Street location in those days. The personnel department sign
alludes to the popularity and high volume of Harkert café job applicants in
those days. Looking at the southeast corner of Fifteenth and Farnam Streets.
Notable buildings include the Harkert House, Daves Clothes, Drexel Shoes,
the Metropolitan Store, and Beaton Drugs in the Barker Building. From the
KM3TV/Bostwick-Frohardt Photograph Collection at the Durham Museum.

ALL IN THE FAMILY

According to the 1937 phone book, Walter's mother, Mrs. Agnes Harkert,
and sister Clara had moved to 311 South Thirty-First Street, Apartment 3,
after Clara became the official bookkeeper for the Harkert House chain.
No longer standing, this original building was in close proximity to the
midcentury modern National Indemnity Company, a personal favorite of
mine at Turner Boulevard and Harney. The Leo A. Daly–built insurance
office is one of our few 1950s buildings left standing, and thanks to the
NuStyle Development team, this structure was recently spared from the
wrecking ball. Todd and Mary Heistand's vision is to develop this solid

but stylish structure into one-bedroom apartments renamed NICO. Long before that, I approximate a mother and daughter Harkert's apartment house stood very near that Indemnity building. Oddly, there was no mention of father Peter, and I believed their move to Omaha was prompted by his death. Later I was surprised to learn from death records that Peter Harkert died in San Diego in 1940. Had the couple separated or divorced? I had thought that mother Agnes lived with the Walter Harkerts while on Martin Avenue, but this was the first time I had found her name listed in the phone books. Of interest to me, the Census records divulged Clara lived with family throughout her life, never married; I estimated her to have been forty-five years of age at the time of this relocation to Omaha. Clara was later named secretary-accountant of Harkert's, brother-in-law Arthur Schwentker was the director of personnel, and their mother, Agnes, continued to make the noodles for the soup, among other recipes. It truly was a family operation. Miss Clara had a big job to do when one considers that brother Walter operated nine hamburger stands. Can you imagine righting the errors on those nightly tallies? It sounds quite nightmarish. It should come as no surprise to anyone that Miss Cassette is not known for her numerical skills.

THE PICKWICK TURNS BURLINGTON

The approach of 1937 marked the beginning of the new Burlington Bus Depot at Fifteenth and Douglas Streets, formerly the Pickwick. Within a short period the new bus depot was seeing forty-two bus arrivals and departures scheduled daily, offering a new, covered loading corridor, and eight big travel buses. The most modern of appointments and furnishings were all under one roof, including a men's clothing and shoe store, tailoring services, shoeshine, barber and shaving, jeweler, and shower facilities for men and women. (Miss Cassette could not ignore the emphasis on the orchid-themed women's lounge. This was the third reference to the orchid hue in this time period, so it evidently was a trend.) The Harkert House was to be included in the new project for a cool eight thousand–dollar construction cost.

73. Burlington Trailways Bus Depot at Fifteenth and Douglas Streets, 1937.
Harkert House and Belmont Jewelry and Loan are also visible. From the
KM3TV/Bostwick-Frohardt Photograph Collection at the Durham Museum.

TO HAVE AND HAVE NOT

Omaha was filled to the brim with nightclubs in the year 1937. If dancing
was how many shook off the stresses of the day, Walter Harkert was in a
good position to enjoy the new booming entertainment; he had plenty
of money for nights on the town and loved to dance, having run the
dancehall back home. It was also the year that my grandparents met and
went steady, a year before their elopement out of town in 1938. I deduced
this was the time period the unseen Harkert had supposedly sent that
ill-prepared messenger to ask my young grandmother for a dance at the
nightclub. From his own words, Walter was known to be "first on the
dance floor and the last to leave." Harkert recounted, unruffled, "And
I danced every song in between." His passion for the new dance craze
elevated the head of the short-order chain to that of first-rate hoofer. I

could find no mention of Mercy sharing his interest in dancing or the nightclubs. This was Walter's lifelong love and prowess, which son Dale would also take up. Dale was rumored to be a fabulous dancer. At one point I even wondered if it was Dale who had asked for my dear grandmother's hand in dance, but their ages did not seem to jibe. Dale Harkert was only thirteen years old in 1937.

Drinking and dancing fun could be found every night at Dixon's downtown, South Omaha's Acme Hotel Bar, and the Wine & Dine Club, Brice's Open Air Gardens way out on 110 West Dodge Road, Benson's famous Krug Park, Cesar's New Country Club at Seventy-Fifth and Pacific, the Chermot Ballroom, the Skyline Lodge—apparently, "Nebraska's finest log cabin dinner club seventeen miles out of Dodge," the Chez Paree, and Lakeside Gardens by the airport, the McDonald Club on Forty-Second and L Streets, Peony Park's outdoor Royal Grove reopened to great success in that year, the Harvard Bar on South Twenty-Fourth, the Mug House and the Races Club by the Ak-Sar-Ben thoroughbred race track. This is but a fraction of the nightlife offerings in the 1930s. It is amazing to imagine that many of these hot spots provided a happy hour, a dinner menu, a full floor show including dancing girls or a bit of comedy, a local orchestra or a touring band, and then dancing all night. What has consistently surprised me is that as hard as people worked back then, they also stayed out late drinking and socializing. The marvels of everyday life, previous to the invention of socially crippling devices such as the television, smartphones, and the internet, astounded me. In late 1937 the Clover Leaf Club officially opened up under the Burlington Trailways Bus Depot at Fifteenth and Douglas, and Walter more than likely danced there also, as it was right under one of his hamburger stands.

ENTER THE ARCHITECT

Very early on I stumbled over the case of Henry A. Raapke. I cannot be sure when our Walter met the Nebraska-born architect, but there is evidence Raapke designed at least one Harkert restaurant in 1937. Henry Raapke would receive his training at Washington University in St. Louis, Missouri; Hamburg Trade and Technical School in Germany; and five additional years of formal education at the École des Beaux-Arts in Paris, France. Thomas Rogers Kimball, another favorite Omaha architect, later employed Raapke. After another study tour of Europe, Raapke would settle in Omaha, hanging his own shingle for the next thirty-eight years. The Nebraska State Historical Society uncloaked this mystery when I found the Harkert job listed among Raapke's historic projects. Although vague, Raapke's archives of letters and applications from this time period intimated the Harkert architectural plan was either a one-time design or a new look to be replicated throughout Walter's franchise. I like the latter. I do not have definitive proof of my inkling. I imagine 1937 marked the year of the invention of the Harkert House, both the name and its complementary branding, including the classic facade Omaha would come to know. Had Raapke designed this "little house" diner look, soon replicated block after block throughout Omaha? I wasn't sure, as some of Wentworth's photographic proof of the infamous checkered tiling predated the Raapke paperwork. With the blue shiny shingles, black-and-white porcelain tiled checkerboard walls, stainless steel fixtures all bolted into place, the welcoming terrazzo entrance, I was in love with the humble, clean implication. The large plate glass windows called to all passing by—revealing the dapperness; the scrubbed quartzite floor; the low everyman counter; the classic, heavy, white diner plates stacked in rows, awaiting a slice of Agnes's to-die-for pie. Like the Edward Hopper painting *Nighthawks* I've always longed to live within, the suggestion of Harkert House pulled at my sleeve. I wasn't the only one.

THE HARKERT HOUSE METHOD

The advertisements from 1937 boldly directed Harkert's Holsum Hamburgers in a new direction:

Now eleven Harkert Houses serving pure-clean food to Mr. and Mrs. Omaha and their children. Count them—

49th and Dodge
18th and Douglas

15th and Harney
16th and Dodge
16th and Jackson
19th and Farnam
17th and Farnam
15th and Farnam
25th and Farnam
15th and Douglas
24th and M

At the grand opening of the new Seventeenth and Farnam location, Walter reputedly brought a chair out to the sidewalk, as his mother wanted to watch the people line up and go in. Agnes Harkert exclaimed something to the effect of "Just look at all those wonderful people!" It was then that Walter came up with his most infamous slogan, "Through these doors pass the nicest people in the world—our customers," the catch-phrase later found promulgated at the stands and in his advertising alike.

According to records, the Harkert House at Sixteenth and Dodge was the fourth built stand. Using my flashlight, I examined the walls for clues. We knew this assessment, or count rather, was not true. I wondered if it was the fourth of the new Harkert House designs. It featured blue shingles and what is now remembered as the classic Harkert look. In the late 1930s seven restaurants encircled its downtown location at Sixteenth and Dodge. A bookstore and a barbershop stood next door, and across the street, on the north side of Dodge, were the Schmoeller & Mueller Piano Company, a couple of the other restaurants, the Ivanhoe Tavern and Meyer's News, and the Omaha Loan and Building Company, with its step-down barbershop.

THE RIGHT FOOD FOR THE RIGHT PRICE

A Harkert manager would commonly clock in for work at 5:00 a.m. Reportedly, 1422 Douglas would go through a full case of thirty dozen eggs and partially into another case a shift, frying up hamburger from nine ten-pound tubs. Hamburgers remained five cents, or one could

74. The Farnam Building at 1607–17 Farnam Street, July 23, 1939. Northrup
Jones Restaurant, a beloved Omaha institution, was stationed on the first
floor. Also at ground level of the Farnam Building: B&G Hosiery and Lingerie,
Mangel's, the "Milwaukee Road" Missouri Pacific Lines ticket office. On
the left is the First National Bank Building, and the Patterson Building is to
the west of the Farnam Building, housing Harkert House. This was Walter's
Seventeenth and Farnam stand, where Agnes infamously sat out front. The
Patterson Building was demolished and the (very uncomfortable) Farnam
Plaza building at 1625 Farnam was built in its place in 1973. From the KM3TV/
Bostwick-Frohardt Photograph Collection at the Durham Museum.

get a "three-in-one Large Hamburger" for ten cents. I am not sure what that meant. People apparently bought the singles by the dozen. In 1937 Harkert House offered frankfurters, pork loin, and cheese sandwiches for ten cents. The cheese 'n' ham and bacon 'n' tomato sandwiches each went for fifteen cents. Classic breakfast diner fare such at bacon and eggs were offered for pennies, but toast, mysteriously, was five cents extra. Agnes Harkert's homemade pies were second to none, ranked in popularity: her apple pie was an easy first-placer, cherry pie second, coconut cream a tidy third, and somewhere down the line, her delicious peach pie.

PRESIDENT OF THE HARKERT BEAN SOUP CLUB

The diners' Mulligan stew, the chili, the chicken noodle soup, and bean soup each went for fifteen cents a bowl. The Harkert bean soup was something to be reckoned with. Father of Miss Cassette evidently was not the only fan. Eugene Eppley, the late hotel tycoon and self-proclaimed "President of the Harkert Bean Soup Club," would reveal years later that even after talking Mr. Harkert out of the recipe, his hotel cooks could not match the original. Eppley's upscale 1915 Hotel Fontenelle at 1806 Douglas was once the crowning jewel of Omaha society. It was Gene Eppley who made the Hotel Fontenelle his flagship as well as his home, in a nationwide twenty-two-hotel conglomerate. It is interesting to think that Eppley had tried to replicate and serve the infamous Harkert bean soup in his fleet of hotels. The hospitality magnate passed away in his Fontenelle penthouse in 1958; the majestic hotel was later demolished, in 1983.

THE BUCK'S BOOTERIE POINTER

Earl K. Buck, well-known owner and president of the Buck's Booterie chain, surprisingly acquired an interest in the Harkert Houses in May 1938. Buck had opened his enterprise at 1503 Farnam Street in 1929, street level of the newly completed, seven-story Barker Building. At that juncture this opening was Buck's twenty-first and largest shoe store in his chain. In fact, he was the first tenant to move into the new Barker

75. Buck's Booterie terrazzo entryway "rug" at 1505 Farnam
Street, now home to the Omaha Lounge. One of those migrating
addresses, but the solid clues remain. Photo by author.

Building. The Buck operation would grow in many directions. His Farnam
storefront entrance persists in announcing the former glory days, by way
of the unremitting, historic entryway. Flanked between gorgeous display
windows, proudly preserved in terrazzo: BUCK'S BOOTERIE. These terrazzo
and tiled Old Omaha entryways were a high school obsession of mine.
The Barker floors above housed a variety of offices. Buck's flagship had
a long reign by downtown Omaha standards, holding court until 1992.
Considered a wealthy, conservative businessman, Earl K. Buck gave a
substantial amount of capital to the Harkert company, in turn becoming the vice president of Harkert Houses. Walter Harkert promoted this
union to "enable us to speed up our expansion program." At the time,
Harkert denied Buck would take an active part in the direction of the
day-to-day business strategy.

Fellow sleuths, I will admit I became suspicious of this business prop-
osition. All of this stratagem may have been very commonplace in the
thirties with entrepreneurial types, or even now for all I know, but I won-

dered why Walter schemed to expand a supposedly successful business with eleven locations during the Depression and why borrow money at that? At the risk of sounding like a Panicky Penelope, I was apprehensive. I puzzled over the prospects of getting a business loan during the Depression. Another detective more versed in Depression era banking could better make sense of these quandaries. Without doubt, Walter was an ideas person. That much was spelled out, and I know from an early life proximity to this churning mind-set, this type of fellow is generally very exciting to be around—always plotting their next big project. I had made some assumptions that were potentially typecasting of a man I had never met. Walter was charismatic, an attention seeker, a braggart at times, gumptious, a gambler. Was I wrong to infer these characteristics? I rationalized that those characteristics might coincide with the pioneering spirit inherent to the American dream, and what did I know about growing an enterprise? If you've got a good thing, why not spread it around, I justified.

MYSTERY EXPANSION

Later on the trail I would hear tell that there were Harkert Houses in Omaha, Council Bluffs, Des Moines, Sioux City, Lincoln, and Denver. Oddly, Walter made no public mention of this Denver location that I could discover. I would read the Harkert's chain of burger stands had eleven links, no twelve . . . wait, was it thirteen? . . . no, make it twenty-one. Every clue read differently. However many, Harkert was known to personally supervise all of the managers by dropping in on them once a month—meaning Walter cooked, waited on customers, washed windows, and mopped the floors. No job was beneath him; Walter was hands on. His intensive training was nicknamed "Harkert University" by his employees. Was the Earl Buck loan in the late 1930s the instrumental capital needed for expansion into other cities?

THE STRANGE CLUE OF *AMOS 'N' ANDY*

A marketing vaunt released an odd bit of 1939 Omaha gossip. The Hamburger King, Walter Harkert, let the press know he had evidently wired

76. The Douglas Block on the southeast corner of Sixteenth and Dodge Streets, December 1936. Harkert's Diner is on the corner, and Kinney's Shoes Store is to the right of it. The negative is damaged but hauntingly beautiful nonetheless. From the KM3TV/Bostwick-Frohardt Photograph Collection at the Durham Museum.

the famous *Amos 'n' Andy* team, "offering to supply a chain of hamburger stands if they would locate their proposed private world's fair in Omaha." This bluster revealed many things, although none are exactly clear. The first takeaway was that in a clever humblebrag Harkert manner, Walter was signaling to Omaha he was looking out for Omaha's best interest and that, as a man of means, he was able to offer up a full chain of hamburger stands to get what he wanted for his town. Was this the financial reality of the situation? Probably not, but it certainly sounded good to the average man.

Amos 'n' Andy was an American radio show set in Harlem featuring two African American characters, although written, created, and voiced by two white actors, Gosden and Correll. The two successfully played

Amos Jones and Andrew Hogg Brown, in the blackface minstrel tradition. The show rose to popularity among whites in 1928. The groundbreaking fifteen-minute nightly series featured over 170 male voice characterizations in its run; the newfangled episodic drama offered suspenseful cliffhanger endings. But to some the show was viewed as moronic, classist, crudely offensive, overt racial ventriloquism. The two would make a popular movie in 1930 called *Check and Double Check*, mentioned earlier in the Harkert print ad. The film highlighted Duke Ellington and his Cotton Club Band. I highly recommend Melvin Patrick Ely's well-documented investigation *The Adventures of Amos 'N' Andy: A Social History of an American Phenomenon*, for a deeper exploration of the show and its reaction by both white and black America. Bishop W. J. Walls of the African Methodist Episcopal Zion Church formally protested the radio show in 1930 and was later joined by the *Pittsburgh Courier*. By 1951 the show would be adapted for television, featuring black actors who were made to imitate the speech patterns of the purposefully idiotic Gosden and Correll characters, meeting even more controversy with the NAACP. These were the first dark-skinned actors seen in a sitcom series. The television show was off the air by 1953, having sparked even more controversy than the radio show.

The second revelation of Harkert's big talk was the bit about the proposed private World's Fair in Omaha. Gosden and Correll had famously been highlighted in the Chicago's World Fair of 1933 by way of the Sky Ride bearing their name. The Sky Ride was the fair ride to behold as visitors were promised a twenty-three story, cable-suspended rocket car ride of a lifetime across a lagoon to an observation platform held up by two sixty-four-story towers. The pair had dedicated the Sky Ride; names on the rocket cars were coined from characters on their show. Now did Gosden and Correll have a hand in the creation of this ride, trade the idea around to various World Fairs, or potentially suggest their own "private world's fair"? I cannot be sure of this, but we do know that Harkert was keen on the idea, whatever it was. Omaha had hosted its own Trans-Mississippi and International Exposition back in 1898, an astounding visual feat, built almost entirely of plaster of Paris.

THE REGULAR JOES OF 1940 AMERICA

The realities of 1940 America were that about only one in five citizens owned a car. Fifteen percent attended college, 60 percent went without central heating in their home, one in seven homes had a telephone, one-fourth of families did not have refrigeration or an icebox, and more than half of all farm homes were still lit by kerosene lamps. The Sears, Roebuck and Company "Big Book Catalogue," also known as the "Nation's Wish Book," only began offering a vacuum cleaner and a toaster model after power lines connected their faithful customers to the 1940s grid. Omaha, like many other large industrial cities, was made up of a great variety of nationalities. The Federal Writers' Project, whose work was compiled from 1935 through 1939, revealed these different ethnic and racial groups had long been arranged into small settlements throughout the city. These enclaves would continue into the 1940s.

SOCIAL STATURE IN THE 1940S

I stood at the end of a row of books, then paused to look right and left. Is it strange to assume, at times, that I have disappeared into the past? I found myself right where I started, admittedly a few months later. During this period of the 1940s the Harkerts were not quite café society, from what I could deduce, but I did find infrequent association and some telltale markers of upward mobility. Walter was mentioned faithfully in local papers as an outspoken businessman; he made his strong opinion clear in editorials regarding civic and city planning. Likewise, reporters seemingly sought him out as a bold, entertaining source. Curiously, Mercedes was not mentioned at all. No boards, no teas, no ladies' lunches, no art committees, no planning or hosting of society soirees gathered in her name. Does that mean it did not happen? This business of studying a life through black-and-white record really does inhibit a sleuth—especially when women during this time did not receive much press unless they were conspicuously well situated. No stone was unturned in my pursuit of Mercy. I wondered how involved she was in the family business, always out of public view on account of the grueling office hours and the extensive orders of raw hamburger meat from local sources. Or perhaps Mrs. Harkert simply had no gregarious blueblood ambition. Maybe she was contented staying behind the scenes? Son Dale Harkert would receive more publicity through his different school events, including election as president of the camera club and excellence in math, theater, and tennis. He was a 1943 graduate of Benson High School, near the family's Country Club neighborhood. But it was daughter Jane who would enjoy the best of good press from polite society throughout her lifetime. Jane was pleasingly featured in acting and dancing performances as a little girl and in her teen years was covered extensively for her fetching involvement in social events and parties of the beau monde. She easily gained access to the prestigious all-girls Brownell Hall. Quite literally, Jane was always at the correct luncheon at the right time. Could it be that Jane's entrance and recognition in the smart set was Mercedes's undivided focus?

Walter and Mercedes's vacations and social entanglements were not as much whispered of until December 1940, when they would spend the winter holiday in Florida and have an "indefinite visit" in Fort Lauderdale. When Mr. Emmett J. Bleger, ex-manager of the Paxton Hotel, moved to the Jung Hotel in New Orleans, his visiting guests for the Mardi Gras of the early 1940s were the Harkerts, alongside the Kunold, Simon, Brun, and Jacobsen families. Fort Lauderdale soon became winter headquarters for the Harkerts. By late 1941 the Harkerts were mentioned helping to plan a "Dutch Treat Party" at the Happy Hollow Club, of which they had recently become members. This breathtaking club at 1701 South 105th Street was opened in 1924 and remains one of the leading thresholds of the beautiful people of Omaha. In those years Walter furthermore found entrance to the Scottish Rite, Shriners, Masonic Lodge, Nebraska Restaurant Association, American Legion, and the Elks. His bases were covered, so to speak. The proprietor of the well-known Harkert Houses would often serve his food at the various clubs' special meetings, "which in itself assured good attendance," according to an old American Legion year-end summary. This certain tip secured that Walter had been an American military service member, a clue I had not yet solidified. Walter's love of dancing continued as well as a flirtation with poker and burgeoning immersion into the world of golf, no doubt helped along by his association with the Happy Hollow Club.

From my dilettante smokescreen under the imaginary rounded canopy of an old downtown Omaha hotel, I continued to spy on Harkert's Depression-proof diner. How would it fare in the oncoming World War II years? Would its staff and clientele change? There would be many invigorating shifts to the Harkert Houses, which we will sift through later, but some things stayed refreshingly the same. For example, in 1940 a hungry fella could still breakfast on bacon, eggs, toast, and a cup o' joe for only a quarter.

THE 1940S DINER STYLE

Stylistically speaking, the American diner would experience changes. The simple kitchen sterility of the 1920s and 1930s, almost medical in feel, would undergo a streamlining and, in some cases, an art moderne period. The classic diner picture in the years before the war and continuing into the 1950s incorporated Formica countertops. The American Cyanamid Company had developed a melamine thermosetting resin, an easy-to-apply plastic laminate resistant to heat, abrasion, and moisture. As important as its function, the decorative Formica was offered in a fantastic, wide assortment of colors. Outstanding tile work, often in two colors in conjunction with porcelain panels and miles of stainless steel trim, gave a crisp but modern look. Inexpensive, quick lunch spots had just begun using the economical fluorescent lights, the bane of interior designers and patrons across America, but from photos I scoured, it would appear that the plain white globes descended from functional chains, and art deco style lighting continued to illuminate most quick spots, leftovers from the previous decades. Stainless steel backbars folded into art moderne shapes as proudly displayed, large metal Osterizer blenders, reflective silver towers of coffee urns, and commercial-grade meatcutters completed the resplendent scene. Even more glorious neon signs, with their catchy insider mottos, would join the ranks of the hep diner. Miss Cassette will proclaim from atop the Woodman of the World,

"There can never be enough neon!" It was no coincidence that Edward Hopper's endlessly mysterious *Nighthawks* was introduced in 1942, his ode to the iconic all-night American eatery.

Here we are in the depths of the investigation, and I tell you I was starving, starving, starving with all of this diner talk. We will forge on, after a moment of self-revelation, I promise. There are times that I miss Cecil's Café at 4971 Dodge Street, and all of the other diners I have known, with such a pining I feel like I could cry. I thank the stars above for Harold's Koffee House, one of the last authentic diners in town. It just feels like home. Psst . . . Harold Halstead of Harold's fame was a Harkert employee at one time. There. Now I promise we will move on with steadfast resolve and magnifying glasses in hand.

CHANGING FOOD COSTS

Simultaneously, the rise in wartime food costs worried local restaurant owners. The Food Rationing Program was set into motion in 1942. Rationing, which deeply changed the American way of life, was introduced by the federal government as a way to control supply and demand of the new shortages in limited food commodity. The long-standing rule of thumb in the restaurant business, the 100 percent markup on food, had helped cover the rent, the staff, shrinkage, utilities, leaving a 6 percent profit, but the newly increased costs of food were making it difficult to ask their patrons to pay the markup. The complaints of the butter pats' thinness and cost of a glass of milk "shook the building," according to local proprietors. In order to keep a pat of butter down to a penny, local restaurant owners had taken to practically shaving a slim slice of chip-thin butter, after having tried the two-cent pat on the angry market. It didn't go over well. Milk prices rose from five to seven cents a glass. Substituting and paring down portions seemed to be the only relief. The famous steak dinners that hotels and swanky restaurants were once known for, a staple in the thirties, now had to trim all of the "starters." Instead of soup, salad, and cocktail, patrons were only offered soup. Pie servings were diminished in order to continue selling at a dime a slice. L. R. Beatty, operator of the Henshaw Cafeteria, commented on how few single women went out for lunch in those days. Office employees also began carrying their lunches to work rather than eating out. "Things are worse now than they were in 1921, when prices mounted even higher." The war was having an effect, apart from prices. Families that used to dine out two or three times a week, especially those with sons who were called to military service, began staying home. "In these troubled times, they seem to want the security that being in their own home implies." Harkert stated the rising costs had affected his burger business, with patrons leaving when they saw the prices listed above the counter. He said they "usually came back a few days later when they found the upward trend was common" at all the restaurants in town. Harkert House offered the "Harkert's Club Breakfast" for twenty cents, complete with choice of fruits or fruit juices, buttered toast, and coffee with "pure cream." I found the same breakfast offered at twenty-five cents in most large cities across the country. Harkert maintained ten locations at that time.

DISGRUNTLED STAFF

Mr. Harkert would say decades later that the secret to good business was to hire good managers, which he paid a salary and commission. The managers, he assured, "worked very long hours but made a good living." Unfortunately, it would seem that not all Harkert employees were afforded a living wage. Harkert House employees, who had been working ten-hour days, seven days a week, went on strike on March 10, 1942. The organized employees were asking for ten-hour days, at a six-day workweek. The employees met with Walter in an effort to settle the strike, ultimately causing the closing of seven of the Harkert locations. Employees were seeking Sundays off, along with a compensatory five-cent increase in wages. Between eighty and ninety employees went on strike; 75 percent of them were married. The all-male staff had been making twenty to thirty cents an hour plus commission and five dollars weekly, from which their meals were deducted. Net wages averaged around one hundred dollars a month. Just a skeletal staff was left on duty at three locations, made up mainly of managers. Des Moines and

Sioux City, Iowa, locations were not involved in the strike. For context it wasn't until 1938 that Congress passed the Fair Labor Standards Act, which limited the workweek to forty-four hours. The forty-hour work-week would arrive in 1940, when the act was amended. It is important to note Omaha jobs were scarce enough that Walter had over two thousand applications on file at his Goodrich Building office, and he was, with-out question, able to fill any opening at any time. I am sure this simple reality was made plain from time to time to keep the crew in order. Two days later an agreement was reached between Walter, Arthur, and the employees. The Harkert employees were granted a day off each week without reduction in pay. Six days a week, a sixty-hour workweek, paid on a weekly basis. The countermen bought it. Soon after, the hamburger prices rose to cover the costs.

HIGH-CLASS LUNCHROOMS AND
A FEMALE WORKFORCE

Right after the employee strike and the rise in burger costs, a new mar-keting campaign began, which I took as a cue of things to come. Ads announced Harkert Houses were now operating "high class lunch rooms." There was also new phrasing, shedding light on the collective wartime attitude. "Do you want somewhere you are paid as you learn, where the depressions of the past years have not affected employees?" I figured this renaming and morale booster aided in explaining the hike in costs, but there was another indication.

For the very first time, in May 1942 Harkert began encouraging women to apply at his diners. Up to that point the lunch counters had employed only men and boys. This was a nationwide first, as one-third of the female population was called to work, particularly into industry after American manpower was lost to the war. "The Grit and the Will to Do It" motto inspired American women and the diminishing number of male civil-ians in the years to follow. According to Gutman's *American Diner: Then and Now*, a 1941 New Jersey diner owner was the forerunner in the hir-ing of women for his counter. By September 1942 Walter had employed more than sixty-five "girls," many with no experience. He proposed the "possibility" of developing them into Harkert managers in the future. I couldn't help but wonder what these girls were paid in comparison to Harkert's striking countermen. I've got it from a good source that women were paid very little during the war effort but were appraised to work much harder and more efficiently than anticipated. Furthermore, the female-served diner environment was discovered to be a more pleasant experience, and this newfound comfort level encouraged other women as consistent patrons. I could only assume profits were increased for one Walter Harkert. Of course, this was no goggle-eyed news to Miss Cassette. I determinedly cocked my fedora to one side.

ONGOING WAR AND THE BUD WILLIAMSEN CLUE

A riveting piece penned by Harkert in December 1942 shed light:

> When our boys return to their former places in the Harkert Organization (which we pray will be soon) their jobs will be waiting for them and the women who have so splendidly carried out their duties that they too will have a steady position with our organization to be made possible through an incomparable expansion program now being planned and to be put into operation when Victory has been won. No doubt you will soon see some Harkert Houses being managed by women trained within our organization to comply with the nation's food rationing regulations, our supplies of meats, sugar, coffee and other products have been reduced. We shall appreciate it if you understand why we are not always able to serve just what you want and in the quantity you may wish. Food will help win the war. By sharing food with your neighbor, everyone should get an equal share.

This article featured photos of all seven locations, with accompanying photos of managers and female employees. Bud Williamsen was the featured manager of 1422 Douglas Street, and in case you don't recognize this name, I'd like you to squirrel away this lead, as he will play into our canvassing of the area much later.

POSTWAR YEARS

The surrender of Japan was announced on August 15, 1945, and formally signed on September 2, 1945, bringing World War II to a close. That November, Walter broadcast that "six boys" had returned to their Harkert House jobs after service overseas. In time the war rationing would end, food prices would fall, people would go out in droves, and the demand for new diners would be high throughout the country as life took on a new color. But it didn't happen overnight. Of note, a melancholic memory from Omahan Bill LeMar was telling of the year shortly after the war. At the time, Mr. LeMar was winding down four years of exhaustive service in World War II, including combat duty in Europe. The war had been over for several months, "but meat was apparently still in rather short supply," LeMar reported. It wasn't really until 1946–47 that many rationed goods would be returned to the American market. "This snippet of a girl behind the counter at Harkert's said, 'We can sell only one hamburger to a customer. It's our policy.'" LeMar claimed the girl looked at the returned veteran coldly, and then ignoring his uniform and denying the current state of affairs, she flatly questioned, "Don't you know there's a war on?"

THE HAPPY HOLLOW CLUB CONNECTION

Walter Harkert's association with the Happy Hollow Club picked up in the following years. His natural leadership abilities and charismatic personality easily won him a position on the Happy Hollow Board of Directors. By 1947 Walt was elected president and habitually played eighteen holes a day. (A revealing annotation: Years later Walter would break his hip and was told by his physician he would never play golf again. He compromised to nine holes, just three times a week.) Later that May, Walter would inform the elite members of a new plan to refinance their organization after a pending lawsuit threatened sale of the club in order to pay out the $210,000 the club owed. The Happy Hollow Holding Company was formed and capitalized at $100,000 under Harkert, newfound president of both the club and company.

77. Farnam Street between Eighteenth and Nineteenth Streets, 1947. Businesses
include Payne and Sons Realtors and the Wellington and Farnam Hotels
on the south side. A Harkert's Diner occupies the corner at Nineteenth
Street. Also shown is the Dixon's Café, complete with a top hat; the City
Club Beer on the Bowl; the Hotel Wellington Key Klub; Harry's Café; L.
C. Smith & Corona Typewriters, Inc.; and Travers Furs. From the KM3TV/
Bostwick-Frohardt Photograph Collection at the Durham Museum.

SECRET NOTES

Months later the Harkert Union Bus Terminal Corporation was capitalized at twenty thousand dollars, filed by incorporators Walter Harkert, Earl K. Buck, R. B. Devor, and E. H. Fitzgerald. I could not figure
out why the foursome was bound under the Union Bus Terminal title.
Revealed later, Buck and Harkert would each introduce an ally to form
a quartern. R. B. Devor was brought in as a partner, and from my med-
dling I uncovered he was both a neighbor of Walt, living in the Country
Club district, as well as vice president and general manager of all the
Buck's Booterie stores. E. H. Fitzgerald was president of the Brother-

hood of Railway and Steamship Clerks, Freight-Handlers, Express and Station Employees. Fitzgerald later became commissioner for the U.S. labor mediation and conciliation board. But it was Fitzgerald's 1940s appointment to the Omaha Restaurant Association board and his affiliation with Walter Harkert that solved the impending mystery. File this away for later—simply put: Devor was Buck's appointee, and Fitzgerald was Harkert's ally.

WHITES ONLY

An *Omaha Star* article from 1948 titled "Violated Civil Rights Bill" drew my attention while I was scouring for news. My interests piqued, I had not found mention of blacks employed by the Harkert Company, although I had no way of surveying everyone the company hired. The article made plain that charges were filed against Frank Clay, manager of the Harkert House location at the "Greyhound Bus Depot at 18th and Farnam," for refusing to serve African Americans in his café. Frank Clay was a longtime Harkert manager, had been moved from counter to counter within the chain, and as of 1942 had opened the depot located near Sixteenth and Jackson. I had attributed the Greyhound depot reference to the Union Bus Depot. According to the *Star*, Mr. Marvin Kellogg and four others entered the Harkert House in the afternoon of March 31, 1948, and were refused in-house service. Mr. Clay told the group "he would not serve them in the café because they were Negroes, however, if they wanted to take the food out, he might serve them." Kellogg and his party refused this arrangement. Clay did not appear for his April 2 hearing; instead, his lawyer requested a continuance. City prosecutor Paxton and attorneys Adams and Howard resisted the continuance, attempting to sway Judge Palmer. Attorney Adams argued that the Harkert House event was objectionable "in view of the fact that Interstate passengers and others were denied their constitutional rights, in addition to the Harkert's organization directly violating the Nebraska Civil Rights statute." The judge granted the continuance. The reporter further wrote: "The matter of the refusal at the Harkert's restaurant to serve Negro patrons at the Union Bus Depot is a matter that has created wide spread interest among Omaha citizens. The Negro Ministerial Alliance, NAACP, Negro Elks, and Negro Shriners have all pledged support in the fight to see that the Nebraska Civil Rights statute will be made affective." Surprisingly, I could find no other mention of this issue or any others with Harkert House in the *Omaha Star* or the *World-Herald*.

It is doubtful that this was an isolated incident of racial discrimination or that Frank Clay, alone, upheld this stance. Was this Harkert House policy? I could find nothing about the company's code of practice in the *World-Herald* or the previous *Bee-News* but assumed that openly prejudiced convention or any variety of racial news even made the mainstream papers in those days. Of note, I did observe numerous classified ads from this time period and earlier specifying employment for "white woman" or "whites only." From the decades of daily Harkert House ads surveyed, I did not find Harkert distinguished employment of a certain race. However, a common, passive practice from that day permitted that if a person of color or anyone else displeasing applied at a Caucasian-owned business, their application was filed squarely in the trash. I wanted to know more about how Africans Americans were treated in Caucasian-owned establishments, which sent me on a long journey. During this time I found a fascinating book called *Black Print with a White Carnation: Mildred Brown and the* Omaha Star *Newspaper, 1938–1989*, by Amy Helene Forss, in which I received a few more details on the Harkert House incident. Forss's well-researched book covered the years of Mildred Brown's ownership of the *Star* and touched upon this particular event. Apparently, Brown's daughter, Ruth Harris, married Marvin Kellogg. Decades later, in a 2008 interview with Kellogg Sr., he reflected that African American Mildred Brown, African American Margaret Wright (Brown's dressmaker), and Caucasian Jean Waite, along with two other white women from the DePorres Club, had accompanied Kellogg to test the racial policy of the Harkert Café.

The DePorres Club was an early civil rights movement organization, having formed in 1947 by a group of Creighton University students, a self-described interracial group with a foundation in intercultural fellowship. Their goal was to improve interracial relations at the Creighton campus, later addressing issues of racism in Omaha as a whole. I tracked them to May 1948, when they began receiving more coverage in the press. Their good works included serving the poor through their fund-raising efforts, painting local homes, as well as bringing awareness to the systemic racist tactics of Reed's Ice Cream, the Coca-Cola bottling plant, Hotel Fontenelle, Paxton Hotel, and Municipal Airport, among other businesses, specifically for not hiring black workers. Through picketing, educating, boycotts, and sit-ins, the group of locals, with the support of Mildred Brown's *Omaha Star*, would go on to change the hiring practices of white-owned businesses in Omaha and even build a community center for low-income families called the Omaha DePorres Center. Interestingly enough, Ms. Brown's Omaha Star building was under the watchful protection of the Black Panthers during the mid- to late 1960s riots, viewed as a North Omaha institution. Through reading Lois Mark Stalvey's *The Education of a WASP*, an eye-opening account of racism in Omaha (suggested by a *My Omaha Obsession* reader), I learned much more about the vanguard DePorres group.

Culture of Racism

American restaurants during this period were, as a whole, segregated. It was commonplace for a black man to be ignored if he entered a white diner and hoped for a meal at the counter, even in the northern states. It was commonplace for a nonwhite but specifically African American to be asked to leave an establishment, or they might be told there was a seat for them in the kitchen, out of view. In the rare case that an order was taken, the food might never arrive, or the bill might be doubled or, worse, the food might be tampered with. In the case of the Harkert House incident, the customers were told their food would be a to-go order. By design many state civil rights laws did not cover eating facilities, including railcar diner segregation, leaving a great deal of leeway for restaurant owners; therefore, white trade–only eateries were the norm. Black-owned teashops, restaurants, and bars held and served their own. Although there is a long, history of African Americans organizing sit-ins and occupation-style protest of Caucasian-owned eateries from the late

1800s through the 1960s, little could be done to alter discrimination policy nationwide within a court of law in which the deck was stacked against minorities. There are many who would argue that the American justice system maintains an inherent institutional racism to this day. It wasn't until the Civil Rights Act of 1964 that confronting discrimination in restaurants and the behaviors of white proprietors began to gain traction.

I never rooted out the details I had hoped to find in the DePorres–Harkert House issue. Around this time I did discover the owners of the B&M Grill were fined for violating the state Civil Rights Law in 1948, after refusing to serve African American would-be customers. By 1960 there were numerous student boycotts of segregated restaurants in Omaha, and on a larger scale Greyhound Bus depots across the nation were the focus of organized boycotts. Restaurant segregation in Omaha was heavily covered in the press after 1962. Regarding our Harkert House investigation, just a few months later, Frank Clay had leased a new site in Atlantic, Iowa, with the intention to open an all-steel drive-in café. I cannot be sure how long discrimination policies were in practice at the Harkert Houses, and I am skeptical that they wholly left town with Clay. I have no proof of this speculation.

THE HARKERT CHILDREN

The Omaha directory revealed Dale and Jane Harkert listed as "students," once again residing in their parent's lovely Country Club home on Fifty-Fifth. Dale would graduate with a business degree from the University of Omaha, after returning from army air corps service. Jane had attended the Christian College at Columbia, Missouri, and graduated from the University of Omaha. In 1948 Jane was selected as an Ak-Sar-Ben Coronation Ball Princess; inclusion in the Coronation Ball was quite the feather in one's cap, as the ball committee honored civic-minded, board-serving, wealthy Omahans. This was an auspicious nod to the Harkerts, signifying their secured social standing. By 1951 twenty-six-year-old Dale was a salesman with Home Realty (his various career moves throughout his life were all related to real estate) and would marry Vernelle Lydia Swanson. The impending nuptials of Jane Carey

Harkert and Richard James Seitner in 1952 alerted me that Walter and Mercedes had taken a surprising new residence. "A small family wedding at the home of Mr. and Mrs. Harkert's Hackberry home," or something to that effect. By the way, the reception was held at my favorite Schimmel family enterprise—the Blackstone Hotel Ballroom, high above the West Farnam district.

THE 710 HACKBERRY FILE

June 1951 marked the first entry of 710 Hackberry Road in the annals of Omaha lore. When 710 was nearly reaching completion, it was featured as one of "Ted Hicks Picks," touted as a stone and frame, red-and-white Fairacres rambler. I couldn't help but wonder what happened to the Country Club home. The clues would fall together later, but I felt satisfied at the time to learn that the Dr. John Aita family moved into the Harkerts' County Club home around 1951. Dr. Aita was a well-respected, local neurologist and psychiatrist, and his family enjoyed the home for many decades to follow. The Harkerts' lovely new home at 710 Hackberry Road maintains its dignified quarters on a northward stretch of stable ranches. The beautiful, tree-lined Hackberry Road runs parallel to Sixty-Eighth, with a boulevard shared between the two, and is just north of meandering Underwood Avenue. Walter, Mercedes, and Jane were presumably the first owners of this midcentury modern gem, although strangely, the Harkert ranch was up for sale the very next summer, in 1952.

THE 1950S DINER

If the driving diner aesthetic of the 1920s and 1930s was tasty, inexpensive food, served in a sanitary, almost medical lab environment, the 1950s diner escorted in a bigger, confident, curvy model. What was once a counter-focused stand with a simple menu had become a diner-restaurant, as they were being coined in 1955. The entertainment factor of highly animated short-order cooks were now enclosed in a back kitchen instead of counter side, front and center stage for all to watch. Newly popular pastel color schemes were unleashed on the soothing-minded dining public, lit from above with the continuing popularity of

78. The charming classic Harkert's look at 101 South Sixteenth Street, 1935.
From the William Wentworth Photograph Collection at the Durham Museum.

fluorescent tubes and fantastic neon signs in bulging windows. There
were so many Johnny-come-lately diners and differing diner aesthetics
during the fifties that I've got to think the Harkert House felt the threat
of competition, although there is proof that more families ate out regularly and more money was being spent consistently. The new modern
shapes expressed through huge metal framing and glass expanses of the
California-influenced shopping malls, drive-ins, diners, and coffee shops
combined with new facades of stone and tile, not to mention those incredible signs using ropes and ropes of neon and all of those crazy fun fonts,
had introduced a futuristic dream experience to the American public. I
do not have photographic evidence that the Harkert Houses' Depression
era aesthetic evolved with the 1950s, and I'm not saying they needed to,
but one thing was for certain: there was an obvious dearth of newspaper
articles featuring Harkert House beautifying updates, whereas previously
even a checkered curtain change had garnered attention. It would appear

for the first time that Harkert had an attitude of leave well enough alone. This would all make sense much later.

Gutman's *American Diner* cited the arrival of such exaggerated titles as "World's Largest Diner" during this period. His suspicion was that the American family was bigger. From my perspective teenagers, for the first time, were out in droves, spending their own money or their pa's, and snacking on burgers and fries was an integral element of modern socialization. Were Omaha teens interested in hanging out at Harkert Houses? There were hints the chain began hiring more and more "boys and girls," signifying perhaps a cultural reflection of youthful staff and patrons. As Ben Peacock, manager of the Harkert House Farnam Street location, just west of the Paxton Hotel, put it: "I've worked there for fifteen years and cook 450 burgers daily. Ninety-nine percent of folks want hamburgers with a pickle." He made mention of another newcomer to the diner—the 1950s cheeseburger. Am I the only one who wondered when the cheeseburger would enter the picture?

THE TROUBLE WITH BUCK

March 1950 declared the beginning of a legal quarrel of what I now know to be the beginning of the end. Dispute over control of the Harkert Houses restaurant chain was taken into district court when Earl Buck brought a startling action against Walter and Mercedes Harkert. I should say, it was surprising to me but not, perhaps, for those involved. As you will remember, the Harkert chain, short on funds, was lent forty thousand dollars by the Buck Stores in 1938. Buck apparently was unwilling to make an additional investment unless he was given an equal voice in the affairs of the Harkert House. An agreement was struck that Harkert sold Buck Stores 40 percent of Harkert stock. Buck then canceled the $40,000 note, which the Harkert chain owed his company. And here is where it got complicated: Mr. Buck then paid $53,625 to Walter and Mercedes. Of the $53,625, $44,750 went to pay outstanding debts on the Harkert Houses, and the remainder went to Mr. Harkert individually. The chain was largely profitable until more problems between the two men arose in 1949. Harkert again felt the expansion bug and pushed

Buck for the funds to supply his insatiable hamburger stand habit. Buck was against this growth in an unsteady financial climate. As strange as it sounds, in January 1950 Harkert had an election (holding ownership and the majority of the stock), whereby he named three directors to bring the number of voting members to five. Mr. Buck's court petition asked for an injunction to prevent Harkert from violating the terms of their initial agreement. Mr. Buck was demanding another new election.

THE FINE DETAILS ANNOTATION

In my pursuit to make clear this entire mug of murk, I would have to dig further into court records. And truth be told, there were some scraps of minutia I knew the most obsessive of you might want to know. Prior to 1937 Walter was the sole owner of his chain of burger joints. I felt guilty for my previous suspicions, but Harkert's finances were indeed impaired, and his business practices were such that his only options were to seek financial aid from sources other than banking institutions. It was revealed later in court that Harkert's salvage plan was to sell his diner fixtures and equipment to a potential investor for cash, entering into an agreement to buy the fixtures and equipment back at the end of five years for a higher price. Several of these sale and repurchase arrangements were written up between various people in Omaha before Harkert became acquainted with Earl Buck. Prior to the incorporation of the Harkert restaurants, Mr. Buck had agreed to four of these sale and repurchase contracts. It was Harkert who had divined the plan between he and Buck in 1937. The incorporation of 293 Harkert shares was filed under the new name, Harkert Houses. The business was calculated to have a net worth of $47,504.38. Documents revealed that Harkert was indebted to numerous entities in the sum of $44,750 and to Mr. Buck for an additional $55,650 total of their four contracts. These were the ins and outs of Buck's proposal to have a percentage of ownership. Now the original four-man board of Harkert, Buck, Devor, and Fitzgerald was its own tidy entanglement. Over time Harkert's ally, Fitzgerald, left the fold, and Mercy Harkert was made vice president. The four members of the new board then consisted of Walter and Mercedes Harkert, Earl

Buck, and Rodney B. Devor. By 1950 Harkert had taken matters into his own hands and evidently wanted an additional boost to his voting power.

THE BATTLE

Harkert came out swinging and snubbed Buck's allegations. In a statement smack of marketing genius, Mr. Harkert declared, "We believe sole leather and food won't mix," an obvious jab to Buck's Booterie fame. In his further signed statement, Harkert elaborated for the courts and anyone with a sense of humor, "There would be no controversy if E. K. Buck Retail Stores and Mr. Buck would continue to confine their activities to the merchandising of shoes." He claimed Buck's petition was a gross exaggeration and misunderstanding on the part of a shoe retailer. Harkert did acknowledge that Buck "was our financial guardian in the past" but stated Harkert Houses was loaned only twelve thousand dollars for the return of eighteen thousand dollars. Harkert went on to say that Buck then capitalized on this situation to get minority stock ownership. Harkert saw the current expansion plan in keeping with the success and progress of the food chain he had developed. He acknowledged that the E. K. Buck firm had certain rights but not the right to steer the ship. While awaiting a formal court date, Walter Harkert assured his hungry patrons "that no leather will be served in Harkert Houses." Now that was good press.

Judge Patton found the 1938 contract between Buck and Harkert valid and binding in the fall of 1951. It was further alleged that Harkert knowingly named three directors, bringing the number to five and essentially giving him control of the chain. The judge ruled the company must return to a four-man board, of whom two could be named by Mr. Buck. In the following months Omaha followed along the court drama, as there were countersuits. It was later estimated that Buck had invested ninety (other accounts said one hundred) thousand dollars in the Harkert chain. I found it interesting that the Harkert Houses had been a nine hundred thousand–dollar a year business, distinguished for its eleven-year run "in excellent financial condition." Modestly, according to an inflation calculator, Harkert's was an eight million–dollar business by today's standards.

248

79. Harkert's in the Farnam Hotel Building at 1821 Farnam, 1935. From the
William Wentworth Photograph Collection at the Durham Museum.

Net earnings of the corporation had steadily and rapidly decreased
since January 16, 1950. Furthering the nail in the coffin, in July 1953, Mr.
Buck filed "one of the fattest briefs in the recent State Supreme Court
history" in his legal battle with Walter and Mercedes Harkert. Divided
into three volumes, the 429-page brief was prepared by the Omaha law
firm of Kennedy, Holland, De Lacy and Svoboda. It answered the Harkerts' appeal to the supreme court. In a real blow the Nebraska Supreme
Court dismissed Buck's $100,000 damage suit in January 1954. One month
later both sides in the suit petitioned the supreme court for a rehearing.
The Douglas County district court later allowed Mr. Buck $33,612 on the
claim, but the supreme court reversed the judgment, stating Mr. Buck
was not entitled to damages. The court ruled that all stockholders, not
just Buck, had suffered damages.

The end of the fireworks display had come to a dismal denouement
when the state supreme court declined to rehear the legal battle between

Harkert and Buck. The court upheld the original contract under which Buck Retail Stores could name two of the directors of Harkert Houses, and the court overruled the district court decision, which had given a $33,612 judgment to Earl K. Buck against Walter and Mercedes Harkert. Both sides were dissatisfied. That was the absolute last word that I heard of the four-year court case.

TIDES CHANGE

Was it any doubt that after the long, drawn-out, expensive court case, a gradual retirement must have sounded good to the Harkerts? Many would give up on the ten-cent hamburger at Harkert's Holsum for a Swanson TV dinner and Johnny Carson on Channel 6, or at least that was Walter Harkert's hindsight summation. My intuition was that Harkert House felt the cold shadow of the Golden Arches and other brands of fast food in the coming years. In retrospect there would be a number of explanations, all conjecture. The few remaining managers supposed that all of the businesses leaving downtown for West Omaha had not helped the diner chain. Additionally, most businesses had moved employees to half-hour lunches, and that put a real dent in the daily diner foot traffic. The older clientele who had always patronized Harkert House had resided in the downtown hotels, and sadly, those were being closed or demolished in the following decades. The young people working in the corporate arena, still mostly housed downtown, were not interested in the Harkert House model. I discovered this was a pattern across the country as people turned their backs on the presumed "old-fashioned" diners. Everyone would have egg on their faces when these vintage diners resurged again to become extremely popular in the 1980s and 1990s, gaining their rightful place of honor. But back to 1954, when the stainless steel glimmer was fading: Walter had yet another good idea, considering what was to come. Rather than shuttering the doors for good, leaving his customers high and dry and long-standing employees without work, Walter Harkert offered to sell each restaurant to those who ran them. His plan was to set up his various diner managers in business by asking "nothing down, payment out of profits."

THE GRADUAL RETIREMENT

Through the 1950s I could track that different Harkert Houses were later identified by their various owners' names—for example, "Myron's Harkert House" was on Fifteenth and Harney. Myron Crabb was a manager-turned-owner for many successful years at that location, until his suicide in 1964. "Wilson's Harkert House" was at Nineteenth and Farnam, and 1720 Douglas became "Mauk Harkert House." "The Clay Harkert House" was located at 2505 Farnam. (Did that denote Frank Clay was still in the fold?) By early 1955 the Greyhound Post Houses franchise, which operated restaurants in most of the Greyhound depots, purchased the Harkert House at the Union Bus Terminal at Eighteenth and Farnam. The Harkert House had held its ground at this location for the past seven years. Harkert would maintain his eight other locations. As of 1955, there was still a good selection of Harkert Houses to be found in Omaha.

BUD AND ANN WILLIAMSEN

In 1955 Bud and Ann Williamsen were ready to buy the forty-two-stool diner they had managed at Sixteenth and Dodge from the Harkert's chain, for which Bud had pegged away since 1940. A review of your notes will show that Bud had previously been located at the 1422 Douglas Street stand, after coming aboard from the Hotel Fontenelle. The Williamsens entered into a three-year buying contract with Walter, the end result securing the couple their own diner. The Sixteenth and Dodge Harkert House, located on the southeast corner, was moored in a magnificent rock of a building. Originally, I had been led to believe that the Kirkendall Boot Company had built and given the name to the massive redbrick Kirkendall Building at 109 South Sixteenth Street. After all, it was one of the city's last vestiges of 1887, proudly one of the city's oldest extant buildings. Stylistically, the Kirkendall was a cohort to the old City Hall, the original downtown Post Office, and the Bee Building, all constructed in the Richardsonian Romanesque style. A deep burrowing into that exact corner in 1887 revealed that Allen's Fish Market, and all of its shrimp, Potomac shad, and haddock were once housed therein. A decade later the Edison Kinetoscope Company was renting out space in the large building, quickly becoming the marvel of the town. This early motion picture peephole allowed individuals to view film shorts, the forerunner to a film projector. The Kirkendall, Jones & Company had its own corner of the world at Eleventh and Harney. It really wasn't until 1949 that the Kirkendall Boot Company pulled up stakes and moved to the Douglas Block, as the Sixteenth and Dodge buildings were called long ago. I could not trace the name Kirkendall Building to that location until the move in the late forties. For its contribution to the corner, the popular Harkert House continued to uphold its classic, white enamel facade, no doubt reminding everyone downtown of the good ol' days, when there was a Harkert's on every corner. The Williamsens were doing all they'd ever done, given themselves day in and day out to this little diner, their second home. Many old-timers still living in multitude of inexpensive downtown Omaha apartments called the Williamsens' diner their home as well.

THE BIG COMBO

Unless I am mistaken, this might have been a time of quiet downsizing for the Harkerts. Walter and Mercedes took up quarters at the modest 4910 Capitol Avenue Apartments, Number 104, in Dundee and later a 1957 Dillon's Fairacres ranch at 835 Parkwood Lane. Walter's mother and sister continued to live downtown, at 311 South Thirty-First Street, until Agnes Lemke Harkert's death in September 1957, at the age of eighty-nine. From the *Council Bluffs Nonpareil* I learned that Walt's mother had been a resident of Council Bluffs for fifteen years before moving to Omaha in 1935. From all accounts Mother Agnes Harkert's early investment and die-hard belief in her son were a huge key to the Harkert House success; after all, it was her secret recipes that had earned a special place in the hearts of the Omaha public. Her wedges of pie, washed down with a cheap cup o' jitter juice, were the home-baked magic. And who could forget those soups? Sister Clara would strike out alone, making a new home at 604 South Twenty-Second Street. The following January, Harkert's favorite location, Number One, at 4924 Dodge in Dundee, fastened its doors for the final time; the little hamburger stand was soon leveled for a parking lot. Walter Harkert was honored at a special Sheraton-Fontenelle Hotel dinner in June 1958 by the Omaha Restaurant Association. More than two hundred gathered in company with Hilltop House's Raymond Matson, to give Harkert his due. Matson was then director of the Restaurant Association, a position that Walter had held over the years.

DEATH OF MERCY HARKERT

In March 1963 Mrs. Mercedes Harkert died at the age of seventy-one in the couple's lovely ranch at 835 Parkwood Lane. She was buried in the family plot at Forest Lawn Cemetery at 7909 Mormon Bridge Road. Mysterious and beautiful, Forest Lawn Cemetery, now called Forest Lawn Memorial Park, was established in 1885, known to be the burial place of Omaha's second generation of leadership—Prospect Hill, being the original cemetery of Omaha's powerful pioneers. Whether it is the rolling hills, the glorious 1913 chapel designed by John McDonald (I dream of engagement photos with Mr. Cassette beneath the chapel, in the old crematorium), or the dark, hidden areas of wondrous trees, the 349 acres of Forest Lawn are some of the favorite wanderings one could ever hope to encounter in Omaha. Sadly, like many women of her day, Mrs. Harkert rather eluded our detective's gaze. Mercy, we hardly knew ye. Walter put their ranch home on the market one month later.

WALTER'S RETIREMENT HOME

As a widower, Walter later relocated to 3000 Farnam Street, Apartment 6R, the infamous Twin Towers, just east of Turner Park. In 1963 the old Western Motor Car Company building–turned–Sears and Roebuck Department Store had been gutted and reconfigured into posh living quarters, with additional floors added after the department store business had earlier packed it up and headed for the new Crossroads Shopping Center on Seventy-Second and Dodge Streets. It wasn't until the later 1960s that a north building was constructed on the former Sears and Roebuck parking lot, becoming a false twin. I thought it quite modern of Walter to set his sights on this happening new abode. For those

80. Mr. Harkert in front of his last house, 1971. Reprinted
with permission from the *Omaha World-Herald*.

no longer in Omaha, the north tower has since been demolished. In the
early 1980s the Twin Towers apartments were reorganized into condos
and became notorious for Larry King and affiliates' parties in the Franklin Credit Union scandal. During his years at the Twin Towers, Harkert continued to enjoy the Happy Hollow Club and is said to have gone
dancing frequently with the mysterious widow of a long acquaintance.

Dale and Vernelle "Nell" Harkert had also moved to the gorgeous 2101
Mullen Drive, a sprawling ranch affair built in 1963 for the Harkerts.
A covetous home, nestled in the hidden Rockbrook area, the Harkerts
were but a hop and skip away from the Happy Hollow Club. The socially
active couple had four children and later grandchildren. This fine home
has remained in the Harkert family ever since.

On September 8, 1967, Sister Clara Harkert died, at age seventy-five.
In October 1967 Walter sold the last of his short-order chain at Fifteenth
and Harney to Ernest Payne. In 1972 Walter Harkert, Omaha's true Burger

254

King, died at the age of eighty-two. His last known address was in the Twin Towers apartments. The man best known for his tasty, quick lunch stands was buried at Forest Lawn Cemetery. Decades later, in 1999, the lovely society darling, daughter Jane Harkert Seitner Muchemore, passed away at the age of seventy-two. Her husbands Richard Seitner and Richard Muchemore preceded her in death. I was touched when I began this investigation to find that son Dale Wallace Harkert had died recently, in May 2017, and was preceded in death by his beloved wife, Nell Swanson Harkert.

HILTON HOTEL AND SIXTEENTH STREET

Although Walt was no longer burdened with the fate of his Harkert lunch counters, being the faithfully obsessed detectives that we are, our inquiry would continue on in his absence. Bud and Ann Williamsen most certainly felt the threat in 1968, when businessmen, city council members, and the Omaha mayor decided that the Sixteenth Street business corridor would best be blocked off for the new Hilton Hotel, plotted just north of the Dodge Street intersection. Executive city planners viewed the prestigious Hilton Hotel as the watershed strategy to the revitalization of downtown Omaha. Many citizens would come to see the Hilton Hotel scheme serve to create a significant barrier between largely Caucasian-owned downtown businesses and the African American community of North Omaha, at an inflection point after the race riots of the 1960s. In the spring of 1968 the construction site of the new Hilton Hotel locked eyes with local favorites Fred's Bar and Horwich Jewelry, the Union Pacific headquarters, and the Omaha World-Herald looking on. Bud Williamsen's Good Food was essentially sealed off at its north end by the new Hilton Hotel and First National Bank complex. Williamsen would later make the comment that Sixteenth Street had become unrecognizable.

HARKERT'S ORPHEUM STAND

A few years later the end would come to the diner Walter had once coined the Orpheum Stand. "The Orpheum Theatre's remodeling destroyed the very last Harkert House," was Bud Williamsen's summation of the Fifteenth and Harney site end days. After a messy exploration I was able to locate the specifics. In February 1974 Ernest Payne did indeed throw in the towel but under interesting circumstances. The little white-enameled steel diner, the last carrying the Harkert House name, was reportedly doing well financially, but the lease had run out. The diner was in the northeast corner of the Orpheum Theatre building, and the space was apparently needed for a new portion of the theater restoration. Payne was under legal contract, having previously negotiated back in 1967 when purchasing from Walt, to not move the Harkert House name elsewhere. Father of Miss Cassette was an adman back in those days and worked for a firm in the vicinity. He and colleagues often enjoyed the Orpheum Stand location for a quick lunch, no doubt indulging in that revered split pea soup. For the record, at the time of its unwelcome demise, Harkert House still offered a hamburger and a cup of coffee for seventy cents.

EIGHTY-SIXED

While Bud and Ann Williamsen kept the light on long enough to out-live all of the neighboring shops and restaurants—including the Union National Bank, a Greek restaurant, the Canopy Lounge, and a Salvation Army store—the couple prevailed, their authentic diner souls intact. In the late summer of 1980 the last of the last of Omaha's Harkert institu-tions latched its doors. Bud Williamsen's Good Food would say goodbye to hamburgers and hash browns as the couple, married thirty-nine years, retired, rumored to be headed to New Orleans. Coincidentally, the Hil-ton Hotel became a Red Lion Hotel that year.

By 1988 a condemnation hearing was set as city officials lined up to demolish the storied Kirkendall Building. The supposed pigeons and homeless transients, falling bricks and crumbling walls, were cited as reasons for the hearing. The Richardsonian Romanesque building was legally considered two buildings and owned by two different parties, both given chance to argue why the structure should not be condemned and torn down. The city housing manager stated the owners would have to make substantial renovations to the building. Interestingly, the owners were well-known Omahans—the Slosberg Company, a longtime family real estate firm, and Neely Kountze, member of the Omaha pioneer family mentioned earlier in our investigation. The one hundred–year–old building had been in the Kountze family since the 1960s.

Miserably, the building carried no historical landmark designation and was torn down in May 1989 without a hitch, after Mr. Kountze sold his portion to Slosburg. In a sad nod to Harkert, the first floor was noted at demolition for its esteemed tile work and the "white front that marked the restaurants of the now defunct hamburger chain." The razed lot was utilized for surface parking until 2002, when workers began removing the old building foundation buried beneath in order to create First National Bank's sculpture park. I couldn't help but wonder what treasures were enclosed there.

SHADOW OF A DOUBT

I had come to the end of my Harkert's Holsum Hamburgers inquest, and as with the quietus of all of my mysteries, I only longed for more. I was left to press my nose against the quickly fogging, imaginary windowpane of the "nothing-fancy, but exceptionally good food" Harkert diner, craning to get a half-look through the steamy mist. I could make out the white-capped countermen and hear the distinct crashing of thick, porcelain plates. Of course, I wouldn't be Miss Cassette if there weren't a bit of melancholy stirring for a time period and life I had never lived. Along the path I discovered a fantastic essay written in 1992 by a like-minded Omahan. I share it here because it is quite brilliant, and it somehow seems appropriate, like a eulogy to the once known Harkert Houses and downtown Omaha.

"Real Downtown Gone Forever"

Omaha, I hope somebody sheds a tear in remembrance of a lifestyle in downtown Omaha that will never be again. The last of the Harkert House restaurants, on a corner of 16th and Dodge Streets, along with the proud old building that housed it, was razed not long ago. Downtown Omaha used to be a wonderful place to shop and dine, and the Harkert Houses were the best, a delight to the eye and sense of smell. Then, suddenly, the powers-that-be caught wrecking ball fever, and most buildings more than 50 years old had to go. Nearly all the landmarks of that pleasant time are gone now, and in their place are smelly parking garages and ugly parking lots, where people grub for the almighty dollar. Talk of revitalizing the downtown area is ridiculous because there is no more downtown area. One by one, businesses have closed their doors and moved. Maybe we shouldn't live in the past too much but always be ready to embrace this thing called progress. Then again, if those sickly-looking Christmas decorations were a sign of progress, I'll take the good old days. —Joseph L. Narducci

CHAPTER 7

The Curse of the Clover Leaf Club

As I remember it, I was eating a hot fudge sundae with my grandmother at a local ice cream fountain. It was an odd little 1950s leftover, the kind of fountain that doesn't really exist anymore in these parts. My grandmother would park her Corvair behind the shop, and we would enter, like any of the regulars, through a creaky back screen door. We'd sit at the metal-edged counter on spinning stools (well, mine was spinning) or in a sturdy vinyl booth, which was sometimes sticky from the previous patrons. If the booth was freshly wiped down, it sometimes offered a top note of sweet, old milk mixed with bleach. The older couple who worked the counter still wore their outdated uniforms, a hairnet for the woman, a funny hat for the man. On this particular day we were in a booth, and my grandmother decided to let me in on one of her little secrets about that ice cream fountain—one that I will never forget.

She leaned in and told me the most colorful story, of which there must have been a lot of explaining to do on her part. My grandmother, apparently, had a very brief, wild period of frequenting a local speakeasy while in early high school. Her boyfriend at the time, not my grandfather, knew someone who knew someone, and the young couple were able to gain entrance into this forbidden club. And the shocker was that the speakeasy had been in the very block of businesses that this ice cream fountain was in. In memory it might have even been in that very ice cream shop. I've already told you I would never forget, and here I am having already forgotten that important fact. What I remember of the story was something of a special knock, a sliding peephole in the door (sometimes called a judas hole or judas window, from old detective novels), a password, followed by the teenage pair being shuffled down a very long hallway, only to walk out into a small but densely filled smoky room. Adults drinking and smoking to their collective hearts' content. The elephant's knees! She must have thought it felt very Big City. I have since estimated that this must have been about 1932. The bar inside was quite shallow, offering only the essentials in liquor, and likewise, only a few men worked there—most likely one bartender, a couple of henchmen, and one at the judas hole. It was dark and windowless, a room within rooms. Not much to look at, elbow room only, perhaps a sawdusted floor, complete with a slender bar, the sole purpose of serving that much in-demand alcohol. It was there that she learned to drink a Sloe Gin Fizz and took up smoking cigarettes. The complexity of the Prohibition era aside, I could not really understand, at my young age, what any of this meant.

We would talk about her very limited but memorable encounters with the speakeasy underworld as I got older. I asked even more questions as my understanding of the early 1930s grew. I assure you, her experiences were all very innocent, but she might have left out the necking parts. So the story goes, my grandmother's father, a well-known businessman in town, put a stop to these teenage escapades in no time flat. Seemingly, a number of his associates tipped him off. Of course, the injustice of it all made my teenage grandmother mad to no end, as these reputed esteemed colleagues had been indulging in the illegal drink and were no doubt "blottoed on hooch" themselves. I am sure it wasn't a very pleasant exchange between my headstrong grandmother and her unyielding father, and it wouldn't be the last.

I was reminded of this whole account very recently when I began reading *Omaha: A Guide to the City and Environs*. This incredible book, part of the American Guide Series, was written from 1935 through 1939 by members of the Federal Writers' Project of the Works Progress Administration. The books and brochures of this series initially gave useful employment to out-of-work American writers and researchers during a difficult time in U.S. history. But what developed was an amazing, ambitious project of large scale, in which writers, editors, fact-checkers, historical societies, librarians, journalists, postal workers, and field workers began to compile a portrait of America, town by town. Apparently, every larger city has a book of its own. The Omaha book is outstanding; a history collected, as told by field workers who walked block by block documenting the local buildings in what they called "tours."

It was in the reading of this at times funny document that I came across a very short vignette that both aroused my ever-operative curiosity and would later remind me of my grandmother's juice joint exploits. The words read: "The CLOVER LEAF CLUB, in the basement at 119 S. 15th St., was opened in 1932. A dine-and-dance grotto, it was for several years a famed resort of night-life in Omaha." I was hooked. And I may be getting ahead of myself, but I kid you not—someone long ago had written in faded pencil alongside that passage, the ∧ symbol and *Snooky*. That stylized script, that cunning little clue from long ago, sent me off and running. This is the story of my adventures in tracking the famous Clover Leaf Club and the secrets buried deep under an Omaha high-rise.

THE EARLY SEARCH FOR THE CLOVER
LEAF CLUB AND SOME DIVERSIONS

With my Federal Writers' book as a pointer, I began looking into the site of the Clover Leaf Club: 119 South Fifteenth Street. I quickly found that this address no longer existed but established that the club would have been on the northeast corner of Fifteenth and Douglas, midway between Dodge and Douglas. Douglas Street, which runs east and west, is one block south of Dodge. From M. B. Newton's book, *Anecdotes of Omaha*, I discovered Douglas Street was named in honor of Stephen A. Douglas, the "Little Giant" of Illinois, who as U.S. senator worked for the bill to authorize the building of the Union Pacific Railroad and ran for president in 1860, losing to Abraham Lincoln. Coincidentally, the Clover Leaf Club address is now the site of the Union Pacific Center, a full city block at 1400 Douglas Street. Within the center the UP also has its credit union, carrying a South Fifteenth Street address.

In my quest to trace the lay of the land at the time of the Clover Leaf, I looked to the one building that still endures in the area. Just northwest of what would have been the Clover Leaf is now the Residence Inn at 106 South Fifteenth Street. My whole life this was known as the Federal

81. Fifteenth Street at the Douglas crossroad, facing north, 2016. On the right is the current Union Pacific Center, which stretches from Dodge to Douglas and Fourteenth to Fifteenth Streets. To the west of the UP Center (left) is the Park One parking garage. A historic aerial view of the nearby plats, courtesy of the Douglas County GIS portal, shows the amazing transformation of the whole four-block area of downtown Omaha from 1941 to 2016. Photo by author.

Office Building or the Old Federal Building. It became a hotel just a few years ago. If you haven't been in this art deco hotel, go walk through the hospitality rooms on the main floor. Amazing bones, and the staff is all very welcoming.

Directly across Fifteenth Street from the current Union Pacific Center is the hideous but I suppose, grudgingly, needed Park One parking garage at 1516 Douglas. This was built in the early 1980s. I uncovered some essential clues that further established the time period and cultural environs of the neighboring Clover Leaf Club. The World Theater had proudly stood on the Park One site from 1922 until the mid-1930s, just one the many glorious theaters in downtown Omaha. This glazed terra-cotta marvel must have been such an impressive structure, boasting round arched windows and Corinthian columns. The center of the

82. Photo of the Old Federal Building when it was erected in 1934.
From the National Archives, RG 121-BS, box 56, folder H.

building and upper three floors was the theater, with ground-level shops surrounding it. What a knockout.

The theater had changed its name in 1935, to the Omaha Theater. They continued to show movies with some live performances. By 1978 it was closed and later demolished, in 1980. I was too young to have remembered this one, but I'd like to think I saw it when we would go to Bishop's Buffet on the next block over. These elaborate, massive blocks

83. The World Theater, later the Omaha Theater, at 1506 Douglas Street, 1923. Its signs read, "Cooled by Frosty Air." From the KM3TV/ Bostwick-Frohardt Photograph Collection at the Durham Museum.

gave me the impression that downtown Omaha had at one time been a place of sheer glory.

Soon after I found a fabulous photograph by Larry Ferguson, taken in 1978 or 1979 on the corner of Fifteenth and Douglas. His photo clearly depicted the last days of the forlorn Omaha Theater (although I've heard people fought to save it) and also showed the emptied ground-floor shops. I stumbled upon this in my library of Omaha books, this particular one an amazing collection called *Omaha and Council Bluffs: Yesterday & Today* by Kristine Gerber and Tom Kessler. In studying this photo, I unearthed what would have been the entrance to the Clover Leaf Club, although long gone by the late 1970s photograph. I could see from Ferguson's lens that the original building that housed 119 South Fifteenth appeared to be quite impressive. I was excited to learn more.

Side mystery: I must also mention that in surveying and salivating over this photo, I spied in the background the location of my dear friends' luncheonette. For those of you who had the pleasure of eating at Rob Gilmer and René Orduña's Dixie Quicks Luncheonette on Fifteenth and Dodge in the 1990s, recall the poor Frenzer Block demolished in 2001. In the early 2000s Dixie Quicks would dress up as the busy Magnolia Room at 1915 Leavenworth Street and later reach full plume at 157 West Broadway in Council Bluffs. RIP René and Dixie Quicks Luncheonette. There will never be another.

THE 1424 DOUGLAS CLUE

The *Yesterday & Today* book gave me an early piece of evidence that was much needed in this case. A tip-off to the old Rialto Theatre sent me tracking a new hint. The Rialto Theatre was one of the numerous, well-attended movie theaters in downtown Omaha. At 1424 Douglas Street, the Rialto was, in fact, right across Fifteenth Street from the World Theater. Much like the design of the World, the Rialto was a large movie house, with seating for twenty-five hundred. Can you envision those days? John Latenser & Sons designed the Rialto with plenty of room for an orchestra space, a full pipe organ, a fetching diagonal corner entrance with three high arches, a ribbon of storefronts along street level with an exterior of ivory and terra-cotta. This huge, stately building opened in 1918 and was quite a success.

By 1929 the Rialto Theatre suddenly closed (was it due to the Great Depression?) and was divided, in time, into additional retail shops. In June 1930 the Pickwick Greyhound Lines was unveiled just as an ever-growing mode of public transport gained popularity. By 1934 intercity bus lines carried almost as many passengers as the railroads. The hit film *It Happened One Night*, in which an heiress was featured for the first time traveling by Greyhound bus, is credited with making bus travel au courant. I would have to find the Pickwick Greyhound station in a photograph of 1930 to imagine the transformation. Surprisingly, the Pickwick terminal waiting room was the gorgeous former Rialto Theatre auditorium. The

84. The old Rialto Theatre on the northeast corner of Fifteenth and Douglas Streets, April 21, 1921. The Rialto Drug Store is to the left of the theater entrance, and the old Moon Theater, yet another theater on the strip, is to the right. From the KM3TV/Bostwick-Frohardt Photograph Collection at the Durham Museum.

theater's proscenium arch and grand chandelier remained intact. Can you imagine what Greyhound travelers thought as they entered Omaha through this glamorous passageway?

OBSCURED BEGINNINGS

The Clover Leaf Club, the famed resort of nightlife in downtown Omaha, was said to have opened in the basement of the Pickwick Greyhound Lines in 1932. By examining the 1932 Omaha City Directory, I could find no mention of the establishment, instead finding the basement environ listed as "vacant." Later I found 119 South Fifteenth Street address within the 1932 *Omaha World-Herald* as home to Jack Guthrie Cigars. The sleuth in me became both suspicious and intrigued by this cigar store, considering the time period in Omaha. I began to wonder about the "cigar store" link to, perhaps, illegal alcohol and gambling. Not to say that Jack Guthrie Cigars was not a fine, upstanding establishment. I would only find mention of it once.

Let's briefly review what was happening in this period. From 1920 to 1933 there was a nationwide constitutional ban on the production, importation, transportation, and sale of alcoholic beverages. Note consumption is not mentioned. In 1920, under pressure from the Progressives, moral groups, and Prohibition supporters, or "drys," the Eighteenth Amendment to the U.S. Constitution made the movement of liquor illegal. It is interesting to note that religious uses of wine were allowed. Additionally, federal law did not prohibit the private ownership and consumption of alcohol, but in many areas local laws were stricter. The Twenty-First Amendment, which repealed the Eighteenth Amendment, lifted the ban on production and sale of alcohol on December 5, 1933. There were some states that continued the ban. Omaha was not one of them. Omaha was known as a "wet" city, compared to "dry" Nebraska. By appearances Omaha only paid lip service to the Eighteenth Amendment, with hundreds upon hundreds of bars still in operation during this thirteen-year period.

Likewise, during Prohibition, Omaha's wide array of cigar stores were often operating bookie joints. The cigar store was the place to stop in and play cards or bet on a game, the horses, or a big fight—and everyone knew it. Placing bets and bookmaking operations through cigar stores and billiard parlors were a steady practice for a good number of Omahans.

So taking this bit of history into account, let us tiptoe further. My second encounter with the 119 South Fifteenth Street address was when I chanced upon a smart advertisement from January 22, 1932, for the Roxy Club: "Play billiards during the noon hour." The Roxy actually predated the Clover Leaf as Omaha's newest billiard room and coffee shop "under the Terminal Building." Located in the same address, the Roxy was a club beneath the Pickwick Greyhound Lines. Of interest, brave ladies were cordially invited to enjoy a free sundae on opening day. This was back when proper women would have to be specially solicited to enter

Here's Relief In Sultry August

I KNOW a place that is always cool . . . that is attractively and realistically decorated like a forest glen . . . where you are always sure of congenial company . , . . and where the sandwiches and drinks are delicious and inexpensive. THE CLOVER LEAF CLUB at 15th and Douglas invites you to drop in for luncheon the mid-afternoon pause that refreshes; dinner; or late evening. Music and entertainment after 8:30 p. m.

＊——＊

Winnie Wise will be pleased to shop for you.

85. "Here's Relief—The pause that refreshes!" A great clipping from 1933. Reprinted with permission from the *Omaha World-Herald*.

an establishment. It was a billiard room, after all. Men were lured with a free cigar upon opening day.

I was a bit uncertain of my chosen path to the Clover Leaf Club until I discovered a fantastic little commendation from July 23, 1933, in the *Omaha World-Herald*: "Here's Relief in Sultry August." I had finally secured a solid piece of evidence.

Upon reading that the Clover Leaf Club was "always cool" (read: air conditioning—this was a big deal in the early 1930s!) and "decorated like a forest glen," I needed to know more. My mind was spinning. A forest glen. I had never heard of anything so dreamy. I had already envisioned it to be a basement "dine-and-dance grotto" from the previous reading. This meant, to me, that amid the downtown Omaha buildings, the Clover Leaf Club was a chilled, cavern-like lounge bedecked with foliage and trees. I began to look into this club concept, and as it turns out, there were countless hep clubs throughout America enhancing their interiors with forest glen style during this period. Who knew? In these years there were also numerous underground clubs called "grottoes." These grottoes usually indicated a club was in a basement or an underground lower level. As you can imagine, this experience of descending stairs or use of an elevator lent itself to a natural, cave-like theme. I was reminded of visits to my grandmother's family friends in very early childhood. This couple, who coincidentally lived very close to the iconic Black Angel memorial statue of Fairview Cemetery, had built grotto-like walls and shelving in their basement—a vestige to the elderly couple's 1930s rumpus room days. The cement of the walls was chock-full of shells and stones from their worldly travels. I remember there being colorful lights in the shelving. Both haunting and mesmerizing, I can only compare it to seeing Mister C's Steakhouse's awe-inspiring decor for the first time. Or third visit.

By 1933 I found a clear listing for the Clover Leaf Club in the city directory. I also found a photograph that shows a daylight accident outside of the club. Signs on the storefront read TULLY'S THE HATTER and STETSON HATS. Tully's offered "the best" in men's furnishings. There appears to be a pharmacy on the left, and there . . . there it is: the fabulous Clover Leaf Club sign above the door.

MAKING HISTORY

The Clover Leaf Club was gaining notoriety as one of the swankiest spots in the city. By all accounts it was the cat's whiskers. The previously repressive drinking laws led to the development of these themed

86. An accident in 1933 brought the firemen and truck to the front of
Tully's on Fifteenth and Douglas Streets. Signs on the storefront read
TULLY'S THE HATTER and HEADQUARTERS FOR STETSON HATS. Photo of
west side of the bus terminal building. From the *Omaha World-Herald*'s
John Savage Collection at the Durham Museum Photo Archives.

nightclubs. Typically, they opened late as other dance clubs and "the
pictures," meaning movies, were letting out, attracting many owls off
the streets. Miss Cassette's favorite period for fashion is the 1930s and
1940s, and I love to daydream of what the guys and gals must have worn
to the Clover Leaf Club.

I located a great little article from the *Omaha World-Herald*, dated
November 9, 1933. In it Hubert McGhee, former waiter at the Clover
Leaf Club, sued Frank Hart and Frank Yousem, proprietors of the club,
for ten thousand dollars. McGhee charged that he had been "falsely
arrested." McGhee also alleged that his boss, Hart, had drawn a revolver
while questioning him and struck him. This was my first indication that
all was not well at the Clover Leaf Club.

87. Clover Leaf Club advertisement, 1935. Reprinted with
permission from the *Omaha World-Herald*.

Dancing was very popular in the 1930s. Not only were there scores of
Omaha venues offering dancing during the week, but many establishments operated most nights of the week. And there were a large number
of dancing classes advertised as well. At this time everyone was doing the
Tango, the Maxina, the Varsity Drag, the Stamp, Jazz Waltz, and Drag Tap.
There were also advertisements that mentioned the Rumba, Quickstep
Waltz, Slow Fox-trot, and old-style dances. And the music? Miss Cassette's absolute favorite time period for music. The Clover Leaf Club was
known for its bands and orchestras (Jack Pettis's Orchestra was a fifteen-
piece!) dancing, lunch and dinner (famous charcoal-broiled steaks and
fried spring chicken dinners), soft drinks, hard liquor, and apparently
gambling. I began to wonder if it had always been a gambling establishment, seeing as the cloverleaf is one symbol on a deck of cards. By 1935
the Clover Leaf Club was being raided frequently by officers looking to
comb through and ransack the premises.

I uncovered a fascinating article in the *Omaha World-Herald* from May
1935. There had been a recent Clover Leaf Club gambling raid in which
seven men were arrested. Three men were held for trial: Ike Levinson,
George "Dutch" Volker, and Fred Sellers, all living at the Loyal Hotel.

Five other men were dismissed for playing a "game of chance," with two others being fined five dollars each. Apparently, the raid followed after two patrons turned in the Clover Leaf for offering games of chance. The officers who conducted the raid reported: "When they entered, Volker ordered Sellers to press a signal light which warned players in the rear room. Levinson denied it was a signal light, saying it was meant to summon the porter. The back room was not for gambling but a dressing room for musicians, he said." Levinson denied there had ever been gambling in the Clover Leaf Club. The proprietors were listed as Ike Levinson, Dutch Volker, and one Charles Hutter.

I would find endless reports on Charles Hutter Sr. from the Omaha papers. As it was revealed to me, Charles Hutter had been a sheriff in Sarpy County in the teens, and by the turn of 1920 Prohibition, Hutter had joined in the lucrative bootlegging business. Big-time. He quickly became one of the three main bootlegging operators in these parts. Hutter would be arrested countless times in sting operations. He was accused of having ties to Al Capone and the Chicago syndicate. One of the many highlights of these never-ending series of articles was the story of Charles Hutter having been shot. Hutter reported being shot in a stickup in front of his home at 4429 South Eighteenth Street. I found through some digging that Lloyd Hutter, a clerk at Paxton and Gallagher, also lived there, as did his brother Marcus, a city fireman, and Tillie Hutter. Charles Hutter was shot in his leg a number of times on this particular night in 1931, leading to him to lose his left leg at the knee. His son, Charles Hutter Jr., also backed up his father's story, but the police were not buying it. They believed this shooting was an assassination attempt in a bootleggers' war. From what I could find, Charles Hutter Sr. and Dutch Volker became partners of some sort in these early years. By the way, the 4429 home was built in 1920, according to the County Assessor, and is still standing to this day. If those walls could talk . . . has never been a more appropriate euphemism. I think we might need to swing by and listen for the whispers.

In July 1935 the Clover Leaf Club's application for selling by the drink was approved. "More Omaha businesses given licenses to sell liquor—state liquor commission issued 26 retail package liquor licenses and

88. The last days of the Pickwick in 1936, when it became the Burlington
Trailways. The Clover Leaf Club sign is visible. United Cigar Store, the
Belmont Jewelry & Loan Company, a safe and lock gunsmith company,
a men's shoe store, Midwest Cleaners, the Pickwick Hamburger shop,
and Town Liquor Supply are featured down the strip. From the KM3TV/
Bostwick-Frohardt Photograph Collection at the Durham Museum.

approved 24 applications for sale by the drink," the *World-Herald* reported.
Dutch Volker, owner of the Clover Leaf, was again arrested in October
1935 for violating a city ordinance prohibiting the "serving of whiskey
after midnight." Apparently, when the patrolmen walked into the Clover Leaf, he was "razzed by Volker, who shouted 'no rookie cop is going
to prevent me from serving liquor to my friend.'" Can you imagine the
shout of cheers from his patrons? That rascal. I was getting swept away
by these characters.

And what characters these fellows must have been. Dutch Volker would
go on to argue that the club's city restaurant permit gave him the right to
operate exclusively as a restaurant after 2:00 a.m. Ads at the time high-

89. Detail of the subtle Clover Leaf Club entrance (magnified from
fig. 88). Miss Cassette just adores this neon sign wedged between the
awnings. I imagine a descending stairwell similar to King Fong Cafe's.
Also note the hinky fellow by the streetlamp on Douglas Street. You might
have missed him the first time, but he didn't miss you. From the KM3TV/
Bostwick-Frohardt Photograph Collection at the Durham Museum.

lighted "no cover charge" and dancing to "Bill McKenna's Orchestra every
noon and night. Your favorite drink at reduced price." Another name I
love was mentioned in an ad to "dance to Synco Hi-Hatters Orchestra."
In yet another colorful article from 1935, a presumably drunken patron
was locked in the Clover Leaf Club accidentally when it closed. The tipsy
fellow fought and bit police officers who came to let him out, leading to
him being held and investigated.

In the year 1937 the Burlington Trailways would take ownership of the
Pickwick terminal. Tully's Men's Store was still in operation. The Town
Theater, formerly the Moon, was still an operating theater to the east of
the bus station at 1410 Douglas Street.

A LONG SERIES OF UNFORTUNATE EVENTS

The *Omaha World-Herald* began covering the action at the Clover Leaf
Club with an almost lecherous frequency, which I suppose was telling
of the times. This was not the only club in town being written about.
Numerous nightclubs and hotels were the scene of games of chance.

In particular I noticed the name the Merriam Hotel with frequency. In one article Mrs. Mae Pruss, proprietor of the Merriam Hotel, merely wanted to clear up that Dutch Volker, who had been arrested in yet another Clover Leaf Club raid, did not live at the Merriam. "The Morals Squad" began raiding and nabbing left and right. I began to see a rise of women being arrested as well. Dice, dice boxes, and tables were also taken in as evidence.

At some point in 1937 Charles Hutter Jr. became a manager at the Clover Leaf Club, as a face of the company along with Dutch Volker. Charles Hutter Sr. and Dutch Volker continued on as holders. In this period Junior was revealed to be named "Snooks," perhaps for the billiard sport. The local papers also began calling him "Young Hutter," which I thought was pretty sweet.

January 1937 found Charles Hutter Sr. in trouble again, when his liquor license was suspended. In a raucous little article of February 10, 1937, I snorted at the headline "Woman Hits Officer over Head with Shoe during Street Melee." In the wee morning hours, two couples were asked to leave the Clover Leaf Club as it was way past everyone's bedtime, and more important, it was past closing hour. A policeman asked the drunken couples to move along, and a fight ensued. "A woman pounded a policeman's head with her shoe while her husband and his brother fought that officer." I like to imagine the shoe that did the pounding, as 1930s women's shoes are My Absolute Favorites. I will not include the delicate lady's name on the slim chance that this might be your lovely grandmother on a rare tipsy night. In a later article I read that the two men were prominent Omaha druggists who had been "in a fight with the morals squad officers."

By this time the Clover Leaf Club and Young Hutter were being collared over and over. In March 12, 1937, Young Hutter was quoted as asking the Morals Squad officers, "What the pinch for this time?" That time it was ordinance 10,444: selling soft drinks without a license. In a lucky break the judge dismissed Young Hutter for selling soft drinks but within months suspended Hutter Sr.'s license for fifteen days. Months later Charles Hutter Sr. was again in court but this time for the big gam-

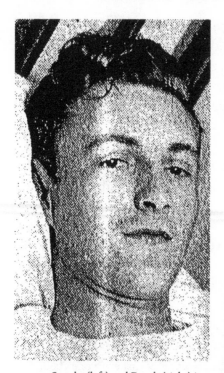 

90. Snooks (left) and Dutch (right) in 1937. "WANTED: George 'Dutch' Volker, above, and Charles Hutter Jr., were sought by police Monday for questioning about the complaint of an Omahan that he lost $1,700 gambling in the Clover Leaf Club, of which they are managers. Young Hutter, arrested last week on another charge, was found to be carrying dice that police said were 'not square.'" Not square! To make matters worse, the box of dice were also said to have been stamped with a cloverleaf. These were among some of the very best stories that I found. Marcus Hutter, Young Hutter's uncle, Senior's brother, again made an appearance when he furnished a $1,000 bond on Young Hutter's concealed weapons charge. Reprinted with permission from the *Omaha World-Herald*.

ing trial. The alleged gaming equipment and tables had been seized in an earlier raid. Hutter Sr. testified that he had bought the club but denied having ever owned or used the gambling equipment seized in the raid. He also blamed unknown storage spaces and rooms adjoining the club "to which entrance can be made only through the club. He said that several months after buying the club he did not look into the storage room where the seized equipment was found."

91. Charles "Snooks" Hutter Jr. (left) and Dutch Volker (right), in what looks like hot water–a court appearance. From the *Omaha World-Herald's* John Savage Collection at the Durham Museum Photo Archives.

UNDER NEW MANAGEMENT

Come May 29, 1937, Charles Hutter Sr., Dutch Volker, and Young Hutter packed up and moved on from the Clover Leaf Club. Fred Barnes, also known as "Tiny," became the new owner. He also owned a bar at 203 South Street. Einar Abramson was involved in the running of the Clover Leaf Club. Coincidentally, I discovered, in June 1937 Charles Hutter Sr. applied for new liquor license for his newest location, 2320 N Street, formerly occupied by, you guessed it, a cigar store: Hupp Cigar Store.

I located countless ads promoting the Clover Leaf Club "under new management." Perhaps an attempt to bring in new customers or to distance themselves from the Morals Squad, the advertising did not seem to work. By September 29, 1937: Tiny Barnes was up on charges stemming from a liquor raid and had to go before the liquor commission. By October 1 his and the Clover Leaf Club's liquor license was suspended.

2 OUTSTANDING PROFESSIONAL FLOOR SHOWS
EVERY NIGHT AT 10 AND 12
Dancing from 8 P. M. to 1 A. M.
No Cover or Minimum Charge

CLOVER LEAF CLUB
119 S. 15TH ST.

92. Advertisement for "2 Outstanding Professional Floor Shows,"
1938. Reprinted with permission from the *Omaha World-Herald*.

Let it be known that Tiny Barnes and Einar Abramson really liked their burlesque shows and performers. It didn't seem like the focus was as much on couples dancing in these times as watching dancing groups perform. I got the idea Al Fanelli's Clover Leaf Club Orchestra was quite an attraction. In October 1938 I found an intriguing article titled "Impersonators Get $25 Fines." Reportedly, four members of the cast of the female impersonation floor show at the Clover Leaf Club were fined and charged with indecent conduct and "wearing clothing of the opposite sex." Oh my. Unbeknownst to me, female impersonators were quite popular in the 1930s and 1940s.

A little too abruptly for my taste, I found a small ad from January 27, 1939, simply stated: "Clover Leaf Club closing; must sell equipment, chairs, tables, safe, etc. Reasonable. 119 S. 15th Street."

By January 18, 1940, 119 South Fifteenth Street had become Empire Shoes. It is hard to imagine all of that colorful intrigue becoming a shoe store. They must have had so much room, what with all of those unknown storage spaces and adjoining rooms. Was it a very chic forest glen shoe shop? Maybe it was a front? See what sleuthing in the underworld has done to my mind. I have become all chary and questioning. At best Empire Shoes was a short-lived enterprise; the address again went vacant for four years, until 1945, when the Dick Ragdale Café opened up. In 1946 it became the GI Club and, later still, the One Nineteen Café and Billiards.

By all accounts the fun continued for George "Dutch" Volker. I found more photographs of him in court. A real trailblazer. What a character he was. Likewise, the adventures of Charles Hutter Sr., the gregarious proprietor of the Clover Leaf Club, would weave ongoingly. (He can be found elsewhere on the pages of this book.) Son Snooks would lead quite the colorful life as well. Would you expect anything less? Apparently, he moved down to Daytona Beach, Florida, and was rumored to have made his way to Las Vegas in the 1970s. Like a magnet. Apropos. Which reminds me, if you want to read the most incredible book about the Omaha underground, check out *Cigars and Wires* by Jon Blecha. I only discovered it near the end of my research for this story. All of the amazing details of underground cigar shop culture. If you call 402-502-0514 and are in town, he will supposedly deliver it right to your door.

The Rialto Theatre building, home to the Pickwick Greyhound Lines, the Burlington Bus Lines, and Union Pacific Bus stations, a bowling alley, numerous retail stores such as Tully's and Natelson's, various cafeterias, restaurants, and of course the once glorious Clover Leaf Club, was razed in February 1986. I would love to have seen the Clover Leaf with my own eyes—that seventy-degree forest glen grotto with a house orchestra beneath the shadows of the city. I imagined the nightlife, the live orchestras, the lit buzzer linked to the tables and the cards in the hidden rooms beyond, the beautiful performers and their costumes, all the snorts, smudgers, tomatoes, and that taboo hooch. The site was paved over for a parking lot and years later became the Union Pacific Center we know today.

CHAPTER 8

Password to the Twenties Club

You and I relish the look of a huge Georgian estate with tall creepers and twine-covered gates. Just imagining walking out on its terrace, crumbly crushed gravel underfoot, sends your heart rapping in your chest for anyone near enough to hear. I can hear it. Fed on a childhood of public television, British murder mysteries tutored us in the important matters. As much as I do love an elegant estate, please understand my equally cavernous curiosity about the strange and unaccountable buildings of Omaha—a compulsion driven by the Not-So-Pretty Pretties. I know you will understand when I explain that these abstruse premises of Old Omaha, still right in front of our eyes, that some unnamed persons might wish would swallow up unto the earth and magically disappear, quietly invite our attentive deliberation as well as the Obvious Beauties. These very kinds of dark mysteries also captivate and send me reeling into fieldwork temptation. Dare I admit, my next investigation has been on my mind since I was a young girl.

I was taken with the Twenties Nightclub at Seventy-Third and Farnam from an early age for several reasons, most explained by an innocent, curious nature. All Omaha children of the 1970s will know what I mean. The Twenties facade and its matching marquee were a fantasy vision of a high-dollar amusement park on a faraway coast or the best pinball machine at Gizmos, a packed disco roller rink with a drop-down mirror ball, an engineering feat as distracting as any Rube Goldberg–designed machine viewed on our woody family television console. The Twenties was the glamorous movie set come to life. At least that was my early childhood view. This may or may not have been the draw for grownups as well. Not only does it remain a fantastical smoke screen, albeit sagging,

93. The Twenties Club entryway as it appears today. Photo by author.

of a midcentury Omaha structure, the Twenties Club is the last vestige of the famous Seventy-Second Street "Strip"—the glittering ribbon once bestrewed with some of the finest of nightlife institutions ever established in this town. Flashy nightclubs, lounges, and steak houses. The fact that the Twenties Club survived when its contemporaries were long ago torn down is a fine mystery in and of itself. Even to my young eyes I could see this was an unusual, glossy Omaha locale. Its shiny red dress exterior trimmed in black boa piping had already been mythologized beyond my grade school comprehension. The smart, flat, midcentury modern roof-line mixed with impressive ropes of neon and seemingly million-bulb casino marquee captivated my believing nature and sculpted my simple, early interest in local signage. "THE 20's." This iconic sign suggested the exotic lights of Broadway, or was it an Old West saloon? Either option was the closest exhibition I would discover, coming from my working-class Benson neighborhood. Back then the employees at Shakey's Pizza Parlor on Ames Avenue appeared quite worldly, donning their Styrofoam boaters. I was compelled to understand the Twenties' sensational multi-bulbed overhang entrance with those subtle, inviting steps. Something magical was behind those doors and yet restrained, almost comically so, by those magnificently crafted 2 and 0 door handles. And why couldn't I go in? It did kind of look like Shakey's or an ice cream parlor in so many ways. Perceivably, all secrets wanted to come pouring out of this grand carnival funhouse entrance, but it was elusive all the same. Was the place always garnished with those opposing black iron 1920s-ish San Francisco ornamental lampposts?

I had to crane my neck to get those meager, time-limited views of this glittering emporium as my father steered down Seventy-Second, headed for one not so intriguing destination or another. There it was, right in the heart of the city. The cloaked clientele always seemed just out of sight from my blurred backseat squinting. As a teen, I was even hungrier to understand the Twenties' magnetic interior and imagined goings on behind the luring doors, especially when a few underground bands played there in the early eighties. I was only allowed a parking lot view from Father of Miss Cassette's automobile—a chance to see older punk rockers duck into this secretive, hallowed environ. How did that inducement come about, or had I dreamed it all? As an adult, I squared the Twenties as two parts muddled 1960s Las Vegas and a splash of small-town razzle-dazzle. This whole block, the winding back roads, the bewildering empty lots, combined with the mixture of small buildings staggered around the Twenties, would become one of my favorite, confusing, hidden-in-full-view quarters of Omaha. And to think, this jumbled hamlet was just a hop and skip from the once most populated intersections in all of Omaha. How could the center of town be so ill conceived and just plain . . . strange? And by that I imply the best kind of strange.

Find yourself a comfortable chair or a blanket in front of the fireplace. Some may want to tuck into their bed with a flashlight. I regret to pleasurably forewarn you this is going to be a long, meandering, some may even suggest digressive tale of a most colorful nature. Curiosity seekers persevere! Onward and upward.

94. The magnificent "20's" door handles, still intact today. Photo by author.

EARLY CLUES

I suppose our investigation really begins with a tour of the grand dukes, so to speak. The R. R. Evans family. Yes, let us start there. In the spring of 1908 Mr. and Mrs. Richard Evans gave a well-attended dancing party at the new Happy Hollow Club on the evening of May 20 for their beautiful daughters, Miss Hazel and Miss Ruth Evans. Originally the site of the glorious Patrick estate, the new private club encompassed the two enormous Patrick homes, over eleven acres of land, and included a golf course. The country club, thought to be on the outskirts of West Omaha at roughly Underwood and Happy Hollow, including the Memorial Park area, first opened its doors on July 20, 1907.

Mr. and Mrs. Richard R. Evans had already stopped the presses for building an eight thousand–dollar residence at Thirty-Eighth and Jones back in 1897—a good chunk of change in those days—and were conclusively positioned in the rising Omaha country set, if you understand these terms. Years afterward, at his deathbed, Richard's brother, John Evans, had famously left his business, the City Steam Laundry Company, stock to Richard, which Richard later incorporated into the widely known Evans Laundry Company. In time the City Steam Laundry site at Eleventh and Douglas Streets would swallow up the Bryn Mawr College at 1013–15 Douglas and expand ever more. According to volume 2 of Arthur Cooper Wakeley's grand book *Omaha: The Gate City, and Douglas County, Nebraska*, the Model Laundry enterprise, yet another professional laundry company, run by Millard Mahlon Robertson, would merge with Evans Laundry sometime in 1912, reincorporating again under the name of Evans-Model Laundry. M. M. Robertson had been an employee of John Evans. I think the detectives in the room will understand when I suggest the Evans family were comfortable.

On September 16, 1914, arrangements were being circulated for the development of the R. R. Evans place, "east of Elmwood Park and just south of the Happy Hollow addition in Dundee." Evans would then purchase seven acres on Fifty-Third Street south of Dodge from Herman La Motte and an additional two adjoining acres from Alma La Motte Bull back in 1908. Why do I obsess? Here's the catch: Mr. Evans already owned thirty-five acres abutting the newly acquired La Motte plots. He was thought to begin to build, "making it among the most valuable property west of Omaha." Evans and his band of friends, including J. E. George, were instrumental in cajoling the Omaha mayor and city council members into formal acceptance of the parks and boulevard system found throughout our city. But bringing us back to 1914, the large Evans tract was being graded and divided into plots, thought to encircle the fine

Evans home, valued at twenty-two thousand dollars. World War I had just started months earlier, and although America would not formally join forces until 1917, it is interesting to imagine why a family would make arrangements to sell their large family estate at that time. Perhaps it had been the plan all along, and as it turned out, the timing was perfect. Omaha would annex Dundee on June 20, 1915.

On the day of the announced development, one Charles H. Harper was found "on the ground to attend to the field work. H. H. Harper, a brother, yesterday closed the deal for taking over the tract," rumored to involve a quarter of a million dollars. H. H. Harper was Hugh Henry Harper, who had graduated from Creighton University Law School a few years earlier, in 1910. One might think that a law degree would keep a fellow pretty busy through the whole of it, but Hugh would prove he was not one to sit idle. In all actuality he only practiced law but a short while, for he had turned his attention to real estate, first in western Nebraska and then in Omaha. From my digging this deal with Evans was his first big break, which I suppose only made me more curious. From the United States Presbyterian Church records I discovered a "Mrs. H. H. Harper" was originally Miss Ruth Evans, clinching my premonition about the R. R. Evans development. A week or so later I came across the local engagement announcement of Ruth Evans, the wealthy laundryman's daughter, to be married to Hugh Henry Harper. As with most formal betrothal photos in those days, Ruth Evans looked dourly frightened but intriguing nonetheless. I can say with certainty that she must have had a much softer, kinder face, although a dour expression reserved for nuptial announcement is a longtime favorite of mine.

All of the wandering detectives will know what I mean when I give this bit of warning mixed with encouragement to our newer, goading friends. Some of our Flowering Impatien(t)s are perhaps sighing loudly at this juncture, being somewhat dramatic with their smacking of lips, wondering when the Twenties Club will enter the landscape. After all, the chapter title implies a story about the Twenties. So here is that warning: the Twenties Club will not be joining us for a while. But please don't stomp off in a fine snit. We've got a lot of history and brambles to traverse and, dare I say, dawdle through. We, as a detective group, have committed to an imagined creed about deliberation and the gathering of clues, free of societal scurry. So, let us unhurry now and turn over each stone just so. We do not want to miss the very path.

SPADES UNEARTH EVANSTON

I am making assumptions that Hugh Harper was tagged to develop the Evans's land because he was to be their son-in-law; perhaps it was the other way around. However fortuitous, this alliance was to establish Hugh in a solid career. By May 9, 1915, H. H. Harper & Company hung its shingle at 1013–14 City National Building, also known as the Orpheum Tower. When this gorgeous building was erected in 1910, it was the tallest building in downtown Omaha, at sixteen stories. Harper had officially entered the landholdings and development market by advertising for Evanston, the newest expansion to the Dundee neighborhood. Dear sleuths, I will confirm I had never heard of Evanston previous to this investigation, which made it all the more compelling. "That high, sightly tract of land south of Dodge Street, overlooking Happy Hollow Golf Course and natural Elmwood Park, is to be known as Evanston." The Evanston district gave certainty there would not be frame buildings, stores, flats, apartment house, one-story buildings or "any undesirable features." A couple could meet with a Harper salesman and reserve a site.

The home featured in the ad was a large affair, in the center of Evanston. I've since learned that our R. R. Evans estate is still standing at 303 South Fifty-Sixth Street. It was in this fine home's living room that Hugh and Ruth would be married, before an improvised altar of palms and ferns. And detectives, this is the information I would like you to file away: other Colonial homes of similar character were to be built in Evanston by George T. Wilson of Browning, King & Company. This house design would come up again.

EARLY COMPLICATED HARPER CLUES

Let us peer at the Harpers a bit and gather our clues as to lay a foundation. Sometimes when I write like this, I envision peeking in on a family having a wonderful gathering around a fireplace or sitting around a long formal table for a traditional Sunday dinner. The house is aglow, illuminated by the amber warm interior. I realize this all sounds rather stalkerish, and maybe it is, but as we look in, you might want to take notation. The Harpers were not a particularly easy group to shadow, as there were some conflicting accounts of their history. Parents Mr. Alfred Harper and Miss Elizabeth Dye married and were rumored to be "pioneer settlers of Kansas," later returning to Illinois, where Alfred once again engaged in his lifelong occupation of farming. Further evidence pinpointed Carthage, a small agricultural community on the western side of Illinois, near the Iowa and Missouri borders. To further jumble the Harper history, a 1930 census conflicted with the family's description that father Alfred was born in Illinois and mother Elizabeth was born in Nebraska. When he died unexpectedly, Alfred left Elizabeth a widow with seven children. In yet another account, that of the Harper children at the time of their mother's death, Mrs. Elizabeth Luella Harper was described as a "Nebraska Pioneer," apparently having "come to Nebraska as a bride in a covered wagon from Illinois." She and Alfred purportedly settled near Fort Kearney in 1875 and lived in the covered wagon while logs were being cut for their home. Did they then return to Illinois? It is unknown when and under what circumstances Mrs. Elizabeth Harper truly moved to Omaha or if she was indeed born here.

According to his United States World War I draft registration card of 1917–18, son Charles Harvey Harper was born in Illinois on November 20, 1883 (later U.S. Census evidence curiously pointed to 1888). In Illinois he would attain the skills of farming, presumably from his father. At least I thought that until, strangely a 1930 United States Census revealed that Charles claimed to have been born in Kansas. Anyone who has toiled in genealogy will appreciate the fulfilling yet hand-wringing nature of this slog. From son Hugh Harper's World War II draft card of 1942, I learned Hugh was born in Jewel City, Kansas, in 1884. He also grew up in Illinois, alongside siblings Grace Harper Blair, Charles Harvey Harper, Lillie Harper Hansen, Earl I. Harper, and mystery sister Mrs. Robert Lawson. I tossed and turned at night over Mrs. Lawson's first name and that of the missing seventh sibling. Mother Elizabeth Harper would live out her Omaha years until her death in 1931 at the home of her daughter and son-in-law, the Robert Lawsons.

MRS. CHARLES HARVEY HARPER

When I set off on the Evanston trail, Charles H. Harper was already married. His bride would duck and hide through the yearbooks, another mystery woman, as elusive as most married women in those days. That is to say, married women were sometimes difficult to track from a historical research perspective, in spite of possibly leading strong, lovely, invigorating lives. I was afforded a small glimpse, however, and could see Mr. and Mrs. Charles Harper had attained some level of affluence and top-drawer positioning as evidenced by their inclusion in the Society column. An *Omaha World-Herald* article from July 1917 announced that the Harper couple along with their four daughters, "Miss Evelyn Harper, the twins Edith and Ethel and the baby, Eola," had just returned from an extended visit to the east, where they had been visiting their parents in Illinois.

Just as suddenly as she had appeared, Charles Harper's wife died of diphtheria in January 1918 at their family residence, 109 South Fifty-Second Avenue. Much later I would finally find her sought-after name— Gladys May. She was the daughter of Mr. and Mrs. Pleasant C. Hughes of Carthage, Illinois. Later still, I substantiated that Gladys was only twenty-eight at the time of her death. It might be odd to admit at a time like this (I have already confessed so many strange little things to you), but when I find a woman had the same maiden name initial as her married name initial, I cannot help but dream of her lifelong monogram and how she might have exhaled a sigh of relief to meet her beloved. Gladys Hughes Harper left behind her four small E daughters: Evelyn, Edith, Ethel, and Eola. I would find later that these girls were as beautiful as their names. From what I could find, the eldest three girls were born in Illinois, lending credence to a suspicion that Gladys and Charles Harper met back in their home state. Private funeral services were to be held for Mrs. Harper, most likely in the home, as was the custom of the day. I was saddened to think of a young husband and his four daughters left alone. It is impossible to imagine what lasting effects this had on our main character and his girls.

THE HOUSE AT 109 SOUTH
FIFTY-SECOND AVENUE

I was chewing the scenery in my pursuit of Fifty-Second Avenue in Dundee. Thanks to H. Ben Brick's book, *The Streets of Omaha: Their Origins and Changes*, I learned Fifty-Second Avenue was changed to Fifty-Second Street sometime later. To make things all the more deliciously complicated, Brick also made mention that prior to its name of Fifty-Second Avenue, it was called Wadsworth Street. So this would mean that the Charles Harper family had lived at 109 South Fifty-Second Street, a lovely, eclectic Tudor with a steeply pitched roof, offering some modest half-timbering. The deep-set, one-story sitting porch appears in the front facade with squared piers and looks like a nice, dark, cool place to sit in the summer months. The house was built in 1916, if the Douglas County Assessor's site is correct, but unfortunately, it was not mentioned in the archives until Mrs. Harper's untimely death. The couple must have moved into the home when it was new. By 1931 the street address had been altered to its current name and just in time for the owner, Mr. M. Charkin, to apply for a building permit for 109 South Fifty-Second Avenue's cement block and stucco garage. If I'm not mistaken, this is the very same garage that stands behind the home today.

I found a peculiar article in the *World-Herald*, dated February 24, 1918, describing a number of real estate sales, including Hugh Harper having sold his residence at 313 South Fifty-Fifth Street "in Evanston" for fifteen thousand dollars and that he intended to move "west of Fairacres into Cedarnole." File this away, detectives. The article also mentioned Charles H. Harper also sold his home at 109 South Fifty-Second Avenue for fourteen thousand dollars. I would find later Alfred C. Ellick had bought the home a month after Mrs. Harper's death. I would imagine it difficult to continue to reside in the family home that one's partner died in and to remember their funeral in one's very front room. However, some find comfort in this very energy.

H. H. HARPER & COMPANY

The following years found the H. H. Harper & Company buying and selling all over town, including the outskirts of Omaha as well. Hugh would go on to have a hand in the development of many fine residential districts in Omaha, known for being able to "fill in" empty pockets of land in a tasteful way. Hugh would eventually move the company offices to the 1713 Howard Street location in the fantastic Flatiron Building, in 1919, and for a very short while, he opened a brick and mortar catch-all store. Dropping the ampersand, Charles H. Harper became manager of this particular offshoot enterprise, operating the H. H. Harper Company, peddling hardware, carpentry tools, stoves, groceries, electrical supplies, auto accessories, wallpaper, and paints in early 1920. I imagine luxuriating in this old-time hardware-sundry store, enveloped in those large panes of glass within the Flatiron. This is to many Omaha Obsessives a very favorite three-sided structure, modeled after the New York City Flatiron Building. Regrettably, by April 1920 the store was having a close-out sale, due to the predicted grading of St. Mary's Avenue and Howard Street. The Flatiron shops would be forced to raise "the floors about six feet," and in preparation for the exhaustive task, the Harpers were selling their entire stock of merchandise. It would appear the sundry business never made a reprisal. However, the Harper real estate and investment venture would continue to great success, and the ampersand remained.

THE EARLY 1920S DIG AND A
QUIET MATRIMONY

In these years the Charles H. Harpers had removed to 2105 Binney Street, currently a remarkable shell of a home, purportedly built in 1900. Its outward structure sends the mind conceiving all sorts of Victorian fantasies. This house has since been assigned to Habitat for Humanity, and renovation is under way. Early on in my hunt I had printed off an article, whereby subtle mention was made of one Mrs. C. H. Harper having received a Chautauqua Reading Circle certificate at the annual "graduating exercise" held at the home of Mrs. W. B. Howard. I properly filed this article in a large manila folder to be properly forgotten about until just now. Founded in 1882, the Chautauqua Literary Circles are regarded as the oldest continuous book club in America (originally correspondence courses), and they were purportedly sprinkled throughout mostly well-to-do neighborhoods. While that is all well and good, the big news is that Charles Harper had remarried—a woman with literary leanings, mind you. I would light on the second Mrs. Harper's clues much later.

7301 FARNAM STREET ARRIVES

The 1925 city directory leaked the 7301 Farnam address for the very first time, but it was only found under the Charles Harper name. I was elated with its formal entrance; however, I wondered, why wasn't it under the street addresses listing? I was also mystified to think of what Seventy-Third and Farnam was like in those days, with the closest neighbor at Fifty-Sixth. Then again, the street address book had not been complete in listing the Harper address, so there were potentially many more homes and family that were not listed. Unfortunately, the site of the Douglas County / Omaha GIS Department does not divulge historic aerial photographs before 1941. Charles Harper was listed in the 1925 directory as a salesman at H. H. Harper & Company. Hugh H. Harper Real Estate and Investments was then located at 717 South Sixteenth Street. This building is non-extant, now an empty lot serving as parking for the incredibly well-designed Gallery 1516.

REGISTER OF DEEDS

A citywide snowed-in day could not hinder my gumshoeing at Douglas County Register of Deeds Office, where my multilayered Spy versus Spy disguise would perform two purposes. Armed with hitherto gathered data "7301 Farnam Street, Cedarnole Addition, Lot 6, Block 9" penciled into my little secret agent notebook, a magnifying glass, and a coating of frost, I clomped into the building. My curiosity was ever piqued to find "Hugh H. Harper + wife" had sold Charles H. Harper the 7301 property on October 30, 1923. I leafed through the whole area, fascinated to see Hugh H. Harper and wife owned all of the surrounding parcels as well.

Anyone who has pored over the large handwritten ledgers at the Deeds Office has no doubt fallen in love with the beautiful cursive curlicues of scribes past. With each study of penmanship and dilettante analysis, I would make up wee stories about each clerk from former times.

NOTES ON LANDS: SECTION, TOWNSHIP, AND RANGE

After discussing the case with the wise staff at the Deeds Office, it was suggested that I review the LANDS SEC-TWN-RGE books. This is usually the kiss of death when investigating a case, as I had learned from past experience one could be buried alive in these stacks, what with trying to make sense of the harried, not so chronological order to ownership. Honestly, I was getting concerned about the time and possibility of the Cassette family car being subsumed out on the street in the impending blizzard. But I committed to finding that blessed trail and not giving up until I could unearth whom Hugh Harper had purchased from.

U.S. land surveying—also called Public Land Survey System, or PLSS—is a very strange thing, and I am certainly not an expert. From my brief time of delving into architectural history, what I have grasped is that many properties in Omaha are divided into parcels and given a number and description after having been platted. Some tracts of land are not so overtly delineated, meaning they have not been platted or plotted and instead are given legal description using township number, range number, and section number. For example there are some parcels in Omaha, which have never been "developed" and will spend the rest of eternity in these LANDS SEC-TWN-RGE books. "My land!" I gasp to all amateur detectives privately. Likewise, these baffling books are also the place to go spelunking for land information before a farm or rural tract was consumed for platting, that is, neighborhood development. Things get further muddled when involving halving, quartering, of smaller squares of acres or the mentioning of the front and back quarter-quarter sections of land, all for the sake of simplifying the surveying of early America. I cry over anything tiptoeing near the language of math or science, so I will choose not to scrabble around in this muck, but it is comical to think that this skull scratching system was developed for those early surveyors not keen on mathematics and was largely thought to be an easier way of doing things. What I am trying to get across (brag about) is that I did excavate this dark hollow in order to make sense of 7301 Farnam. If our roles were reversed, I know you would go down that rabbit hole equipped with a headlamp for me.

THE WEAR PROBE

I could see in the delicate handwritten LANDS SEC-TWN-RGE book entries that Joseph Wear, Mary V. Wear, and Elizabeth Wear had sold their land to Hugh Harper in February through March 1916. The Wear property appeared to be a vast one. I had jotted down the year 1906 next to their names in my notations from that snowy day visit. Of course, I promptly forgot what 1906 signified. Misery me. At the library weeks later I was able to backtrack through the press archives to discover numerous real estate transfers within the Wear clan in late October 1906, including yet another member I didn't find in the original ledgers, Ellen E. Wear. Odd transfers from Wear relations all over town. From an obituary of 1907 I would discover that Emma J. Wear died in that year. (Both G. and J. had been denoted as her middle initial.) Who were these early Omaha landowner-investors? There were decades of the Wear family real estate dealings discovered, but I tripped over a clue from back in 1900 that broke the case open. Elizabeth and Joseph Wear were listed as new administrators of the estate of Francis Wear and Catherine Kennedy. Elizabeth and Joseph purportedly brought suit against the city of Omaha, having taken issue with the tax assessment made in the paving of the Twenty-Fourth and Vinton area, owned by Francis.

I traced this suit to its original 1898 public notice where Francis Wear was listed, among many property owners, including Catherine Kennedy, and ordered to "construct permanent sidewalks" by the city of Omaha. I am not sure what became of this case, but I did have confirmation that Francis Wear died a year later, in August 1899. Although interesting to me, none of this evidence gave much information until I looked into the thick "Omaha Bible," or at least that's what I lovingly call volume 2 of

Arthur Cooper Wakeley's tome, *Omaha: The Gate City and Douglas County, Nebraska.* According to Wakeley, Francis Wear was an Irish native straight from County Westmeath. A farmer throughout his life, the book did not make mention of the fact that Wear had curiously acquired large tracts of land all over Omaha and western Iowa, including a savory sprawl just west of Elmwood Park. John D. Wear, son of Francis, was Wakeley's true focus, as he was an early Omaha attorney, having begun his practice in 1900.

It wasn't until I came across Mrs. Elizabeth Wear's obituary from 1934 and a further scouring of the Family Search ancestry files that I would put the pieces together. Mr. Francis and Mrs. Elizabeth Wear evidently arrived in Omaha in 1884 and would do very well for themselves. Mrs. Elizabeth was buying up lot after lot throughout the early 1900s subsequent to Francis's death. The couple had six children, including attorney John D., Nellie, Frances, Mary (who went by May, sometimes Mae), Emma, and Joseph. The name I could not solidly identify was one Catherine Kennedy. The members of the Howard Kennedy line were early real estate moguls in town, and other Kennedys were attorneys and judges. While I discovered Ms. Kennedy also owned abundant parcels throughout the city, I could not directly connect the Wear clan. The Irish tended to stick together, possibly a Wear-Kennedy marriage.

THE EARLY CEDARNOLE ADDITION

Thanks to a Deeds Office staff member, I was able to ferret out the original paperwork on Cedarnole, confirming my suspicions that Hugh and Ruth Harper had developed this addition. As "owners and proprietors" of the Cedarnole addition, the Harper couple signed the plat document on April 4, 1916. A review of an early Cedarnole map, which I estimate to have been drafted between 1916 and 1920, shows that the new development bordered Dodge Street on the north, Sixty-Ninth Street on the east, Howard Street on the south, and Seventy-Fourth on the west—not a perfect, even square plot. Within a year of the first sale of the Evanston addition, all but two of the lots had been sold, earning H. H. Harper & Company an enviable reputation. By May 1916 the Cedarnole addition was touted as having larger tracts "just west of Evanston," and its new

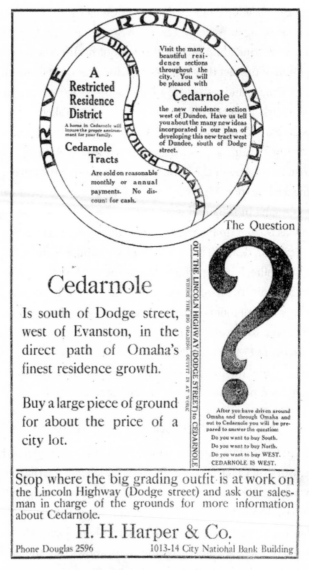

Visit the many beautiful residence sections throughout the city. You will be pleased with

A Restricted Residence District

A home in Cedarnole will insure the proper environment for your family.

Cedarnole Tracts

Are sold on reasonable monthly or annual payments. No discount for cash.

Cedarnole

the new residence section west of Dundee. Have us tell you about the many new ideas incorporated in our plan of developing this new tract west of Dundee, south of Dodge street.

The Question

Cedarnole

Is south of Dodge street, west of Evanston, in the direct path of Omaha's finest residence growth.

Buy a large piece of ground for about the price of a city lot.

OUT THE LINCOLN HIGHWAY (DODGE STREET) to CEDARNOLE. WHERE THE BIG GRADING OUTFIT IS AT WORK

After you have driven around Omaha and through Omaha and out to Cedarnole you will be prepared to answer the question:

Do you want to buy South.
Do you want to buy North.
Do you want to buy WEST.
CEDARNOLE IS WEST.

Stop where the big grading outfit is at work on the Lincoln Highway (Dodge street) and ask our salesman in charge of the grounds for more information about Cedarnole.

H. H. Harper & Co.

Phone Douglas 2596   1013-14 City National Bank Building

95. Curious 1916 marketing design for early Cedarnole. I dare you to spin around this hidden gem just west of the University of Nebraska Omaha.
Not many know Cedarnole is concealed there except for its grateful inhabitants, who no doubt smile to themselves every time they pull into their drives. The stately brick Colonials, the confident spacious ranches, the studious upright Tudors, the smiling hush postwar small houses of the forties. Reprinted with permission from the *Omaha World-Herald*.

building codes were restricted to brick, stone, and stucco. The first Cedarnole home was being constructed that July 1916 as folks were drawn to
the finer selling points—"an exclusive refuge from the noise and dust of
the city," complete with winding boulevard streets, where hundreds of
cedar trees were soon to be planted.

THE CEDARNOLE MAP RABBIT HOLE

Now I may be getting ahead of myself, but a thorough review of a portion
of the early Cedarnole plat map displayed many interesting things. I do
apologize for the rash of technicalities so early in our investigation, but
it is all rather difficult to describe streets in Omaha without an accompanying handheld tutorial. Moving from east to west, one can see that
Seventieth Avenue was renamed Seventy-First Street. Also Douglas Street,
directly south of Dodge, used to sway upward and connect on the diagonal of what is now the Scooters Coffee (7149 Dodge Street)–Fuddruckers
burger chain–U.S. Cellular corner (7059 Dodge Street). Most interesting is that Seventy-Second Street was once called Cedar Avenue, a fact
that I double-checked using my favorite tool, Brick's *Streets of Omaha:
Their Origins and Changes*. Indeed, this north-south Omaha staple was
once called Cedar Avenue, giving further elucidation as to the coining
of Harper's Cedarnole. As it turned out, Seventy-Second was only ever
called Cedar Avenue for a very short run between Dodge and Howard
Streets, exactly in the Cedarnole addition. So, who was named after
whom? So much for simplification, my dear Watson.

After some arduous obsessiveness, I traced backward until I found
Seventy-Second Street was called Von Hindenburg Avenue, an "old county
road intersecting Dodge about a mile and half west of the city limits of
Dundee." This simple dirt road was rechristened Cedar Avenue by none
other than the H. H. Harper Company, agent of the Cedarnole addition,
in April 1917. Harper claimed to have renamed the county road after platting Cedarnole without much interest in the old wooden signboard, most
likely hand-painted, VON HINDENBURG AVE., posted near his property.
Hugh Harper trumpeted, "The official name of the street was, is and will
continue to be Cedar Avenue, regardless of signs." Apparently, motorists

96. 2017 map of the Cedarnole addition and surrounding area. Google Map.

along Dodge Street had come to view the sign, sharing a name with Germany's foremost military leader, with a new distaste, a perception that Harper took full advantage of. America had entered World War I in 1917, and German statesman Paul von Hindenburg had clearly overshadowed Omaha's judgment of ol' Von Hindenburg Avenue. Hugh stepped in and apparently, with ease, changed the street name to promote his new development. I continue to stand in awe of early Omaha and how ingenuity, money, prominence, lack of restrictions, and brazen confidence shaped development and city planning. I guess they still do. But it seems that in Old Omaha a fella in the right place, at the right time, could become a pioneer to lasting effect simply because no one had previously dared in that particular arena. Such was the story of short-lived Cedar Avenue. With my question squarely resolved, I couldn't help but steadily turn over the revelation of the Von Hindenburg Avenue ticket and images of that rickety hand-painted sign covered in dust.

There was yet another clue unturned, that of Harper Avenue, also laid out on the diagonal, on the southwest corner of what was then the Dodge and Cedar Avenue intersection. The naming of Harper Avenue was another bold decision, this one more overtly related to the H. H. Harper Company. This short avenue was not mentioned in my H. Ben

97. Scan of the Cedarnole Subdivision plat map. Map
courtesy of the Douglas County Deeds Office.

Brick go-to book. To view the older map and compare it to the newer,
one can see that Harper Avenue had divided what would now be the Do
Space Community Center at 7205 Dodge Street. For those no longer
living in Omaha, this was once the site of the late 1990s–mid-2000s
Borders Bookstore and, before that, the Omaha Famous Kenny's Steakhouse, sometimes called Kenny's Restaurant, unfortunately shuttered in
the fall of 1988. Harper Avenue was named back in 1916 at the time of
the original platting of Cedarnole, but I am not absolutely sure of when
the street name fell from the books. I did find a 1988 city council request
"to vacate a portion of Douglas Street, formerly Harper Avenue, between
72nd and 73rd Streets." This request was a few months after the demise
of Kenny's Steakhouse; the soon to be demolished property was bought
by neighboring First Westside Bank, and perhaps, in an attempt to recon-
figure its business, the angled street had become a problem for the bank.

CEDARNOLE WEST

What this early plat map truly showcased for this Nancy Drewer is that
Cedarnole West, as I will call it from now on (the development where the
Twenties was later situated), at one time made perfect sense. That is to

98. Aerial image looking southwest over the intersection of Seventy-Second and Dodge Streets before the Crossroads Shopping Center was built, 1955. The large building at the top is the Cargill facility. Goosebumps ran up and down my arms as I finally discovered this descript photo, after hungrily clawing my way through the Durham archives. And was that a carriage house east of the house? Like happening upon a treasure chest or a warehouse filled with unworn 1940s women's shoes, I felt like doing the Cyd Charisse *Party Girl* dance! It was well worth the hungry clawing. From the *Omaha World-Herald's* John Savage Collection at the Durham Museum Photo Archives.

say, it was not always a vague, hodge-podge ghost town of city planning. There were numerous parcels all arranged in a pleasant, winding, park-like fashion. There was an overall balance. From my assessment of the Deeds Office records, most parcels to the west of Seventy-Second were not sold until 1924. That is, except for the large sale dated October 30, 1923, when Hugh and Ruth sold Charles Harper 7301 Farnam Street (Lot 6) in addition to Lots 3, 4, 5, 7, 8, 9, 10, and 11 on Block 9—fundamentally, the whole south side of what is now Farnam Street, flanked by Seventy-Second and Seventy-Fourth. The investigation gained a bit of traction. I wondered, what had Charles calculated with all of that land?

THE 7301 FARNAM STREET FISH ABOUT

I mentioned earlier that the 7301 Farnam Street address first entered the Omaha City Directory in 1925, but we now knew Charles Harper purchased the Cedarnole land, future home to the Twenties Lounge, in late 1923. Now friends, I know this photograph was taken decades later, in 1955, but I include it here so that you will not have to languish as long as I did, wondering what sort of abode Charles Harper built. Most enticing.

COLONIAL REVIVAL STYLE

One can assume that Charles Harper built his fine home between the window of 1924 and 1925. I had observed this proud Colonial style peppered throughout Midtown for as long as I could remember. This home was similar to the treasured family domain in the *Sixteen Candles* movie, oddly located in another Evanston. Oh, and the *Ordinary People* home . . . or was that a Georgian? No matter, the Colonial Revival home found around Midtown had always seemed to symbolize a traditional, clean ease. Badminton rackets might just be laying in the yard. The R. R. Evans home, central to the Evanston development, resembles this Colonial. Tour up and down, north and south, Dundee and count the Colonial style homes you find. By the end of World War I, America moved again toward traditional architecture. It has been suggested that influence was due to American soldiers having been abroad and experienced the mystifying domestic buildings of Europe. A new concentration on accurate architectural details drove the blanket term *period houses*, as the American public was able to view bona fide photographs of traditional housing from Europe. American architects often created an eclectic mixture of English, Italian, and French styles within the Revival movement. In the early 1920s masonry techniques were developed making brick and stone exteriors more affordable, furthering architects' and craftsmen's ability to produce an Old World doppelgänger. Virginia Savage McAlester's *Field Guide to American Houses* clarifies that the specific style Colonial Revival "is used to refer to the entire rebirth of the interest in early English and Dutch homes of the Atlantic seaboard." The Colonial Revival style dominated the American housing market from 1910 through 1930.

OBSESSING ABOUT THE 7301 ELABORATIONS

The Charles Harper Colonial at 7301 Farnam Street was side gabled with a strong parapet edge. The gable-ended Colonials in these parts often have simple straight sides and slightly overhanging eaves. In Harper's case the gable end projected above the roof level, forming a defining parapet. I had originally found the very large home and confounding shadow of this very parapet through aerial views on the DOGIS mapping site. I marveled to see that it cast quite the shadow and had three solid dormer windows protruding from the second story. Of course, I wouldn't truly understand how impressive a sight it must have been until I found the actual photos. Charles's parapets must have given a Londoner's mystique. The brick home was most likely red. Three strong dormer windows were visible and what looked to be prominent pedimented features. These details, if I'm not imagining things, were rooted in the Greek and Roman columns and would run vertically alongside the windows' edges, "holding up" the triangle of the dormer roof. Very attractive, if I do say. I spy a steeply hipped roof with shallow eave overhang. A shallow but accentuated front entry porch, most likely displaying a simple crown and pilasters combined with slender columns that most likely supported the entry roof. As one can make out, there are rectangular windows throughout, probably double-hung sashes with the main floor shown in frequently adjacent pairs. The Colonial Revival is usually focused on symmetry, balanced windows, and a central, formal door. Harper's home more than filled the bill. From the 1955 photograph there appear to be a number of outbuildings to the west of 7301 Farnam, with open land directly south. Come to think of it, there were only a few other homes visible. Did this mean that the Cedarnole West lots were never really sold to buyers, or was it kept purposely spacious and rural? What emerged was an elaborate Colonial dwelling on the rural edge of town.

COINCIDENTAL NEIGHBORS

If you will recall from the Rose Lodge investigation, William and Rose Rose's residence in 1926 was listed vaguely at "74th and Douglas." Theirs was described as a palatial home "just off Dodge Road in a neighborhood of expensive homes." We now know this was a reference to Cedarnole West. Theirs was a "large two and a half story structure, handsomely finished inside," where the couple kept their moonshine still, estimated

99. Detail of previous image, 1955. The Harper home is magnified for your delight. In June 1955 Farnam Street was still a dirt road. From the *Omaha World-Herald*'s John Savage Collection at the Durham Museum Photo Archives.

to have cost $10,000 (about $135,000 by 2017 calculations) installed in the Roses' basement. It is most promising that Charles Harper and the Roses knew one another.

If you are in the mood for an investigative jaunt, tour by 7447 Farnam Street when you are able. This portion of Farnam winds deceivingly behind the entire hullabaloo in a western direction. According to the Douglas County Assessor's site, this Colonial was built in 1926. This brick cutie is actually located in the Tobias first addition development, west of Seventy-Fourth being the boundary line, but it clearly would have been a concurrent structure of 7301 Farnam, just a hop down the lane. This is one of only two residential buildings left standing of the whole area, now utterly committed to industrial and commercial enterprise. The address 7447 Farnam currently houses the Crossroads Massage Clinic and is wedged between the Consulate of Mexico in Omaha and the Missouri River Valley Presbyterian ranch style church. Anyone might easily miss this little tract but not us. The Plant House at 7337 Douglas Street is another neighbor, still standing. I tracked this modified American foursquare back to the Hannon-Hopper family, another cohort of the Harpers. This frame house, as it turns out, was not in the Cedarnole development, explaining its construction. On that note I would learn how very serious the original Cedarnole neighborhood residents were about their brick and stone code when a well-meaning woman from north Dodge Street attempted to move her massive frame house across the road to an open lot in Cedarnole. One might have thought the circus was asking to pitch a tent next door to a mansion. Let it be known, her huge wooden foursquare, gorgeous by all estimations, was not to pass!

A MYSTERY MARRIAGE AND
THE SCHEUER FAMILY

Charles continued on as manager-salesman of the Harper real estate company. To my happy surprise I located "Charles Harper and wife" buying and selling abounding real estate plots in 1926. Charles had been married right under my snooping nose, dating back to at least 1920. I was left to create all sorts of fantastic imaginings, looking out on the snow, as I drank cup after cup of hot tea. I figured some folks liked to be private. An article dated March 31, 1927, cleared up some of the haze. Apparently, an engagement ring of 2.85 carats valued at fifteen hundred dollars was stolen from the Henry Scheuer home at 7301 Farnam Street. The theft was reported by Miss Muriel Scheuer, who stated the ring was taken from "her hiding place in her home" between Monday and Tuesday around 4:00 a.m. How very specific of her. We may never know which suitors' ring was pilfered, but more important, why were the Scheuers living in Charles Harper's Colonial?

There were so many fascinating winding roads regarding the Scheuers, and as I followed each lead, I could hear a few of you whispering from backstage, "There she goes again . . . we're headed toward the weeds." A 1930 census displayed Henry and Anna Scheuer were both born in Berlin, Germany; a 1940 census led on the couple were immigrants from Denmark. If their surname was any indication, my money's on Germany. The couple had two daughters, Effie and Muriel, born in Omaha. I cannot say for certain when Effie Scheuer married Charles Harper, but with confidence I report she was eighteen years his junior. Or wait . . . yet another census illuminates that she was twelve years his junior. I was beginning to think the Harpers were not faithful historians, or perhaps the census takers had butter fingers. The 1930 census revealed Effie Harper to be Charles's wife, eighteen years his junior and eleven years older than his daughter. Effie's age was recorded as "29." "Age of marriage" was recorded as "22." This does not square with my 1920 wedding date . . . unless Charles was married to yet another woman—between Gladys and Effie. When researching a house and its people, there are so many potential opportunities for error.

We know from Mrs. Charles Harper's Chautauqua Literary proclivity that Charles was coupled by at least 1920, possibly earlier. I would guess his marriage to someone precipitated the Cedarnole multi-parcel purchase and perhaps motivated Charles to build such a spacious home at 7301 Farnam. What we can sew together is that Effie's parents and sister also moved into the dwelling, which might have been somewhat cramped by today's standards, considering the four young Harper girls. However, a family of nine wasn't too terribly crowded for those days.

DEATH OF EDITH HARPER

Moving around in a very flexuous, brambling way led me back to the sad news I discovered when my unescorted investigation began. These explorations come about at their own speed and nearly always out of chronological order. So I warrened this away, possibly not wanting to find it again. On November 5, 1927, a brief pronouncement showed "Edith E. Harper, 14-year-old daughter of Mr. and Mrs. Charles H. Harper of 7301 Farnam Street, died Friday at a local hospital, following an operation for appendicitis." From what I have perceived of the twins in my life, this had to have been devastating news for Ethel, let alone the family.

THE GIRLS

In the following years the Harper girls made the newspaper by throwing birthday parties for one another in their large home. These sorts of In Society news clippings have always made me tingly, just by description alone. Evelyn Harper would graduate in a class of seven from Underwood High School in 1931, a school this amateur detective had never even heard about. Miss Cassette spied the school at Seventy-Eighth and

Underwood Avenue. An article from 1952 made plain that Underwood High was reconfigured into the West Side High with a new building being erected at Eighty-Seventh and Pacific. At that time the old Underwood building would be converted for grade school use. Youngest daughter Eola Harper would switch from Underwood and graduate from Central High School.

CEDARNOLE FARM

Charles Harper's "chicken house caught on fire," fanning my suspicions that he was, indeed, managing a small farm on his Cedarnole property. I have written on my website about the popularity of the urban farm during this time period. Harper was also noted for his 1938 grand champion hen, a Barred Rock pullet, in the poultry division at the local fair. By all accounts Charles continued on with the real estate business under brother Hugh. It is interesting to note that both Effie and Charles had only attained eighth grade educations. This admission meant something very different in the decades past. Take into account that by the 1940 United States Census, more than ten million people in the country had less than a fourth grade education. Of the American population twenty-five years and over, 60 percent had only an eighth grade education or less. Only 10 percent of our population would go to college, with less than 5 percent graduating from said college.

POLITICS

Within the era of both Prohibition and the Great Depression, I found evidence of Charles H. Harper endeavoring into local politics. As of March 1932, Charles was running as Democratic candidate for county commissioner while still working in real estate with is brother Hugh. This campaign photo tagline reveals more details of Charles than I could have hoped to find. "Experience in real estate, newspaper and radio field—early life on the farm." I yearned to know about his media days. I envisioned that due to his involvement in local real estate, having met so many different community people and leaders and observed the various

100. *Omaha World-Herald* campaign photo of Charles H. Harper,
March 20, 1932. At last we get to see what Mr. Harper looked like.
Reprinted with permission from the *Omaha World-Herald*.

policies, Harper must have desired involvement in the administration of the budget and overseeing spending.

A position in politics was not ultimately in the cards for Charles, but in September 1932 Charles and Hugh were involved in planning and reception for Governor and Mrs. Franklin Delano Roosevelt. The Democratic presidential nominee and wife were to be toured throughout Omaha in a slowly driven car whereby interested parties were encouraged to view, well-wish, and wave hello along a route, focusing on Farnam Street, Happy Hollow Boulevard, Fifty-Second Street, and Military Avenue. The Harpers and a handful of other Omaha Democrats were to greet the couple's "arrival at the station," which I tracked to the Burlington Station, and carry on to a private party at Sumnick Farm. Shortly thereafter, Governor Roosevelt would become the thirty-second president in 1933, subsequently continuing his winning streak after three more successful presidential elections.

THE BEAUTIFUL HARPER GIRLS GET MARRIED

Charles and Effie Harper's daughters—Evelyn, Ethel, and Eola—all became engaged within a year and half of one another, right in the middle of the Great Depression. In this period of higher unemployment and great strife, the United States marriage rate fell significantly, especially in the years spanning 1929 to 1933. I imagined few young people felt they could start their own family as many continued to live at home with their parents. Often two or three families would live together under one roof to combine resources, as we detected with the Scheuers and the Harpers. Marriage rates began to rise again in 1934. Miss Ethel announced her betrothal in September 1934. She was to marry Harold "Hal" Morgan of Lincoln. The youngest, Miss Eola, became engaged to Orvis Neely of Lincoln in July 1935, a month after graduation. December 1935 brought the announcement of Miss Evelyn's espousal to Ivor C. Ingraham. All three girls were such beautiful brunettes that I need to include their engagement photographs. I could see the girls' slight resemblance of Charles Harper, but I couldn't help but imagine what their biological mother, Gladys Hughes Harper, must have looked like.

Returns to Omaha

Married Sunday.
Before her marriage Sunday,
Mrs. Harold Morgan was Miss
Ethel Harper, daughter of C. H.
Harper. Mr. and Mrs. Morgan
are on an eastern motor trip and
on their return will be at home
in Lincoln. Skoglund photo.

Skoglund Photo.
Miss Eola Harper

101. Evelyn Harper, Ethel Harper Morgan, and Eola Harper.
Reprinted with permission from the *Omaha World-Herald*.

CEDARNOLE TAKES A STAND

In 1938 the homeowners living in the Cedarnole addition were still considered residents of the outlying country. The neighborhood took up a
petition, asking the City of Omaha for zone protection exclusively for
residential use under city provisions—the first of its kind. By law Omaha
was able to offer this protection up to three miles distance beyond the
city limits. But it wasn't until I learned more about the winter of 1939
that I got to the bottom of the scuff-up. In a dispute over whether the
Dundee Realty Company could develop a Dundee Golf Course within
an "exclusive residential zone," that of Dundee proper, the planning
board further established the boundaries of this restricted, protected
area. By aligning with Fairacres, Dundee, and Sunset Terrace, among

others, Cedarnole won its hard-earned protection. Downtown Dundee, of course, was allowed for commerce.

A 1938 *World-Herald* article mentioned that Seventy-Second and Dodge was already occupied in part by filling stations, which would also be an exception to the rule. To be revealed later, the real fear of Cedarnole residents was the proposal for a "trailer and cabin camp" on a triangular tract south of Dodge, near Seventy-Second. Rumor had it that the Knott family of ten had very recently asked a filling station employee on the nearby corner if they could "park a couple of trailers." In their defense this junction was discernibly out on the edge of town. Thinking that the Knotts meant truck trailers, the attendant gave permission. Apparently, the Knott couple and their eight children settled down for a night of washing, setting up a clothesline, and driftwood burning all on the private property of a very hot Cedarnole resident. The people of this select neighborhood "saw red" when they learned of the grading of a travelers' camp down the road and quickly initiated the Cedarnole Improvement Club. Now I think it was very likely a case of weighted journalism when the Knotts were quoted as saying they "were from nowhere and going nowhere," but I include it here as a touchstone to 1938. Exploitive or not, this storyline probably said more about the writer and public perception of the time.

There was an awful lot written about "gypsy camps" in those days as well. This was the tail end of the Great Depression, after all, and "the unwashed masses" had apparently worn out their welcome in the Cedarnole area and maybe everywhere, according to the haves. As of the late 1940s, the northwest corner of what is now the Crossroads parking lot maintained a similar makeshift trailer court–camping ground sales display area. It is fascinating to wonder if this Cedarnole struggle potentially pushed the campground–sales area north or if it was another site altogether.

AN ACCIDENT

The last time I was able to find any news reports alluding to Charles Harper's real estate management and transactions were from 1945. The 1945 city directory listed the 7301 Farnam house and elaborated that four people resided there. Charles, Effie, and her parents, Henry and Anna Scheuer, were the remaining inhabitants. Charles H. Harper's place of employment was unaccountably missing from the directory. A 1944 article pinpointed an unfortunate automobile accident, which clarified a good deal and, in my interpretation, wheeled Charles's prospects in another direction. The *World-Herald* wrote: "Charles H. Harper, 60, of 7301 Farnam Street, will receive $15,000 from Burlington Transportation Company for injuries received in an auto accident, through a settlement reached in District Court Monday. Mr. Harper represented by Attorney George Boland had sued the company charging that he suffered fractures of both legs and a fractured skull March 11, 1944 when a Burlington truck rammed the rear end of his car as both vehicles were moving east on Dodge at about Sixtieth. Mr. Harper appeared in court on crutches. A former employee of the Martin Bomber Plant, he has been unable to work since the accident." The Burlington Company settled as the trial of Harper's damage action was about to begin. I could not be sure of the severity of his skull fracture—potentially, he had suffered brain damage, including traumatic brain injury. We know so much more about brain injury now and its related, often cruel symptoms. The meager breadcrumb markers along the course of his life could point to Charles having been impaired with a life-altering condition.

MARTIN BOMBER PLANT

The article had let on a hidden clue that Charles Harper was a Martin Bomber Plant employee prior to his accident. The Glenn L. Martin Bomber Plant is still located in Bellevue on the Offutt Air Force Base, one of its last remaining buildings seen near the flag entrance on Fort Crook Road. In its day the plant was an impressive twelve-acre factory, three football fields in length, where a workforce of more than fourteen thousand would build an astounding amount of B-26 and B-29 bombers in just three years, beginning in 1942. Architect Albert Kahn designed the seventeen-building plant with local company Peter Kiewit Sons beginning construction in March 1941. How Harper became involved in the war effort is not known but not surprising for this time period, during which many left stateside gave a hand in supporting the country. The Martin Bomber production lines ended in September 1945 at the end of World War II. Only a few of the buildings are extant, with the largest one scheduled to be demolished due to expense of upkeep and proximity to the Offutt landing field.

FOR THE LOVE OF PIGEONS

The spring of 1947 gave my first hint that Charles was running with a new crowd, enjoying a new pastime. He might have been following a lifelong passion for all I knew. "A pigeon owned by C. H. Harper set an Omaha Flying Club record for 112 miles today. It averaged 1,662 yards a minute in a flight from Frankfort, Kansas. 81 birds competed." Charles landed other victories with his winning pigeons in that year. I am not sure how he did it or the pigeon protocol for this sport, but Charles Harper was consistently winning pigeon races throughout the eighteenth season.

SELLING LAND

After hearing of his debilitating accident, it wasn't surprising to find parcels of land for sale in Cedarnole West during the mid- to late 1940s. I am not sure how Charles was making a living in those days, and it made sense that he wanted to unload parcels of his share; Effie Harper was then employed as a stenographer at the Farm Credit Administration. Meanwhile, the Harper Real Estate business continued on without Charles. I shadowed Hugh and Ruth Harper to their residence at 6009 South Forty-First Street. Charles's mother-in-law, Mrs. Anna Scheuer, died in the 7301 Farnam Street Colonial in March 1947 at the age of seventy-three. Father-in-law Henry Scheuer continued to live with the Harpers.

In April 1949 a brand-new five-room brick Cape Cod style home was built and assigned the fresh address 7211 Farnam. It wasn't until October 1949 that the home found an owner in the Mr. Wilson F. Sroufs. The Sroufs spent no time turning that little Cap Cod into the Cedarnole Chinchilla Farm enterprise. It appeared the couple offered up choice breeding stock and no doubt saw the potential for this rural lot right in the middle of an ever-expanding town. I couldn't help but wonder what the Cedarnole Improvement Club thought of that chinchilla farm. Now Miss Cassette is not here to judge chinchilla farming, as I am sure that it is all very well and good, but as quickly as they blew in, the Sroufs moved within a year, leaving the home on the market once more.

THE DEED MYSTERY

Oddly, by July 15, 1949, I found a "QCD" written on the historic 7301 Farnam Street deed from "Charles H. Harper and wife" to "P. G. Lawson." Lawson had bought other property in Cedarnole in that year, according to the *Omaha World-Herald* archives. In my short time of learning to investigate properties, I have stumbled over this QCD: quitclaim deed. My limited understanding is that a quitclaim is often used to take someone's name off of a deed, for instance in a divorce situation or if one partner dies. It is also used for family gifting of property. The quitclaim also operates to show a legal interest in the property, which is where it gets tricky, in my estimation. This QDC can show that a person does not own the property and nothing is actually transferred. I took that to mean that P. G. Lawson showed interest in the Harper home. After further examination, I speculated that the Harpers potentially lost 7301 Farnam in a "sheriff's deed" sale denoted as "ShD" back on December 30, 1948. A sheriff's deed gives ownership rights to a property purchased at a sheriff's sale. After a failure of mortgage payment, a sheriff's sale serves to sell the property in a foreclosure situation. The person owing on the home often has the right of redemption of the property until confirmation of sale is signed by the judge and filed by the court. The unnamed sheriff then signed it over to P. G. Lawson. This sheriff's sale, although completed in December 1948, was not entered on the deed until September 1954. I did not have absolute proof but suspicioned Charles had incurred financial troubles after his accident, was trying to sell parcels, and eventually lost 7301 Farnam to foreclosure. Concurrently, Charles Harper maintained dominance in the pigeon racing province, operating from the expansive 7301 Farnam property. I continued to read of his winnings into 1956.

THE 1954 PUZZLE

There were no satisfying explanations when I discovered 7301 Farnam Street had fallen from the books. Likewise, there was no city directory listing for Mr. Charles Harper under surnames. On a whim I searched for Effie Harper, whom I found living at 4291 Wirt Street. Had the couple divorced? I would learn from Henry Scheuer's obituary from February 1954 that father Henry had lived with his daughter at 4291 Wirt that year. Perhaps not so coincidentally, this was the year that the sheriff's sale was entered on the 7301 Farnam deed. Apparently, Charles had kept the Wirt home all along and later sold, rented, or gave the property to Effie and her father. Or were Charles and Effie still together and the home was listed in Effie's name? What with all of the pigeon obsessing, I had, perhaps wrongly, assumed Effie had filed for divorce. Miss Cassette is living proof of obsession in full, unabated throttle, but it can be taxing on loved ones. Considering all of the evidence to that point, I came to believe that the Harpers had unfortunately divorced. Effie never resided with Charles again, living at 4291 Wirt for many years to come. She later was a stenographer at United States Farm Credit Administration.

A SINGLE MAN

The house at 7301 Farnam was not traced in the 1957 or 1958 Street Address Directory. I was able to shadow Charles Harper by the surname listing, discovering that he still lived at 7301 Farnam and was "manager of the Grigaitis Rest Home." Through reviewing the business directory, I found the Grigaitis Rest Home owned by Mrs. Emily, widow of Vincent Grigaitis. She lived at 4004 South Twenty-Sixth Street and operated her nursing home along with three nurses and, apparently, Charles Harper. Decades earlier Mr. and Mrs. John W. Koutsky had called 4004 South Twenty-Sixth home, as did George Kubik, a 1930s grocer and restaurateur. Of note, a rival syndicate member shortly thereafter gunned down Kubik when Kubik continued to work as an independent liquor dealer during Prohibition. A thorough search of this address revealed that many,

many older Omahans had died in this nursing home throughout the 1950s until the end of the 1960s. I guess that goes with the territory. Sophie Ann Zegar was the last person to die in the house, in May 1969. The address seemingly disappeared from the archives after her death, and I wondered if they had closed up shop, the home torn down. This address is no longer extant, but it must have been one of those Grand South Omaha Dames.

THE SLIP

The July 26, 1959, entry on the 7301 Farnam Street deed showed the home went from "P. G. Lawson" back into Charles H. Harper's name. (Was I reading the G initial correctly?) I began to wonder if there was a lien on the house or some agreement between the two parties. This negotiated arrangement potentially allowed Charles to reclaim his property after he got back on his feet. After all, there was evidence Charles Harper continued to live in the home even when it was in Lawson's name. A few weeks later I would find an article from 1934 in which Eola Harper, Charles's youngest daughter, was mentioned as traveling to Illinois with her uncle and auntie, Mr. and Mrs. Robert Lawson, to see Charles's late wife's mother, Eola's grandmother Mrs. P. C. Hughes, in Carthage. I would have to reverse course and redis-cover that Charles's sister was Mrs. Robert Lawson. His mystery sis-ter, first name unknown, just might have been the enshrouded "P. G. Lawson" on the deed, who stepped in and bought the property from the sheriff's sale in order to help Charles get established again. Yes, a wonderful sister just might do a thing like that, I surmised. I unearthed wondrous corroboration of a Pearl Harper Lawson born in Kansas in 1887, reared in Carthage, Illinois, daughter to Mrs. E. L. Harper, furthermore whom was married to one prodigious Robert Lawson in Burlington, Iowa. Mrs. P. Lawson was involved in Omaha theater and taught piano lessons in the couple's home. "Glory Be, this is a tidy turn of events!" I may have exclaimed. With delight in finding a shipshape resolution in the form of Pearl Harper Lawson, I returned to my bed. Had I dreamed it all?

STRANGE CHANGES

The 1959 Omaha City Directory presented many baffling clues. On that date 7301 Farnam was home to the Delmar School Photographers. Strangely, this business also had Charles H. Harper's name listed in smaller print. To make things all the more blurry, the address also lodged: "Will's Studio Photos" and "William H. Oliver." There was only one telephone number listed: 393-2521. I wondered if Charles has rented out the large home to businesses to help cover expenses. Meanwhile, he was still manager of the Grigaitis Home. I could not find any information about the Delmar School Photographers anywhere. Oh, how I toiled! When I think of the Delmar during this period, my mind races to the Delmar Hotel, 213 South Twenty-Fourth Street (RIP), or the Delmar Café at 2240 Farnam Street. My walking around money is on Oliver having operated both the Delmar School Photographers and Will's Studio Photos out of the home. For all I know, Jack of All Trades Harper likewise dabbled in photography. It was no stretch.

DEATH COMES TO CHARLES HARPER

On October 26, 1959, at 5:30 p.m. a rescue squad was allegedly called to 4004 South Twenty-Sixth Street, Grigaitis Nursing Home, for a C. H. Harper. It was thought to have been a possible stroke. Harper was taken to County Hospital. Two months later Charles H. Harper died at the age of seventy-seven, and 7301 Farnam was listed as his residence at the time of death. He was "survived by his three daughters: Mrs. Walter Scovil, Omaha; Mrs. Vern Brooks, Colorado Springs, CO; Mrs. Harold Morgan, Lincoln." Please take note of his daughters' new names, detective friends, as this will come up again shortly. As you might recall, daughter Evelyn was originally married to Ivor Ingraham. She would remarry Walter Scovil. Likewise, Eola had married Orvis Neely but was remarried to Vern Brooks. Sadly, the obituary did not mention Charles's siblings, other family, or Effie. I wondered what had happened that not even brother Hugh was mentioned in the obit? I felt a sadness after trailing the ghost of a man I could never know.

Hugh and Ruth Harper would continue to run the simplified Harper Real Estate. Sister-in-law Ruth Evans Harper died in 1967. Hugh Harper died at the age of ninety-four, in 1978, a well-respected real estate mogul, having developed Evanston, Cedarnole, Creighton's second addition, Fontenelle Park, Westmoreland, Harper Subdivision, and Weir Crest neighborhoods, among others. Charles Harper's ex, Effie Scheuer Harper, died in 1995.

THE CROSSROADS SHOPPING
CENTER AND THE STRIP

Isn't that the way of life? Charles Harper finally secured his lovely Colonial home back in his name and passed away months later. When he died, in 1959, the whole Seventy-Second and Dodge area was in a state of transformation. The Colonial address would disappear from record in 1960 or 1961, although the property upheld Harper's name through these years. Meanwhile, big news on the horizon was the construction of the Crossroads Shopping Mall, just north of the Harper home, at Seventy-Second and Dodge. Rumblings had begun back in 1956, when the Brandeis Investment Company had acquired a forty-acre tract west of Seventy-Second. Except for that pestering issue of zoning, the successful department store was champing at the bit. Sixty heated homeowners turned out to a council meeting, with Mrs. Michael Crofoot of 502 North Seventy-Second Avenue pointing out that if second commercial zoning were granted, the Brandeis delivery trucks would be "coming and going all night." The neighbors were none too excited in the face of progress. They fought a good fight, and the mall was circumvented until September 1960. In the aerial, looking northeast from about Seventy-Fourth and Farnam Streets, one can see that 7301 Farnam is a large house shrouded in trees, with the huge Cargill building to the west. The Cargill Elevator Company and the Minneapolis Moline Implement Company were large industrial ventures surrounding the Harper home. The landscape was changing.

The writing was on the walls in 1961, when the Cape Cod at 7211 Farnam became a commercially zoned property. The brick house remained, but owners would promote the merits of the additional vacant lot attached with "space for a business" or the suggestion to "move the house" for an even larger business plan. This scrape phrasing had taken another tone altogether as the owners began advertising the valuable proximity to the Crossroads Shopping Center, no longer promoting the intrinsic value of the brick house as family-owned residence or the Cedarnole neighborhood.

THE STRIP

I suspect *On the Strip* or *The Strip*, hip jargon for the Seventy-Second stretch between Dodge and Center, entered the local dialect in the late 1950s. No doubt lifted from the Las Vegas Strip and the Sunset Strip, the idiom gave this expanding ribbon of restaurant row, hotspots, and midcentury-themed lounges the marketing panache Omaha demanded, and as with all great expressions, this one happened organically. While every Regular Joe had been referencing Seventy-Second as a "strip of road" for years, Ross' Steak House at 909 South Seventy-Second appeared to be the first business to formulate the common term into its marketing framework in 1960. Ross' also flaunted the exotic Cleopatra Lounge as its adjoining cocktail den. Sam and Ross Nisi's SpareTime echoed the catchphrase when they relocated their twenty-three-year-old South Omaha operation to 707 South Seventy-Second Street in 1962. Their new restaurant presented temptations such as the Sultan's Chamber, the Stage Bar, and the festive Taormina Rooms.

These adult nightlife options were publicized as the cocktail hour gateway to the Ak-Sar-Ben Race Track and Coliseum events just down the road. Ak-Sar-Ben celebrated two big shows a year and the yearly event for the well-heeled Ak-Sar-Ben Coronation Ball crowd. The Strip manifested as Omaha's playground for some of the most expensive dinners, themed nightclubs, lounge acts, and nightcaps for after-show fun. The Strip competition was keen, but the club owners would also come together as a fraternity of business owners, aptly named the Strip Association. This alliance of executives pledged to a strict code of quality and ethics. Early on it was the Prom–Town House, Kenny's Restaurant,

Sam and Ross Nisi's SpareTime, the Ranch Bowl, Caniglia's Venice Inn. Alert for your notepad: the Twenties Club was given a charter membership even before it officially opened its doors. The association numbers would grow. The Lamplighter Motor Inn at Seventy-Second and Center laid claim to being the "First Motel on the Strip" in 1963.

Years later there were even restaurants luring the big spenders "just off the strip" or claiming to be on the strip but truly located a few blocks away. By early 1964 the John Markel Ford car lot at 103 South Seventy-Second and Dodge gave the Las Vegas wink with his clever advertisement: "There's No Gamble . . . When You Purchase a Used Car from John Markel on the Strip." Markel's nod to jazz and nightlife was not lost on me, when a year later he advertised, with my personal favorite, his "Birdland on the Strip" sale, offering the '63 Falcon and '63 T-Bird at reduced prices—a wordplay on the famous New York City Birdland nightclub, named for Charlie Parker, largely regarded as the Jazz Corner of the World.

This was at a time when Omaha, like any larger city, had oodles of jazz combos, crooners, piano players, easy listening vocalists, and any variety of stand-up acts. These local musicians were able to make a real living and support families from their regular gigs as a house band, often playing two or three shows a night—sometimes moving from club to club juggling different set times. Regional acts also toured a circuit run from Chicago to Kansas City and all points in between. The local flavor of Rat Pack knock-off shows of the mid-1950s and early 1960s confirmed an audience found something to love in a variety show after a couple of nice stiff drinks. And yes, national acts passed through. I've heard tell it was not uncommon for the big Ak-Sar-Ben celebrities to roll down the Strip and end up at one or another of Omaha's candlelit dens, shoulder to shoulder with the local suited-up elite. We do love a chance brushing with a celebrity in this big small town, but by and large Omahans were more than satisfied with the local talent, of which there was a plethora.

DIGGING THROUGH THE DEED

I tell you the Register of Deeds staff are saints, as I can be a little pest time and time again. A curious entry caught my attention. Even though the 7301 Farnam home was still in Charles's name years after his death, "Ethel E. Morgan et al." presented on the deed selling to "Vern V. Brook [sic] and wife" in May 1962. Essentially, sister Ethel sold to sister Eola, also called "Lee" as an adult. I sifted and combed, but it looked as though Lee and Vern Brooks lived in Colorado Springs, and I could not understand why they would want the property.

MYSTERY SOLVED

I could find nothing about the plans for razing the Colonial at 7301 Farnam in the cobwebbed archives, and other than a sad, little garage sale notification in the summer of 1963—offering a two-piece sectional, a desk, drapes, brand-new Venetian blinds—the tall brick home departed without fanfare. It all made me a bit glum. By that August the Omaha City Council okayed a Class C liquor license at the 7301 Farnam address, and the next thing I knew, announcement of new construction signaled the beginning of an altogether different architectural phase.

MY TAKE ON CEDARNOLE

We have all dallied for a very long time with the Harpers and the initial stages of the Cedarnole neighborhood—or I should say, I dallied. But I found the dalliance was a necessary examination, essential to the foundation of what was to come next. I will share my impression that the Harper Real Estate Company never did fill all of those forty perfectly laid-out residential plots in Cedarnole West. It seemed there were possibly eight houses at best on the west side of Seventy-Second Street at its height in the 1940s and early 1950s. The few residences were large in scale, compared to those on the east side of Seventy-Second, this observed through the lens of the Douglas-Omaha GIS aerials.

Now this is just my take on things, but the geographic separation by way of Seventy-Second appeared to have precluded any sort of family-focused, community neighborhood association for the simple fact that Cedarnole West became an unscheduled satellite left to its lonesome. The unexpected commercialization of Seventy-Second Street and Dodge further cut this little niche from Cedarnole proper and the rest of Midtown

Omaha in a way that Hugh Harper could not have prophesied. From a strictly practical point of view, I could see that the hodgepodge enclave lay vulnerable due to its lack of density, and the Crossroads Shopping Center was the binding coffin nail. It is my estimation that there are twenty-two commercial lots in this district as of this writing.

A FORMAL INTRODUCTION

By August 1963 the Omaha City Council approved a Class C liquor license for the 7301 Farnam address, and I knew we were finally seeing a formation on the horizon in our search for the Twenties Club. The licensees were detailed as Andrew Greco and Allan Weinstein. Now rumor had it, Andrew Greco, along with his wife, Lucia, had long been in the spirits business. I had also discovered Mr. Weinstein's Auditorium Bar had just closed that very March. It seemed, at the outset, a likely pairing of entrepreneurial types. I did not realize just how extensive the shadowy web would grow to be, still largely unmapped.

If one investigation was to reveal just how big of a tenderfoot sleuth I am, it was this very one. The thick, intricate weaving of old-school Italian and Jewish businessmen, their unseen, interlaced connections and the nightlife environs their association created, about toppled me into a snowdrift. It was all so fascinating to me. But here I have run off ahead of the suited-up parka pack. We will need to traverse quite a bit of ground in order to see these relationships, and unfortunately, there is a layer of snow covering our notes.

The first *Omaha World-Herald* article to officially breathe word of the new lounge didn't come until October of 1963: "The owners of Omaha's new Twenties Club—now under construction at 7301 Farnam Street—could make good use of Wills. Another Charles Stark creation, this four hundred–seater will serve Tin Pan Alley specialties instead of food." The cultural reference to Maury Wills, a banjo strumming sensation, found singing in the Jane Powell show at the Sahara in Las Vegas during this era, and nod to Tin Pan Alley entertainment, the name assigned to a vague but popular musical style heralding from New York City, was like a dog whistle to lovers of nightlife. The hint at the 1920s-themed vaudeville nightclub seating four hundred must have caused purring in some. Named for both a specific neighborhood in Manhattan and collective of musicians who wrote upright piano sheet music, the Tin Pan Alley genre enjoyed popularity from the late 1800s until the start of the Great Depression, when the public's love affair with sheet music fell from fashion. These keywords, coupled with the new club's name, motioned directly to the musical stylings of the 1920s, piquing gasps by design. And then there was that overtly off-handed mention of Charles Stark.

To my surprise, Charles Harper's daughter Eola "Lee" and husband Vern Brooks continued to own the 7301 Farnam parcel. Did they have a hand in the Twenties Club? I delighted in imagining if the Harpers were in on the business planning and fancied myself a cocktail waitress at a private club as these fine details were hammered out around a table with highballs and cigarettes. I would have to suss out those truths later.

THE GRECOS OF OMAHA

Let us agree we need to start somewhere. There is a whole cast of characters I need to introduce you to before we can pass behind the Twenties' doors, and I can hardly refuse the beckoning call of the wonderful Greco family. Andrew Greco and his wife, Lucia, an immigrant from Carlentini, Sicily, were married in Omaha in 1925. Lucia, having moved to Omaha at age twenty-two with her three sisters, had taken a job in the M. E. Smith Company, a clothing factory. Andrew made his living as an oil station operator. The couple's son, Anthony R. Greco, was born in 1926, and their daughter, Rose Greco (Wilson), came later. Andrew and Lucia hatched a plan and bought three lots on the southwest corner of Forty-Fifth and Center Streets with a notion to build a family home as well as move into the bar business, after finding an ad offering three acres. This was thought to be a choice location for its proximity to the highway. There was a building already on the site, originally serving as a confectionery in the late 1920s. I soon discovered this very building still stands, now identified as Paddy McGown's Pub and Grill, having taken over since the McFly's Center Street Tavern closed. Miss Cassette was at one time obsessed with the interior of this Perfect Neighborhood Corner Bar before the renovations came, a favorite haunt of long ago.

As mysteries ever tangle the further one digs, I found the Grecos did not immediately move into the nightclub business. I would imagine Prohibition possibly dampened that plan. It would appear from a police report that Sebastian Greco, a grocer, and his wife, Mary, were peddling foodstuffs and packaged goods out of 4503 Center in the year 1932 under the name of Sunnyland Confectionery. I guessed Sebastian to be about nineteen or twenty years of age, possibly a young brother or cousin of Andrew. I have known so many fantastic Grecos in my life, and I promise you, they are all related in one way or another. I could trace an addition to the corner building in 1934 by Andrew Greco, and it would appear the Ritz NiteClub was born, a year after Prohibition ended. The Ritz Nite-Club carried the address of 4501 Center Street while the family resided at 4503 Center, perhaps an example of addresses migrating over time. Sometimes the addresses were interchangeable. Currently, empty parking lots can be found to the west and to the south of the bar; I suspect that 4503 Center was the old Ritz and that the family home was later demolished. In 1935 newly divorced Sebastian Greco would move his venture, that of Greco's Highway Garage, down the road to Forty-Sixth and Center, where he would perpetually annoy neighbors for turning his place "into a junk yard" when he "started wrecking old autos" without much of a neighborly notice.

Andrew Greco continued to make building additions to the Ritz Nite-Club, later becoming the Ritz Night Club, through the Great Depression and into the 1950s. Business must have been good. Unexpected as it was, I was tickled to find the Ritz customarily advertised specifically for "Middle Aged Women" to work the bar. Possibly the largest stroke of luck was when those hardworking Grecos acquired a large swath of land on the Forty-Second and Center corner, sealing their financial fate. Originally, a Texas filling station planned to build a business on the corner, after agreeing to a sublease through the Ambler Realty Company, which had a ninety-nine-year lease on the property through the Grecos. The lease forbade the operation of a tavern on the property, and construction was not to detract from the neighboring buildings, including the Veterans Hospital across the street. The sly ones in our snowshoed audience have already guessed the Greco land would eventually become Omaha's strangest, most fascinating shopping emporium, the Center Mall, at 4101 Center Street. I say that with complete and devout love. If you have ventured to the upper levels lately, the wavering music is still piped down the halls. It is a sort of dated heaven. Andrew and son Anthony would later operate the Panther Room Cocktail Lounge located therein. I have a very strong affection for 1960s mall lounges. Perhaps they had written the tavern clause into their leasing agreement to keep away the competition—strange because, according to Father of Miss Cassette, there would be a number of fun lounges in the Center Mall over the years. Maybe they owned them all?

A Panther Room bartender had been pinched for taking bets early on. Was the unnamed bartender running his own side operation, or were the Grecos in on the ticket office? Were there other bookmaker hints? *Fuggedaboutit*, said with a Brooklyn accent. There were loads of fascinating anecdotes on Andrew Greco—the kinds of things I love to get all snarled up in. Mr. Greco was charged with shooting a game bird from a public highway in 1950. For the record, the bird was a dove, and the highway was at Seventy-Second and Center. In 1966 son Tony Greco was helping father Andrew to remodel once again and move into the restaurant business; they would rename the Ritz the Twinridge Lounge. In the late 1960s Greco's 4501 Center club, the name recently changed to Hey Jude, was consumed in flames to the destruction tune of fifteen thousand dollars. Although the Grecos owned the bar, Yano Caniglia and Peter Bonacci were operating Hey Jude. The fire chief suspected arson immediately upon finding the entrance door and a window smashed in, the prominent smell of petroleum, and the fortuitous early closing time due to the Thanksgiving holiday. I'm not sayin' nothin' about it.

THE YANO CANIGLIA CONNECTION

You have probably picked up on this familiar Omaha famous name. Sebastiano "Yano" Caniglia's family also emigrated from Carlentini, Sicily, and the Caniglias' lore is a proud Italian American story forged in the commercial enterprise of their family's Little Italy bakery near Seventh and Pierce. But as I would discover much later, this wasn't our Sebastiano "Yano" Caniglia.

Yano Caniglia of our story was also a well-known Omahan but within the nightclub domain. Our Yano was bartender at the Town House at the time of a vice liquor raid in 1955, when he, the doorman, a waitress, and the proprietor were arrested for selling illegal hooch. Also called the Town House Motor Hotel at 7000 Dodge Street, this was once a posh, society gathering spot, particularly the Hawaiian Room. Prom Motor Hotel out of Kansas City would buy the Town House and Diplomat Hotel in downtown Omaha in 1963, explaining the cool ads I sometimes came across for the Prom–Town House. The motel and accompanying entertainment spots, including a liquor store, were destroyed in the horrible tornado of 1975 and are now, regrettably, the site of another vacuous strip mall. Yano spearheaded a number of bars over the years—the Guys & Dolls Lounge at 1519 Farnam and the Cheetah Lounge at Seventieth and Dodge, among others.

ENTER PETER BONACCI

Peter "Pete" Bonacci comanaged Hey Jude with Yano Caniglia. Bonacci was well connected but, from what I could tell, largely worked behind the scenes, if you catch my meaning. Early in his life Pete Bonacci had gotten into some trouble with the law, having served time by age nineteen and later still, when he accidentally hit a small child with a truck. In the mid-1940s Bonacci landed a solid gig as proprietor of the Junior Bar at 414 North Sixteenth Street. Bonacci subsequently was found operating the Capri Club in the Carter Lake area in the mid-1950s, quietly running the nightclub until it was raided by law enforcement for selling bootleg liquor with improper Nebraska stamps on the bottles. There were other busts to follow at Bonacci's Capri Club, and I would puzzle out later that Snooks Hutter was also a "special partner" in this operation. (The fine details on Snooks Hutter are featured elsewhere in this book.) I had wrongly assumed Mr. Bonacci was just an extra in a long Twenties script, but I would discover his name sewn into the inner lining later still, elevating Pete Bonacci to a proper person of interest.

THE ALLAN WEINSTEIN DOSSIER

The other early licensee of the new Twenties Club was one Allan Weinstein. As it turns out, the Andrew Greco–Allan Weinstein alliance was not such an obvious pairing, although their drive to succeed in the liquor game was similar in some regards. Weinstein was a young man, still in his twenties, in the late 1950s. The Omaha cocktail lounge scene in the late 1950s and 1960s provided an easy entry point for newcomers wanting a cut of the lucrative profits. I wrongly assumed that young Allan was looking to hone his chops in the tavern business by opening Al's Bar at 1623 North Twenty-Fourth Street not long after his wedding. After a day of disguised gumshoeing it through the archives, I happened upon the Nathan Weinsteins, an Omaha family with a successful proprietary past. Nathan Weinstein had operated a wholesale grocery store at Ninth and Capitol in downtown Omaha. Along with his wife, Lillian Stoller, an immigrant from Russia, the couple would incorporate a delicatessen and fish and poultry markets to their growing empire. Between the daily operations of their multiple businesses, the couple managed to raise four children, their youngest being our Allan Weinstein (sometimes spelled *Allen*). I tracked the family's brick home at 1711 North Fifty-Second Street to the beautiful Metcalfe Park neighborhood. As it turned out, Al's Bar initially was the family fish market, a one-story concrete block building at Twenty-Fourth and Franklin Streets. Lillian and her sons, Herman, Harold, and Allan, would operate the bar after husband Nathan's poor health no longer allowed him to manage the market.

Allan Weinstein and Joyce Brunner would marry in the summer of 1955; approximately two years later, Joyce would give birth to their only son, David. There were some rather strange articles about Allan, such as the time he and a younger woman were the victims of "leg cuts" while at Al's Bar. A year later Weinstein was collared for selling mixed drinks to some minors. Miss Cassette deduced this flavor of misfortune might regularly befall a watering hole proprietor from this time period. But there was more. Yes, it is true Weinstein did hit a young fellow's eye out of the socket using a concealed weapon in a 4:00 a.m. street fight in downtown Omaha. The young fellow was Robert Winters, a twenty-two-year-old University of Omaha football player and former Golden Globes boxer, out for a fun night with his gal and another couple. Reportedly, Winters and Weinstein exchanged words in a small café, accelerating to a fight outside. Now, to hear Weinstein tell it, Winters had challenged him to go outside and take up the brawl. When Winters's eyeball was knocked clean out of his head, Weinstein claimed to have struck him with a brass garden hose nozzle. I suppose it wasn't all that clean. I found inclusion of the nozzle such a perplexing, far-fetched excuse—why would he be carrying such a thing? That is, until I read Omaha detectives did eventually find Weinstein's bloody pistol and, oddly, a brass nozzle hidden in a trashcan in front of the State Theater downtown. I had not hitherto considered a brass nozzle an ineffective weapon, but I suppose, in a pinch, it is a half-brother to brass knuckles, now that I think about it. I couldn't help but be reminded of a lovely man I know who collects antique brass garden hose nozzles. Winters soon filed suit against Weinstein for $200,000. I am not sure what came of that court case, but I do know Mrs. Joyce Weinstein would file for divorce.

I admittedly fell under the spell of Allan Weinstein, a habit that is somewhat dangerous for a sleuth. For my fondness is somewhat fated in trailing another time, and I suppose I am standing here as some type of warning against falling for the past. Shortly thereafter, Allan Weinstein would take ownership of the sometimes sordid Auditorium Bar at 117 North Sixteenth Street, one of a string of small fitful inns along that strip. The bar would endure until March 1963, when Weinstein officially shuttered it. For reasons unknown, Weinstein was taking a pause, but most likely it was the hope of a new direction.

That August 1963 Andrew Greco and Allan Weinstein had penned a fresh deal in the form of the Twenties Club. I cannot be sure how long the group was arranging this project. Two months after the announcement of the Twenties Club liquor license, Allan Weinstein died in a terrible accident when his vehicle was struck head-on by a car north of Denison, Iowa. Allan was only thirty-three years of age. He was driving a load of fish for his uncle's market. His seven-year-old boy, David, miraculously lived after escaping the fiery vehicle. It is always such a shock to follow with such fervor, binoculars focused, tiptoeing with care through the archives . . . only to discover your focal point obsession was killed.

A PROPER TONY GRECO INTRODUCTION

Although the senior Greco attained the liquor license, it was actually son Tony who was behind the origins of the early Twenties Club, after further scrutiny of the 7301 Farnam Street deed. This made more sense to me as I considered the ages of Weinstein and Junior Greco, certainly contemporaries and possibly friends. Tony Greco went to Creighton Prep High School, then served in the navy for two years during World War II, subsequently attending Creighton University for two years with the intent to study law. It is more than likely his various restaurant and lounge jobs, including an infrequent stand-up comedy routine at his parents' Ritz NiteClub back at Forty-Fifth and Center, taught him many lessons in thinking on one's feet. Greco worked at the Ritz until 1955, where he learned to book bands, tend bar, stock liquor, and cook, but his favorite job was management. Despite his law school leanings, the lure of the nightlife was in his blood.

I had come across the name Tony Greco earlier as manager of the Panther Room Cocktail Lounge at the Center Mall, which we know Pa Greco owned. According to Father of Miss Cassette, this Panther Room Cocktail Lounge was a real cool affair in the early 1960s, a jazz club featuring live combos six nights a week. With Andrew's help, Tony would get his footing at the Panther, exploring the role of tastemaker. He was a natural. Likewise, my father seemed dazzled with another nightclub supplying entertainment, food, and booze on top of the Center Mall. It must have been the Cimarron Room and Terrace? After all, "Top o' the Center" was its slogan, and the dates did line up.

THE HAROLD M. KLEIN AFFAIR

Mr. Harold M. Klein was a dramatis personae I would not be introduced to until the opening night advertisement for the Twenties Club in 1964.

I disclose his identity here, as it seems to make more sense to broach these tangled relations earlier than later. When I tracked Klein to a long history within the mysterious coin-operated machine distributing business, my interests were immediately piqued. In 1951 he had arranged the Midwest Coin Machine Show in the Paxton Hotel in downtown Omaha, where the recent commotion was the red-hot persecution of local jukebox operators by way of the Office of Price Stabilization. The OPS, as it was called, demanded that jukebox owners reduce their ten-cent record plays to five cents. This offending group was a protective agency put in place by President Harry S. Truman in the fall of 1950, under the Economic Stabilization Agency (ESA). Signed into law as a response to the Korean War, this measure of control was created to oversee the American economy, similar to the price controls and rationing by the Office of Price Administration during World War II. President Eisenhower called an end to the ESA in April 1953—but not before one thousand people had attended Klein's Paxton affair, displaying various new coin machines and a chance to join the ruckus over a pinched nickel a tune.

The coin-operated machine distribution business had been a solid bet in those years, no matter what side of propriety one found themselves drawn to. Solidly fabricated, coin-activated machines had allowed for the rise of the vending machine–amusement games, including pinball machines, music "juke" boxes, and slot machines—in the 1930s and 1940s. Before World War II, plant and factory operation guides recommended that workers needed a refreshment break every ten or so hours, establishing vending machines as a good source of prepackaged snacks and sodas. My perception that this coin-operated business could be a bit perilous only came after reading tales of lore about operators and distributors. Cigars + candy + coin-operated machines could sometimes = Gambling, Liquor, and Underworld Omaha. And this is where a seemingly innocuous pleasure had an underbelly rooted to the illegal vice racket in the controversial coin operator sphere. State laws were either against gambling or seemed to heavily regulate any form of it, but the slot companies quickly developed their way around this issue, eliminating taxes. In later years the machines rewarded their winners with chewing gum, in lieu of the cash payouts of the early years. Pinball machines were another suspicious game of chance in that there was great debate over whether they, too, were gambling devices. Vice squads throughout the nation had a healthy dubiety of vending machines, their operators, and distributors.

It is in light of this sometime societal skepticism that I divulge this next account, discovered while eavesdropping along my detective's path. Mr. Harold Klein's coin-operated machine company, Mayflower Distributing, at 1209 Douglas Street, was bombed in March 1952. This is in the current neighborhood of the Holland Performing Arts Center. Of consideration this was, apparently, Omaha's third bombing of early 1952. For his part Manager Klein said he was "mystified" as to the reason for the blast that took off the front of his store, as the firm "had no gambling devices— stock was mainly jukeboxes and pinball machines." If we are to take Klein at his word, or not, regarding the absence of slots, it is unknown if this explosion was the act of his competition, an organized crime ring that Mayflower had wronged, a personal vendetta, or pure accident.

Perhaps a sign of the times, the Mayflower headquarters were in hot water just months later with yet another issue. Herman Paster, head of the Mayflower Distributing Company headquarters out of St. Paul, Minnesota, was busted by vice, along with two employees, for transporting thirty-eight slot machines from Davenport to St. Paul on a new law prohibiting the interstate shipment of slots. Soon after, the Mayflower Omaha branch at 1209 Douglas Street would clean up its facade and hang a new shingle—the Central Music Distributing Company—congruent with Klein's original defense, that he mainly stocked jukeboxes. Was Klein's Mayflower small fish or a major player in the Omaha underground?

From what I got wind of, the mysterious Mr. Klein exhibited panache as manager and resident of the Commodore Hotel and Surf Room in downtown Omaha at 2410 Dodge Street, just west of Joslyn Art Museum. This corner site is now home to the Physicians Mutual headquarters, complete with expansive gated grounds.

Harold Klein had many irons in the fire, as all my obsessions appeared to have. On paper Mr. Klein bought a club from Stella Sittler in 1956 up in the Carter Lake area. Stella Sittler was a Rotella by birth and maintained association with numerous gamblers and nightclub owners. Don't you love this? In company with a Teamster organizer and another man, Sittler bought Pete Bonacci's Capri Club. The 311 Locust Street location featured an underground room, recast as the Ivy Club's illicit home. Stewart's Airport Parking now occupies this site, largely maintaining the industrial no-man's land sense. Of course, spin down the block, and one can understand why this was the perfect place for a hidden nightclub. Stella Sittler had dreams of creating a members' bottle club, complete with private cards, but a few months in, she was raided and found with numerous bottles of illegal whiskey. The basement Ivy Club was padlocked until Klein entered the scene.

From outward appearance Harold Klein had merely wanted to reopen the Capri Club as a restaurant, to be called the Steakhouse, but in January 1957 the Carter Lake Town Council turned down his bid. His restaurant application was suspected of leading the way to further permit problems. Bonacci and Sittler's former gambling spots were perceived to give Carter Lake a bad name, and the community was "too unsettled" to allow the club to reopen. Did Klein retain deep vice ties, and was the board ginned up? According to Jon L. Blecha's book, *Cigars and Wires: The Omaha Underworld's Early Years*, Pete Bonacci was involved in the club all along, although not traced to paperwork. I would find another raid from March 1957 in the *Herald*, exposing Bonacci, Klein, and Marion Bruno when they were arrested for illegal possession of liquor and for operating their establishment without proper restaurant and dancing permits, just as the Carter Lake board had predicted. It appeared that they had not formally opened the Steakhouse but, rather, tried their hand at a low-key Ivy Club spin-off. Raiders confiscated forty-one bottles of whiskey and eight to ten cartons of cigarettes without legal stamps. Evidently, Marion Bruno served as bartender, Harold Klein was the owner-manager, and Pete Bonacci part owner. While Klein and Bruno would plead guilty, a later article revealed no charges were ultimately filed against Bonacci, after hard proof of his connection never materialized. Pete Bonacci would go on to open the infamous Pee Dee's Supper Club on the South Omaha Bridge Road, later facing a 1959 raid for after-hours liquor violations.

I would curl up in my library one night and give audience to the snowfall against our 1940s windows. I let my mind roam and contemplated how Harold Klein became enveloped in the Twenties Club deal. I would find his name as co-owner, along with Tony Greco, when Klein was interviewed about the 1964 opening of the club. I calculated the Twenties Club business treaty was occasioned by the untimely death of Allan Weinstein, but I would find subsequently, in a 1963 *Sun* newspaper article, that Anthony Greco, Allan Weinstein, and Harold Klein had forged the 7301 Corporation early on. I had no way of knowing what other connections were shared between Tony Greco and Harold Klein. I had found a Harold H. Klein buried at Temple Israel Cemetery, but this gentleman had died in August 1966, which didn't seem to agree with the storyline. Months later I discovered Harold Klein had also possessed the Club New Yorker at 6703 West Center Road; years later he would change the name to the Kings' Row Lounge, offering a chuck wagon–style buffet.

THEMED NIGHTCLUBS, CONVENTIONS, AND COCKTAIL CULTURE

There is just one more stop. One more glowing thread to pull out of this tangled yarn before we arrive upon the Twenties Club. A bit of cultural history. Miss Cassette just loves the vintage nightclub themes throughout American history. Such allure. The time, money, intention, and design devoted to these privately owned, local clubs before the days of the flinching franchise is astounding, let alone the sad, national trend of LED forensic labs and industrial bars that pass for nightlife today. I shudder to realize most contemporary lounges look and feel the same.

Through my Clover Leaf Club expedition I would learn that America had long loved a good supper club and nightclub theme, a fantasy world for adults. My previous Fabulous Fireside Restaurant investigation (on my website) had taught me how much we longed to escape to a beautiful interior dream decor. But the smaller downtown show clubs and burlesque reviews across America were being replaced in the postwar years as nightclubs gussied up, with a new emphasis on polish, technology, and upward mobility. This was a new era focused on the seduction of big convention money, the traveling conventioneers, the happy hour businessmen, and the tourist trade secondary to automobiles, motels, and the popularization of luxuries, such as airline flights. I would find the convention nightlife obsession spread through every larger American town as city councils and mayors competed for their cities to be seen as cultured places, earning even more tourism dollars.

Meanwhile, the American people were trying on a new persona, marked by sophistication, wealth, glamour—the ability to look the part, even if one's bank account did not mirror the image. New levels of decadent pageantry were observed in clothing, cars, and frequent nights out. Hat-check, cocktails, live music, a stand-up show, cigars, cocktails, dinner, cocktails, dancing, valet—can you bring my car 'round—a late-night snack at another club. I continually marveled at just how many Regular Joes as well as Omaha high society painted the town red for nightly rounds, late-night meals, and drinking multiple nights a week, often winding down the festivities at two or three in the morning. For one thing, these meal and drinks were not as expensive. I understand that beers and mixed drinks were under a dollar then. But bigger still, America had a healthier distribution of wealth after World War II, and people wanted to celebrate. Celebration included dressing up and meeting with friends or business associates for multi-course meals, often including steak and lobster, cocktails and desserts, paired with live music and dancing. Another undeniable factor was that strict drunk driving laws had not yet entered the picture—the police often waving drunkards home with a knowing smile. From what I have read, it was common for an adult to have six or more mixed drinks on a weeknight out. There is evidence that we were hardier people all around then—a hardier people who died younger. Tougher law enforcement, although desperately called for, impeded big club business and the cultural perception of kicking one's heels up throughout the week.

While the drink-dinner-dancing trend exploded in popularity, huge clubs on the coasts, influenced by the Las Vegas shows, would pack them in by the thousands. The Mardi Gras Supper Club, the Old South theme, the ever popular Hell theme, the Latin Quarter, the Diamond

102. This blurry architect's rendering is our earliest pointer to the Twenties Club to come. Image from the now defunct *Sun* newspaper, November 14, 1963.

Horseshoe, Dixieland themes, Tiki Bar Mania, Tropicana, Cuban themes, the Copacabana, circus-themed lounges, the Golden Slipper Restaurant and Nightclub of Long Island, African jungle themes, Island Paradise, or outer space themes mimicked the instrumental lounge music sound of the time. These concept clubs were considered lively, exotic, cheeky. A well-developed concept integrated a catchy club name, a jingle, a slogan with print ads, architecture, interior appointments, fixtures, entertainment, and uniforms all synced up. The themed clubs and their marketing were not viewed from the same lens of cheesiness or distaste that some would endorse today.

Many of these nightclub themes and complementary interior designs were culturally appropriated from indigenous people and minority groups, by our contemporary standards. African American musicians and performers could often find work on these stages and were sought after as entertainers, but many were not allowed in the front doors as paying customers. President Lyndon Johnson's Civil Rights Act of 1964 forbade discrimination by race, color, religion, or national origin in restaurants, hotels, motels, theaters, and stadiums; however, private club owners found ways around this act by way of special "members-only" clauses ensuring that people of color, or anyone they deemed unworthy, could

103. The impressive exterior of the Twenties Club. The cars
aren't too bad either. University of Nebraska Omaha Photograph
Collection, Archives & Special Collections, Criss Library.

be kept out. Female hospitality staff were objectified as a general rule.
I have heard from an insider that "girls," meaning young sex workers,
could be ordered up to a room at the Prom–Town House motel by a
simple phone call to the concierge desk. A smile or wink excused many
things in those days. None of these particulars were discussed or noted
as standouts for many years to come.

THE BUILDING

There was great drive in 1964 Omaha to get in on the national convention circuit. The Twenties Club undeniably presented itself in the spotlight under this guise, using phrasing such as "Omaha's bid for national
recognition as one of America's leading dining, entertainment and convention cities" in its announcement. The Midcentury Modern cocktail lounge, with its broad, flat roof, looked very much as it does today,

reviewing an architect's 1963 rendering. Looky-looers wanting a peek at the Reckless Decade were promised a handsome bronze plaque at door side (still there!) and the "ever-widening entertainment pursuits of discriminating patrons." Boasting three bars with space to serve three hundred, the 7301 Farnam Street address was the new entertainment spot Just Off the Strip. Co-owners Harold Klein and Tony Greco had spent "a year of patient research and planning" to coordinate the "brilliant concepts of nationally-renowned designer Charles Stark." The owners explained the club's 1920s motif with framed photographs of silent film stars, playbills, and billboards to reflect that period. The exterior was to be covered with five-by-eight-foot panels, lighted from behind with portraits of showbiz folks.

A key point of my fervent obsession, here in the eleventh hour of this investigation, was a savory quote by Charlie Stark, found in a November 14, 1963, *Sun* newspaper interview, shared by a *My Omaha Obsession* website friend, Ron Hunter. Stark commented that the Twenties Club was "being built around a Georgian house that was on the lot." The Twenties was "built around" the Harper house, as in they shared some the same interior walls? Did they have the same basement? What exactly did that mean? Or was it just an offhanded expression? I was ecstatic. (Now Miss Cassette is not really here to split hairs with anyone, certainly not a well-known designer, but the Harper home was not a Georgian Colonial by my estimation.) But the bigger news was the acknowledgment that Charles Harper's original home had been at the heart of the Twenties Club, in some kernel of a capacity. Another focus of elation was learning the "out-of-date lampposts," my black fantastic lights that continue to flank the Twenties entrance, were salvaged from the "OPPD warehouse" in 1963. They were original Omaha streetlamps. Mama mia, I would have loved to get a gander at this Golden Ark of the Covenant OPPD Warehouse of yesteryear!

Twin City Neon Company, at 1807 Vinton Street, designed and fabricated the incredible neon work for that infamous 20's sign. The Universal Terrazzo & Tile Company handled the tile work in the restrooms. I had recognized the name as the company who had floored the Harkert

TOMORROW! A SPEAKEASY BLOOMS ON OMAHA'S FAMOUS "STRIP!"

104. An advertisement for the Twenties Club's opening night, January 26, 1964. The most fantastic news in all of this image was the inclusion of those black iron San Francisco ornamental lampposts that flanked the front entry. Another mystery solved. Those beauts had been there from day one! Reprinted with permission from the *Omaha World-Herald*.

Houses. I would have loved to find the architect and builders' names, but I could not uncover those clues.

OPENING NIGHT MONDAY, JANUARY 27, 1964

And now . . . the moment we've all been waiting for. Drum roll, please. Ladies and Gentlemen . . . the Twenties Club. The club would have its grand opening on a Monday night, very telling of the party atmosphere in Omaha in those days. Boasting of its Strip Association charter membership, the Twenties Club press described a speakeasy with Charleston Dancers shimmying up a storm, complete with the enticing Prohibition drama of a potential police raid, and a heavy ax's slam on the front door! It is funny to think that one of the Twenties' owners had experienced this true-to-life scenario. A full-page ad suggested an opening the likes of which Omaha had never seen: "A bright new dimension on Omaha's night life scene . . . the Twenties Club created as a living tribute to the great stars of the show business, whose names and fortunes lighted up that gaudy, lusty, exciting era remembered as the roaring twenties. You'll

105. Opening night toast from the Sol Lewis Engineering
Company, 1964. "Omaha's bid for national recognition as one of
America's leading dining, entertainment, and convention cities."
Reprinted with permission from the *Omaha World-Herald*.

be a part of the sights and sound of this flamboyant era the minute you
cross the threshold of the new Twenties Club. Dance to the velvety music
of Hal Pryor and his Original Memphis Five."

To hear Emil Vohoska describe it from the *Sun* article dated January
30, 1964, the crowd turnout was unlike any Omaha society had ever
witnessed. Uniformed policemen were posted out on Seventy-Second
Street entry points, while the Twenties doorman was forced to turn away
would-be patrons, until the capacity crowd could squeeze enough room

106. In April 1968 the University of Omaha (ou) Concerts and Lectures
Committee sponsored Midnight Slapstick, a salute to the silent film era.
That year the films of Leatrice Joy were featured, and the actress traveled
to Omaha to take part in the event. After arriving in Omaha, Joy made an
appearance at the Twenties Club. Midnight Slapstick organizer and ou
Professor of Special Education Walter Beaupre at right. Look at that outstanding
Twenties Club interior! Very Las Vegas lounge. University of Nebraska Omaha
Photograph Collection, Archives & Special Collections, Criss Library.

for a few more socialites. The main lounge area was thick with happy,
tipsy Omahans enjoying the live combo tunes as they danced underneath
bubbles suspended in the air above. A wide-eyed crowd was held back,
atop the stairs, by a velvet rope, left to enviously observe and await their
turn on the dance floor below. Vohoska wrote, "Everybody was there . . .
almost like the whole city had been brought inside, under one roof."

The interior elaborations were the real showstopper. The Charles Stark
Corporation planned, designed, and equipped the Twenties Club, quite
possibly the exterior ornamentation as well. Outfitted in red, I understand, red on red vinyl, red padded velvet with black-and-gold details.

339

The look was a flocked wall, with midcentury modern tables, chairs, and booths, accented with antique furniture. I've heard tell there were portraits of the silent film era stars, surrounded by flickering lights, as well as framed playbills and sheet music. Stained glass ceiling lights were nestled above, and there was even a glass-enclosed telephone booth that appeared to have been sprayed with machine gun bullets. I am not sure if these details came later or if they were original, but apparently, the Twenties featured a huge mural of old-time stars painted on the outside of the building. Inside, there were more murals of 20's scenes as well as a Mr. C's Steakhouse–type mock city street scene, where a sexy mannequin leg could be viewed revealing itself from behind an "upstairs window curtain" on the west side of the large room. In the words of Mother of Miss Cassette, "Back then the Twenties Club was considered racy but definitely not sleazy." Taking into consideration this period in American history, I perceived the Twenties theme as invitingly risqué. Reputedly, the decor was so spot on that George R. C. McFarland, the actor who had played Spanky in *Our Gang*, wanted to use the lounge as an on-location spot for his movie *The Fatty Arbuckle Story*. Arbuckle had been in the nightclub business in the 1920s, after being exonerated in the death of beautiful starlet Virginia Rappe. Although most likely flattered, manager Tony Greco apparently was not interested in the dark shadow this affiliation might cast on his brand-new club.

By April 1965 the Twenties was already expanding. An eight-foot-deep band shell was attached to the south side of the building, essentially converting the old bandstand into a dance floor. This would serve to double the dance floor. The female performers, attired in 1920s garb, had previously danced on the floor and would be moved to one-foot-high platforms that slid out from under the band shell. The walls and multiple bars on the west and east sides of the main room were moved, adding seating for another one hundred patrons.

Mother Cassette was one of the many curious Omahans who ventured to the Twenties Club in its early days. "It would have been in '64 or '65, as I recall—before I met your Dad. I had a few dates, and we went there. Back then it was a nightclub, a rather respectable place, racy as it was.

It was nicely furnished and did not seem sleazy. Frankly, in those days, it was just considered provocative dancing." The last sentence was in reference to the previously mentioned platform dancing that took place near the band shell.

Father Cassette remembered the Twenties Club in its earlier form: "Yes, the Twenties was a first class nightclub when it opened. Before going to boot camp, I double-dated with a buddy, and we took two nursing students from the Lutheran Hospital. We all got drunk and had a great time. I think I spent all the money in my savings account for my half of the bill—huge gin gimlet hangover the next day!"

CHARLIE STARK

Allow me to introduce the Roaring Twenties interior designer, Charlie Stark. Most days Charlie Stark could have been described as an unorthodox, swanky-dressed, wise-talking New Yorker. And he was. In my experience this strain of personality can really shake things up in reserved, often mumbling Omaha. Stark had a flair for both storytelling and an artistic eye for design. At the time, he was a fifty-three-year-old redheaded dreamer. This charisma carried over into his personal attire—dapper, cigar smoking, and, I would venture to guess, Stark used his hands when he detailed his various, expansive schemes. Solidly grounded Omahans were said to find it difficult to discern between his tale tales, his actualized designs, and his dreams for the future. I like to imagine them holding on for dear life during one of his overlong Jimmy Durante–style narratives. And yes, they ran around together. There's a great story about Charlie entertaining Durante and cast after-hours at Sam and Ross Nisi's SpareTime. Mr. Durante had appeared in an Ak-Sar-Ben show earlier in the night. Charlie dazzled, giving a humorous report as chairman of the Lower East Side, while Sam Nisi poured. Oh, to have witnessed that night, sitting in the corner with a cigar. Apparently, his sports coat was stuffed with 'em. There was something larger-than-life about Charlie Stark, and the press loved him because his quotations were amazing. A journalist wrote, Professor Charles Stark is available for lectures on such titles as "Outstanding Gangsters I Have Known." Confidence, coupled with crazy talent, Stark should have been celebrated every time he walked in the room. A standing ovation, I reckon, if Omahans weren't so dang buttoned-up . . . and, I would later find, threatened.

A *My Omaha Obsession* reader, Ron Hunter, introduced me to Charlie Stark, and I followed up by purchasing Karen Stark's book, *World on a String*, about her father's upbringing in 1920s New York. A fascinating man, Charles Stark was born into poverty, the son of Jewish immigrants. His father made a meager living as a pushcart vendor, while his mother stayed in their two-room tenement with her nine children on the Lower East Side. According to Charlie, a self-taught artist and set designer, he got his start working backstage, shifting scenery and eventually designing scenes for the theaters of Second Avenue, "the Broadway of the Yiddish Theater." Stark later began decorating speakeasies for the "mobsters" and the "notorious Italian neighborhood gangsters"—he was particularly sought after for his painting abilities. There were also rumors that he was a song and dance man, earning roles with a host of 1920s celebrities. Other fantastical tales described Charlie as a fourteen-year-old nurse-maid to six foot two Billy Kimball, one of a stable of boxers in New York, some of whom young Stark was hired to train and keep an eye on. Years later Charlie used his theater set design skills as he began decorating and designing restaurants in Kansas City. In following his trail, I would often find Charlie darting between Kansas City and Omaha, living and designing in both places through the years.

Designer Charlie Stark could also lay claim to the decoration of many of Omaha's nocturnal hotspots, considered institutions. What follows is the list I have found to date. Unbeknownst to me, the Twenties Club was thought to be an updated complement to Stark's original concept at the Colony Club. The Colony Club was the very first nightclub my father went to, down on Twentieth and Farnam. It was later destroyed in an explosion and fire in 1963. The Brewery, a short-lived club located at Fifth and Pierce, was in Sam Nisi's old SpareTime Café building, later reopened as La Tropicana. Stark decorated Angelo's Restaurant right at Seventy-Second and Pacific, Ross' Steak House at 909 South Seventy-Second Street, Caniglia's Venice Inn at 6920 Pacific Street, La Casa Piz-

107. Charlie Stark in profile, 1963. Photo from the *Omaha Sun* newspaper.

zeria at 4432 Leavenworth Street, the Italian villa scene and decor of the SpareTime party room at 707 South Seventy-Second, Angie's Restaurant and Cocktail Lounge at 1001 Pacific Street.

I was given another *Dundee and West Omaha Sun* newspaper article by Ron Hunter, dated 1964, which illuminated an Omaha mystery—one of jealousy and prejudice regarding our man Stark. Through the years his interiors and taste making had made numerous friends and business associates a bushel of money, and now Stark understandably wanted to try his hand in the nightlife business. Diamond Lil's was Stark's elegant dream of a nightclub–steak house, a controversial supper club that had been trying to find a home along the Strip since Stark's plan was hatched. By a seven-to-zero vote, Stark's application for a Class C liquor license for his proposed restaurant at 900 South Seventy-Second Street was flatly denied, city council's second brush-off. The mystery presented itself when one considers the prior Omaha liquor license rules. Previous to this particular vote, when a new hotel, bowling alley, or steak house was constructed, the owner was automatically granted a Class C liquor license. Additionally curious on this date, the city council voted to eliminate its own hotel–bowling alley–steak house exception, originating with the Stark case. Charlie Stark was blocked all the way around.

The 900 South Seventy-Second Street address does not exist, but I believe Stark's monumental edifice would have been on the west side of the street, directly across from Ross' Steak House at that time. Currently, the Boot Barn Western Wear is housed on the proposed parcel. The fact that Stark's grand club had already been kicked down Seventy-Second, away from the College of Saint Mary's (the sisters had a problem with a three million–dollar risqué supper club being situated near their girls' school), was one blockade he had already come to terms with. Charlie Stark had never owned his own club, but the idea of being shoulder to shoulder, right across from Ross' Steak House, among his other contemporaries, was one he surely relished. However, it would appear this proximity was probably more than his "friends" could bear. Competition on the Strip was fierce, and Charlie Stark presented a large threat. The Diamond Lil's dream club, and Stark, himself, became a big problem.

108. The Twenties Club band shell stage, featuring Hal Pryor
and his house act. University of Nebraska Omaha Photograph
Collection, Archives & Special Collections, Criss Library.

After Diamond Lil's second rejection, even Stark's attorney said it was
time to move on, the application withdrawn. Charlie Stark would continue to dream of opening Lil's and pen angry missives entitled "Open
Letter to Omaha." It would have been hard to swallow.

THE TWENTIES STYLE

The Twenties brought in a wide range of acts: comedy and singing teams,
ragtime piano players, old-time revue, Broadway stars, one-man shows,
live jazz combos, soft rock combos, lounge singers, melodramas, cabaret
acts, a children's puppet theater, burlesque. Through it all the Hal Pryor
Band worked full-time and backed all of the entertainment acts as the
house band. The Twenties bartenders, barbacks, and waitresses were
rumored to sing throughout the night as well. Tony Greco auditioned all
of the entertainers personally by scouting their various acts in other cit-

345

ies. Touring acts would remember Greco and stay in touch; Greco would even manage a few artists in his stretch at the Twenties. With regard to the risqué nature of the Twenties, years later Greco would say: "I never had topless dancers or smutty comics. I never thought smut was funny. I never wanted to have a place where I'd be ashamed to take my family." Many of the Twenties' performers became bigger names later. The *Omaha World-Herald* reported that "one of them, Rich Little, made a tape giving his impressions of how famous people might read the Nebraska drinking laws. The tape was played every night at closing time to remind customers to drink up, clear out and drive home safely."

A problem the Twenties Lounge experienced early on was very telling of the times and just how commonly Omahans would go out socializing. Greco reported Twenties customers would typically arrive to the club about 8:30 p.m., subsequent to dinner elsewhere. After drinks and entertainment, patrons would leave the Twenties between 11:30 p.m. and midnight to stop somewhere else and eat again before heading home. The Twenties was challenged to keep customers spending their money without going into the steak house business, something its owners recognized Omaha had an abundance of.

THE STAFF

Tony Greco was the ultimate successful host. Known to hobnob with the best of them, Greco knew the key elements to a classy, party atmosphere, as evidenced by his tailored, conservative suits, fancy sports cars, flamboyant attitude . . . even a white Rolls Royce. "America's most elegant speakeasy" gave Tony an esteemed position as Omaha tastemaker, proudly "a club operator, not a restaurant man," in his own words. Rick Cockston was the floor man. In his role, between the infamous rollicking and swaggering staff, Charlie Stark bragged that Cockston had once been towed one hundred miles on the Missouri River while balancing on a single ski. Sam J. Corrado had already earned a reputation as being among the fastest bartenders in town. Barman Corrado handily clinched his title at several clubs, including the former Prom–Town House, Colony Club, and Gorat's. Andre Flores was the hatcheck girl at the Twenties Club, having traveled to Omaha just four years earlier as one of the seven "Pearls of the Pacific." The Pearls were a touring Polynesian dance act. The troupe left town with just six Pearls, when Andre married local Omaha fella Dick Flores. A former employee of the Chicago Playboy Club, Dick Flores was a floor greeter, rumored to give out frequent pointers on how to bunny hunt. Whispers from the grapevine suggested singer Pat "Sophie" Murphy came to the Twenties Club by way of the Hot Springs, Arkansas, crackdown on gaming dens, where she had worked as a lounge act at one the padlocked casinos. Twenties vocalist Cara Lynn, known as the "lass with the lowdown New Orleans voice," was tittle-tattled to have been straight off the farms of Iowa.

TWENTIES ATTIRE

In the early years the cocktail waitresses, coat check girls, and female dancers were said to don satin, silk, lace, flowing boa feathers, of the Roaring 1920s. I would conjure silent picture starlets and Ziegfeld Follies girls. But from advertisements it would appear that the costumes would resemble a saloon style in reality, more of a burlesque attire with fishnets and a comical feather springing from a bun. Of course, this just seemed perfectly over-the-top 1960s to me. Do you recall the cowboy movies and westerns from the 1960s? All false eyelashes, fishnets, bouffants, and hairspray. An ad from 1964: "Cocktail Waitresses. Must be attractive. No experience necessary. Age 21 to 30. Will be costumed. Must have nice figure. For the fabulous new Twenties Club opening January 20." I suspect the male staff—bartenders, bar porters, security, and floor attendants, for their part, wore bow ties or neck scarves with a short suit jacket or suspenders. However, I have no real proof of this, as there were no men featured in print ads, of course.

GO-GO DANCING

There were many beautiful women shown in the Twenties Club print ads with stage names the likes of Bee Palmer, Dolly Dawn, Gladys Glad, Kiki Roberts, Flo Ward, Linda Gale, and Misty Wilson. I assume those were made-up names. Lord knows, Miss Cassette is in no position to judge elusive identities. Were these gals go-go dancers or cocktail waitresses? I am not entirely sure. The go-go dance craze sprang from the nightclub scene, where women were found dancing "the Twist" in miniskirts and knee-high boots. Popular clubs on the coasts began hiring dancers to get up on tables, platforms, and later cages, to go-go dance for nightclub patrons. By 1964 this trend had exploded and reached every major city, including the downtown Omaha bar scene. Although donning something filmy or the bikini style would become the vogue as the decade contin-ued, American go-go dancers were usually fully clothed in hip, albeit little, getups. The shimmy and twist were risqué enough. There was rare reporting of topless go-go dancing on the coasts; oftentimes these gals would go on to become celebrity-styled feature dancers working a tour circuit. In 1964 one must figure bleached blonde hair, large earrings, and even kohl eyeliner sent a message of promiscuity to the conservative mainstream; a miniskirt coupled with slim-fitting go-go boots, merged with gyrations, were just plain racy. An informant gave inkling of what I suspected: the women at the Twenties Club were in a 1960s spin on 1920s attire and did not bare their bodies, although they were thought to be Quite Appealing.

THE MAYOR, MR. COLEMAN, AND MR. GRECO

Under city filings and new incorporators, I had found 7301 Realty Cor-poration of Omaha had formed an alliance in January 14, 1964, with ten thousand dollars, under the names of Harold M. Klein and Anthony R. Greco. The Twenties Club would eventually have two corporations, 7301 Realty Corporation and 7301 Corporation. Additionally, Tony Greco would obtain both Tower West Corporation and KOLT Corporation for his real estate operations. These names would enter the picture five years later.

An interesting complication transpired concurrent to the Twenties inception. Back in the fall of 1964, Chicago investor John B. Coleman claimed that former mayor James J. Dworak solicited a twenty-five thousand–dollar bribe from Coleman to prevent a veto of the Coleman rezoning application for an apartment he intended to build in Omaha.

Coleman claimed that Mayor Dworak told him if he did not make a campaign contribution to him, Dworak would veto the zoning even if it passed with city council. The mayor then proposed the payment go to a dummy firm, the KOLT Corporation, so that Mr. Coleman could get an income tax deduction on the expenditure. Our man Greco happened to own the KOLT Corporation. Coleman began recording the Blackstone Hotel meetings on multiple occasions in September 1964. Meetings were held at the Blackstone Hotel and Eppley Airfield, but apparently, Greco would not take the money in hand. The case would go to court in 1966.

Tony Greco reported, from the courtroom stand, that back in September 1964 Mayor Dworak had rung him up at the Twenties Club. Greco said the mayor "talked rough" and sounded like he'd been drinking, asking that some of his friends be able to get a good table at the Twenties. Early the next morning Greco was awakened by Mayor Dworak calling again, this time asking if Greco was still in real estate. Greco explained that he held four corporations, KOLT being one of them. KOLT, Inc., was a corporation held with Greco's wife to buy land and construct an apartment building. To that point there had never been a business transaction under KOLT. Greco claimed to be confused by the mayor's questioning and was further perplexed when warned "not to accept any check or cash if contacted by an outsider." Tony Greco said he was later contacted by John Coleman but did not accept monies from him.

For Mayor Dworak's part, he claimed he did not receive anything, in fact turning down Coleman's offer three times. The mayor claimed Coleman was entrapping him. On the stand Dworak did admit to having called Tony Greco, asking for "help and assistance" even though he was not very well acquainted with Greco. Dworak admitted he had asked the name of Greco's corporation because Coleman wanted to make his payment to a corporation so that cost could be deducted as a business expense. He had told Greco not to receive money from Coleman but, instead, to call Dworak directly or (henchman) Mr. Gugas. According to Dworak, he then went directly to city attorney Fitle to ask what evidence was needed to prove a bribe offer.

DEED CONFUSION AND NORMAN BORTOLOTTI

March 23, 1966, revealed an article in which a board approved the purchase of outstanding Twenties Club shares by the club operators. My immediate (mis)understanding was that a Norman Bortolotti had bought out Tony Greco. A strange quitclaim deed was penned into the 7301 Farnam record in March 1966. It looked as though Tony Greco was able to bow out of the Twenties, or so I thought. After months of acclimating to the case, I learned it was actually Charles Harper's daughter Eola and her husband, Vern Brooks, who were bought out. Their identities were shrouded and not announced in the press.

In the same month Greco was taken off of the deed, which is where I was initially befuddled. The A. S. Battiato Construction Company entered a QCD instrument on the deed—but who were the early investors? Like a tidy shell game, Norman Bortolotti then signed the deed over to 7301 Realty Company in the same month. I know now Tony Greco and Norman Bortolotti were equal shareholders in that corporation. Harold Klein had never been on the deed, and I can only assume from frequent newspaper articles about his business, the Club New Yorker, Klein had most likely pulled up stakes and signed off the Twenties early on.

I was not sure of how deep their connections ran, but I did know that in the summer of 1964 Tony Greco and Norman Bortolotti owned a mystery twenty-five-foot cruiser, named the *Normador*.

THE FABULOUS BORTOLOTTIS

I traced Norman Bortolotti to his 1910 residence at 9900 Florence Heights Boulevard. Pioneer Omaha real estate developer N. P. Dodge Sr. had lived in the large home at the time of his death in 1950. Bortolotti worked for the Universal Terrazzo & Tile Company in all capacities, primarily as secretary and treasurer. Norman's father, Isidoro Bortolotti, was an immigrant from Udine, Italy, founding the Universal Terrazzo & Tile Company in 1924 in Omaha, having learned the terrazzo trade when he was a young boy. Norman, his brother Doro, and sister Norma would grow up working in the Omaha tile company. Still family owned by the

Bortolottis, Universal Terrazzo & Tile Company can be found at 4225 Florence Boulevard, although it is now named G. M. S. Werks. Surprisingly, it was Isidoro Bortolotti who had gotten the family into the nightclub business. Story goes, back when he was laying tile on-site in the Twenties, Isidoro had overheard a conversation indicating the early club's investors could use additional capital.

PROBLEMS AT THE TWENTIES

The dirty laundry aired on the Twenties Club was that the club was losing money by 1968. My simplified overview: Greco owned 50 percent of the 7301 Corporation stock and N.N.D. Investment Company held the other 50. I suspect N.N.D. was the Bortolotti family. Differences of opinion of how to manage the club arose, leading to a lawsuit, the very first of its kind under the 1963 Nebraska Business Corporation Act. In a new precedent the court would appoint a receiver to manage the corporation until the Twenties Club could be sold or a suit decided upon. Days later John C. North, attorney and Creighton Law professor, was appointed the task of operating the Twenties Club. Soon after, North announced the Twenties was officially for sale.

NEW DIRECTION

Although themed nightclubs were still wildly popular with the older set, it isn't hard to imagine the youth of the late 1960s were not interested in their parents' Twenties Club, amusingly outfitted with what must have seemed an extravagantly garish red-on-red environment. Small impromptu clubs as well as auditorium venues would allow the younger set to "hang out," in environs not overtly decorated or as pretentious as in the past. In typing these words, please understand Miss Cassette embraces all flamboyance and vulgarity of the 1940s through mid-1960s decor but with recognition these ostentatious displays became passé by Baby Boomer standards. A raw warehouse, colorful blacklight psychedelic playgrounds, rustic themes, turn-of-the-century cowboy clubs, and outdoor festivals were vague designations for late 1960s music lovers turned inward, seeking their own personal experience, desiring straightforward entertainment. The Vietnam War was in full swing, and the Summer of Love was on the horizon.

GRECO'S 8 LTD.

It appeared Tony Greco had staked up at a west outpost. In December 1968 Greco dropped a few clues he was scouting a large space in the basement of the Westroads Shopping Center. He sounded hopeful as he described to a journalist the possibility of two lounges fitting into the space and his dreams of having a cool club geared toward the younger set, twenty-five to thirty years of age, and their accompanying tastes—five to six musicians in a group, offering "fast-paced" singing and dancing. I think we all know what that was code for: rock 'n' roll! That summer Tony began working with architect Gary Goldstein on an interior featuring a hexagon-shaped stage and runway, which could be moved with "automatic controls." The dominant color scheme was magenta, and *psychedelic* was thrown around in later reviews. Greco's 8 Ltd. was a hit for ten years to follow.

NEW PHASE OF THE TWENTIES

Universal Terrazzo & Tile Company officially owned the Twenties after March 1969. Doro Louie Bortolotti stepped up as manager. During this phase the club's spelling had simply been altered to The 20's. Designer Charlie Stark was summoned for renovation. A month later there was a new design for a room near the entrance called the "Police Gazette Room," but two months later The 20's incorporated an L-shaped room at the east end of the club curiously named "Harry the Gent's," where Stark envisioned walls covered in vintage, blown-up newspaper photographs. The additional room was projected to have an intimate bar, serving the cocktail hour, when the rest of the club was darkened. Ragtime piano player Johnny Maddox was hired to perform at The 20's Club, displacing Turkish belly dancer Ozel Turkbas.

CONSTANTINO BEAUTY ACADEMY
AND OTHER NEIGHBORS

In the fall of 1970 Joseph Constantino took out a building permit for 7330 Farnam Street, west of The 20's. That address was the West Omaha satellite of the Constantino beauty empire, established at 1409 Douglas

Street. Forecast to be the New Constantino Beauty Academy and Salon, this building was, I mistakenly assumed early on, an original Cedarnole residence, albeit a peculiar one. Then again, there wasn't anything routine about this enclave. The tall white structure can be observed on any given day squaring off with Seventy-Second Street, its closest parallel opponent. It couldn't have initially looked like this, I questioned. I seem to remember a girlfriend starting beauty school right after graduation. That summer a group of us girls were sitting in a circle in a parking lot, most likely affecting a collective bored look, smoking and listening to music. I am not sure why this was a good idea at the time, but I recall this gathering in the lot adjacent to the 7330 Farnam building, at the 7317 Douglas building, around the corner to the northwest. I discovered this address once housed the Beauty and Barber Wholesale Supply Warehouse throughout the 1970s, until Beauty Mart Discount Supply took over the lease in the 1980s. By the late 1980s, 7317 Douglas became home to the brilliant Gadgeteer shop, Rita Danielson's design-focused housewares store. With exhilaration I finally tracked the Salvatore "Mr. Rudy's" Cosentino College of Hair Styling to 202 South Seventy-Third Street, an east-facing address to the 7317 Douglas building.

CHARLES HARPER'S LOTS

Cedarnole West was leaning decidedly more commercial. The Cedarnole Shopping Center, to the south of The 20's, at 314 South Seventy-Second Street (Harney cross street), opened in March 1971. The Cape Cod house at 7211 Farnam changed businesses a number of times until it was razed in March 1973. Norman Bortolotti bought the parcel and constructed a new retail rental space in January 1974. Salon Constantino's Beauty Shop and the Joseph B. Constantino Beauty Academy were successes at 7330 Farnam. Meanwhile, 7333 Farnam, built in 1968, operated as Dr. Thomas Plank's dental clinic. The Richard Coyle and Donald Polsky Associates Architecture group was new to the area in the 7337 Farnam location, built in 1970. The building at 7444 Farnam, home to the Fish Bowl Tropical Fish store, seemed familiar. All of Charles Harper's original lots on the south side of Farnam Street had been filled in, but notably, the northern swath was still empty. The 20's had ushered in the late 1960s–early 1970s commercial buildings, but because of their positioning on the curvy Cedarnole neighborhood streets, there was no cohesion, no density, and it remained a pocket of disarrange. Perhaps that is why it was the perfect setting for the next undertaking.

THE CAESAR'S WEST NIGHT CLUB

Shockingly, Mr. Bortolotti closed The 20's in the spring of 1971, until he could find "something the public will support." Doro Louie Bortolotti had split his time between the club and the family's terrazzo and tile business, in what must have been an overwhelming commitment. As it turned out, the "something the public would support" was topless dancers, then legal within city limits.

TOPLESS DANCING

There was a very brief window in late 1970s when Omaha police and city attorneys had loosened their view of exotic dancing as entertainment and turned a blind eye. No longer perceived as lewd, OPD openly stated there was "nothing that can be done under the current laws" about topless dancing "unless someone files complaint." The Douglas County sheriff saw little wrong with the topless shows in Omaha, amounting to entertainers taking the stage in bikini-type outfits, removing the upper garment, and go-go style dancing with an occasional "bump and grind." During this period of exotic dancing, the classic striptease, emphasis on the slow tease, was popular, seemingly innocent by today's standards. Not surprisingly, there was a dedicated local team of officers willing to document these clubs and keep an eye on the quality of their dancers. I am sure their motives were pure. By the summer of 1971 a topless ban suit was filed due to public outrage (a vocal few?) as well as council members who were divided on the moral compass. In retrospect The 20's decision to move into the topless realm was a point at which there was no turning back. Ask anyone around to this very day, and they will either turn up their noses when The 20's Club is mentioned, find its history oddly fascinating, or harbor a personal story about an adventure enveloped within. For better or for worse, the public would view the once well-respected Twenties Club as a strip club from that day forward.

When the Bortolottis began presenting topless dancers in 1971, they also decided it was time for a new name as well. The Twenties Club–20's Club, once home to Marilyn Maye, Rusty Draper, a puppet act, and Little Egypt, had morphed into Caesar's West Night Club. I couldn't help but wonder how employees explained the HUGE 20's sign? By all accounts this marvel continued to light the whole Cedarnole West enclave—perhaps the candle that singed the moth. There was a Caesar's Palace offering topless dancers down at 2920 Farnam Street, but I am not sure if they were related. At this time Bortolotti turned the management keys over to Bert Reid Howard, who made the club quite a success, securing the Bortolotti family investment and relieving Doro Louis of his management duties.

THE BERT REID HOWARD FILE

Bert Reid Howard was a fascinating character, the type this girl detective loves to trace. In the late 1950s Bert Reid Howard was a self-proclaimed fifty-dollar-a-week costume jewelry salesman. He was also arrested in one of the biggest hauls of questionable gambling devices ever made by Omaha vice, topping that of his good pal's, Howard W. Lansing's, arrest from two years earlier. The two young fellows were well known in the Omaha arena as gamblers. Bert Reid Howard caught Omaha's attention when a box of crooked dice, cards, and equipment was confiscated at the Rocket Recreation parlor in downtown Omaha at 1521 Farnam Street. There the twenty-six-year-old Howard was arrested, and papers later found showed he had been picked up previously with crooked gambling equipment in Lincoln, Nebraska, and St. Joe, Missouri, as well. Young Howard had a pocket full of $270 and a vial of white powder. His apartment at 3509 North Thirty-Sixth Avenue was chock-full of a large quantity of "crooked dice"; decks of cars with the backs marked in a way that was only visible with special tinted glasses (which were also found); notebooks filled with club meetings and parties in Iowa, Nebraska, Missouri, Illinois, Kansas, and Minnesota; two more $100 bills and ten $100 money orders; an unregistered Beretta; and even more vials of the white powder. Howard's car was plumb full of metal dice and twelve more marked decks of cards. The St. Joseph police rang in with their confiscated goodies from Howard, including four magnetic kneepads. The vials of white powder turned out to be plastic cement used in loading dice.

I tracked Bert Reid Howard (let's just call him Mr. BRH from now on) to the Ak-Sar-Ben Bookstore down at 1517 Dodge Street in the late 1960s. I had come across this store in my Muse Theater research and discovered it to be an early Omaha adult store, featuring mostly books and magazines. Now that location serves as a parking garage, at Fifteenth and Capitol, across from the Residence Inn. Mr. BRH, his wife, Susan Siegal Howard, and other employees were arrested a number of times for exhibiting and selling "obscene material" at the Ak-Sar-Ben Bookstore. These frequent police busts would yield over 830 magazines from the shop in one year's time, garnering the Howards quite a bit of attention.

Shortly thereafter, topless dancing would become illegal, and the dancers had to start wearing "cover-ups," essentially bikini dancing. But the times had changed, and the Caesar's West crowd no longer wanted cabaret and mixed entertainment shows; they seemed dated and hokey. The club couldn't seem to pack in the audiences it once had with the topless dancers and one of Omaha's top bookmakers, Mr. BRH, running the show.

Caesar's West Night Club would limp along until a lawsuit forced the Bortolottis to change the name back to the Twenties Club in 1973, as a result of legal action taken by Caesar's Palace of Las Vegas citing infringement. For his part Mr. BRH would be forced out of the Ak-Sar-Ben Bookstore business in 1974, not wanting to fight with the city anymore. He would get into the bonded auto sales business. By the time I had to leave the hot trail of Mr. BRH, I found he had been charged with conspiracy, along with fellas named "Boogers" and "Socks," for allegedly trading automobiles for tips on forthcoming OPD raids with the former assistant city prosecutor Anthony Troia. Later Mr. BRH would be discovered as the man behind the curtain of the Bittersweet Lounge and the Lusty Lady at 1512 Howard (another investigation from my website). I longed to know more, and honestly, I could have followed him to the end of his short, exuberant life, but I felt a pressure to keep on our Twenties mission. By

December 1973 owner Louis Bortolotti announced he would close The 20's due to "lack of interest in the shows." The family closed down the club, once the most handsome room in Omaha, under ten years old.

ROCK 'N' ROLL TWENTIES

The club stood empty for one full year. In January 1975 Louis Bortolotti made the news again by telling Peter Citron, once famous *World-Herald* entertainment writer, he wanted to bring The 20's back, this time focusing on live music. It would appear that the scantily clad dancing girls continued during this period but held shows in another private part of the club.

In the 1970s Mother- and Father-in-Law of Miss Cassette attended some concerts at The 20's, where a bevy of soft rock groups, light southern rock, and live country acts were touted on the bill, as was "Mayor Benson," aka Tom Freberg. Freberg reminisced about the River City All-Stars band playing a number of concerts at The 20's Club in the late 1970s. He was quick to note the All-Stars had splintered off from Bumpy Action, a famed Omaha bluesy rock band from the 1969–74 time period. Bumpy Action was composed of Michael Pryor, or MojoPo to the McFoster's crowd (RIP); Bob Ganey; Mike Haas; Doug and Denise Fackler; Richie Thieman; Mike Ganey; and Chris Winquest. The Bumpy Action would infamously pack a crowd of five thousand in the huge Aquarius Lounge, south on Seventy-Second and Pacific Streets, known for having fifteen separate bars within its circular interior. This new carnation featured the laidback, cool melodies of Doug Fackler, Ron Cooley, Brian Sampson, Rich Walter, and Jack Greer. In fact, checking Freberg's information, I came across a live recording of the River City All-Stars performing "What I Need" at the actual 20's Nightclub in 1978. Find it on YouTube and marvel. Such a perfect late 1970s sound.

Freberg remembered the River City All-Stars playing in the larger room of The 20's with the bigger stage: "It was red and over the top." He recollected there were statues to the sides of the stage. "It was all shiny and gaudy to the tastes of this particular music crowd." He seemed to suggest the scene was on a natural, straightforward 1970s vibe. In looking back, Tom thought there were maybe only tables and chairs in the room and didn't seem to think an audience would stand for shows at many places in those days. The "smaller room" was where the exotic dancing took place. The two crowds were distinctly different and didn't interact, to his memory. I imagined this smaller room must have been the intimate bar on the eastern side of the building, created in 1969, as part of Stark's remodeling plan. Mysteriously, by the late 1970s The 20's Club would go dark yet again.

THE TONY GRECO SCORE

After the Westroads Shopping Center's management took over the 8 Ltd., turning it into more retail shops, Tony Greco would be forced to shutter his basement rock shop in 1979. Greco had already purchased Cheeta(h) on the southeast corner at Seventieth and Dodge in 1978, the Yano Caniglia creation that had undergone many name (the Heet, the Cheetah, and Dirty Sally's) as well as format changes (top name entertainment, go-go, topless, and revue). Reconfigured as Bacchus, named for the god of wine, Greco would make a solid bet and move on to a discotheque theme, a venue mimicking the likes of Studio 54 in New York City. Disco was sweeping the nation. By the late 1978 most major American cities boasted disco clubs as well as disco dancing lessons; after all, *Saturday Night Fever* had been released the year before. New emphasis was put on the club DJ, who would seamlessly mix the seven- and twelve-inch disco records into a stylized show, perfect for crowd dancing. The dancing, costumes, and culture were a return to the extravagant themed nightclubs of the past, with a new emphasis on sexuality and excess. Even Miss Cassette's parents took disco dancing lessons and could be found out in these local disco infernos till the "Last Dance." Sadly, disco's death by public shaming concluded many dancing clubs. Tony Greco sold Bacchus in 1984 along with the valuable adjoining land to Omaha's pizza king, Willy Theisen, who later opened his gourmet hamburger restaurant, Flakey Jake's.

THE EIGHTIES MYSTERY

A paging through the well-worn Omaha City Directory of 1982, 1983, and 1984 mysteriously exhibited 7301 Farnam as unoccupied, at least on the days city directory data collectors came knocking. Addresses 7215, 7301, and 7305 Farnam were listed as vacant as well—a very barren Cedarnole West. I imagined this dearth of business and ghost town–like atmosphere, hidden in the center of town, offered the proper ambience for a den of artists, wanderers, the curious, and the lonely. Was it any wonder that The 20's Club would spin into its next incarnation under these blank, uninhabited circumstances?

The Nosy Nelly in me was particularly intrigued with these years because within this period I clearly remembered the Ramones, a seventies punk band, had played The 20's Club—a scarcely recalled, confounding profundity in the annals of Omaha's punk history. I remember this night as if I was allowed within those forbidden doors of lore. The truth is I was not permitted to go to this show, as I was too young—once again missing my chance at this peculiar, enticing environ. On a lucky whim my father drove me to that Ramones concert, where we sat in The 20's parking lot, in a Volkswagen, and I was allowed to play homemade mixed tapes as I studied the cooler-than-cool older kids entering the club. So, when I could find no proof that The 20's was open in those years, it justified my fears that I had dreamed up this whole experience.

Terry Click, then a thirty-year-old drummer from Cincinnati, must have seen a gold mine when he surveyed the abandoned 20's Club in the early summer of 1983. Click had formerly been a sales manager for Montgomery Ward but moved to Omaha to become the new high school program director for Junior Achievement. Click marveled at how Louis Bortolotti had kept the building up, including heating and air-conditioning it, even though it had been shuttered for about fourteen months. Terry Click agreed to lease the building, with an option to buy, and began formulating a new plan. He installed a new sound system, extended the stage, and would look into installing an elaborate lighting system. He would refocus the club on live music, a diverse offering of big names not found at other Omaha nightspots. The 20's would be open every night, with local bands playing Thursday through Sunday. The Comedy Shoppe was on Wednesdays, and anyone could hop onstage. Click's big dream was to host weekly national acts.

THE BANDS

In a state of Sherlockian rapture, I tiptoed through the archives in hopes of discovering the truth about The 20's Club with Terry Click at command. A *World-Herald* article from May 29, 1983, did prove there was a Tuesday, May 31, 1983, Ramones concert for a mere $8.50 cover charge. You've gotta love a door fee involving quarters. "Hastily arranged appearance in newly reopened 20's Club," read the article. The Ramones had already performed at the Music Box ballroom in Omaha in 1978 to 650 fans. Then in 1980 they played the Music Hall before an audience of 1,400. The 20's capacity was set at 425 for the band's May 1983 show. I believe this "hastily arranged" Ramones concert was Click's first national act for The 20's and a real feather in his cap. The show was sold out.

Click would bring Ricky Nelson, rock 'n' roll singer and actor, to The 20's soon after the Ramones. The "Be-Bop Baby" and "Poor Little Fool" star would pull in another sold-out show. Weeks later a little-known indie group from Athens, Georgia, R.E.M., would hit the stage on June 29, 1983. The band's debut record *Murmur* had just been released two months earlier, and although it would be named *Rolling Stone's* best album of the year, upon its release, Murmur had only a small but cultish college radio crowd following. Omaha favorites Digital Sex were approached to open for R.E.M. Click had a third sold-out show in a month's time. He was on a winning streak. Is anyone else wondering what happened to the dancing girls during this period? I would surmise, based on word of mouth, that the Bortolottis continued to run the smaller bar within The 20's, complete with dancers' stage, for that separate clientele.

There would be a wide mix of talent, just as Terry Click had promised, to follow in the next months. Chicago industrial band Ministry possibly played The 20's Club on July 9 on its With Sympathy Tour, but they definitely played on September 2, 1983. Country artist Tanya Tucker had two well-received shows in one night in July 1983. Hard rock band Zebra had also just released its mainstream debut record, and the band got its chance under The 20's lights sometime in early July. Spyro Gyra, a New York jazz fusion band, came to town on July 16. Unbelievably,

Michael Bolton performed on July 22, followed the next night by Men Without Hats. Singer-songwriter Dave Mason performed on July 29. The Greg Kihn Band played on July 30, showing off its recently released hit "Jeopardy." August 21 brought southern rock group the Ozark Mountain Daredevils to the stage. During this period there was a rumor that Def Leppard would be taping a video at The 20's on August 11, 1983, the day between the band's two scheduled concerts at the Civic Auditorium— this was one story I could not confirm.

FIRSTHAND REPORTS

Omaha musician Dereck Higgins shared his memories from The 20's Club. In those days Higgins was playing bass in Digital Sex and, not long after that, RAF. "I attended and played shows there. I do remember the decor feeling out of sync with the proceedings. Backstage with R.E.M. was very memorable. The Ramones' 20's show was way better than the one at the Music Hall but still nowhere near what happened at the Music Box. I remember meeting Al Jourgensen of Ministry at The 20's. He still used a fake English accent back then. Another outstanding show was The Alarm."

Omaha musician Stephen Sheehan was vocalist of Digital Sex during those years. "I recall a red-on-red-on-red interior. I remember how confusing it was that The 20's was offering live music of this kind, which back then was regrettably called 'alternative music,' a term which later morphed into 'indie rock.' It should be noted that The 20's had two areas. The main area (The 20's itself) and adjacent to it was a much smaller room called Showgirl Lounge, I think, where the strippers did their thing, which didn't involve much stripping due to local laws. I stuck my head in there once and exited almost immediately. Bands played on a stage inside The 20's recessed into the building, like you'd imagine inside a small theater. I recall seeing shows by Ministry, with local band Disco Ranch opening; the Ramones; and R.E.M. (Digital Sex opened the R.E.M. show). I seem to recall Michael Stipe asking the bar to use their blender so he could make a protein smoothie. Ministry was probably my favorite show. The Alarm did play there and are often forgotten within that period. It seemed so weird that we were watching great touring bands in a local stripper bar, which probably wasn't *that* weird considering at the same time we were also seeing bands at a bowling alley down the street." Sheehan was referencing the non-extant Ranch Bowl on Seventy-Second Street.

Music fan Andrew Ireland was at a few of The 20's concerts: "I saw Men Without Hats there. You could dance if you wanted. I also saw R.E.M. and the Ramones there. I remember The 20's as a long room and the stage and bar being on the long sides, opposite of each other. At the end of the bar was the door into the other room. It was tiered. I think two tiers, bar on the top. I think it had a red and gold curtain. I recalled seeing scantily clad waitresses from the strip club side coming into the music show side to pick up drink orders from the bar."

Another music fan, Greg Wees, rang in about his 20's experiences, after having seen numerous shows including R.E.M.: "It was a packed show; everyone was listening to *Murmur* in those days. We were having lots of fun that night. I believe there was no bar, so we had flasks. What I remember most distinctly was how low and small the stage was. We were basically standing right next to Stipe and crew, and you could practically chat with them between numbers. I think it was a girlie club then too, but not a nude thing like now (or so I've been told). Bikinis. The big room was for kids' shows, the little room was for depressed men, go-go dancing. I was in a band back then, so I got a lot of exposure to those clubs. The 20s was just a kind of anomaly."

A PUZZLING DEMISE

And then, as mysteriously as Terry Click's concerts began, all fell silent at The 20's. Terry Drea was a regional booking agent, promoting concerts in Omaha and western Iowa at the time. Drea, along with Click, brought the Ministry show on September 2, 1983. From what I would unravel, The 20's folded up shop after that show. The only tip-off I could trace was a problem Click had alluded to early on. Unfortunately, the 300–375 capacity venue meant "a zero profit margin" for the club. The sold-out shows' money all went to the bands, production costs, and advertising.

The bar was where Click had hoped to make some money, and surprisingly or not, the music crowd he was drawing for these national shows "was averaging seven and a half drinks apiece." Wow . . . the good ol' days of the bar business before strict DWI laws. For whatever reason this business model only lasted one blowout of a summer. The bar at 7301 Farnam Street sadly sat empty for another year.

THE YEAR 1984

An interview from September 1984 broke the silence at 7301 Farnam Street. New owner Mickey Sparano spoke with such charm and courtesy that more than a few nightlife fans must have perked up their ears—and didn't his name sound familiar, after all? The one-time coach of South High School intended to bring a touch of Atlantic City and Las Vegas to Omaha, minus the gambling. He acknowledged The 20's had not been successful for more than a few years at a time since its first five-year run in the 1960s.

Sparano had taken over the dormant 20's with a scheme to bring back the shows, the glitz, and the dance bands—the kinds of acts he had personally scouted in the casino lounges. It all sounded like good clean fun until a journalist's further probing revealed the shows to be of the Playboy Club variety, topping off with scantily clad cocktail waitresses. Sparano was quick to counter with his ideas for a Michael Jackson impersonator, a belly dancer, a new breakdancer, a flash dancer, and a group modeled after television's Solid Gold Dancers. He invested in a fifteen thousand–dollar video system for The 20's. Cameras were promised to film the dancers and even interview patrons of the new club.

THE MICKEY SPARANO STORY

Michael "Mickey" J. Sparano had experienced a rich and varied life by the time he had taken up with The 20's. Born in Iowa, to Italian immigrant parents, the Sparanos moved to Omaha when Mickey was eleven years old. Young Mickey had been a *World-Herald* carrier as a child, a Tech High School student as a teen, and a combat veteran in World War II, in which he served as a navy aerial gunner fighting in the South Pacific.

When he returned to the States, Sparano penned a new chapter, becoming a conference wrestling champion at the University of Nebraska and coach of five state championship wrestling teams at Omaha South High from 1953 to 1960. By then Mickey had married Mary, and the couple had children, Cheryl and Mickey Jr. Although he was a devout family man, his daughter's assessment was that her father liked the image of being seen around attractive women. It didn't take a detective to note the connection to his later line of work, eventually turning his life in a new direction. Sparano began to manage a nightclub in 1961.

Mickey Sparano was a well-known, well-loved personality and grand host in the early 1960s downtown Omaha nightlife scene. I knew I had recognized his memorable Italian name—a name plucked from a 1940s film noir whodunit. I had come across his catchy name in lights handle when I was investigating my "Cave under the Hill" story (which you can find at my website), as Sparano is widely known as the man who brought go-go to Omaha. A pioneer, so to speak. However you sized him up, either as an outspoken, amusing advocate, a provocateur, or a selfish promoter focused on his own predilections, Sparano—standing all of five foot three—would give Omahans what they wanted and would support: a wide variety of nightclubs and supper clubs over the years, including Mickey's Nite Club down at Fifteenth and Harney, Romeo's in the Diplomat Hotel at 1516 Harney, Mickey's Twist Club at Sixteenth and Jones Streets, San Moritz, the Pink Tiger, Mickey's Vegas at Forty-Fourth and Dodge Streets, Lynn Russell's Bunny Club, the Razzle Dazzle Go-Go Club at 3339 West Broadway in Council Bluffs, Mickey's Aquarius, and the former Mickey's at 8437 West Center Road, later changed to Wild Jack's.

Sparano also knew a thing or two about the horses and was known to study the Ak-Sar-Ben Daily Racing Form. His partner and friend Dennis Konvalin made a definitive comment in June 1988, "I don't think Mickey Sparano feels comfortable unless he has a go-go place in the city of Omaha." Konvalin spoke from a position of confidence—Konvalin would manage The 20's, as he did most of Sparano's joints. The two had, in fact, co-owned the Razzle Dazzle. I could trace "Denny" way back to the original Mickey's Nite Club and the Diplomat Hotel.

During the later 1970s Mickey Sparano's son, Mickey Jr., was struggling with mental illness. Mickey and Mary had evidently tried to get their only son psychiatric help. I was saddened to learn that on July 4, 1978, Mickey Jr. beat and stabbed his mother to death in the family home at Fifty-Second and Blondo. Voices had apparently told Sparano Jr. that his mother was a demon. To add to the sorrowful story, in 1985 Mickey Jr. killed himself at the Lincoln Regional Center, where he was living after being deemed "mentally unfit for incarceration." I cannot imagine the pain and loss that Mickey and daughter Cheryl must have endured. Cheryl Sparano Wild would go on to focus her adult life in her Christian faith, her family, serving on local boards, chairing events, and working regionally to educate the community about mental illness. From what I could find, Cheryl maintained a loving relationship with her father and always spoke of him in the highest regard. It is interesting to think of Cheryl's early assessment of her father and that Mickey Sparano possibly found solace in the company of beautiful women the rest of his life.

THE NEW FORMAT

How unforeseen and yet perfect that Mickey Sparano, pioneer of the Omaha go-go, would end up at the well-lit entrance of my 20's investigation. Back in 1985, Mickey Sparano boasted of having remodeled The 20's building, adding a few smaller bars around the room, but the basic layout remained unchanged. The club still featured a street scene interior, red decor, brick, and a garish style interior. He had hoped to offer revue bands and even tried a supper club approach with tableside service by tuxedoed servers, but apparently there was not enough traffic to keep these ideas afloat. I couldn't help but assume the perception of The 20's was so soured at that point that it scared away the well-heeled customers Sparano was hoping to attract.

However one squared it, The 20's entered its exotic dance club period in those years. Denny Konvalin said at the time there are some strip club customers "too shy to head into the big room" or "older customers who feel out of place" or some who didn't like contemporary music of the concert room. Meanwhile, he recognized, "there are also a lot of people

109. The formal Showgirl canopy west entrance as it appears today.

who wouldn't be caught dead going into a go-go place." The main room of The 20's was maintained for larger concerts and the "younger crowd's nightly rock bands." The 20's Showgirl "Gentleman's Club," on the west end, was developed to cater to these shy types, as a small lounge, a self-contained room seating fifty people, essentially keeping the groupings of customers apart. Mickey would add a separate entrance so the Showgirl patrons wouldn't feel uncomfortable walking through the rock room. The Showgirl opened at 4:00 p.m. The weathered orange canopy of the

Showgirl can be seen at the west entrance of the club today. There are also some great hand-painted signs found on the south side of the building, much in the Times Square–Broadway–Pussycat variety.

MICKEY'S DANCER

Conforming to the standards of the early 1980s through the 1990s, The 20's dancers typically wore a mixture of bikinis and fantasy lingerie outfits, their bodies covered, albeit by revealing attire. In those days a dancer's set onstage, of one or more favorite songs, could hopefully generate great tips, keep her customers on-site buying drinks, and build up a loyal clientele. There would often be a rotation of dancers in a given night, and a DJ would emcee the proceedings. Strip clubs were forced to move into high security in those days, which was blamed for cutting into profits—a uniformed policeman out front, a fire marshal at the door with the bouncer, ten floor men, management staff on premises, as well as cocktail waitresses, who did not strip, and bartenders. The 20's also offered side rooms for private dances, where the dancer and the patron would agree upon a payment. Mickey Sparano would bring in the pole dancing, which had become popular by the 1980s. Pole dancing introduced a new level of athleticism to the art form, as 1980s and 1990s exotic dancing became unequivocally more graphic; there was not as much as a smidge of tease, the burlesque or the humor left to endure, as audiences desired a candid experience for their money.

All the while The 20s remained popular with its hard rock concerts and various mix of acts. It was all a little hard to believe—then again, I was a kid obsessed with small punk clubs and running around in ghostly warehouses in downtown Omaha. What did I know about the popularity of The 20's? In 1986 Herman Woody Herman and his Thundering Herd, a clarinetist of the big band era, performed to a good-sized crowd in the larger room, as did a Dixieland jazz band. By the time I had left Omaha in 1990, the Omaha Symphony Musicians' Organization surprisingly presented its sixth annual Big Band Concert at The 20's. Performers included Preston Love, the Gulizia Brothers, Liz Westphalen, the Nebraska Jazz Orchestra, and the Resurrected Swing Big Band. Master

110. The once impressive Twenties Club entrance as it appears today, now refashioned into Club Omaha. Photo by author.

of ceremonies was local Dale Munson. By the mid-1990s slow business had forced Mickey Sparano and Denny Konvalin to close The 20's big room most nights of the week, but The 20's Showgirl Gentlemen's Club was going strong.

A PERSONAL ACCOUNT OF THE TWENTIES

Miss Cassette has a dear friend who worked as a cocktail waitress at The 20's during 1998 through 2008. She was willing to share her memories, as long as she remained anonymous. I will call her "Miss Twenties." Miss Twenties helped me seal more indispensable details on the club. Miss Twenties explained that in the time of her employ "Mickey Sparano was the owner and Dennis 'Denny' Konvalin was the manager, later becoming owner after Mickey died." (I would uncover that Mickey had died from the effects of Lou Gehrig's disease at age seventy-eight, in 2002.)

111. The iconic 20's marquee as discovered in the fall of 2017. Photo by Ron Hunter: "Several months ago I was scrounging around the yard at A&R Salvage, 2820 Vinton St., and spotted the massive sign from the Twenties. John at A&R Salvage has a lot of bits and pieces of old Omaha." Photo used by permission.

The Twenties interior was still very red and pretty gauche. It had preserved its Las Vegas interior. Framed photos of old 1920s silent movie stars could be found in the top dart room. As to the layout, upon entering, a doorman would meet a patron. To the left was a little room that had a small bar (but was not used anymore when I was there) and a small cloakroom, which was then used for an electronic dartboard area. To the right of the doorman was the "entry floor," which had the ATM, a few high top tables and two low tables, one of which was Mickey's "Personal Table." Upon this "perch" Mickey would sit at his Table with Denny, then manager and his guests, most of which were personal friends or Fran Hoffman, the manager/partner of his other Council Bluffs venture, the Razzle Dazzle. Walk down three steps and there was the main stage area, which consisted of a raised platform. There were no statues that

I remember. The backstage was a small separate area. The stage, itself, was like a 5x5 square with poles on each corner.

SCANDALS

Unfortunately, The 20's would be met with a number of scandals in the following years. An off-duty police officer would open fire at someone outside the club. Two people were arrested on drug charges in the parking lot. While working as an off-duty fire marshal at The 20's Club, an Omaha fire captain was fingered as having conspired with cocaine dealers in 1991. When the two drug dealers, who were government informants, led investigators on a long chase involving The 20's, the club entered a new unwanted spotlight of scandal. A bar fight in 2004 drew even more attention when a man slashed another man's face with a broken glass. Tragically, a fifteen-year-old was shot and killed in The 20's parking lot in 2006. It was just as Mickey Sparano had alluded to back in the 1990s; because of changes in the business and the clientele, a full-time security staff was needed. To paraphrase his words, a go-go club simply wasn't the carefree business it had once been.

TRIPLE MYSTERY

After having scurried through the snow to come back to my library and find the remainder of the deed sitting in my Twenties file, there it was in black-and-white. Doro Bortolotti had owned the Twenties / The 20's all along—all through the 1980s, the 1990s, and the 2000s, including the Mickey Sparano and Denny Konvalin years. Did that mean the partners were leasing the club from the Bortolottis? I was impatient with the facts. I could see in July 2011 Universal Terrazzo & Tile Company was taken off the Twenties deed. This served to separate the club from the Bortolotti tile business. Doro and his wife, Vera Bortolotti, signed the deed into Jo Ter Ran Investments LLC in August 2011—another of the couple's businesses. Jo Ter Ran, I deduced, was a combination of their children's names. In March 2015 Jo Ter Ran sold the 7301 Farnam Street property to its newest owner, who now operates a private club out of the location. Spellbinding.

To this day I savor the stakeout at the neighboring U.S. Bank parking lot—the chance to observe the collective uncertainty as newcomers pass by, wandering by those forlorn, unaccountable back buildings, 'round the ol' red-dressed Twenties Club. Did they take a wrong turn from a Pier One visit? I wonder. The mystery of city planning continues to baffle the uninitiated. The two parts muddled 1960s Las Vegas and a splash of small-town razzle-dazzle unceasingly beckon, although now called Club Omaha—the sturdy flickering lights, the black antique streetlamps, the red flat-roofed lines, the very last vestige of the famous Seventy-Second Street Strip. I'm smiling at the evidence that some might wish would swallow up unto the earth and magically disappear. And I love it just the way it is.

Epilogue

I awoke as if from a long ago, luxuriant nap upon my grandmother's bed. I can still remember the cool, pure-white tufted cotton chenille, stretched to perfection across her bed, framed by a dark-stained wood, caned headboard. Never wanting to disturb her divinely folded, crisp sheets, as a child I would sleep atop that bedspread like a happy caterpillar on my stomach. Inevitably, small indentations from the nubbly design were pressed across one side of my face as the familiar sound of *The Mary Tyler Moore Show* roused me, floating down the hall from the small television in her kitchen. I could smell butter warming in a pan, hear her gentle movements, and imagined that soon she would be calling me to her.

Acknowledgments

First and foremost I want to thank all of my wonderful Omaha Enthusiasts, Detectives, and Confidants I have met through the website. If you like to stray, then you understood the *My Omaha Obsession* website from the beginning. The fact that we found each other—with our collective recreation invested in memories; mysterious architecture; Old Omaha; fascinating people; photos of the past; ghosts; winding off the beaten path; and queer, little buildings long forgotten—is important. We needed to talk. To all of the beautiful homeowners who agreed to meet off the record and shared their incredible family histories, enthusiasm, and neighborhood stories, I have treasured your time and kindness. I found out very quickly I would not be able to meet with everyone who extended invites or my identity would become public. To those who have taken the time to make comments, give hints, tip off leads, and written, I thank you for your time, passion, and interest in historic preservation. This expression has meant the world to me.

I would like to thank Mr. Cassette for enduring all of my stakeouts, drive-bys, and 3:00 a.m. obsessions. I am grateful you include me in Your Big Obsession: gardening and love of the natural world. I continue to grow with you. Big thank-yous to the Mothers and Fathers of Miss Cassette for the customary morning-after grammar and punctuation correction emails but also, more important, the lifetime of shared family history and Omaha memories. I would not know to be interested in the city around me had it not been for parents who nodded and signaled out the car window and cared enough to explain what once was.

Thank you to Martha Grenzeback, Lynn Sullivan, Mark Sorensen, and the incredible librarians at the W. Dale Clark Library in downtown Omaha for their time, attention, wisdom, and like-minded obsessiveness. Their collective humanitarian action in helping everyone who walks through their doors with professionalism and compassion is inspiring. I continue to learn from you. Long live public libraries!! Thank you to senior editor Rob Taylor, copyeditor Elizabeth Gratch, project editor Joeth Zucco, and the staff of the University of Nebraska Press. To Michael Leahy, Bill Eustice, Stephen Sheehan, Kris and Tom Bartel, Drs. Chris Harding Thornton and Maria Buszek, Marq Manner, and Amanda Lynch for early guidance. To Syd Reinarz for the much needed arcane advice. To Jesse Hutmaker, Bruce Karlquist, John Jordan, Wolfman, and Jim Hofmann for ongoing encouragement and continued supportive words when you didn't have to. Much thanks to Detectives J. Lund, E. Foley, T. Besch, M. Soener, S. Mundt, A. Hepburn, Marnie, M. McCormack, Z. Drakulich, Beymer, A. Hayes, L. Olson, M. Smith, and M. M. for ongoing investigations, theories, laughs, and conspiring with my Need for Intrigue. My true PI friends, I love you.

I would have no book without our forebears, the local journalists and historians of Omaha's past, which I quote freely in my writing. I am so grateful. A toast to the incredible foresight and keen vision of the Omaha photographers, mostly deceased, who captured the breathtaking architectural images that continue to draw us in. Thanks to the Durham Museum, various county and state historical societies, and University of Nebraska Omaha archives, we have these glorious photographic collections. But I shower specific attention and praise upon Bill Gonzalez, dear friend and keeper of the Durham Museum Photo Archives—someone whom I enjoy very much. I have treasured our conversations, your wealth of knowledge, your compassion, and your assurance that "what is said at the Durham, stays at the Durham." With utmost respect and admiration to those who compiled current and historical data for the various reconnaissance surveys of Omaha's neighborhood studies, particularly the Nebraska State Historical Society, Omaha City Planning Department, and various architecture firms. Outstanding ovation to those architects and aids who wrote the numerous National Register of Historical Places registration form documents. What a city treasure.

Thank you to Scott Barnes, Mary Barnes, Susanna Nunes, and all Omaha staff at the Register of Deeds Office for tolerating my pesty, inquisitive ways. To Taylor Korensky and the Appsky Labs team for helping to design my website. To Kristine Gerber, previously of Restoration Exchange Omaha, for her incredible books (a true gift to Omaha), knowledge, and generosity. To Ron Hunter for your great photographs and for sharing the historic *Sun* newspaper with me. To Amy C. Schindler, director of Archives & Special Collections at University of Nebraska Omaha. To Gail Knapp and Mike Schonlau of the Omaha City Planning Department. To Martha Miller of the Nebraska State Historical Society for her patience and help. To Sherri Moore and the Joslyn Castle staff for the opportunity to investigate for hire. To my contacts at the Omaha Police Department, you know who you are. To Joseph A. Knapp with Historic Preservation at the City of Omaha Planning Department for spending time to help me dig and dig further into my passion. To Tim McMahon of Lazy-I fame and Mike Kelly of the *Omaha World-Herald* for sharing their spotlight with me. To Michelle Gullett of the *Omaha World-Herald*. To Trina Westman, former city planner, Urban Design Division, Planning Department of the City of Omaha, for her knowledge and generosity in sharing the department's archives. To Lynn Meyer, my Omaha photographer obsession, now retired Omaha planner, photographer, and preservation advocate. To Renee Ratner Corcoran of the National Jewish Historical Society for helping me with my early questions and turning me onto some great books.

Thanks, too, to my favorite Omaha writers of the past, Margaret Patricia Killian, Eleanor Hicks Murray, and B. F. Sylvester, for giving me countless hours of pleasure. To Carolyn Keene, aka Mildred Wirt Benson, for creating my life inspiration, Miss Nancy Drew. Character Veronica Mars and real-life character Nicole Curtis, both of whom have shaped my adult Miss Cassette. To Raymond Chandler, Dashiell Hammett, Dorothy Sayers, Arthur Conan Doyle, Agatha Christie, Wilkie Collins, Phyllis Dorothy James, and Margery Allingham for a lifetime of reading beneath the covers. Inquisitive amateur sleuths everywhere, unite.

Thank you to Trey and Lallaya Hicks Lalley at Brothers Lounge, my heart. Brothers, along with all of the fantastic Omaha mom-and-pop shops out there, is fighting the neutral concrete slab national franchise landscape. They give Omaha its distinct flavor. To all of the neighborhood associations sprinkled throughout our city, they build connection, educate, and empower. Thank you for keeping your focus on historic preservation of our city's architecture while finding balance with new cohesive, high-quality development.

CPSIA information can be obtained
at www.ICGtesting.com
Printed in the USA
LVHW030512181220
674481LV00002B/2

9 781496 207616